Managing Career Development

Marilyn A. Morgan

**The Wharton School
University of Pennsylvania**

D. VAN NOSTRAND COMPANY
New York • Cincinnati • Toronto • London • Melbourne

Cover illustration by Colos/Business Week Magazine.

D. Van Nostrand Company Regional Offices:
New York   Cincinnati

D. Van Nostrand Company International Offices:
London   Toronto   Melbourne

Published by D. Van Nostrand Company
135 West 50th St., New York, N.Y. 10020

10 9 8 7 6 5 4 3 2 1

To My Parents,
Whose Constant Encouragement
and Support Have Enhanced
The Development of My Own Career

Preface

This book is about our past, present, and future experiences in organizations. This series of separate yet related experiences through which a person passes is known as a career. Some of us have long careers, others have very short careers. Some pursue multiple careers, others have only one dominant career. Some of us are successes, others are failures. Some are very involved or absorbed by their career, others are only remotely involved. But the point is that we all have careers. A better understanding of basic career issues is the focus of this book.

Two main themes related to careers are developed. First, careers develop over time; that is, they change and mature over the course of a person's work life. In spite of differences among people, occupations, and organizations, there are several predictable phases and transitions through which we pass as our careers unfold. Within each of these phases, there are several dominant issues and concerns that need to be considered in order to enhance career effectiveness.

The second theme is career management. While we do not have complete control over our careers, they can be "managed." The ultimate responsibility for career management rests with the individual person, although the responsibility is shared by the supervisor and the organization. The supervisor and the organization serve to enhance and facilitate a person's career development.

The organization of the book reflects the two themes of developing and managing careers. In the first section an effort is made to consider the basic parameters and frameworks used in understanding the dynamics of careers in organizations. The next four sections focus on careers as they develop or mature in organizations. Section 2 provides an overview of adult development and the concept of career stages. Sections 3, 4, and 5 deal with the specific issues, problems, and activities in the early, mid, and late stages of careers. Career success is the theme in Section 6. An effort is made to challenge some of our narrow traditional definitions of success and to consider some of the consequences of the "Success Ethic." The issue of special career concerns for women and minorities is raised in Section 7. The book concludes with two sections that identify specific activities and strategies to enhance career management. Section 8 focuses upon individual tasks relating to career management and Section 9 suggests organizational strategies to enhance career development.

This book has been made possible by the generous assistance of a number of persons. The students in my classes have reacted with insight to much of the material. Two research assistants, Kathryn Coleman and Eliot Marx, helped throughout the various phases of the book's development. The comments and suggestions offered by the following reviewers were most useful: Lloyd S. Baird of Boston University, Sam Gould of The University of Texas at San Antonio, W. Clay Hammer of Duke University, Jay Kim of Ohio State University, Meryl Louis of The University of Illinois at Urbana—Champaign, John P. Wanous of Michigan State University, and Uma Sekaran of Southern Illinois University at Carbondale. And finally, the facilities and assistance of the Department of Management at the Wharton School were extremely valuable in supporting my efforts to complete this project. I express my deepest gratitude to all of these persons.

Table of Contents

Developing a Career Perspective

Managers have always had careers, but until recently little attention was directed at a systematic assessment of managerial career issues. Within the past few years work careers have become the focus of both scholarly attention and popular concern. Issues of career management and development have become increasingly important to both individual employees and organizations.

Work plays a key role in a person's life. An individual needs to understand career processes in order to manage his or her own career more effectively. This understanding and appreciation of career processes can be a great aid to the individual's self-awareness and sense of identity. In addition, while the manager's prime responsibility is to manage a group of subordinates, one of the subordinate's prime concerns is to manage his or her own career. Therefore, the manager who can understand career interests and career dynamics will be more effective in managing and developing people.

Organizations can better cope with many human resource management problems through creative techniques for career management. More effective corporate career planning systems can begin to answer questions such as, How can we reduce turnover among recently hired employees? How can we increase the number of high-potential candidates for management positions? How can we increase promotion opportunities in a stable or contracting organization?

The purpose of this first section is to help the reader develop a career perspective. This is accomplished by focusing on three main questions: How can we examine the interaction of the individual and the organization in terms of a career perspective? What are the career-oriented values and concerns of today's managers? What are the demographic trends which are likely to affect the careers of managers in the next decades? The three readings in this section address the issues raised by these questions.

In the first reading, Van Maanen, Schein, and Bailyn examine the individual, organizational, and societal forces that shape the development of careers. In presenting their framework for the study of careers they argue that "by using the career as a fundamental unit of study and action managers will be able to learn substantially more about why people in organizations behave as they do and, more critically, discover how to do something about it." Thus, the career perspective is important to further assure managerial effectiveness.

Renwick and Lawler present the results of their study on the "new job values" of American workers. They describe a mobile generation of managers who attach great importance to their personal career growth. The authors portray today's workers as being highly desirous of more opportunities to learn and grow, use their talents and skills, accomplish something worthwhile, and exert more controll over decisions in the work force. Renwick and Lawler conclude that "most workers are generally satisfied with their jobs for now, but that there is an unmistakable undercurrent of restlessness that may well create problems for employers as the American economy rambles toward the 1980's."

According to the authors of the third selection, the United States is going through some fundamental demographic changes which are likely to affect the careers of organizational members. The most immediate change relates to the incoming "baby boom" managers. The large influx of these managers will create a dramatic shift in the ratio of inexperienced to experienced managers—"too many Indians and not enough chiefs." In addition, these young managers are likely "to experience continuing difficulties in satisfying career and income aspirations simply because of the competitive pressures generated by their sheer numbers." A second element of the shift in demographic patterns is the fact that the U.S. population is growing older. Between the years 1970 and 2000, the median age of the American population will shift from 28 to 35. Such a change will have dramatic effects on the number of workers entering and moving through our organizational hierarchies. Unfortunately, few companies have given much thought to the particular management problems which may result from these demographic shifts. Insightful managers, however, will begin to consider the implications of such trends for the management of their organizations and their careers.

The Shape of Things to Come:
A New Look at Organizational Careers

John Van Maanen

Edgar H. Schein

Lotte Bailyn

People have always had careers. But only recently has serious attention been directed to the way careers actually develop, and to the forces—individual, organizational, and societal—that shape this development. Yet, managers in organizations need the results of such inquiry if they are to utilize their human resources most effectively and deal with such recurrent topics of managerial concern as turnover, morale, motivation, and productivity from both a long- and short-term point of view. It is our contention that by using the career as a fundamental unit of study and action, we will be able to learn substantially more about why people in organizations behave as they do and, more critically, discover how to do something about it.

The key to our developing framework on careers is found not in the person, the organization, or the work task itself, but rather in the ways in which cultural, organizational, and occupational demands interact with individual aspirations, family concerns, and work demands across time. Throughout this paper we will try to spell out the implications of this perspective and to make clear why we believe the study of careers must encompass this complex whole. We begin in section I with some examples of current issues and problems in organizational careers. In section II, we extract from these examples the requirements for the systematic study of careers if that inquiry is to have the far-reaching consequences we believe possible. And, finally, in section III, we discuss the implications of this view for career development systems and for what we see to be the shape of things to come.

I THE SHAPE OF THINGS PRESENT

We live in an era in which a great variety of life-styles is realistically available. But as the possibilities expand, so do the painful necessities for choosing, and so also do the difficulties that individuals have in meshing various, and often conflicting, needs and desires. As people introduce more intricate considerations into their personal career choices, managers of organizations are faced with new and unexpected complexities in their traditional ways of mobilizing and directing human resources.

The evidence is everywhere, individuals refuse to be promoted or to move to another city. Young couples will not accept job offers unless

3

both are placed satisfactorily. The problems of mid-life are increasingly met not by a quiet, internal crisis, but by a radical, external change in life-style, including, at times, permanent career transformations. Organizations report having problems with young workers who are not responding in the time-honored fashion to traditional assignments and rewards. Some companies seem to be having enormous difficulties in successfully recruiting and upgrading the careers of women and minority employees. And tales regarding the ineffectiveness of "plateaued" personnel with long service and multiplying. Things have been moving so rapidly that some firms have even gone so far as to hire outside consultants to advise their own employees on whether, in light of personal needs, the employees in question should or should not accept an offered transfer or promotion within the organization.[1]

In general, our cultural understandings of the "proper" organization of work are undergoing change. More and more people, for instance, are ignoring the traditional conception that professional work is more valuable or worthwhile than nonprofessional work. Indeed, very talented people are taking jobs for which they are overeducated. Take, for example, the growing number of trained and licensed architects who are becoming involved in the "hands-on" jobs such as stonemasonry or carpentry, in the construction trades. Or consider also the many students who are avoiding certain professions—such as engineering and other applied sciences—because the work is viewed as potentially harmful to society. Further, numerous employees are putting a positive value on staff, technical, and skilled craft positions which involve responsibility and influence through the practice of

certain occupational skills but which explicitly do *not* involve managing others. The idea of rising in an organization is no longer limited to the idea of "getting into management" but is increasingly associated with having more influence through one's practical competence.

At the same time, we see more people who put little effort into their jobs and great effort into their hobbies, sports, social life, or other leisure-time activities in which they feel they can more fully express themselves. In other words, the concept of work itself has undergone a considerable transition from something sacred and unquestioned in a bygone society to a set of activities whose "meaning" has become a major concern in today's society (Berger, 1964). People now have many choices about their work and career, and it is no longer possible to make uniform assumptions about how any person will approach his or her work.

In some occupations and organizations, which almost invariably promote tension between work, self, and family concerns of employees, this uncertainty about the meaning of work is particularly evident. There is the Willy Loman syndrome of social isolation common to the proverbial traveling salesman; there is the confusion that accompanies the jet-set, "if-it's-Tuesday-it-must-be-Belgium" international executive; there is the rootlessness of the geographically mobile corporate manager of whom it is asked, if not demanded, that he shift communities time and time again, disturbing, in the process, his family and coterie of friends and acquaintances.[2]

Difficulties also arise when organizational rewards are perceived by individuals to be inappropriate to their particular career phase or stage. Indeed, many organizations are learning that for some people in mid-career, financial rewards are not enough to maintain commitment and motivation. Nor is "job enlargement" or an increase in work challenge welcomed by all. What many people require at this stage is an

---

[1]Career development appears to be at least one area in which practical applications have outrun supportive research. Indeed, research seems to be playing "catch up" to the new programs which are being implemented with increasing frequency. While this is in many ways a happy state of affairs, it does beg the question of the worth of these programs, not to mention the perhaps unintended consequences of such a quick leap from *problem* identification to *program* solution.

[2]At least one writer has suggested that it is, in part, the brutalizing effects of rootlessness arising from corporate mobility that has led to a significant increase in the suicide rates among the middle-aged (Seidenberg, 1975).

opportunity to engage their abilities in something new. In fact, some executives have turned down generous bonuses and promotions just for the opportunity to try their hand at something different (Beckhard, 1977). And some technical people at mid-career (as well as the organizations that employ them) are better served by being allowed to place their work in a secondary role than by attempts to rekindle their involvement in work (Bailyn, 1977).

A new order of complexity is also introduced by the changing role of women. A wife can no longer be viewed merely as an appendage to her husband: the foreign service no longer "requires" wives to follow orders from the wives of officers at higher positions than their husbands; companies no longer automatically evaluate wives when their husbands are up for promotion. And yet the supportive roles that a woman does play in her husband's career—in what has been called the "two-person career" (Papanek, 1973)—are beginning to be seen as more important, as is evident in the expense some multinational firms incur when entire families are sent on trial visits to countries in which the husband may someday be asked to work. Further, as more women enter the higher work ranks on their own, these changes are likely to accelerate. If the husband of a female college president is given a title, salary, and function, it seems likely that sooner or later the important ancillary roles that wives play will also come to be recognized formally by the institutions that employ their husbands. Finally, for the growing number of "dual-career families" (Rapoport & Rapoport, 1969), work decisions made by one member of the family obviously have a significant impact on the other. Without question, organizations will have to recognize that such "extraneous" forces play a powerful role in the careers of their employees.

What all these examples suggest is that careers must be examined within the total life space of a person. Personal and family constraints cannot be viewed as unrelated to work concerns. People do not live neat, compartmentalized lives in which each separate concern operates within a closed system. For too many

years we have studied and made proclamations about such issues as work satisfaction and job motivation as if they existed somehow outside of an individual's full and rich life in progress. It is clear that a broadening of perspective is required.

II A NEW PERSPECTIVE ON ORGANIZATIONAL CAREERS

This contextual emphasis—the realization that one cannot look at work and career in isolation from other aspects of people's lives—is the basic element of our perspective. From the point of view of the individual, this may seem obvious—though it has more often been paid lip service than incorporated into systematic investigation. But we are saying more than this: we are implying also that this contextual element is crucial to employing organizations and to the larger social institutions that affect all our lives.

Educational programs and opportunities, for example, which create and subsequently sustain many of the available career paths in society, will not be successful in their professed goals if they are not matched to the overall goals of the people they are designed to help. Moreover, if federal and state statutes governing such diverse topics as manpower training, welfare assistance, unemployment insurance, affirmative action programs, and day-care centers are to be effective, they must rest on an understanding of this broader context.

Nor can employing organizations afford to ignore the role that work plays in the total lives of their employees. The growth and productivity of organizations is now, more than ever, dependent on the effectiveness of human performance, which is less and less likely to be predictable in traditional ways. Organizations that cannot respond to their employees as total human beings may stagnate, and become less efficient than those organizations better able to manage their employees' careers.

A second major attribute of our perspective is its emphasis on *development*, on the *changes* that occur in all aspects of a person's life throughout the adult years. Every person goes through a series of stages in his or her career, each of which may require different involvements and capacities. This "career cycle," further, evolves side by side with a "personal cycle" of changing needs and abilities and with a "family cycle." The latter is determined both by the structural stages of the family (as defined primarily by the number and ages of children) and by the developmental needs of spouse and children. At any given point in time, each of these cycles makes its particular demands upon the individual in the form of growth opportunities to be seized, vulnerabilities to be dealt with, and constraints with which the person must cope. It is the *interaction* of these opportunities, areas of vulnerability, and constraints that creates the particular life issues that the person must resolve at any given time.

If individuals and the organizations that employ them are not sensitive to these complex realities, they may find themselves in trouble. For example, if management decides to deal with an alienated engineer by giving him a more "people-oriented job," it may be helping him personally with his problem of low job motivation, but the new role may also require increased commitment to his organization. If this happens at a time when his children are leaving home and his wife requires more of his time, this seemingly "obvious" solution to his work problem may backfire. Or, to take another example, consider the manager who has worked very hard to attain a high position in his organization, but at a certain stage in his life begins to question the value of career advancement as his major life goal. He is perhaps ready to become, in Erickson's (1959) words, more "generative" to others in the organization, more desirous to act as a guide and mentor to younger employees, and more willing to meet the previously ignored needs of his family. On the other hand, his wife, who has been generative or supportive of others all her life, may be ready to enter an independent and autonomous phase of life no longer centered solely on the family. Thus, what might have been an integrative move by either one at an earlier phase now

merely reverses the sources of strain in their lives.

But the lack of congruence of cycles need not only occur between husband and wife, or between employee and organization. It may also occur *within* the individual. It is an intriguing hypothesis, for instance, that strain in one area can be handled by a person provided he or she is not simultaneously under strain in any of the other areas. "Failure"—broadly defined as a problem that is not dealt with effectively and which has led to more or less irreversible consequences—may, therefore, be partially explained by the coming together of periods of vulnerability in more than one cycle, causing more stress than the person can handle.

These considerations make it clear why it is important to distinguish between those issues that have to do with a career as defined externally by society and organizations, and those that have to do with a career as it is perceived and lived internally. This "internal" career evolves from the particular combination of forces, out of the many possible, that impinge on a person at a given point in time. These forces emanate from a person's "career anchor,"[3] from the needs and tasks associated with the particular life stage which the individual has reached, and from the circumstances of the immediate family, particularly the needs and stages of spouse and children. Because of the uniqueness of these forces, it is obvious that people will experience the same external career

[3]Schein's notion of career anchors is a way of summarizing those factors that might be said to "drive" the internal career. Career anchors are seen as syndromes of personal interests, abilities, needs, values, talents, and motives that organize and give stability to the career. Such anchors may be latent or unconscious in the person when he or she first chooses a career, but become manifest both to the individual and to others as actual work experience accumulates. They are clearly "inside" the person, functioning as a set of driving and constraining forces. Hence, if people move into settings in which they are likely to fail, or move into settings in which their values are compromised, they will be "pulled back" into something more congruent with their skills and beliefs; thus, the metaphor of "anchor." (See Schein, 1975b, 1977.)

events (such as a raise, a promotion, or a geographical move) in very different ways. Thus one must be prepared to find multiple patterns in the way people live out and experience their careers, and in the manner in which they balance career concerns with other life concerns.

Our research has confirmed the existence of such multiple patterns at every point. A longitudinal study of alumni of the Sloan School of Management, for example, showed that this group exhibited five different career anchors: managerial competence, technical-functional competence, autonomy, creativity, and security (Schein, 1977). Engineers at mid-career, to take another case, were found to be people-oriented, or technically and professionally oriented, or not very strongly oriented to work at all but more accommodative to families (Bailyn, 1977). If such pluralism in the "human resources pool" is not recognized by multiple reward systems and multiple career ladders within an organization, difficulties are bound to occur.

A vivid example of the lack of recognition of such multiple patterns occurred in a career workshop held in a large financial organization for its general managers. Among this group of managers, there turned out to be three distinct patterns of "ambition," even though the company value system clearly put the emphasis on only one of these patterns. Some of the managers, all currently at the regional level, did want to climb the corporate ladder to positions of group vice-president, executive vice-president, and ultimately president—the traditional pattern. However, some equally talented managers in the group wanted to remain at the regional level because they wanted the autonomy that this level of management made possible. These men saw movement up into corporate headquarters as undesirable and were willing to trade rank for autonomy and the ability to really run their own show. They wanted to be promoted to larger regions but not into headquarters. Finally, a third group of managers wanted to leave line management responsibilities and enter corporate headquarters in senior staff roles where they would have an opportunity to influence policy through con-

ceptualizing how certain areas of the business should be handled. Of greatest interest was the fact that these men were surprised to discover the diversity within their own group (their initial assumption had been that they all wanted to be president), and were shocked and dismayed to find that the second and third groups did not feel free to tell their bosses what they wanted from their careers because it would violate traditional career expectations.

It is such mismatches between employers and employees that have prompted us to argue that the central problem of career development in organizations is how to match internal career needs and external career opportunities (Schein, 1975a, Van Maanen & Schein, 1976). It is to the implications of our perspective for the success of such an endeavor that we now turn.

III THE SHAPE OF THINGS TO COME

An adequate matching of individual needs and organizational opportunities will not occur unless individuals, organizations, and other social and governmental institutions *all* take some responsibility for the things they can control. For example, no successful matching can occur unless both employee and employer know what the needs and opportunities of the other actually are. Yet, the prevailing practice in many organizations is for decision makers to guess at or assume the needs and values of their employees and then simply move them about at will (Alfred, 1967). Clearly, such a practice can never assure success. To be sure, employees themselves may not know their own desires, but in many work settings they are made to feel that to ask for or to initiate a career shift, however slight, will bring suspicion of disloyalty and hence adversely affect the course of their entire future. Thus, one of the first and most important changes to be made is to alter this unilateral concept of career development—the organization must define its available career paths, the employee must learn more about his or her internal career needs, and a climate of mutual trust necessary for the sharing of this information must be established and maintained.

But one must further assume that government will have to play a key role in this matching process as well, because some mismatches will not be resolvable within a given organization. For example, if an organization has to terminate employees because they have the wrong mix of talents or needs, or if employees discover that a given organization cannot provide them with the opportunities they seek, they may well need help of an institutional sort in making a career shift, particularly if such a shift requires additional education and training or a period of extensive search for new opportunities. The creation of mechanisms to aid this process may be particularly important during mid- and late-career periods because so many organizations are biased against investing in older employees (Fogarty, 1975).

Only by the joint action of individuals, the organizations that employ them, and government will it be possible to achieve an optimal utilization of human resources. In the remainder of this paper we outline some specific actions and directions for the future that we feel are necessary to reach this goal. First, we examine the sorts of things that government and other societal institutions might be expected to undertake. Second, we suggest several directions in which organizations might move. And third, we consider the kinds of issues individuals will have to deal with to further develop their own careers.

A What Government and Other Social Institutions Can Do

It is becoming obvious that as political, economic, social, and technological conditions change, so do the needs for different kinds of talent within a society. Societies differ with regard to the extent to which they centralize planning, both economic and social, but the interrelated issues of what kinds of competence are needed and how they are to be stimulated and controlled are major problems no society can long ignore. We would expect, therefore, that the future will bring improved procedures for forecasting manpower needs and the

creation of various mechanisms to recruit and train talent pools.

At present, the dissemination of career information has become a multi-million dollar governmental activity in this country. But along with information dispersal must come appropriate institutional structures to support and promote entrance into various career paths. Job fairs, work-study programs, and support for education and on-the-job training represent the beginnings of such governmental support systems.

At another institutional level, what is now primarily a private activity—aptitude testing and vocational counseling—will perhaps come to be offered on a much broader scale through the public educational system. Already the counseling function as practiced in the high schools is undergoing significant alterations as an increasing number of employing organizations are taking a more active part—particularly in minority communities. We would hope also that counseling, in general, will shed the "classification of people" approach and pay more attention to the classification of the actual features of work careers, allowing more and more students to make their own career choices on more realistic grounds, unencumbered by restricting labels regarding what they are or are not "fit" to do. Thus, counseling in educational institutions must begin to emphasize "process consultation" models in helping people *enact* better career decisions rather than rely on the traditional "expert consultation" models in which a young person is implicitly or explicitly *told* what he or she should do on the basis of a profile of interest and attitude tests (Schein, 1969).

Yet, no matter how carefully people choose their careers, there will inevitably be mistakes. People may misread their needs, or their needs may change; job opportunities may be inaccurately perceived or may undergo actual transformations. It is too much to expect that employees and employers can, by themselves, solve all the problems of mismatch. New mechanisms that permit people to reassess and change their careers and to obtain additional education or training are necessary. Such mechanisms are in fact already becoming available (Pascal, Bell, Dougharty, Dunn, & Thompson, 1975). The job corps, teacher corps, and subsidized adult education are recent examples of governmental support in this area. Relatedly, we would also expect to see governmental restrictions placed on such organizational practices as coercive pension plans that discourage employees from leaving their present organizations except at great financial cost. And, insofar as schooling is concerned, we expect that the present bias of graduate schools against those people who are ten or more years out of college will slowly disappear, resulting in an easing of the problems associated with career shifts.

In summary, it should be clear that many different sorts of institutional support systems and policy changes are needed if we are to improve significantly utilization of our human resources. Not only must we as a society assist people in selecting, preparing, and entering into appropriate lines of work, but we must also be prepared to aid those people who wish to redirect their work efforts at later points in their careers.

B   What Organizations Can Do

Organizations will have to grow increasingly sophisticated in the design and implementation of human resource planning and forecasting systems. They will have to learn to identify correctly the career needs of their employees, and match them with organizational requirements. The procedures and systems to achieve this matching will necessarily be complex and will have to be carefully monitored and evaluated. Such systems are likely, also, to increase the sharing of responsibility for career development between organizations and individuals since effective manpower forecasting and planning cannot be carried out without such sharing. Organizations need information not only about their own manpower requirements, but also about employees' aspirations. Mechanisms such as job posting elicit such information, and also stimulate employees' initiative to develop their own careers by actively seeking new assignments. Job posting also stimulates the organization to do more honest performance appraisal, because employees who do not qualify for a particular job must be told precisely why they did not qualify and what they would have to do to rectify the situation.

Career counseling, in the widest sense, is likely to be expanded and closely linked to performance appraisal. This will require a variety of activities designed to help employees identify their own job needs and aid the organization in finding positions to fit them. Such counseling will increasingly be conducted within the confines of internal or external "assessment centers" (Bray & Grant, 1966). Such centers, instead of trying to infer future performance from personality traits as revealed on projective or other tests, make the assumption that assessment can be improved by putting candidates into situations that simulate the actual jobs to be performed. Evaluators, in most situations, are people who are familiar with the job because they have performed it themselves. Feedback relates assessment to observed behavior and thus permits candidates to perceive themselves more accurately and to develop a more realistic sense of their career chances. Whereas in the past such centers have primarily served the needs of the organization, increasingly their focus will have to shift to considering the needs of the individual employee as well. They will become *development centers* instead of assessment centers.

Special temporary assignments and job-rotation programs which help employees make career choices and help the organization assess their talents are also likely to become more salient in the future. This kind of program is broader than the assessment center approach because an individual spends time in a consequential situation and is thus provided with a more elaborate taste and test of his or her abilities.

Another form of "counseling" lies in the adoption of a workshop program to aid people in thinking about their careers. Such programs were initially focused on improving the process of bringing new employees into the organization by smoothing the transition from school to work (Kotter, 1973). But they also provided opportunities for larger career issues to be raised. Mid-career workshops are logical extensions of the "joining-up" workshops and have already been tried in a number of organizations. These workshops can help people learn how to make a life plan, how to think about the role of their work career within that plan, and how to develop concrete action steps toward implementing the plan.

Finally, a whole series of innovations will have to be introduced to make organizational reward systems more flexible, and more responsive to the wide range of needs of employees. For example, organizations in the future will have to become more involved in supporting educational and training activities at all levels in the firm. Further, it is likely that they will have to offer time off and financial support for such training if they are to keep their best workers from leaving the organization. One can even see prospective employees evaluating particular job opportunities on the basis of the kinds of educational opportunities promoted by several competing companies. Very clearly, educational and training activities are becoming more and more important elements of an organization's overall reward system.

Organizations will also have to provide support such as sabbaticals and flexible working hours for off-work activities. Extended leaves to pursue community service or teaching activities, already available for senior people, may well become the norm for employees at all levels. Law firms, for instance, are already finding that they must promise time for public service work (*pro bono publico*) in order to attract top law students. And, in the case of plateaued employees, such policies may actually come to represent the major rewards for individuals throughout the remainder of their careers. With the growing emphasis on self-awareness, leisure, and social relevance, "time off" may well become one of the most important benefits a company can offer its employees.

In the financial area, giving employees a choice among several forms of rewards (such as salary, bonus plans, benefit packages, stock options, or paid leave) will have to become a central feature of personnel policies. In terms of promotional policies, organizations in the future will need to develop multiple promotional ladders to reflect the fact that not all employees want to be supervisors or general managers, nor, given the flattening out of organizational growth curves, can all employees reasonably expect to be supervisors or general managers. Hence, the increasing importance of developing multiple tracks in the effort to reward the horizontal as well as the vertical careers. Little attention, for example, has yet been given to upgrading such roles as financial analyst, computer programmer, staff specialist, purchasing agent, secretary, or the skilled and unskilled worker on the factory floor.

The objective of all these activities is to widen options so that employees can make more meaningful career choices, and so that organizations can allocate their human resources more effectively.

C What Individuals Can Do

It would be a mistake, however, to assume that government and employing organizations can sweep away all the career problems confronting individuals. Organizations promoting change are vulnerable. Businesses can lose money, educational innovations may fall by the wayside, and governmental agencies can undergo major budget cuts. One might hypothesize, therefore, that the movement toward and through change will not be linear, but uneven; the forces of change and resistance will probably interact continually. The result may be a kind of seesawing between tradition and originality as various forces gain temporary advantage. What are the issues facing individuals as a result of this situation? What tensions are likely to arise?

We suspect that there will be a growing sentiment toward increased personal accountability for careers: individuals are likely to become more directly answerable for the incompetent performance of their duties as well as more demanding of more appropriate rewards for competent performance. In other words, with increasing choice will come increasing responsibility. While we recognize that individuals can never control all the forces that determine their careers from the outside, we expect that people will be forced into doing more about their own careers than they are now doing.

Toward this end, it will be necessary for people to become more attuned to their own needs, their values, and their personal goals. In this, they are supported by other trends in the society, including the so-called personal growth movement—which has created a desire in people to understand themselves more completely—and the general tendency to decrease the arbitrary power of organizations over people. In such a climate, particularly if employers continue to offer more options to their employees, it is not unrealistic to assume that people will develop considerably more insight into their own particular career experiences and desires. To the extent that they do so, their future career accomplishments, experiences, and work circumstances will benefit.

The aim of career development for individuals, therefore, is to increase their awareness of their beliefs and preferences about a career, and to have them expose themselves to personal examination. As this happens, individuals will require more varied career paths, and organizations will have to respond to the resulting pluralism. It is primarily the impetus of employees themselves, pushing for increased options and for more control over their own career destinies, that will lend organizations and other social institutions to respond in the ways we have outlined above. And, ultimately, no equitable allocation of employment opportunities will be possible without the joint efforts of government, employing organizations, and individual employees.

REFERENCES

Alfred, T. Checkers and choice in manpower management. *Harvard Business Review*, January-February 1967, 157-167.

Bailyn, L. Involvement and accommodation in technical careers: An inquiry into the relation to work at mid-career. In J. Van Maanen (Ed.), *Organizational careers: Some new perspectives.* London: Wiley International, 1977.

Bailyn, L., & Schein, E. H. Life/Career considerations as indicators of quality of employment. In A. D. Biderman & T. F. Drury (Eds.), *Measuring work quality for social reporting.* Beverly Hills, California: Sage, 1976, 151-168.

Beckhard, P. Managerial careers in transition: Dilemmas and directions. In J. Van Maanen (Ed.), *Organizational careers: Some new perspectives.* London: Wiley International, 1977.

Berger, P. Some general observations on the problem of work. In P. Berger (Ed.), *The human shape of work.* Chicago: Regnery, 1964, 211-241.

Bray, D. W., & Grant, D. L. The assessment center in the measurement of potential business management. *Psychological Monographs*, **80**, 1966.

Erickson, E. H. Identity and the life cycle. *Psychological Issues,* **1**, 1959, 1-171.

Fogarty, M. *Forty to sixty: How we waste the middle aged.* London: Centre for Studies in Social Policy, 1975.

Kotter, J. The psychological contract. *California Management Review*, Spring 1973, 156-165.

Papanek, H. Men, women, and work: Reflections on the two-person career. *American Journal of Sociology*, **78**, 1973, 852-872.

Pascal, A. H., Bell D., Dougharty, L. A., Dunn, W. L., & Thompson, V. M. *An evaluation of policy related research on programs for mid-life redirection.* Santa Monica, California: The Rand Corporation, R-1582, 1975.

Rapoport, R., & Rapoport, R. N. The dual career family: A variant pattern and social change. *Human Relations,* **22**, 1969, 3-30.

Schein, E. H. *Process consultation.* Reading, Massachusetts: Addison-Wesley, 1969.

Schein, E. H. Career development: Theoretical and practical issues for organizations. Paper read at Conference on Career

Development, International Labor Office. Budapest, Hungary, April, 1975a.

Schein, E. H. How career anchors hold executives to their career paths. *Personnel, 52,* May-June 1975b, 11-24.

Schein, E. H. Career anchors and career paths: A panel study of management school graduates. In J. Van Maanen (Ed.), *Organizational careers: Some new perspectives.* London: Wiley International, 1977.

Seidenberg, R. *Corporate wives—Corporate casualties?* New York: Doubleday, 1975.

Van Maanen, J. (Ed.) *Organizational careers: Some new perspectives.* London: Wiley International, 1976.

Van Maanen, J., & Schein, E. H. Career development. In J. R. Hackman & L. Suttle (Eds.), *Improving life at work.* Pacific Palisades, California: Goodyear, 1977.

What You Really Want From Your Job

Patricia A. Renwick
Edward E. Lawler
The *Psychology Today* staff

Toward the end of the 19th century, when trade unionism and radical socialism were competing for the soul of the American worker, the country was asking what labor wanted. Samuel Gompers' simple answer was "*more.*" The first president of the American Federation of Labor expounded a vision for labor of "more opportunities to cultivate our better natures, to make manhood more noble, womanhood more beautiful, and childhood more happy and bright." The theme became a litany in Gompers' campaigns on behalf of craft unionism. "We want more, we demand more, and when we get that more, we shall insist upon again more and more," Gompers said in a 1902 speech.

Psychology Today's survey of our readers' work satisfaction reveals that you, too, want *more.* But not simply more money and benefits—you were raised in affluence and tend to take these for granted. Instead, you want more psychological satisfactions. More opportunities to learn and grow. More chance to exercise to the fullest your talents and skills. More possibility of accomplishing something worthwhile.

Like your parents, you are willing to work hard and even put in long hours. Although you value your leisure, our survey suggests (in contrast to some other national studies on broader populations) that you still find much of your identity in work. But you want more control over the decisions in the workplace, especially those that affect your own jobs. And you want more freedom to set the pace of your own work, to control your own hours and schedules, to get in an hour of tennis before work or take a long skiing weekend. You have a whole hierarchy of needs, which you see as necessary for what Abraham Maslow called self-actualization.

This emphasis on personal growth has also been noted in previous studies of your generation. What is surprising in our data is that if you do not get what you want, you may just bug out, take French leave. No less than two-thirds of those who answered the *PT* questionnaire reported there was some likelihood they would change occupations within the next five years (and only a small portion of the sample were young people who are beginning their careers and tend to make more changes).

A total of 23,008 readers returned the 77-item questionnaire in our September issue that asked, "How Do You Like Your Job?" From the survey results and the letters that many of you who wanted to comment in detail sent in, we conclude that most of you are generally

Reprinted from *Psychology Today Magazine.* Copyright © 1978 Ziff-Davis Publishing Company.

13

Who You Are: Profile of Survey Participants

Because of the sheer volume of response to our survey, we took a sample of questionnaires for analysis. By a random-selection process, we assured that the sample would be statistically representative of the whole. We included every 10th survey form we received, in the order that they came in, for a total of 2,300 questionnaires. The table below shows the characteristics of the PT readers participating in the survey, compared with 1977 figures for the nation provided by the Bureau of Labor Statistics.

PT SAMPLE

Occupation
Executive or manager	15.9%
Professional	43.4%
Salesman	4.3%
Foreman or skilled worker	9.2%
Clerical worker	13.7%
Semiskilled or unskilled	5.7%
Other	7.9%

Full time	92.7%
Part time	7.3%

Self-employed	6.3%
Wage and salaried	93.7%

Sex
Female	51.5%
Male	48.5%

Age
Under 18	1.2%
18–24	19.3%
25–34	43.5%
35–44	21.8%
45–54	11.5%
55+	2.7%

Marital Status
Single	30.4%
Married	48.3%
Living together	7.7%
Separated	2.3%
Divorced	10.6%
Widowed	.7%

NATIONAL WORK FORCE

Occupation
Manager and administrator	10.7%
Professional and technical	15.1%
Sales worker	6.3%
Skilled worker	13.1%
Clerical worker	17.8%
Nonfarm labor	5.0%
Operatives (of equipment and transportation)	15.2%
Service workers	13.7%
Farm workers	3.0%

Full time	85.6%
Part time	14.4%

Self-employed	8.4%
Wage and salaried	90.7%
Family business	.9%

Sex
Female	40.5%
Male	59.5%

Age
16–17	3.4%
18–24	19.2%
25–34	25.6%
35–44	18.8%
45–54	17.9%
55+	15.2%

Marital Status
Never married	22.1%
Married, spouse present	65.6%
Married, spouse absent	3.1%
Divorced	6.2%
Widowed	3.0%

All categories except "Married" include in their numbers persons who are living together. The Census Bureau estimates that 2% of the nation's 48 million "couple households" are "living together."

PT SAMPLE		NATIONAL WORK FORCE	
Annual Income (before taxes)		**Total Money Earning of Persons Employed (1975 figures)**	
Less than $5,000	6.5%	Less than $5,000	40.9%
$5,000–$9,999	23.4%	$5,000–$9,999	26.1%
$10,000–$14,999	28.6%	$10,000–$14,999	17.9%
$15,000–$19,999	19.2%	$15,000–$19,999	8.6%
$20,000–$29,999	13.9%	$20,000–$24,999	3.2%
$30,000–$49,999	6.0%	$25,000+	3.2%
$50,000+	2.4%		

Last Year of Education Completed		**Last Year of Education Completed**	
Grade school or less	.3%	Grade school or less	10.0%
Some high school	2.3%	Some high school	13.7%
High school diploma or equivalent	9.6%	High school diploma or its equivalent	40.8%
Some college	25.5%	Some college	17.2%
College degree	20.1%	College degree	10.8%
Some graduate or professional school	14.8%	Some graduate or professional school, or	
Graduate or professional degree	27.5%	graduate or professional school degree	7.5%

satisfied with your jobs for now, but that there is an unmistakable undercurrent of restlessness that may well create problems for your employers as the American economy rambles toward the 1980s. You are potentially quite a mobile generation, with only loose loyalties to a particular corporation or a particular occupation.

The questionnaire, developed jointly by the authors and the *PT* staff, also tells us where you stand on a number of social issues related to jobs, ranging from whose career comes first in dual-career families; to who feels discriminated against on the job, and why; to how men and women are dividing the household tasks these days, and how people regard the ethical standards of their companies. Since we drew some questions from items in previous surveys by the Institute for Social Research at the University of Michigan, we can compare what you think with the opinions of other Americans.

Among the more intriguing results of the *PT* survey:

• 43 percent of *PT* readers felt that they had been victims of job discrimination in the past five years. Yet 82 percent oppose programs of affirmative action to make up for past discrimination against women and members of minorities.

• 78 percent would like to be able to set the hours that they start and leave work—suggesting strong support for plans such as "flextime."

• 44 percent feel "locked into," or trapped in, their jobs.

• Most people would continue working even if they could live comfortably for the rest of their lives without doing so.

• The most popular method of relieving tension from the job was not alcohol or drugs but physical exercise.

• Despite the influence of the women's movement, men's careers still come first in two-career families, and women are still stuck with most of the housework.

YOU LIKE YOUR WORK—MAYBE

Of course, we could not cover everything, and some readers complained, quite rightly, about our omissions. Gays, for example, pointed out we had not included them in an item about job discrimination. Other readers wrote to us about the tensions of having to work at two jobs. A number of people pointed out the special problems and pleasures of work in a small, family-owned business. A few offered some good advice about the importance of having work experience before graduating from school and beginning a career.

As a group, *Psychology Today*'s readers are closer in composition to Daniel Yankelovich's New Breed than to the country as a whole. They tend to be younger, better educated, and higher paid, with a heavy concentration of professionals (43.4 percent vs. a national average of 15.1 percent). In the sampling of questionnaires we analyzed, almost half earned between $10,000 and $20,000 a year. About 44 percent were 25 to 34 years old, which means this group was overrepresented in comparison to the nation.

There were more women than men (52 percent vs. 48 percent), reflecting the population as a whole but not the labor force, which has approximately 12 percent fewer women than the *PT* sample. The racial composition was 92 percent white and 8 percent non-white, similar to the ratio in the national labor force. (For a breakdown on the survey participants, compared with the national work force, see chart on page 14.)

The majority of our sample had fairly positive attitudes toward their present jobs and were notably free of depression. Their reports on how satisfied they were break down much like the results of the myriad other large-scale

"How likely is it that you will change your occupation in the next five years?"

Occupation	Likely	Some-what likely	Not at all likely
Semiskilled or unskilled	59.7%	24.8%	15.5%
Clerical workers	59.4%	26.5%	14.2%
Other	52.5%	27.7%	19.8%
Salesman	50.6%	21.6%	27.8%
Foreman or skilled worker	38.7%	31.4%	30.0%
Executive or manager	30.5%	28.1%	41.4%
Professional	25.9%	31.4%	42.7%

national studies of work satisfaction done in recent years: 21 percent said they were *very* satisfied, 20 percent registered some dissatisfaction, and, of these, 6 percent were *very* dissatisfied.

Not surprisingly, managers, executives, and professionals were more satisfied, less often depressed by their work, and less likely to feel trapped in their jobs than semiskilled, unskilled, and clerical workers. The most dissatisfied workers were the young (under 24), blacks, and those with an annual income between $5,000 and $10,000. These groups also reported the highest levels of depression. (We asked nine questions related to depression, such as, "How often do you feel down-hearted and blue?" and "How often do you feel more irritable than usual?")

Women generally tended to be as satisfied as men, which contradicts some other studies that show them to be more dissatisfied; the evidence from various studies on this point is inconsistent. By the same token, women did not report more depression than the men in our sample.

But men report higher levels of satisfaction than women in five aspects of their work: the opportunities it offers them to learn new things; the freedom they have on the job; the degree of participation in decision-making; their chances of promotion; and monetary rewards.

Through a series of questions, we checked to see if there's any truth in the assertion that female bosses have a negative effect on the job satisfaction of their subordinates. We found no evidence of it. Women with female supervisors, women with male supervisors, men with female supervisors, men with male supervisors—all tended to report roughly the same amount of job dissatisfaction.

COMPLAINTS ABOUT THE CORPORATION

In general, *PT* readers were dissatisfied with the way rewards are distributed and their performances evaluated in their organizations. As might be expected, they ranked pay and lack of advancement as chief causes of dissatisfaction, but they frequently complained as well about the share of praise they receive for doing a good job and the amount of information they are given about their job performance.

Previous studies also suggest that the rewards provided by an organization and the way they are allocated are a major source of worker dissatisfaction. Of course, they probably always will be, so long as budgets are limited and only a few can advance. But there is also evidence that many organizations often aggravate the situation by deciding who gets what in secretive and authoritarian ways—a style hardly calculated to attract the New Breed.

Cynicism about corporate processes was also apparent in the response to a question about how people get promoted. Almost half the people in the survey think that getting ahead in an organization depends more on whom you know than job performance. (Some of this reaction may have been defensive: people who were dissatisfied with their jobs and less involved in them were more likely to believe that knowing the right people was most important.)

Some writers have argued that most workers have about as much say in decision-making as they really want, and that only social scientists are concerned with giving them more. What did *PT* readers think? Overall, they tended to agree that such influence was desirable and that they wanted more of it. The majority said they had most influence on decisions directly related to their own work— but wanted more. They also said they had relatively little influence on corporate policy in general and on the division of work in their organization. Here, too, they wanted more say. Finally, they reported having the least say in personnel matters, such as firing and promoting others, but they were ambivalent about whether they wanted more influence in those decisions.

Men also reported having more say than women in every area of decision-making except in the scheduling of their own work routines. Women seemed less interested in opportunities to make decisions than the men in our sample, for reasons we could not determine.

Readers on Work

"Individual managerial leadership no longer exists. . . . Decisions are compromises made by groups, too late to be effective. Even the younger executive is a great believer in 'don't make waves.' "

"I'm not here to make a moral judgment—I'm here because I have to eat and pay my bills. I'll take whatever job fulfills that end the best—no matter how offensive I may find the company's practices. It's too damned hard to find jobs now. I can't afford to be so picky as to turn down a job because of pollutants or discriminatory personnel departments."

"I work for the Social Security Administration, which has implemented a flextime system. . . . All of us at SSA love it, and it is the reason many of us are still hanging around, even though we all hate our jobs."

"I am the first and only female working as a laborer for a fire department in a major city. . . . I am the most capable and responsible worker on my crew, which began with eight males plus myself, and dwindled to four. The thing that so intensely irritates me is that the supervisors all know this, yet they resist giving me any responsibility. . . . If other women are treated as I have been, their employers are going to lose enthusiastic, hard-working people."

"Each time I reentered the work force, my extensive résumé always elicited the response 'That's fine honey, but how fast can you type?' Financial desperation would finally get the best of me and I would submit doctored-down résumés, playing down the education and experience and building up my office 'skills,' with the misguided thought that once I got in, I'd show what I could do. I've discovered that being intelligent, hardworking, and ambitious is an excellent way for a woman to starve."

WHAT'S MOST IMPORTANT?

PT readers seem to make a sharp distinction between what they liked about their jobs and what they thought was most important about work in general. When asked how satisfied they were with various aspects of their jobs, the thing that pleased the largest number was the friendliness of their fellow workers.

But when asked to rate the things they felt were most important in work, they told another

---

"How satisfied are you with each of the following aspects of your job? And how important to you is each of them?"

Respondents were asked to choose among different degrees of importance and satisfaction for each job feature. Based on averages of their responses, the numbers below rank each from 1 (most important to the group or most often satisfying) to 18 (least important or least often satisfying).

	Importance	Satisfaction
Chances to do something that makes you feel good about yourself	1	8
Chances to accomplish something worthwhile	2	6
Chances to learn new things	3	10
Opportunity to develop your skills and abilities	4	12
The amount of freedom you have on your job	5	2
Chances you have to do things you do best	6	11
The resources you have to do your job	7	9
The respect you receive from people you work with	8	3
Amount of information you get about your job performance	9	17
Your chances for taking part in making decisions	10	14
The amount of job security you have	11	5
Amount of pay you get	12	16
The way you are treated by the people you work with	13	4
The friendliness of people you work with	14	1
Amount of praise you get for job well done	15	15
The amount of fringe benefits you get	16	7
Chances for getting a promotion	17	18
Physical surroundings of your job	18	13

story. It was the possibilities for self-growth that crowded the head of the list, including opportunities to develop their skills and abilities, to learn new things, and to accomplish something that would make them feel good about themselves. Among the least important things (though not necessarily unimportant) were fringe benefits, chances for promotion, the physical surroundings at work—and the friendliness of co-workers.

Was self-actualization really more important than money? We pressed people on the issue by asking them if they would accept a higher-paying job if it meant less interesting work. Almost two-thirds of the sample were unwilling to do so.

On the other hand, 46 percent said they would not accept a *more* interesting job if it paid less than their present one (41 percent were willing to make such a tradeoff). Those least likely to take a pay cut for more interesting work were divorced women (55 percent), widows (47 percent), women living with someone (47 percent), and married men (49 percent).

The data suggest that people have in mind a level of compensation that they consider adequate for them. If their pay falls below this level, then money becomes more important than interesting work. If wages or salary are above this level, then whether they consider their job interesting assumes more importance.

WHO PLANS TO CHANGE?

The majority of *PT* readers in our sample appear to be having second thoughts about their occupations. Many of those who think they might make a change in the next five years are, of course, the same people who express overall dissatisfaction with their jobs. Though women seem to be no more dissatisfied than men, they are more inclined to make a change in the next five years.

People are restless for a number of reasons that we can only speculate about. Some go through a mid-career crisis and are forced to reevaluate their previous values and goals. Others discover that because of changes in the

"If you would continue to work, what is the one most important reason?"

	Male	Female
I enjoy what I do on my job.	29.0%	28.6%
I derive the major part of my identity from my job.	25.8%	27.5%
Work keeps me from being bored.	17.4%	18.2%
My work is important and valuable to others.	13.9%	10.8%
I enjoy the company of my co-workers.	5.3%	8.1%
I would feel guilty if I did not contribute to society through gainful employment.	4.4%	3.4%
I would continue out of habit.	4.2%	3.4%

economy, their skills are simply no longer in demand and they must learn new ones.

The *PT* survey suggests another reason may be that their choice of career was poorly thought-through in the first place. Almost 40 percent of the reader sample said they had happened into their occupation by chance, without much deliberation. Still another 16 percent reported that they had settled for their present occupation because they couldn't get a job in another one they preferred. Only 23 percent were working in their occupation of choice.

As for the 44 percent who feel "locked in," most of them may think the time isn't right to take a risk or that they have too much at stake in the present job to move. Pay plans, seniority advantages, and fringe benefits are powerful incentives for staying with a company—even if an employee isn't happy there. A tight labor market and high unemployment may contribute to nervousness about a hasty move.

More than half of our sample (54 percent) were optimistic about their ability to find another job at about the same level of pay and benefits as their present one. Managers and executives felt most keenly that they had too much at stake to leave their present positions now. However, it was the semiskilled and unskilled who expressed the strongest feelings about being trapped and thought it would be very difficult to find a job equal to their present one.

Readers on Work

"We working mothers (especially the ones who would rather be with their children for a few years after they're born) are bitter. My present job is a good one—although it is clerical, it offers me a wider range of responsibilities than I've ever had in the past. However, no matter how good I've got it, there isn't a day that goes by that I don't long to be with my child and watch her develop. . . . I work on Capitol Hill and I strongly feel that at least the government should set up day-care centers for the children of working mothers."

"Your question about feeling trapped in a job really hit home. Somehow, I find myself earning $21,000 a year doing work I never meant to get into. . . . Now I'd have to take a cut to start over in a new field—a big cut—which I'm willing to do, but prospective employers either think I'm crazy or want to keep me in the same occupation to use my experience. I'm about ready to drop out altogether!"

"Dirty looks from my boss are common. Never in nine months has anyone come right out and said, 'Could you do it this way? I much prefer it.' That's too easy. The method here is *not* to tell you, just to talk about what a lousy job you are doing."

"During my eight years as a secretary, I went through a lot of changes in attitude. . . . I discovered that the typical boss wants very little—and very much—from a secretary. He wants his coffee black, his errands run, no independent thinking, no personal life on the job, punctual arrivals, late departures, an exact lunch hour, and God forbid you should leave your desk and he doesn't know where you are, even if you are running 10,000 copies of his report. . . . I now have found an employer who believes in me. I feel like a human being again instead of an android typist. I have been handed responsibility without experience and performed superbly . . . just because someone up there had faith in me."

HOW YOU COPE

The data on job mobility only affirm that work is to this generation of adults more than an economic necessity to be avoided if at all possible. Only 9 percent said they would stop working if they could live as comfortably as they liked for the rest of their lives. Almost 75 percent reported that they would continue to work; and women were as likely as men to want to continue, which suggests, in part, that work now is as important to their identities as it is to men's.

The average *PT* reader spends between nine and 10½ hours a day on work and work-related activities. To be sure, attitudes toward work have changed. For the most part, this generation agrees with Douglas McGregor, author of *The Human Side of Enterprise*, that "work is as natural as play." But work also causes pressures and tensions. How do our readers cope with them?

They appear to make a conscious attempt to separate home and work. Almost 70 percent in our survey said they like to keep the two separate. But the attempt to compartmentalize doesn't always succeed. Three-fourths of those in the sample said they brought their work, troubles, and frustrations home with them.

For our survey members, work was rewarding, but not when it cut into leisure or time with family. About 24 percent of them complained about excessive hours. Another 28 percent felt they had to start work too early or leave too late. Some 20 percent found it difficult to complete assigned work during office hours; 13 percent objected to excessive overtime. And 21 percent reported that their work schedules interfered with their family lives. (Executives and managers complained most about long hours and the impact on their families.)

The data suggest there is considerable potential support for a system such as flextime, which has been successfully introduced in some

About 43% of the sample felt they had been victims of job discrimination within the past five years. Below, a breakdown of the reasons for discrimination and the forms that it took.

FORM OF DISCRIMINATION   *REASONS FOR DISCRIMINATION*

	Sex	Race	Ethnic Origin or Religion	Age	Physical Handicap
Affirmative action guidelines led to my not being hired although I had sufficient qualifications.	18.0%	32.7%	24.1%	16.7%	31.0%
My salary was lower than for other workers doing comparable work.	48.5%	15.5%	17.2%	28.1%	17.2%
I was expected to do more work, different work, or less prestigious work than other workers who had similar jobs.	28.0%	21.8%	27.6%	25.1%	17.2%
I could not get the job for which my skills qualified me.	37.2%	34.5%	31.0%	44.8%	37.9%
I was not accepted or invited to participate in informal social activities like lunch or a drink after work.	12.8%	7.3%	19.0%	7.4%	6.9%
I was not encouraged or allowed to participate in in-house training programs.	16.2%	15.5%	12.1%	9.4%	6.9%
I did not have access to informal communication or sources of information relevant to my job.	25.3%	29.1%	43.1%	24.6%	34.5%

Because respondents checked as many of the forms of discrimination as applied to them, all categories add up to more than 100%.

government and company offices. Under flextime, an employee must work a set number of hours per week (usually 40), but is given a choice of a few different schedules.

With their long hours and desire for career growth, this generation has its share of tensions and frustrations. They have found their own ways of coping.

In his novel *Something Happened*, Joseph Heller describes salesmen as a "vigorous, fun-loving bunch" who "drink heavily until they get hepatitis or heart attacks or are warned away from drinking for some other reason. . . ." Salesmen are more likely to drink on and off the job than other occupational groups, our survey shows, but they are also more likely to engage in physical exercise. Indeed, physical exercise is the approach to handling job stress cited most frequently by our whole sample.

The next most frequent methods are eating, daydreaming, and buying something for oneself. Women are more likely than men to use all three methods. Along with professionals, they are, as a group, also more likely to seek counseling or therapy to relieve job stress.

Managers and executives are somewhat

"All in all, whose career is given more weight when making decisions that affect both careers?"

	Male	Female
Mine	65.2%	9.4%
Partner's	1.4%	40.7%
Equal weight	15.7%	32.6%
Does not apply	17.6%	17.2%

"If your partner were offered a better job in another city, how likely is it that you would move even though you might initially be underemployed or unemployed?"

	Male	Female
Unlikely	69.9%	25.3%
Likely	18.6%	63.5%
Undecided	11.5%	11.1%

more inclined than others to drink after work. Foremen and skilled workers are more likely to use drugs on and off the job. In general, clerical workers are more likely to buy something for themselves and, along with professionals, to eat when under stress. Unskilled and semi-skilled workers are more likely than others to smoke or daydream. The younger the person, the more likely he or she is to use drugs as a means of coping—including tranquilizers, amphetamines, and marijuana.

THE OLD ETHIC—NOT DEAD YET

Although women as well as men seek the psychological satisfactions of work nowadays, this apparently does not spare women from the housekeeping chores. The reports of both men and women on how they divide household tasks indicate that women still do most of the grocery shopping, cleaning, cooking, and clearing away after meals. When there are children, women generally take care of them, including driving them to activities, or, they share the responsibilities with their mates. The younger the woman, the more likely she was to report that the household work is shared equally—a sign that changes may be coming, though slowly.

Readers on Work

"I am recently married and have moved to a small town outside Davenport, Iowa, from Chicago. In Chicago I had my own business, supervised two full-time employees, and made approximately $25,000. I am now handling responsibilities similar to those I had in Chicago, but I am working for someone else and my salary is an unbelievable $9,600.

"My dissatisfaction with my salary and the influences it has upon the family budget are major factors in the real push we are making for relocation.

"If women in the cities think that they have it had, they ought to try it out here. In the cities, while sexism still exists, there is an acute awareness that there are legal sanctions for equal opportunity and there is a nervousness about meeting guidelines. People here are blissfully unaware of the entire issue."

As for household finances, most people reported that they handled the bills themselves or shared the task with their mates. It seems likely that in most cases each partner managed different aspects of the family budget.

The men and women in our sample also displayed traditional attitudes on the issue of whose career comes first when both partners work. Almost all the women in the survey (93 percent) and most of the men (59 percent) were in the dual-career category. About 65 percent of the men said that their careers came first in decisions affecting both parties, while only 9 percent of the women said theirs came first.

Similarly, when we asked men and women whether they would move if their partner were offered a better job in another city—even if it meant that they might be initially unemployed or underemployed—women were much more likely to pick up stakes and follow their men (64 percent of the women vs. 19 percent of the men would move). The higher a man's income, the more resistant he was to moving under these circumstances. His mate's income had absolutely nothing to do with what he said he would do. It seems that reports of the death of traditional sex roles are greatly exaggerated.

Although a majority of our sample described their politics as liberal (47 percent) or moderate (34 percent), their views seemed conservative on some social issues. For example, 82 percent of the sample opposed a program on affirmative action that would give preference in hiring to women or members of minority groups if their qualifications were not as good as those of other applicants. There was no significant difference in the male/female response to this question. Our readers took this position even though 43 percent reported that they themselves had been victims of some form of job discrimination within the past five years.

Complaints about discrimination were most numerous among women, blacks, and the young (though people between the ages of 45 and 54 also reported a relatively high incidence of discrimination). Their most frequent complaint was that they had not been able to get a job commensurate with their skills and abilities because of discrimination. Next in frequency,

> **Readers on Work**
>
> "I'm addicted to business. . . . Retailing is like the stock market, and a little like gambling. Invest in an inventory and gamble on selling at a profit. What a wonderful game . . . I bought a gourmet shop, and I love it. It would be rough to work for a large corporation again."
>
> "I love my work. . . . I am an ombudsman at a university. There are, in this country, only 140 of us. The charge to this office calls for us to 'provide justice' to the members of the university community, 'to investigate grievances concerning abuse of power.' It sounds noble. It *is* noble, and the satisfactions, therefore, immeasurable."
>
> "The employer is, surprisingly, absent from this questionnaire (except if he's engaging in immoral or illegal activity or when we disagreed). Yet the boss can destroy a good job for an employee, or make tolerable, even enjoyable, a dull one. I've had it both ways. Of course, it is most desirable to be the boss oneself."

people complained about being denied access to informal communication or other sources of information vital to their jobs. Some people also reported that they had not received equal pay for equal work.

Women were more likely than men to report that they had been expected to do more work or less prestigious work than other workers who had similar jobs. They also said that they were often not invited to take part in informal activities, such as lunch or a drink after work, when they might pick up information useful to their jobs, and were not encouraged, or in some cases even allowed, to join in-house training programs. On the other hand, men were much more likely to complain of "reverse discrimination"—that they had lost out on some opportunities because of preferential treatment of women or members of minorities.

Why do those who themselves have been discriminated against lack sympathy for affirmative action? We suspect this seeming

"I often feel trapped in my present job."	
Strongly disagree	16.5%
Disagree	21.9%
Slightly disagree	7.6%
Neither agree nor disagree	10.1%
Slightly agree	18.6%
Agree	14.1%
Strongly agree	11.3%

contradiction might reflect older and deeper values, going back to the Protestant ethic. If so, we would expect those in our sample to endorse the values of hard work and individualism. The results support this interpretation. More than 50 percent of the respondents felt that hard work makes you a better person, and more than 75 percent believed that people who were capable of working and chose not to were a drain on society.

Attitudes toward ethics in business were more ambivalent. About 86 percent rejected the suggestion that it was necessary for them to themselves engage in illegal or immoral behavior in their jobs. But when asked if they would report illegal or immoral behavior by their employers, they were generally uncertain. Although 37 percent were quite likely to do it, 26 percent said they were not at all likely to—and the remaining 37 percent were ambivalent. We got similar responses when we asked people if they would confront their employers with such behavior, rather than go to the authorities.

Letters from readers suggest that the main reasons for which they were unwilling to act against their employers were worries about getting another job and supporting their families. One woman wrote that she would be

"All in all, I am satisfied with my job."	
Strongly disagree	7.8%
Disagree	10.6%
Slightly disagree	7.5%
Neither agree nor disagree	5.7%
Slightly agree	15.1%
Agree	35.6%
Strongly agree	17.6%

guided by loyalty to her employer in such cases, and would quit her job before turning him in. On the evidence of the *PT* survey, it seems that potential whistle-blowers in the corporation are a minority.

TOMORROW'S TURNOVER

Many of the views of *PT* readers seem to represent a healthy new commitment to the importance of work. But it would be wrong to conclude that their attitudes represent a return to traditional feelings about job values. Healthy, yes; traditional in the spirit of the 40s and 50s, probably not. *PT* readers do not have the strong commitment to working for a particular organization or in a particular occupation that was characteristic of the old days. They appear to be very willing to change jobs if they can better themselves. They also seem very concerned about the decision-making opportunities, interest, and challenge in their jobs. Further, they seem to have little of the social consciousness that was so important to young people in the 60s.

It seems to us that the best term to describe our respondents' approach to work is "self-oriented." The phrase expresses a turning inward that is taking place in the nation as a whole. Americans today seem to have less interest in social reform than they do in securing a satisfying job for themselves.

This high self-orientation should, in some way, make management of organizations easier than it was in the rebellious 60s and early 70s. People seem to believe again in the value of hard work and in developing themselves at the workplace. On the other hand, they are not likely to be easy to satisfy or retain as employees. They are likely to demand a great deal, and, if they don't receive it, will look elsewhere.

We may be in for a period of increasing instability, because of the turnover of those who can find better jobs and the turnoff of those who can't. Particularly disturbing is the fact that our data come from a sample that contains mostly professional and managerial employ-

Readers on Work

"In my case (36-year career with the same
organization), I deliberately chose, at my 27th
service year, to 'shoot my way' into organiza-
tional-development consultation. This required
considerable personal risk, abandoning my
former technological field (engineering administration). . . . While I enjoy my work, and am
involved in a client-centered way, I try (and
usually succeed) in keeping my ego involvement low."

"My present husband and myself left Baltimore, Maryland, two and a half years ago to
live in Olds, Alberta, Canada, because he
wanted a better life. He left a lucrative dental
practice, a wife, and two children; he was in
Who's Who in the East. I left a husband and a
child because of these pressures you talk about
in your article. It is a *very* difficult decision to
leave, but we have never regretted it. We have
two stores and a dental practice—but we go
camping practically every weekend. We really
enjoy life and each other—and there's very
little stress running two stores in a small
town."

ees—who are essential to any large organization and who have traditionally had a low rate
of turnover. Equally unsettling is the amount of
discontent among other critical groups—
foremen, clerical personnel, skilled and unskilled workers. They, too, want a satisfying job
that offers prospects of personal growth.
Instead of seeing opportunities ahead, however,
many express feelings of being trapped and
show signs of psychological withdrawal.

One thing that organizations can do, in
response, is to pay more attention to the needs
of their employees. If they want to make the
most of their human resources, they had better
understand the new job values—and start
thinking of ways to improve the quality of work.
Even if they do, however, some people will
continue to move—and there will be little
corporations can do about it. Under the
circumstances, the only alternative may be to
develop training and recruitment programs
that are designed to deal with the turnover from
a generation that wants more, more, more, and
may worry, above all, about standing still.

Americans Change

Business Week

The structure of a nation's economy, the problems it faces, and the solutions it devises for those problems are determined in large measure by the people who compose it. Everyone who will be a mature worker, pensioner, or executive in the U.S. in the next 20 years is already born. By looking closely at who these people are, what they will want, and what they can do, business and government can tell a great deal about what sort of country the U.S. will be in the next two decades and what sort of challenges it will face.

Even economists consider demographics—the study of populations—a rather unexciting and unrewarding branch of their science. Business executives, distracted by inflation, shifting markets, and increasing government intervention in the private sector, have had little time to listen to the demographers.

The U.S., however, is going through some fundamental demographic changes that forecasters and policymakers will have to take into account. The economy is already feeling the impact of these shifts, and there is more—much more—to come in the future. "Demographic statistics make dull reading," says economist Michael L. Wachter of the University of Pennsylvania's Wharton School, "but they helped lay the groundwork for our current economic problems."

The most obvious change in the U.S. population is simply that it is growing older. In 1970 the median age was just under 28. Within three years, it will reach 30, and by the turn of

the century, it will hit 35. Such a change means a shift in patterns of consumption and incomes. And, inevitably, changes in social attitudes as well. "The growing mood of conservatism in American society is probably related to the maturation of the population and the waning of the youth culture," says Jeffrey Evans of the National Institute of Child Health & Human Development.

But the steady upward march of the median age gives a deceptive impression of orderly progression. Actually, the structure of the U.S. population is due for some sudden and disconcerting shifts, which have their origins in changes in the birth rate years ago. The various age groups that make up the total population—the "cohorts," as the demographers refer to them—will expand dramatically and then shrink abruptly as these waves occur.

Baby Boom, Then Bust

Three drastic shifts in the rate at which the U.S. population reproduces and increases itself have occurred in the past half century. The first was the "birth dearth" of the Depression years, when total births dropped to about 2.5 million from an average of close to 3 million a year. At the time, the fertility rate (the number of children born to the average woman in her lifetime) dropped close to 2.1—the replacement level that would lead to a stable population if maintained indefinitely.

The second shift was the well-publicized

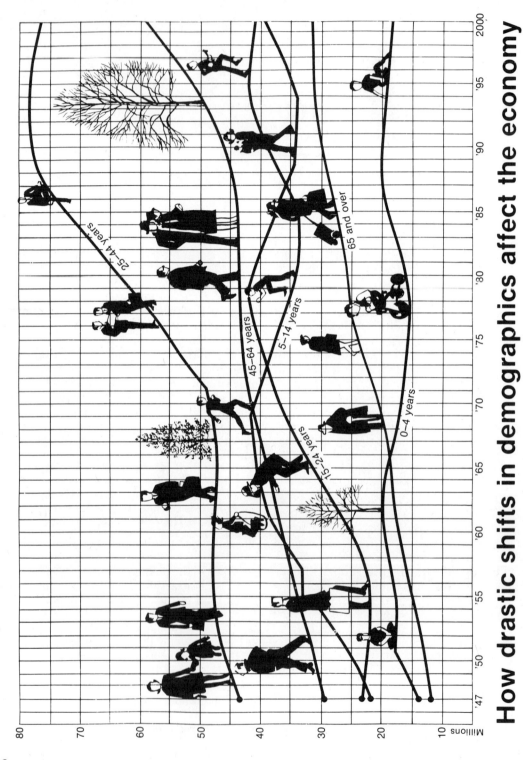

How drastic shifts in demographics affect the economy

"baby boom" of the postwar era, which continued into the early 1960s. In the mid-1950s the fertility rate shot up to 3.8, and the number of births each year surged past the 4 million mark.

Then came the third shift—the "baby bust"—marked by a progressively steep decline in the fertility rate, which had fallen to 1.76 by 1976—far below the population replacement level. And this, in turn, brought the number of births down to 3.13 million in that year.

The unstabilizing effects of such a baby boom, preceded and followed by a very low birth rate, are the source of many of the problems the U.S. has faced in recent years. And the problems are by no means ended. "Because of the low birth rates both before and after its occurrence, this group of cohorts is like a melon being digested by a boa constrictor," says demographer Denis F. Johnston of the Census Bureau. "It will undergo strains and pose a succession of problems for the nation's institutions as it moves through the age cycle."

The baby boom cohorts made their mark on U.S. society and on U.S. markets long before they left home. School districts will be paying for years on the bonds they have floated to provide educational facilities that may or may not be needed in the future. Manufacturers of stereo sets and blue jeans will have to hope that tastes will not change with age.

The real impact of the baby boom on the U.S. economy, however, began to be felt in the late 1960s, when the first cohort entered the labor market. The problems were masked for a while by growing college enrollments and by the manpower needs of an overheated economy and the Vietnam war. But by the early 1970s, rising unemployment figures brought the issue into sharp focus: The U.S. economy must create jobs and incomes for a rapidly expanding mature labor force in the next decade. After that, it must adjust to a slower rate of growth and eventually, perhaps, to very modest growth by historical standards. Beginning after the year 2000, the economy must find ways to keep the mounting costs of pensions and retirement income from overwhelming the producing workers.

Declining Population

The immediate problem—and the problem of the early 1980s—is to produce jobs that will absorb these new workers into the economic system. This may become somewhat easier as the baby boom cohorts grow older, since the tremendous acceleration in the growth of the working-age population will soon be behind us. The growth of the 18-to-24-year-old group is now slowing sharply, and by the 1980s, this cohort will be declining steadily—a process that will continue for another 15 years. Over the next 12 years, the most rapidly increasing element of the population will be 25 to 44 years old. On the whole, of course, this is the most employable age group in the U.S. labor force and the most productive. It is also the group with the highest spending profile. Its numbers will jump by 35% to 78 million in 1990 from 58 million today. After 1985, however, the 25-to-34-year-old segment will top out, and it will decline throughout the 1990s.

Meanwhile, the 45-to-54-year age group will shrink a bit until the second half of the 1980s, when it will enter a period of rapid growth. By 1995, the baby boom generation will begin to swell the ranks of the 55- to 64-year-olds. Throughout the 1980s and 1990s, the over-64 group will grow steadily, but as a percentage of total population, it will remain steady at 11% to 12%. The enormous increase in this group will start in the second decade of the next century, as the baby boom cohorts become senior citizens.

The 1980s, therefore, shapes up as a decade of enormous opportunities for growth as well as for severe strains on the economy. In the 1990s, with an older and more slowly expanding labor force, growth will come harder, but the quality of life may be easier to improve. After the year 2000, the U.S. will enter a new period of economic and social strain as the number of people no longer working increases in proportion to the number still on the job.

After the year 2000, however, the labor force will consist increasingly of people who are not yet born. And demographers, who failed entirely to foresee both the baby boom and the

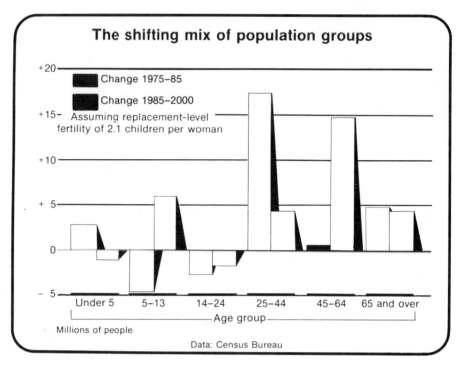

The shifting mix of population groups

+20

■ Change 1975–85

□ Change 1985–2000

+15 — Assuming replacement-level
fertility of 2.1 children per woman

+10

+ 5

0

– 5

| Under 5 | 5–13 | 14–24 | 25–44 | 45–64 | 65 and over |

Age group

Millions of people

Data: Census Bureau

subsequent baby bust, are qualifying their predictions about the future of the birth rate with a lot of caveats. Most think that the birth rate will rise somewhat as the baby boom generation enters its 30s and as women who have postponed childbearing face a now-or-never choice. But though birth and fertility rates did pick up a bit last year, few experts see a dramatic surge in fertility ahead.

The Census Bureau's official view is that the fertility rate will eventually move up and stabilize around the replacement level. But Robert L. Clark of the University of North Carolina thinks the figure will be even lower. "Of course, the picture could change overnight," he says, "but the current social and economic trends suggest that fertility will tend to stay somewhat below the replacement level."

Among the trends cited by Clark and others are such social phenomena as the falling marriage and rising divorce rates, deferred childbearing, the upswing in single-parent, two wage-earner, and individual households, and higher education levels. Add to that the

increased work experience among young women and their greater career opportunities, the high cost of rearing and educating children, and the ever-increasing usage of effective birth control techniques. Says Clark: "All of these trends tend to reinforce each other."

Given such powerful factors, demographers can draw some tentative conclusions about the future:

The over-all rate of unemployment should begin to drop in the 1980s as the rear guard of the baby boom generation enters its mature working years. Productivity should increase for a while, reflecting a more experienced work force. This, in turn, may help dampen inflation. By the mid-1980s, however, labor surplus will give way to labor scarcity. Economic growth will slow, and inflationary pressures are apt to rise.

Government spending on education and crime prevention is likely to slacken. In the wake of sagging birth rates, primary school enrollments have already plummeted in many localities and secondary school attendance is also beginning to decline sharply—both as a result of the baby bust and of the increasing number of dropouts. At the same time, college enrollment rates have also been declining, particularly for males. "If present trends continue," says the Census Bureau's Johnston, "the number of undergraduates will fall faster than the college-age population for at least another decade."

Similarly, crime rates are beginning to subside in many areas. More than 75% of such crimes as burglary, robbery, and auto theft are committed by youngsters under 25, and their numbers are beginning to wane. "Because crime is associated with unemployment, and because joblessness among teenagers may be expected to lessen as their numbers decrease, the crime rate could fall significantly in the 1980s," speculates psychologist Eugene Winograd of Emory University in Atlanta.

The aging of the baby boom group may eventually dampen the population shift from the Northeast and Midwest to the Sunbelt. "In the past," says Rand Corp. demographer Peter Morrison, "high birth rates often hid the fact that migration was occurring. But when rates dropped sharply in the 1970s, a lot of areas suddenly found themselves losing population." Since the young adult group most prone to migrate will be declining in size in the 1980s, Morrison expects the tempo of migration to slow somewhat—particularly if the trend toward two-paycheck families continues.

The baby boom cohorts are likely to experience continuing difficulties in satisfying career and income aspirations—simply because of the competitive pressures generated by their sheer numbers—just as they had faced heightened unemployment in their teens. To be sure, the lack of seasoned managers to oversee the flood tide of younger workers will create a problem for business. And it will provide rapid advancement for a lucky few (and delayed retirement for some managers). But most of the baby boom cohorts probably face the prospect of heightened competition as well as relatively depressed incomes and advancement opportunities during most of their working lives, particularly in the context of slow labor force growth.

Compounding the problem is the fact that

this group is the best educated in the nation's history, with more than 40% of them estimated to have attended college by the time they are 30. At the same time, their ranks include a number of youngsters, primarily blacks and other minorities, whose educational attainments have been falling sharply in recent years. In both cases, the situation spells frustration: The college-educated are having to settle for lower-level positions than they anticipated, and the disadvantaged are having trouble finding any jobs at all.

As a result, some experts see "severe social disruptions" in the decades ahead, with little chance that the economy (which may then be on a permanent slow growth track) will ever supply enough high-level jobs to match the educational attainments and aspirations of the baby boom group. The Census Bureau's Johnston, however, is more sanguine, predicting a variety of responses to the new economic realities. "Many young people will work harder and seek more education in their adult years to boost their chances of advancement," he says. "Others may downgrade material affluence and the work ethic. And a few may seek an outlet in efforts to change the system."

The Wharton School's Wachter feels that the chief problem may lie with the disadvantaged. "We are in danger," he says, "of creating a permanent group of marginal workers whose lack of skills and early job experience, combined with high welfare and jobless benefits, will keep them chronically unemployed."

Notwithstanding the frustrations of the job market, the outlook for consumer spending appears bright—at least during the near term. As Leon W. Taub of Chase Econometric Associates Inc. puts it: "The new consumers may feel poorer, but they will be better off in real terms as the economy continues to grow. And with fewer children to support and more two-wage-earner families, discretionary income will rise." To give some idea of the pending surge in purchasing power, Conference Board economist Fabian Linden estimates that the U.S. will add 7 million families in the 25-to-44-year age group in the decade ending in 1985. "By that year," he says, "the income of that group will have risen 80%, and it will account for half of all consumer spending."

Demographic trends suggest where much of that income will go. Housing demand should be particularly strong in the next few years, "both for the single-family homes that are typically purchased by young families in their early 30s, and for apartments that cater to the growing number of single-adult, one-child, and childless households," notes demographer James A. Sweet of the University of Wisconsin. Adds consumer economist Carol Brock Kenney of Loeb Rhoades, Hornblower & Co.: "Houses will be smaller, better-insulated, and will require smaller appliances with multipurpose functions. And their sales will spur demand for household durables, textiles, and do-it-yourself products."

For marketers, though, the trick will be to look beyond the gross age shifts in the population to changes in living patterns. For instance, to deal with a slowing birthrate and with increased competition for the food dollar from fast-food outlets and convenience stores, supermarket chains are now altering their product mixes and interior designs. And a recent study unveiled by the Coca-Cola Co. indicates that although teenagers consume more soft drinks than their elders, those in their 40s now consume more of the beverages than they did in their younger years. "This suggests that demand for many so-called youth products can continue to grow as the population ages," says a Wall Street consumer analyst.

In general, the experts feel that demographic trends suggest a stress on quality, durability, and variety in future purchases, with more dollars going to small consumer durables, entertainment, travel, recreation, adult education, and other convenience- and experience-oriented goods and services.

A Need for Added Capital

Behind such optimistic appraisals of tomorrow's markets, of course, lies the assumption that the government can devise and implement economic policies appropriate to the changing economic and demographic climate.

And to economist Wachter, that means the recognition that aggregate demand stimulus will worsen, not solve, the stagflation dilemma currently facing the nation. Following the lead of George L. Perry of the Brookings Institution, Wachter argues that the failure to recognize that structural changes in the labor force—the influx of low-skilled teenagers and young women—had changed the unemployment-inflation trade-off in the mid-1960s permitted policymakers to overheat the economy, sparking a sharp rise in inflation. "We're all paying the penalty of that mistake now," he says.

What is more, the problem is still with us. Wachter and his economist wife Susan have calculated that structural shifts in the labor force, together with high jobless and welfare benefits and a rising minimum wage, have now pushed the noninflationary unemployment rate to the 5½% range, compared to 4% in 1955. "And due to a continuing lag in capital investment by industry," Wachter says, "it could be as high as 6%."

The solution as he sees it is clear. Because labor force growth is about to slacken as the baby boom completes its entry into the prime work force, structural unemployment can be expected to decline. But taking advantage of this favorable shift requires added capital spending, since a failure to expand physical capacity now could result in supply bottlenecks well before the economy reaches its new full employment potential. Thus, Wachter favors vastly expanded incentives for investment, far beyond what President Carter is proposing in his current tax package. "We should be thinking," Wachter says, "about things like a 12% tax credit, accelerated depreciation, and allowing companies to expense the added costs of new health, pollution, and energy usage regulations that may be imposed after a new plant is built."

At the same time, Wachter argues that there is an immediate need for upgrading the skills of disadvantaged youngsters in the 16-to-24-year age group so that they will be in a better position to take advantage of improving job opportunities when the labor market tightens in a few years. "Time is running out for this group, which has suffered extraordinarily high rates of unemployment in recent years," he warns. Rather than public service employment, which takes youngsters off the streets but provides few skills that are transferable to the private sector, Wachter favors financial inducements such as wage subsidies and tax credits to encourage industry to hire and train the low-skilled. "Such programs would not only alleviate human suffering but would pay off for industry in the coming decade when labor supplies will tighten."

And what of the era beyond 1985? Assuming that the U.S. is now on a permanent path leading toward population stability, most economists who have looked at the implications of such a scenario are not overly concerned. "Higher immigration, delayed retirement, and increased labor force participation by women may well soften the blow of a reduced flow of domestic workers," says Larry Neal of the University of Illinois. Neal also points to the practice of such countries as West Germany and Switzerland in importing "guest laborers" to supplement their work forces.

Nor do economists worry—as they did during the depression—that the economy will suffer "secular stagnation" because of a lack of adequate demand to stimulate investment. "If there's one thing we've learned—perhaps too well—it's how to maintain aggregate demand," says Wachter. While overall economic growth will eventually slacken in line with slower labor force growth, Neal notes that per-capita income and the ratio of capital to labor would both tend to rise. "With zero population growth, productivity would tend to increase as the result of greater investment in physical and human capital, and we might even improve the rate of advance of technological progress," he speculates.

Intergenerational Conflict

Perhaps the most serious problem in the current demographic scenario is the burden that a large retired group imposes on the working population when pensions are financed on a pay-as-you-go basis and when the ratio of retirees to workers increases. The hefty increases in Social

Security taxes mandated by recent legislation are only the first taste of this problem, which will take on massive proportions in the next century—when the baby boom generation reaches retirement age.

In another 60 years, the so-called dependency ratio (the ratio of wage earners to beneficiaries) is expected to fall from its current level of 3.2 to 1 to less than 2 to 1. Many observers fear that the prospect of ever-escalating payroll taxes will spark a rebellion among younger workers, who will eventually balk at paying the tab for their elders. Since the political clout of the elderly will increase with their numbers, such a conflict could tear apart the nation's social fabric.

Even if the intergenerational conflict is contained, economists see the possibility of serious economic effects. Harvard University's Martin Feldstein believes that the scheduled rises in Social Security benefits will inspire workers to reduce their savings for retirement, resulting in less capital for business investment, and thereby slowing productivity gains and the advance in real wages.

Chase Econometric's Taub also worries about the impact of a growing tax burden on individual incentives. "At some point, people may simply stop working as hard," he says.

Weighty as these problems are, however, they are not intractable. Joseph J. Spengler, economics professor emeritus of Duke University, believes that one key answer is extending the retirement age. Another solution might be to scale back the growth of future retirement benefits, allowing the replacement of wages to decline on a percentage basis during a period when everyone is more affluent.

"The important thing," says Spengler, "is that analysis of demographic trends allows us to see clearly the dimensions of future problems, and that is the essential first step toward their solution."

AN UNEVEN FLOW OF MANAGEMENT TALENT

The population patterns that are now straining the U.S. economy will confront corporations with a peculiar management problem in the 1980s. But even though most companies can see trouble coming, few of them have given much thought to what to do about it.

The problem is summed up by Arch Patton of McKinsey & Co.: "In the years 1985 to 1990, managers in the 45-to-65-year age group, a group that has traditionally held 60% to 70% of senior management jobs, will number only between 11% and 18% of the total population segment in management." Or to put it another way, says Patton, "management's ranks will contain 88% more 20-to-34 year olds than 45-to-59-year olds, an inexperienced-to-experienced ratio of almost 2 to 1."

And the curious unwillingness of business to prepare for the day when there are too many Indians and not enough chiefs is explained by a senior vice-president for personnel at a New York bank: "It is hard to govern a business by the bottom line if you stockpile staff to cover peaks and valleys. We react to the labor pool as it appears in our daily lives."

Business Week reporters got the same reaction from executives at computer companies and manufacturers as well as at banks. Most personnel executives refused to let their names be used because, as one put it, "We've simply not given much thought to the subject, and anything I say may turn out to be embarrassingly wrong."

The stubborn arithmetic of demographics, however, is not going to be dismissed so easily. In the 1980s an extraordinary number of ambitious young men and women will crowd onto the first step of the management ladder, but the number of seasoned executives to supervise them will not grow correspondingly. In the 1990s the situation will reverse. There will be more experienced, fully qualified junior managers than there are spots in senior management to absorb them.

Isolate the "Superstars"

Patton, who has done some careful thinking on the subject, says, "It is astounding how few corporations recognize the shortfall" that will develop in the 1980s. Dealing with it, he predicts, will involve some massive changes in

company organization: "Jobs will require simplification, particularly in the lower management levels, so that they can be effectively handled by less experienced people. Organizational relationships, as a result, will necessarily change. Whether this means more levels of supervision or a broader span of control will depend on the decisions involved in the individual company and the availability of talent."

He adds: "What [this] will do to that great favorite of the industrial psychologists a few years ago, job enlargement, I leave to your imagination."

One solution might be to delay retirement of older executives. But even if companies ask senior workers to stay on and Congress raises the mandatory retirement age to 70, chances are slim that many top managers will choose a longer career. At American Telephone & Telegraph Co., for example, slightly less than 25% of managers work through until 65 now.

Most companies, therefore, will have to think in terms of restructuring jobs, giving intensified training to junior management, and picking some of the most promising younger talent for fast advancement. Management will have to learn to isolate "superstars" early and put them on a fast track for promotion, while keeping the majority of their good-but-not-great colleagues in jobs that may never lead to the top.

The surplus of young managers, however, could have some significant effects on the job market in general. It could lead to:

• Wider differentials in pay between junior management and supervisors.
• More job hopping by experienced managers and recruitment of senior executives by hungry companies.
• More "perqs" for senior management, such as insurance policies and fringe benefits.
• More government rules to protect the job rights of young employees, and even, says Patton, government pressure to limit a company's right to fire workers.

That pressure may not only come from the government. Certain businesses such as retailing, where store managers may find their careers throttled in mid-stream, could be particularly vulnerable to executive unionization, Patton warns. Middle-aged executives, he says, will both want to protect their jobs against the influx of youngsters and will recognize that they need support in getting more money if promotions are not forthcoming. "Remember, the labor unions got their big toehold during the Depression, when jobs were less available than people," Patton notes. "That is what's happening now in management—people outnumbering jobs."

Still, most companies think they can handle the problems because they are used to training managers and know how to keep those they really want. "Better than 80% of our top executives came with GE out of college, and we experience pirating all the time because we're known as a company that develops good managers," says Robert N. Mills, manager of recruiting and entry level programs operations at General Electric Co. "Inevitably there will be some frustration among people who want to be on a fast track, but there always is," adds Gene E. Kofke, director of human resources planning at AT&T. "And our senior management people have traditionally been long-time employees who've worked their way up from the bottom," he says.

One reason that companies like GE and AT&T are less fearful of the future than Patton and others might expect is that the types of employees they seek are not likely to be swamping the market. Kofke says that AT&T plans to hire more than 16,000 graduates from now through 1982, and that "a high proportion of them will have technical degrees in physics, math, and the like." For its part, GE is looking to hire engineers, a group that is still in short supply. "There's a tremendous oversupply of liberal arts and business graduates for our needs, yet the competition among recruiters for engineers is very tough," Mills notes.

Overcrowded B-Schools

Such comments spell trouble for B-school administrators and placement officers, not to mention their graduating students. The number of MBAs spewing forth from B-schools has skyrocketed to upwards of 30,000 in 1976 from about 6,000 in 1964. And despite a general dip in the total number of undergraduate students, applications for MBA programs—many of them from women—continue to increase. Even the most prestigious B-schools are seriously considering braking their own growth. "We already had a 30% increase in MBA applications last year, but we've decided not to expand our program," notes William Dill, New York University's dean of business administration. "Yet there are a whole flock of smaller schools that, for financial reasons, are advertising aggressively for MBA students and turning them out to a very uncertain future."

At Long Island University, one of the schools that is expanding its MBA program, a worried Robert V. Johnston, director of career planning and cooperative education, already sees the handwriting on the wall. "We're seeing placement officers actively competing for corporate recruiters," he says. "Companies by and large are having a problem finding meaningful middle-management positions for those people they hired in the last few years, and there is already a distinct trend for MBAs to take jobs that were originally slated for undergraduates."

This is a continuation of a downward-bumping trend that is already plaguing undergraduates. The 1976-77 edition of the Bureau of Labor Statistics' *Occupational Outlook for College Graduates* notes that "between 1970 and 1974 the proportion of workers having four or more years of college has increased by more than 60% in clerical, service, and blue-collar occupations, areas which traditionally had very small proportions of college graduates." It goes on to predict that over the 1974-85 period, "Problems for college graduates will center on underemployment and job dissatisfaction, which will likely result in increasing movement among occupations."

More Mobile Executives

Many observers predict that those graduates who do carve out careers for themselves will increasingly do so in service-oriented industries—insurance, real estate, and the like—

rather than in manufacturing. But they will have to learn to be more geographically mobile, warns David Birch, director of a Massachusetts Institute of Technology program to study neighborhoods and regional change. "In the last few years professionals and managers have stayed close to cities because that's where corporate headquarters were," he explains. "But the service sector is more evenly distributed across the country, and they will have to move where the jobs are."

That may be the best answer for disconcerted job seekers, but it does little to answer the big question facing industry: where to find a good-sized crop of seasoned managers in the next 10 years that are able to cope in an environment of sophisticated technology, increased government regulation, energy and materials shortages, and relentless consumerism. Many companies will simply have to grow their own—through beefed-up in-house training programs and through tuition refunds for older executives who want to continue their education.

In many areas, this is happening already. "The demands on managers are changing so much that we have already been offering more executive courses for people who have been out of school for 10 or 15 years," says Arjay Miller, dean of the graduate school of business at Stanford University. "We may actually train middle managers for second careers in different areas of the company to respond to management scarcities," adds one personnel executive.

"Management has always been one of our scarce resources," sums up Stanford's Miller. "And even now that the supply [of MBAs] is finally exceeding demand, there's still a shortage of really good managers. Executives who know how to cope with external change, to handle really big assignments, will always be in short supply."

LABOR'S BIG SWING FROM SURPLUS TO SHORTAGE

"Presently the younger generation will come knocking at my door."
        —Henrik Ibsen, *The Master Builder.*

In Ibsen's famous play, the aging architect Solness perceives too late that the younger generation is not still outside his door but, symbolically, already on the inside. Similarly, workers born during the "baby boom," though still newcomers, already dominate the labor force. But labor and management have failed to adjust to the changed social values that this has brought to the workplace, both in blue-collar and white-collar jobs. The main conflicts, however, will occur in the unionized segment of the labor force, where workers are demanding more leisure time and less authoritarianism on the job, as well as high levels of wages and benefits.

Between now and the mid-1980s, the major problems are likely to arise from the labor surplus that will be caused by the enormous size of the 25-to-44 age group as it bulges through the economic arteries. The competition for decent-paying jobs in a slower-growing economy will be intense. Blacks, other minorities, women, and older people will face continuing difficulties in the job market over the next few years. But their situation may improve by 1985 or so, as labor force growth slackens considerably.

The people who already have jobs will try to protect them by tightening seniority and other union rules or by shortening the hours of work. Many workers will be forced to take jobs for which they are overqualified. This will cause much personal frustration among workers who are better educated, more individualistic, and more likely than any previous generation to demand a voice in job-related decision-making.

In the 1990s, the nature of the problems will begin to shift. As the much smaller age group born in the 1960s and 1970s begins to move up the job ladder, labor shortages may develop. And a new problem will loom ahead. As the baby boom generation reaches retirement age after the turn of the century, the ratio of dependents to active workers will increase markedly, straining the ability of the economy to support nonworkers.

Trends That Add to Stress

These sudden changes will pose some tough questions for labor-management relations. It could well be that solutions applied to the problems of the 1980s will create other problems in the 1990s. One example is a possible trend toward shorter working hours. To alleviate the job shortage over the near term, unions will demand job-spreading measures such as a reduction in the 40-hour week. This is particularly likely if the inflation rate declines, enabling unions to stress leisure time over money demands. The United Auto Workers is already moving in this direction in the auto industry (BW—Feb. 13), and there is little doubt that the baby boom workers put much more stress on the value of nonwork activities than older workers do.

But such a trend in the next few years might complicate life later on. "The danger is," says Audrey Freedman, a Conference Board economist, "that if we institutionalize various contractions of work hours in the 1980s, there might not be enough productive workers coming along as the baby bust generation enters its mature working years. Then we'd have to lengthen the work week."

Until recently, relatively little serious thought had been given to solving problems raised by the demographic changes. Union leaders in particular, and labor relations practitioners in general, tend to be highly pragmatic people who are concerned largely with day-to-day problems. There is now some evidence of more concern for the future.

For example, the AFL-CIO's Industrial Union Dept. recently devoted an entire issue of its quarterly magazine, *Viewpoint*, to problems in the '80s. It proposes no specific solutions to these issues, but IUD President Jacob Clayman warns unions that they may have to shift bargaining objectives to cope with an aging work force, rising divorce rates, smaller families, and the increase in women and part-time workers. In April, management consultant Peter F. Drucker will conduct a symposium on demographics and labor relations issues, and the Work in America Institute will hold one in May.

Despite the relative lack of discussion about demographics, problems brought by the entrance of the baby boom generation into the labor force began surfacing years ago. This generation, having no remembrance of the Depression and economic hardship, grew up in the affluent—and permissive—atmosphere of the 1950s and matured during the social upheavals of the 1960s. Not only did it bring marijuana to the workplace; it also brought a dislike for union and management bureaucracies and a demand for more challenging work.

"It's a generation that won't accept Prussian authoritarianism at work," says sociologist Arthur B. Shostak, who specializes in studies of blue-collar workers. "In fact, these youngsters have caused a major change in the American workplace, and they won't permit a reactionary pullback as they grow older."

The Shift in Motivations

Some critics, however, say that companies and unions have not yet adjusted to the new generation. The Work in America Institute, a nonprofit organization supported by unions, companies, and the government, was founded two years ago to promote innovative labor relations programs. The institute's president, Jerome M. Rosow, points out that a Daniel Yankelovich poll last year found that 54% of Americans believe they have a "right" to share in decisions that affect their job. But business, by and large, is not responding to this demand, Rosow says.

"Workers today are not less motivated than before," Rosow says. "But their expectations of work have risen, and work has to compete with other values in their lives more directly than ever before. They want to participate in job-related decisions, but our managers are technocrats who don't think in terms of the individual. By the mid-1980s, only a minority of companies will have increased worker participation."

Another problem that will increase job tensions is the projected oversupply of college graduates. Between 1974 and 1985, the number of graduates will exceed job openings that require degrees by some 950,000, according to the Bureau of Labor Statistics. The degree-holders will gravitate downward to lower-income and lower-status jobs. Already large numbers of college graduates have moved into blue-collar jobs or into white-collar service-type jobs that do not call for a college education. In 1976 some 656,000 graduates were in blue-collar jobs, compared with only 179,000 in 1970.

"Clearly, you're going to have a lot more mid-career disappointment because of that hump in the 24- to 44-year-olds," predicts Arnold R. Weber, a labor economist and provost at Carnegie-Mellon University. "There will be a greater sense of personal frustration, and a lot more competition as more women and minorities come looking for jobs."

Corporations such as General Electric Co. are trying to devise strategies for dealing with this problem. "The American idea of onward and upward on the job—higher pay and more responsibility—will have to change for a while," says one GE analyst. "We're going to have to put increasing emphasis on alternate rewards such as lateral transfers, and convince people that there are different ways to get ahead."

As it becomes clearer that schooling will not repay the investment put into it, enrollments may continue to decline and dropouts increase. The recent recession produced an alarming increase in high school dropouts, and Peter Drucker believes that the psychological effect, in a time of relative prosperity, could be crippling. He notes that Walter P. Reuther dropped out of college during the Depression, turned to the labor movement, and eventually became president of the UAW. "Reuther blamed it on the system," Drucker says. "Today's dropouts don't have that motivation. These kids feel they've blown it. They blame it on themselves, and the unions will pay the price."

A Changing Retirement Age

Drucker also points out that organized labor and management have barely begun to cope with such major changes as the influx of part-time workers into the labor force and the likely raising of mandatory retirement to age 70. While Drucker supports the higher retirement age, he says workers over 65 do not need as much income as younger workers, and it is questionable whether they ought to retain

seniority rights to promotion and wage increases, as well as relative immunity from layoff.

If large numbers of workers over 65 stay in the labor force, it most likely will be in low-wage service industries, where pension rates are not very high. But major industries such as steel and autos foresee no change in the current trend toward earlier and earlier retirement. Indeed, the participation rates of workers aged 55 to 64 have declined markedly in recent years. "The older workers are moving out of the workplace rapidly," says Melvin A. Glasser, director of the UAW's Social Security Dept. "There is nothing to lead me to believe that this is going to change."

Unions will continue to put large emphasis on ever higher pensions at ever lower ages. As retirees increase in number, their influence over union decisions will expand. This raises the possibility of increased conflicts within union ranks between the militant young worker who wants more money in his pay envelope and the middle-aged worker who is looking ahead to retirement. But some unionists say this rift is exaggerated. "Ten to 12 years ago, I absolutely expected this to happen, but it did not," Glasser says. "The younger workers find the pressures of the job such that they are willing to give up part of their wages for retirement benefits. They know that after 30 years they can get out of their jobs and live respectably."

One certain objective for unions in bargaining is a cost-of-living escalator clause for pensions. The United Steelworkers pioneered with such a provision in aluminum contracts four years ago, but it proved so costly that it was modified last year. Nevertheless, company officials expect it to become a prime union demand. Says a senior steel company executive: "Workers will soon realize they're getting killed by inflation when they retire, and if inflation doesn't subside in the next decade, they'll have to get some sort of additional retirement protection."

Structural Economic Changes

All the problems caused by the dramatic demographic shifts over the next 20 years will be exacerbated by major structural changes in the economy. The long-term decline of employment in goods-producing industries will continue as service industries expand. By 1985, says a Joint Economic Committee study, 8 of every 10 workers could well be employed in providing services, particularly in information-processing industries such as finance, education, and communications.

The archetypal blue-collar industrial worker is passing from the American scene. This has large significance for labor relations. For 40 years, the dominant pattern of bargaining over wages, benefits, hours of work, and working conditions has been established by blue-collar unions, such as the USW and the UAW, and for factory workers. Now this will gradually change.

It is unclear, however, whether unions are prepared to take this change—along with the changed composition of the labor force—into account, either in organizing or in bargaining. "Many unions still seem to think they represent a white, male, blue-collar worker," says the Conference Board's Freedman, a former union economist. "But only a minority of families fit the stereotype of a dad with a blue-collar job, mama at home with an apron on, and a 10-year-old boy, and a 7-year-old girl."

Organized labor's membership is shrinking. Only 24.5% of the nonfarm labor force belonged to unions in 1976, down from 31.5% in 1950. And the economy is growing precisely in those areas—the service industries—where unions are weakest. There will be some increase in organizing efforts, particularly if Congress passes the labor reform law. The structural changes also will produce union mergers as traditional areas of strength decline. In the next decade, the new demographics also will bring to the fore new, younger union leaders, better educated than their predecessors, more militant on newer issues such as environmental concerns and flexible working patterns. Whether they will be any more successful may depend largely on how today's leaders respond to the coming changes.

THE PROBLEM GOVERNMENT REFUSES TO SEE

The population of the U.S. and the economic system that sustains it will undergo profound changes in the next half century. Some of the consequences of these trends are predictable—indeed, they are inevitable—but business and government have done very little serious thinking about them.

In the 1980s, the problem for economic policymakers will be to provide jobs—good jobs, not makework—for the biggest, best educated, and potentially the most capable labor force in U.S. history. In the 1990s the problem will be to maintain production and economic growth in a labor-short society. And sometime after the year 2000, the U.S. will face the critical question of whether a stable or slowly growing labor force can sustain the increasing number of retirees and their dependents.

The public's needs. The great demographic changes that the U.S. faces will put new demands on business and new strains on the social structure of the nation. As the population grows older, markets will change, and so will the public's idea of what it wants from the economy and from government.

For one thing, older customers will demand better products. "Companies have to become more concerned than they have been about the gap between the promise of products and services by marketing and what the public perceives and is receiving," says Stephen A. Greyser, a marketing professor at Harvard University and executive director of the Marketing Science Institute.

Older customers will also tend to be more conservative in their tastes. Most marketers think that new products will be harder to introduce in the future and less effective in building sales. Says Dan Ailloni-Charas, president of Stratmar Systems Inc., a New York marketing research company: "There will be a slowdown in product obsolescence, which in turn would mean fewer new products introduced into the marketplace."

But older customers are likely to be good customers, and accommodating their tastes will force marketers to make thousands of small shifts in strategy. For instance, John P. Wyek, director of marketing for Levi Strauss & Co., predicts, "As the male population gets older, sportswear that is less casual will become important." Levi Strauss also expects the older women to be somewhat bigger and stouter than today's customer but no less interested in good clothes. To get a foothold in this market, Levi Strauss next year will introduce a line of women's sportswear that will come in sizes 32 through 46.

Tensions.   What happens in the markets, however, will depend in large measure on how the U.S. economy responds to the challenges it faces. The 1980s and 1990s do not shape up as tranquil periods for U.S. society. If the students who trashed the dean's office in the 1960s, when they were 20 years old, find themselves at the age of 40 dead-ended in the lower ranks of corporate management or out of a job entirely, the reaction may be explosive. Management consultant Arch Patton sees such a group of discontented middle-managers as a fertile field for union organizers. Alternatively, the baby boom generation could take the political route and use its voting power to press for restrictions on what corporations can do and a sweeping expansion in the role of government.

The basic question is whether the U.S. can step up capital investment fast enough to provide jobs in the 1980s, maintain growth in the 1990s, and sustain the increasing burden of retirements after the year 2000. For in an industrial society, it takes capital to make jobs, and it takes still more capital to keep production rising at a faster rate than the labor force. To ride out the great waves now surging through its population, the U.S. needs an offsetting surge of capital into its economy.

At present, the U.S. is not getting anything resembling an upswing in capital spending. Investment has lagged throughout the three years of economic recovery that began after the 1974-75 recession.

The problems that the U.S. faces as its population changes, therefore, call for an economic policy that will give some real stimulation to capital investment. The starting point for such a policy is a sweeping revision of the tax system. To get adequate levels of investment, the U.S. must scale down the corporate income tax, which, in effect, doubles the amount that a corporation must earn on investment to get an acceptable rate of return. And it must reduce the tax load on the upper-middle income groups, which do the saving and provide the funds for corporate expansion.

Anticipating Problems

No such philosophy is reflected in President Carter's tax cut proposal, which would give a small reduction to corporations and practically nothing to middle incomes. Nor did Congress give any thought to investment when it passed the Social Security financing bill that shifts most of the load to the middle incomes.

Even if the Administration clearly foresaw the problems that are emerging, the political trend toward egalitarianism in the U.S. would make it harder—if not impossible—to take the necessary actions. As government imposes sharply increasing tax burdens on the middle class (more than $20,000 a year in income), it squeezes out the resources and kills the incentives for the savings that sustain investment.

Neither business nor government has yet made any estimates of the kind of capital spending it will take to adapt the economy to the shifting center of gravity in the population. Planning is much in vogue with corporations today, but most of it is geared to market forecasts rather than to the economic needs of the future.

And the U.S. government has never been noted for anticipating problems. Administrations tend to think in four-year cycles. And as one longtime government worker sums it up: "The longer-range the work you do, the lower your rank. The boss thinks about next year, and his boss thinks about next month. The top guy thinks about tomorrow's problem."

Section 2

Stages in Career Development

Adults go through fairly predictable stages as they "grow up" in organizations. Many people within broad age groups face the same types of opportunities, problems, and issues as a function of their psychological/physiological development and their social environment. Information about these developmental processes provides a useful framework for better understanding the individual-organization interaction in terms of a career perspective.

Managers do mature and age during their years in organizations. As the result of this maturation process, one's personal and professional life structures are in constant evolution over the course of adulthood. Times of crisis, transition, disruption, and constructive change are not only predictable but desirable, for they indicate growth and movement from one phase or stage to another. Within this developmental paradigm the notion of career stages becomes important because each stage is characterized by distinctive tasks, concerns, needs, values, and activities.

The purpose of this section is to clarify the career stage perspective. The first task is to identify the various stages through which individuals move during the process of their personal and professional development. In addition, an effort is made to identify the primary issues and tasks involved within each stage.

The first selection presents a brief overview of the six stages in adult development. Establishing their foundations in the life-cycle work done by Erik Erikson, several recent scholars have attempted to explore the major transitions during one's adult life. It is apparent that as the study of adult development progresses, we are becoming increasingly aware of the interaction among work, family, and self concerns.

While the first selection focuses on adult development in general terms, the second reading identifies the developmental phases related to one's career. Dalton, Thompson, and Price propose a career stage model for managers and professionals which is based on performance-related criteria. Each of the four stages—apprentice, colleague, mentor, sponsor—differs in the tasks an individual is expected to perform, the types of relationships required, and the psychological adjustments which must be made.

In summary, the concept of developmental stages has received increased attention in our efforts to understand behavior in organizational settings. In addition to providing an important theory of career development, this framework provides managers with a useful tool for explaining how and why people react the way they do to their jobs and to other organizational members. Thus, managers who are attempting to increase the performance capabilities of their work force would do well to be responsive to various employee needs incurred at different stages in the growth and maturation of members of organizations.

New Light on Adult Life Cycles

Time

Freud, Spock and Piaget have charted almost every inch of childhood. Psychoanalyst Erik Erikson put the final touches on a convincing map of adolescence. Yet until very recently, most of the charting stopped near the age of 21—as if adults escape any sequence of further development. Now a growing number of researchers are surveying the adult life cycle.

The research so far has been narrow, concentrating largely on white, middle-class American males. But in separate studies, three of the most important life-cycle scholars—Psychiatrist Roger Gould of U.C.L.A., Yale Psychologist Daniel Levinson and Harvard Psychiatrist George Vaillant—have reached some remarkably similar conclusions that add new dimensions to the topography of post-adolescent life. The main features:

16–22: LEAVING THE FAMILY

In this period, youthful fantasies about adulthood slowly give way. Young people begin to find their peers useful allies in an effort to break the hold of the family. Peer groups, in turn, tend to impose group beliefs. Emotions are kept under wraps, and friendships are brittle; any disagreement by a friend tends to be viewed as betrayal.

23–28: REACHING OUT

Following Erik Erikson, who found the dominant feature of the 20s to be a search for personal identity and an ability to develop intimacy, Gould, Levinson and Vaillant see this period as an age of reaching toward others. The growing adult is expansive, devoted to mastering the world; he avoids emotional extremes, rarely bothers to analyze commitments. To Levinson, this is a time for "togetherness" in marriage. It is also a time when a man is likely to acquire a mentor—a patron and supporter some eight to 15 years older.

29–34: QUESTIONS, QUESTIONS

All the researchers agree that a crisis generally develops around age 30. Assurance wavers, life begins to look more difficult and painful, and self-reflection churns up new questions: "What is life all about? Why can't I be accepted for what I am, not what others (boss, society, spouse) expect me to be?" An active social life tends to decline during this period. So does marital satisfaction, and the spouse is often viewed as an obstacle instead of an asset. Marriage becomes particularly vulnerable to

infidelity and divorce. Vaillant sees a crass-
ness, callowness and materialism at this stage.
Levinson detects a wrenching struggle among
incompatible drives: for order and stability, for
freedom from all restraints, for upward mobility at work. Says he: "If a man doesn't start
to settle down by age 34, his chances of forming
a reasonably satisfying life structure are quite
small."

35–43: MID-LIFE EXPLOSION

Somewhere in this period comes the first
emotional awareness that death will come and
time is running out. The researchers see this
stage as an unstable, explosive time resembling
a second adolescence. All values are open to
question, and the mid-lifer wonders, is there
time to change? The mentor acquired in the
mid-20s is cast aside, and the emphasis is on
what Levinson calls BOOM—becoming one's
own man. Parents are blamed for unresolved
personality problems. There is "one last chance
to make it big" in one's career. Does all this add
up to disaster? Not necessarily. "Mid-life crisis
does not appear to portend decay," says
Vaillant. "It often heralds a new stage of man."
The way out of this turbulent stage, say the
researchers, is through what Erikson calls
"generativity"—nurturing, teaching and serving others. The successful mid-lifer emerges
ready to be a mentor to a younger man.

44–50: SETTLING DOWN

A stable time: the die is cast, decisions must be
lived with, and life settles down. There is
increasing attention to a few old values and a
few friends. Money is less important. Gould sees
married people turning to their spouses for
sympathy as they once did to their parents.
Levinson notes that men tend to have fantasies
of young, erotic girls as well as of older,
nurturing women—all part of a final attempt to
solve childhood problems and cut free from the
mother.

AFTER 50: THE MELLOWING

These years are marked by a softening of
feelings and relationships, a tendency to avoid
emotion-laden issues, a preoccupation with
everyday joys, triumphs, irritations. Parents
are no longer blamed for personal problems.
There is little concern for either past or future.

Like Freud and Erikson, the life-cycle
researchers argue that personality disorders
arise when, for one reason or another, the
orderly march of life stages is disrupted.
Vaillant's studies suggest, for instance, that
men who fail to achieve an identity in adolescence sometimes sail through life with a happy-
go-lucky air, but never achieve intimacy,
BOOM or generativity. "They live out their
lives like latency boys," he says, not mentally
ill, but developmentally retarded at the childhood level.

The researchers' findings are tentative. So
far, few minority group members or working-
class men have been studied, and the data on
women is limited. Vaillant believes, however,
that the female life pattern is much the same as
the male, except that the drive for generativity
that appears in men in their late 30s or early 40s
may show up a decade earlier in women.

In any event, a thoroughly detailed portrait
of adult life is still "many years away," as
Gould concedes, and there is much skepticism
in the academic world that one will ever appear.
Yet the life-cycle researchers are confident that
the threatening 30s and the mellowing 50s will
some day become as universally accepted as,
say, the terrible twos and the noisy nines of
childhood.

The Four Stages of Professional Careers—A New Look at Performance by Professionals

Gene W. Dalton
Paul H. Thompson
Raymond L. Price

A person has to be able to change or he'll stagnate, but it is so hard to change in this organization. I'd like to move up or pursue a related career, but I'm cast in the role of radio-chemist and I don't know how to move out of it. I have to go outside of work to get my rewards. [40-year-old engineer]

I really wonder what to do. I like technical work, but when I look at the specialists 15 years my senior still in those little cubbyholes, it scares me. I think I'll get a chance to try management, but if you let yourself get too far from your field, you're out on a limb with no way back if it doesn't work out. [28-year-old scientist]

I manage nearly three hundred professionals; and by all practical standards, I'm very successful. But I'm not satisfied. I feel it is time to make a change and try doing something new. However, it might mean that I wouldn't directly manage anyone anymore. I wonder what would happen to my career and my influence around here. [52-year-old manager]

These are some of the concerns we've heard expressed as we have talked with several hundred professionally trained employees over the past three years. These are the knowledgable workers, the fastest growing part of our workforce, who at present constitute 32 percent of the workforce. (Blue collar workers are 33 percent of the workforce.) Their initial training was as engineers, scientists, accountants, MBAs, and so on, and they have spent their working lives as employees of large, complex organizations dependent in large part on their professional skills. Having done well in college and graduate school, they entered these organizations with high career expectations. They brought with them scarce and valued skills, but few had any clear understanding of what forging a career in an organization is like. Few came with any understanding of the constantly changing activities, relationships, and emotional adjustments they would have to learn to manage if they were to remain highly valued contributors throughout their careers.

Perhaps it should come as no surprise, therefore, that we so often perceived a sense of frustration, bewilderment, even betrayal, as these people spoke about their careers. Any career guidance they may have received in college or graduate school was usually limited to helping them choose courses or majors. No one had given them an accurate preview of what life in a complex organization would be like.

Nor did many of them feel they had received much more help in career planning after they entered organizational life. A few talked about getting some valuable training or advice from a supervisor or a friend. But a large number expressed feelings that are captured best by a comment from a young financial analyst in a bank: "Nobody has helped me do any real career planning. I suspect it's because they're not sure of where they are going themselves."

We have in fact encountered uncertainty among managers of professional employees about how to guide the careers of their subordinates. From these managers we constantly heard comments such as these:

> We bring in about a dozen of the best young people we can each year. Two years later, about eight are contributing. The rest are floundering and usually leave. I wish I could understand it. Those who floundered came with records as good as the others. [Laboratory Director]

> We have some men in their 40s or 50s who are among our lowest performers. Their salaries are out of line with what we get from them, but they have been here so long we aren't likely to bring ourselves to fire them. We've told them to take courses to get current, but I can't see it's had any effect. What will we do with them for the next 15 or 20 years? [Chief Engineer]

CAREER MODELS

Those of us who study careers in organizations have found ourselves perplexed by these same questions. Several years ago we began examining the relationship between age and performance among engineers. In a study of 2,500 engineers in seven large organizations, we found a negative correlation after age 35 between age and performance rating. The older the engineer after the mid-30's, the lower his performance rating was likely to be.

But the message seemingly implied by these statistics was brought sharply into question when we examined our data more closely. Not all older engineers had low ratings. In fact, the top third of the engineers over 50 were almost as highly valued as the top third in any age group. Many engineers had remained highly valued contributors for the duration of their careers. But more of those in their 40s and 50s had low ratings than did younger engineers.

Why have some professionals remained high performers over the years while others have not? What have they done differently?

Existing Career Models

We have concluded that part of the confusion about careers has grown out of the career models we have all used, explicitly or implicitly. The first and most influential of these is of course the pyramidal model of organizations (and of careers), so graphically illustrated by most organizational charts. Authority, status, and pay all increase as the individual moves up the chart.

Implicit in this model is the concept that career development consists of moving as rapidly and as far up the pyramid as possible. As professionals first moved into industrial and governmental organizations, this was the sole career model they encountered. Many professionals with advanced degrees became prime candidates for management positions.

But there were also many who were dismayed to find that the ability and willingness to manage seemed almost the sole criteria for advancement, recognition, or reward in their organizations.

Similarly many organizations found that the pyramidal model failed to take important realities into account. Too often, they found themselves promoting a key technical specialist to a management position because it was the only way to reward him. More and more firms began to set up special new pay and promotion schemes such as the dual ladder for their professional employees in order to recognize the critical contributions they could make as individuals. In almost all those organizations, however, professionals began griping about the realities of the dual ladder:

> "Ours isn't a real dual ladder; it's been bastardized. It's been filled with ex-managers."

> "The men in the upper technical slots don't do real technical work. They prepare proposals and brochures."

> "The real rewards don't go to those on the technical ladder."

These criticisms have not subsided. Instead, they have persisted and indeed increased in recent years.

The Obsolescence Model

As the number of professionals with 20 and 25 years' experience grew, a new problem and a new model of professional careers began to emerge. The low performance ratings of many of these senior employees led to use of the metaphor of obsolescence. The picture projected by the metaphor was that of a rapidly changing technology in which the skills of the older professionals were rapidly outdated and in which recent graduates who had mastered the latest tools and techniques were at a premium.

Interestingly, the model carries with it an implied solution to the problem. When it is assumed that professionals become obsolete like machines, when we begin to talk as if a professional education has a half-life of so many years, like a uranium sample, the obvious solution is to update or reeducate professionals and to restore them to the state they were in when they came out of school—on top of the newest and most sophisticated techniques.

Millions of dollars have been spent on continuing education programs in companies and in universities. In addition, professional groups have pressed for legislation that requires continuing education as the price of continuing professional practice. For example, lawyers in Minnesota are required to take the equivalent of 15 course hours a year to avoid being placed on a restricted status. The

Engineering Foundation of Ohio recently suggested a law requiring almost the same qualification of engineers. Accountants in several states face the possibility of having to return to the classroom in order to retain their professional status.

All this money and effort rests on a questionable model. It has not been demonstrated that courses improve performance. Our studies have in fact shown repeatedly that the high performers are no more likely to have taken continuing education courses than the low performers.

A NEW MODEL

If the high performers are not taking more courses than their peers, how *are* they different? What, if anything, are they doing differently? In what respects have their careers been different?

To answer these questions, we interviewed 550 professionally trained employees: 155 scientists in four laboratories, 268 engineers in four organizations, 52 accountants in three firms, and 75 professors in three universities. We selected our subjects to give us representative samples of high- and low-rated performers. We began by simply asking them to describe their own careers and those of their fellow professionals. What, we asked them, characterized the high performers they knew? We coded their responses carefully and compared them with the way the high-rated and the low-rated performers described their own careers.

Our early analysis yielded only frustration. Each promising uniformity exhibited too many contradictions. Each new hypothesis failed to find support in the data. It was only when we began to look at the effects of time that a clear pattern began to emerge. High performers early in their careers were performing different functions from high performers at mid-career. And both these groups were different from high performers in late-career.

As we investigated further, it became increasingly clear that there are four distinct stages in a professionally trained employee's career. Each stage differs from the others in the tasks an individual is expected to perform well in that stage, in the types of relationships he engages in, and in the psychological adjustments he must make.

It was the individuals who were moving successfully through these stages who had received the high performance ratings. Conversely, individuals who had remained in the early stages were likely to be low-rated.

In Stage I, an individual works under the direction of others as an apprentice, helping and learning from one or more mentors.* In Stage II, he demonstrates his competence as an individual contributor. In Stage III, he broadens and acts as a mentor for others. Those in Stage IV provide direction for the organization. Figure 1 shows some of the central features of each stage. It is important to realize that while the stages can be thought of as distinct, there are elements in each stage that are present in each of the other stages, although in a different form. Our description of each stage focuses on the issues that clearly differentiate one stage from the next.

STAGE I

When a young professional joins an organization, he is immediately confronted with several

*We would like to acknowledge the helpfulness of the ideas of Daniel Levinson and his associates at Yale University. Their concept of the mentor helped us understand much of the phenomena we observed in this stage.

challenges. He must learn to perform at least some of the organization's tasks competently. He needs to learn which elements of the work are critical and which activities require the greatest attention. He must learn how to get things done, using both formal and informal channels of communication. Finally, he must do this while he is being closely observed for indications of competence and future potential.

Because he lacks experience, and because others do not yet know how much they can rely on his judgment, he works under the fairly close supervision of a more experienced person. In other words, he must usually begin by helping someone else do the work for which no supervisor is responsible.

Activities

Much of the work in Stage I may involve fairly routine duties. One manager observed:

> There is a lot of detailed work to be done between the time a project is conceived and its actual implementation. A new person is often stuck with many of these detailed tasks. I like a subordinate who recognizes that someone has to do the routine work and therefore doesn't complain about it all the time.

However, it is important for the person in this stage not to become completely bogged down in this detail work. He is also expected to show some initiative and be innovative in finding solutions to problems. So another manager commented:

Figure 1 Four career stages

	Stage I	Stage II	Stage III	Stage IV
Central activity	Helping Learning Following directions	Independent contributor	Training Interfacing	Shaping the direction of the organization
Primary relationship	Apprentice	Colleagues	Mentor	Sponsor
Major psychological issues	Dependence	Independence	Assuming responsibility for others	Exercising power

I like a subordinate who has an aggressive attitude. He has to show initiative, be innovative, and be willing to take some risks. With an aggressive attitude, I can normally guide him in the direction in which he needs to go.

The differing views expressed by these managers illustrate the fact that it is often difficult to achieve the optimum balance in Stage I between willing acceptance of routine assignments and aggressive searching out of new and more challenging tasks.

Another characteristic of the work in this stage is that the individual customarily gets assignments that are part of a larger project or activity directed by a senior professional or a supervisor. Many young professionals find such a relationship frustrating. They are eager to have their own project or their own clients.

Such an attitude is understandable, but a person who tries to escape the subordinate relationship too quickly will miss out on an important aspect of career development. He will fail to learn what others have gained by experience. More important, if he undertakes sole responsibility for work he's not prepared to do, he may soon acquire a reputation for mediocre performance, which will be hard to overcome.

Relationships

As we have just indicated, the primary relationship in Stage I is that of being a subordinate. Our interviews suggest that the individual's skill in managing that relationship may be a critical factor in building an effective career. Ideally, in this stage he will work with a mentor who knows how to design a study, structure an audit, or analyze the critical risks involved in a loan. He works closely with the mentor, learning from observation and from trial and correcting the approaches, the organizational savvy, and the judgment that no one has yet been able to incorporate into textbooks. He follows instructions and carries out detailed and sometimes boring work in exchange for the things he learns and the sponsorship of his mentor.

If he learns quickly and well at this stage, he will be given increasing responsibility. If he fails to do so, however, he may continue to do the routine work under close supervision as long as he remains with the organization. Tom Johnson's experience in a large research organization illustrates this point:

In my first two years in the company I was unhappy with my job. I worked for a man that I disliked and did not respect. He provided very little assistance or guidance. As a result, I made little or no progress. Then I began to work with another engineer who could get things done; he protected me from the flack coming down from above. He provided a climate that I enjoyed and he was willing to go to bat for me. When he became a formal group leader, I insisted on being transferred into his group, where I became the informal leader. Later, he recommended me for a supervisory position.

Tom's experience points out some of the benefits of having a good mentor in the early stages of a career as well as some of the problems of having a poor one. The mentor knew the right people and could show Tom how the system worked—how to lay out a job, how to get computer funds, how to requisition necessary equipment and travel funds, how to negotiate faster delivery from suppliers, and so on. A mentor is also extremely helpful when anyone is learning the ropes in a complex organization.

A good mentor often becomes a model that the Stage I person can follow whenever he is unsure how to approach a problem. He instructs and provides the subordinate with a chance to try his hand, while making sure that he doesn't make important errors. These and other benefits suggest that finding a good mentor should be a key agenda item for any professional entering an organization. Providing him with the opportunity to find such a mentor is an equally important responsibility of higher-ups in the organization.

Psychological Issues

The psychological adjustments a person makes in Stage I are as critical as the way the activities are performed or the relationships that are developed. One of the major problems is adjusting to the dependence inherent in the role of subordinate. The people we interviewed said that in this stage a person "is expected to willingly accept supervision and direction . . ." and "is expected to exercise *directed* creativity and initiative."

Many professionals looked forward to completing their education so they could be free of the demands of their professors and find the independence they believed their profession provides. It is easy to understand their irritation when they find themselves forced once again into a dependent relationship. A physicist in a highly respected applied research laboratory described his feelings during his first year:

> My first year here was frustrating. I had a good record in graduate school. I was ready to go to work and make a contribution. But for a year, no one paid much attention to my suggestions. I almost left. It took me a year to realize that I didn't yet understand the complexity of the problems we were working on. Now I try to take enough time with new people to help them understand the dilemma of that first year.

Another difficult adjustment is learning to live with the never-ending routine work. A recent MBA described his frustrations in this area as follows:

> My job is very boring. All I'm doing is routine financial analysis. This work could be done by a high school graduate with a calculator. They didn't tell me in the MBA program that I'd be doing this routine work. We spent our time in the program discussing cases with important problems to be solved.

Many young professionals find themselves in a similar position, and it is a risky one. If they lose interest in the job and do sloppy work or lay down on the job, they may acquire a reputation that will compromise their future career development.

STAGE II

The primary theme in Stage II is independence. The individual who makes the transition into Stage II successfully does so by developing a reputation as a technically competent professional who can work independently to produce significant results. John, a young financial analyst, describes his transition into this stage:

> After about a year and a half with the company, I was capable of working on my own and therefore was placed in charge of monitoring the procurement accounts. Before this time, whenever a person from another department came in to ask a question, I had to consult with my supervisor before making a decision. When I was in charge of the accounts, this was no longer necessary.

Activities

Most professionals look forward to having their own project or area of responsibility. This does not mean that they are allowed to work completely on their own, because most projects must be coordinated with other projects and activities, but they are no longer closely supervised on the specific methods of getting the job done.

In this stage, a person is expected to hone his professional skills to a high level. One way to achieve this competence is to develop an area of specialization. The major career dilemma in this stage is how much to specialize. There is a great deal of discussion and dissension on this issue—with most people taking a strong stand in favor of their particular point of view. An article in *Business Week* (October 12, 1974) offers this advice to aspiring managers:

> Get experience in several fields—engineering, sales, manufacturing—right off, and be sure to get your ticket punched in finance early. If you're heading for the president's office, become a generalist fast. . . . Get out of your specialty fast, unless you decide that's all you ever want to do. This means rapid rejection of the notion that you are a professional engineer, lawyer, scientist, or anything but a manager.

Our data suggest that this advice could be misleading if a young professional interprets it to mean that he need never develop and demonstrate solid competence in some critical task of the organization. For in doing so, he will fail to establish a major building block to his career.

The environment in which most professionals operate is changing so rapidly that it is nearly impossible for any one individual to develop expertise in all areas of his field or profession. Therefore, it is often advisable to become a specialist, at least temporarily, and gain a reputation for competence within that specialty.

Using this strategy of focusing his energies in one area enables the individual to develop a sense of competence. In addition to increasing his self-esteem, the individual also tends to enhance his visibility in the organization. A person who has done outstanding work in one area is more likely than a jack-of-all-trades to gain visibility in a large organization.

There are two primary approaches to selecting an area of specialization. One strategy is to choose a content area in which to specialize, such as a CPA who is an expert on tax problems for banks, or a scientist who focuses on nondestructive testing, or a banker who concentrates on loans to utilities. The other is to develop a set of specialized skills and apply those skills in solving a variety of problems. People who are skillful in computer applications, statisticians, and those who are particularly effective in dealing with clients all fall into this category.

There are risks of specializing, of course, such as becoming pigeonholed in one area, or ending up in a specialty that's being phased out. But our research suggests that a carefully selected specialty in Stage II has usually formed the base for a productive and successful career. Failure to establish such a base is a risk few professionals can afford to take.

Relationships

In Stage II, peer relationships take on greater importance. A person at this stage continues to be someone's subordinate. But he comes to rely less on his supervisor or mentor for direction. This transition is not easy, involving as it does a change in attitude and behavior on the part of the supervisor as well as the individual himself.

Some supervisors are unable to make this switch, and the subordinate may need a transfer to accomplish the transition. Ray's experience as an electrical engineer with two supervisors illustrates this point.

My first project engineer taught me a lot about basic engineering, but after a while I didn't need all the handholding and direction. So I was happy to be transferred to a new project. The new project engineer was a better manager. He helped me to expand my sphere of influence. He encouraged me to develop contacts with people in my field, both inside and outside the company. He showed me how to interact with these people as well as how to make presentations to management and customers. I also learned how to write papers while I worked with him, and several of my papers were published during that period.

Psychological Issues

It seems logical that everyone would want to move from dependence to independence; the transition should be easy. Far from it. By age 25 we have usually had a great deal of experience and indoctrination in being dependent, but little preparation for real independence. From the first grade to graduate school, to ensure a good grade the student has to find out what the teacher wants him to do and then do it. Similarly, on the first job the task is to find out what the boss wants done and then do it.

To move into Stage II, a professional needs to go beyond that dependence and begin to develop his own ideas on what is required in a given situation. He needs his own standards of performance. Some help in developing those standards is available from peers and from professional standards, such as generally accepted accounting principles or engineering safety standards. Still, judgment is necessary in applying any professional standards.

Developing confidence in one's own judgment is a difficult but necessary process. One scientist's experience with this process may illustrate the point:

> I had been working with my mentor on research projects for three years before I developed the necessary confidence to submit a proposal on my own. But I found that my confidence was short-lived. I had been used to making decisions, but I had always checked them with my mentor; and he made the final decision, wrote the final draft, and so on. Now that I had my own project I lacked the confidence to make any of the important decisions. He was unavailable for about six months, and I was almost paralyzed during that period. I made very little progress on the project. Eventually I discovered that I could get the opinions of other people in the department and then make a decision using their input. It was a major discovery for me to find I didn't need a boss to approve my decisions.

This quotation came from a scientist, viewed by others as a very promising young man, who later became a successful professional.

Some people find Stage II uncomfortable and spend too little time in it to develop the skills that have to be acquired in this stage. This often happens when an individual takes on a supervisory position before he has had a chance to establish himself as a competent professional. Often the organization and the individual conspire in moving the person into a management position too soon.

The opportunity may be enticing, but it involves a high degree of risk. Time after time in our study, we encountered first-level managers who were not effective in their positions because they did not understand the technical aspects of the work they were supervising. This tended to undermine the manager's self-confidence as well as the confidence of his subordinates.

Our research indicates that doing well in Stage II is extremely important in the process of career development. Moreover, many people remain in Stage II throughout their careers, making substantial contributions to the organization and experiencing a high degree of professional satisfaction. However, the probability that they will continue to receive above-average ratings diminishes over time, if they do not move beyond this stage.

STAGE III

We have sometimes called Stage III the mentor stage because of the increased responsibility individuals in this stage begin to take for influencing, guiding, directing, and developing other people. It is usually persons in this stage who play the critical role in helping others move through Stage I.

A second characteristic of persons in Stage III is that they have broadened their interests and capabilities. The tendency to broaden comes about quite naturally for many professionals as part of the work process. One researcher who had been very specialized described his experience this way:

> When you are very close to the data, you are able to see the small differences. If you are observant and in a fruitful area, you soon have more ideas than you can possibly pursue by yourself. You run the risk of eliminating some potentially good ideas unless you get others to help you.

From dealing with two or three clients, a bank lending officer or a public accountant may develop knowledge and skills that have applications throughout an entire industry. We have seen engineers learn or develop a new type of computer technique to solve a particular problem, for example, only to find that the approach has wide application to a range of problems facing the organization.

The third characteristic we observed of individuals in Stage III is that they deal with people outside the organization (or organization subunit) for the benefit of others inside. They obtain contracts, get budgets approved, secure critical and/or scarce resources or project funds, help others get salary increases, and so on. The reputation an individual has developed for results and solid achievement in Stage II is initially the keystone to this part of Stage III work.

Activities

We identified three roles played by those in Stage III: informal mentor, idea man, and manager. These are not mutually exclusive; one individual may play all three roles. The point that deserves emphasis here is that a person can carry out Stage III activities from more than one role base.

Informal mentor. Often an individual begins to play the role of informal mentor as an outgrowth of his success in Stage II. He is asked to do more work because of his increased capabilities and contacts, which means that he needs more assistance. He begins to find others who can help do the detail work and develop his initial ideas. In doing this, he becomes a mentor for the people who assist him.

One informal technical mentor described his role in these words:

> Right now I find the sponsors for our work. I do the conceptual thinking, develop the project, and then get someone to support it. After I get the job, then I must supervise and collaborate with others who do most of the actual work.

He remained the force behind the project and also worked closely with those doing the detail work.

Idea man. Some professionals are exceptionally innovative. Often this kind of individual becomes an idea man or consultant for a small group. Others come to him for suggestions on how to solve current problems. Sometimes he originates an idea and then discusses it with others, who may pursue it independent of his supervision. Either way, he is involved with and influences more than his own individual work. John Jensen, a 59-year-old scientist, described his work in this way:

> I sell ideas. I would describe myself as an innovative scientist. When I work on a problem, it starts to bug me. At some time, I will read something and apply it back to solve the original problem. Others often come to me with problems they cannot solve. Generally I can pull some information from my experience or reading and give them a direction to follow in solving the problems.

Manager. The most common role in Stage III and the one most easily understood is the formal role of manager or supervisor. Usually the management role for a Stage III person is not more than one or two levels in the organizational structure away from the work itself.

Professional competence usually continues to have some importance in the performance of the manager's work. Often the formal management role is given to a mentor who already has been informally performing many of the functions expected of a manager.

Transition to the formal role of manager is not dramatic. Bob Smith, a 37-year-old manager, described a fairly typical pattern of a professional moving into a Stage III management role:

> I gained knowledge of other programs and began to develop outside contacts. Finally, I discovered I could sell programs. With more programs coming in, I managed several long-term projects under time and money constraints. The business was expanding, and I was directing more and more technical people. Soon I became acting section manager and, after three months, the section manager.

Relationships

Probably the most central shift that occurs as a person moves into Stage III is the nature of his relationships. In Stage II he had to learn to take care of himself. In Stage III he has to learn to take care of others, to assume some form of responsibility for their work. When the mentor receives an assignment on which he needs the collaboration of others, he quickly learns the importance of tapping additional skills. To get even a small group of professionals working together effectively requires more than technical skills and an interesting problem. A scientist who had been doing a lot of independent work described the process:

> I wrote a successful proposal for basic research in energy. Now there are three other people working on the project. We are going full blast and having a ball. But there are new questions. I have always asked my boss to give me independence, and I gave him loyalty in return. Now I have to learn to do that with the people under me.

He finds that he needs interpersonal skills in setting objectives, delegating, supervising, and coordinating.

At this point he also has begun to accept the fact that he has to satisfy a number of people—multiple bosses. He experiences a shift in the relationship with those above him in the hierarchy. He now has responsibilities downward as well as upward, and he feels some of the tugs of the proverbial man in the middle. He must learn to cope with divided loyalties. If he is seen as only looking upward, he will find it hard to retain the loyalties of those working for him. At the same time, unless he has strong influence—and is perceived as having such influence—he will be ineffective at influencing the people he directs.

Psychological Issues

Moving into Stage III requires a number of internal changes as well. The individual must develop a sense of confidence in his own ability to produce results and to help others do the same. He needs to be able to build the confidence of junior people, not tear it down. If he is threatened by the success of his apprentices, he will not be able to provide them the guidance and freedom they need if they are to progress. There must be a delicate balance between directing them and providing them with the freedom to explore and to test their skills.

Second, he must be psychologically able and willing to take responsibility for someone else's output. As a mentor he assumes an obligation to both the apprentice and the customer. Implicitly he promises both parties that the output will be satisfactory.

Some competent people experience formal supervisory responsibility for others as confining and uncomfortable. Whenever this occurs, the question for the individual and his superiors is whether he can find a role in which he can still exert a broad influence without supervising others or whether he should move back into Stage II work.

Those in Stage III also often find themselves pulling away from technical work. The question is: How far? Some move fairly far away from it without ambivalence. Others, like Bill Rivers, make a great effort to stay close to their field. He describes both the feeling and the effort as follows:

> I assumed when I came here that being a good scientist was all that was necessary. Later I found that science was more than just research. You have to conceive, sell, and direct a program. I began to do all those things and found myself in management mainly because I didn't want to work for the other guys they were considering. I want to stay close to technical work and maybe move back into it. Because I know it is difficult to move out of management into technical work, I have stayed close to my field, written papers, and still consider myself to be a scientist.

Some, like Rivers, are able to meet these combined demands better than others, but the tension of keeping a foot in each camp is a problem for almost every professional at this stage of his career.

One further adjustment a person in this stage must make is learning to derive satisfaction out of seeing his apprentices move away from him, become independent, or take on new mentors. This can be a major source of gratification or of difficulty. Even though the mentor expects and looks forward to such eventual movement, differences in expectation about timing and methods may constitute a potential source of conflict and disappointment.

Not surprisingly, this adjustment seems to be harder for the Stage III individual without a formal supervisory position. The formal supervisory position carries certain psychological supports and a role clarity unavailable to those in less traditional roles. Counseling and dealing with the outside on behalf of others inside are part of the role definition of the supervisor. For the informal mentor, it is often less clear that these things are part of his job. On the other hand, the lack of an official boss-subordinate role often allows the nonsupervisor to enter into richer, more comfortable counseling relationships.

Along with conflicts, Stage III also brings long-term satisfactions. Challenges come from broadening the individual's thinking, increasing his knowledge by moving into new areas, or applying his skills to new problems. There is adequate social involvement, recognition from peers, and the satisfaction of helping junior professionals further their careers. Generally, the organizational rewards—both money and status—have reached a fairly satisfactory level. Some people find Stage III, with its combination of counseling, technical proximity, and recognition and rewards, viable and satisfying until retirement. Some find that they are stagnating and are hard-pressed to keep up with younger competitors. Others move on to a new stage.

STAGE IV

Finally, as our study progressed it became clear that the careers of some individuals contain a definable fourth stage. The key characteristic that identified people in this stage was the influence they had in defining the direction of the organization or some major segment of it. Many of these Stage IV people occupied line management positions; others did not. But each had come, in his own way, to be a force in shaping the future of the organization.

A stereotype of organizations pictures this influence as being exercised by only one person—the chief executive officer. But this influence is in fact more widely distributed among key people than is commonly thought. They exercise this influence in a number of ways: negotiating and interfacing with the key parts of the environment; developing the new ideas, products, markets, or services that lead the organization into new areas of activity; or directing the resources of the organization toward specific goals.

Because these functions are so critical to the growth and survival of the organization, those who fulfill them are highly valued, and only those persons whose judgment and skill have been proved in the past are trusted to play these roles. Stage IV people have gained credibility by their demonstrated ability to read the environment accurately and respond appropriately.

Activities

The Stage IV people we encountered usually played at least one of three roles: manager, internal entrepreneur, idea innovator.

Upper-level managers are usually but not always in Stage IV of their careers, while a number of middle-level managers are making the transition to this stage. Unlike the Stage III supervisors, they are usually not involved in guiding Stage I people or even supervising people in Stage II. They are not close enough to the details of the daily work to perform in these roles. Instead, they formulate policy and initiate and approve broad programs.

One Stage IV manager described how he had changed his activities in order to work on directing his part of the organization as follows: "I have tried to develop my staff so that I could concentrate on where we are going instead of where we are at the moment. Consequently, things are running more smoothly, and I have more time to myself."

By no means are we implying that Stage IV managers spend all their time doing long-range planning. But the work they do and the decisions they make shape the direction of the organization, or at least a significant part of it.

There are others who, through their entrepreneurial activities within the organization, exercise an important influence on the direction of the firm. They are people with new ideas and a strong sense of the direction in which the organization should go. They bring resources, money, and people together in the furtherance of their ideas. One professional who seemed clearly in Stage IV described his work this way:

> I had an idea for a new product area and was getting very little support through the formal channels. So I talked to a couple of people on my level and convinced them it was a good idea. We went ahead and did it. Today it is bringing in a significant part of our sales. Luckily, it worked out all right.

Entrepreneurs like this are often considered mavericks in their organizations. As long as they are successful at it, however, it is legitimate to be a maverick.

The third type, the idea innovator, seems distantly removed from the manager and the entrepreneur, but he has one thing in common with them—innovative ideas. The biggest opportunities, the most significant break-throughs, probably most often originate with an individual contributor. He may puzzle over a problem or an idea for years before the solution finally presents itself.. Such individuals may work quite closely with a manager or someone else to sell their ideas. Don Jones is an example of the technical or individual contributor. His department manager described him as follows:

> Don is one of the brightest people I know, but he doesn't like to talk. His knowledge of the field, however, is outstanding. He is talented, hardworking, and disciplined. He sets goals for himself on a technical project and achieves them. Every two or three years he has a new direction he wants the company to follow, and he is almost always right. He is not a salesman; he gets people like me to sell his ideas.

Often, the Stage IV individual contributor has also established a reputation outside the organization by his professional achievements and/or publications. This enhances his credi-

bility inside the organization and may enable him to play a key role in recruiting and business development.

Relationships

One of the major ways in which those in Stage IV influence the direction of the organization is through the selection and development of key people. One of the managers we interviewed described this part of his work as follows:

> Since I first moved into management I have consistently tried to develop my staff. Just as others have sponsored me and made it possible for me to take their positions when they moved up, I have done the same.

There is of course a similarity between Stage III and IV in this respect. But there is also a difference. The individual in Stage IV is not concerned with getting new people started. Instead, he selects those who show promise of performing Stage IV activities in the future and grooms them. The focus is on opening up opportunities, assessing, and providing feed-back rather than on teaching and instruction. He watches these people, notes their strengths and weaknesses, counsels them, and tries to guide each one into areas where he is most likely to be effective.

The development of key people is not restricted to Stage IV people in management roles but also forms a significant part of the work of Stage IV nonmanagers. The entre-preneurs and the idea men also tend to spend a considerable amount of time and energy in the development of key people and, interestingly, often not into their own mold. In one of the large laboratories we studied, the director and two of the associates had been mentored by one senior scientist. He noted that he had suggested they move toward management because their great-est strengths seemed to be in that area. We frequently found that these nonmanagerial Stage IV people had played a major role in developing many of the most able managers.

Another characteristic of Stage IV people is that they are heavily involved in key relationships outside the organization. One of our Stage IV interviewees described himself as multi-organizational because he worked on so many external boards, committees, and associations. These outside contacts are critical not only because they bring into the organization current information about events and trends in the environment but also because they give the organization the visibility it needs to market its goods, services, and people. Senior partners in CPA firms, for example, are expected to be involved in professional associations and to have developed extensive relationships in the banking and legal communities.

We often found, particularly among non-management Stage IV people, that, writing and publication had been and continued to be a means of achieving visibility and contact. But extensive publication or extensive contact of any kind with the outside is no guarantee of Stage IV status inside the organization. Unless the publications or the outside relationships are structured and focused in areas of major concern to the organization, such activities are not likely to be viewed positively by others in the organization.

Psychological Issues

The psychological shifts a person must make to move successfully into Stage IV are even greater than the changes he must make in his activities and relationships. As we indicated, managers in Stage IV remove themselves from day-to-day operations and transactions. Even as a Stage III mentor it is possible to stay close enough to the operations to retain a sense of personal control. But that must be relinquished by managers moving into Stage IV. Nonmanager Stage IV people often stay closer to some aspects of operations, but they are also relentlessly pulled away. One of the essential psychological shifts in moving to Stage IV is to learn not to second-guess subordinates on operating decisions. It is necessary to learn to influence by means other than the direct supervision of ongoing work—through ideas, through personnel selection, through reviews, through resource allocation, and through

changes in organizational design. The need for this mode of influence is even greater for nonmanagerial Stage IV people.

Another critical shift for those moving into Stage IV is a broadening of perspective and a lengthening of time horizons. These individuals must learn to think about the organization as a whole and act in terms of that framework. They must learn to think about the needs of the organization beyond the time period during which they will personally be affected, to think not about next month or next year but about the next five to ten years—or beyond.

Last, because the issues are critical, because they affect the lives of so many people, and because the decisions must be made on the basis of personal judgments, people in Stage IV must also become accustomed to use power. Even if the individual himself is not initially comfortable in the exercise of power, he will find himself forced to exercise power because so many others depend on him to fight for their programs. He also needs to be able to form alliances and to take strong positions without feeling permanent enmity toward those who differ with him.

QUESTIONS RAISED BY THE MODEL

Whenever we discuss this model with professionals and managers, a number of questions arise. One, for example, is whether our data predict that a person who skips a stage will be a failure. We can only answer that we have interviewed a number of successful people who said they did not experience Stage I and a few who said they did not go through Stage II. Some people replied that they did not have a mentor but learned "how the system works" and so on from their peers. In some cases a group of new people joined the organization at the same time, and they helped each other learn what they needed to know.

The preponderance of our interviews suggest, however, that this alternative strategy is usually not as effective as working with a competent mentor. The mentor is better equipped to help the new employee make the transition from the academic setting into a professional career.

Some people say the model implies that the only successful people are those who have progressed to Stage IV. That is not our position. People in all four stages make an important contribution to the organization. A number of people in each stage are necessary for organizational effectiveness. However, our research indicates that as people grow older they are less likely to be highly valued if they don't move beyond the early stages.

The data in Figure 2 provide an illustration of that point. We asked managers in two research and development organizations to classify the people in their departments in one or another of the four stages. Figure 2 contrasts stage and performance for all individuals over age 40. This figure suggests that only a small proportion of the people still in Stage II are rated as above-average performers. The implication is clear: To maintain a high performance rating throughout his career, an individual should seek to move at least to Stage III.

Another frequent question is, do people only move forward in these stages? If they do revert to an earlier stage, what is the likelihood of their being able to make the eventual transition to one of the later stages? That seems to depend on the climate of the organization. In some organizations, there seemed to be enough flexibility in both the formal and the informal systems to allow people to do some moving back and forth between stages. Even in these organizations, however, the thought of moving from Stage IV implied demotion, and people were reluctant to make such a transition. An example will illustrate the point.

At age 50, George Dunlop found himself in an uncomfortable position. He had been department manager of a group of 300 employees for eight years, and he realized the job was losing the challenge it had once had for him. He thought it unlikely that he would be promoted to the next step in the management hierarchy, and he felt that he might end up holding that position for the next 15 years. About that time he was given an opportunity to make a shift, which he describes as follows:

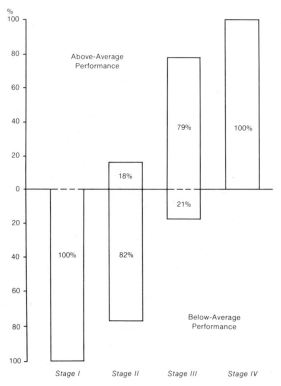

Figure 2 Relationship between stage and performance level for people over age 40

I was asked to do a major study for the president that would require my full-time effort. I was reluctant to accept the assignment if it meant giving up my position as department manager because I didn't know where it would lead. I agreed that I would work on it full time for six months, but I would only take a temporary leave from my position as department manager. In order to do the study I had to go back and learn a lot about surveys, interviews, analyzing questionnaire data, and so on. After I finished the study, the president asked if I would take a position in which some of the things proposed in the report might be implemented. He invited me to become his assistant and work out of the office of the president. It sounded interesting, but I still had a lot of questions. There was the question of status. When I was head of a large department, I had secure status. I expected it to be difficult to assume a staff position with no one but a secretary reporting to me. It took time to adjust to the idea.

After some extensive soul-searching, I decided to take the new position, and it has worked out very well. I enjoy my work, and I believe I'm having a major impact on the whole organization.

George accepted a position which, in our terms, temporarily moved him from Stage IV to a variety of Stage II activity in which he specializes in a new area of research. However, he made the transition successfully. He learned to exert considerable influence in his new role and clearly moved back into Stage IV, but in a different kind of work. This was done in a large laboratory where a precedent had been established by a former laboratory director who had made a similar move. In other organizations, we found less movement of this sort.

Some people have asked if the stages are merely another way to describe the management hierarchy. Stages III and IV are not limited to people in formal management positions in most organizations. Figure 3 shows the percentage of managers and individual contributors in each stage in five organizations. Figure 4 indicates the proportion of professionals and managers who were described by their superiors as being in each stage.

Upper-level managers described many nonmanagers as doing Stage III and IV work. We believe that any effective professional organization will have many nonmanagers in Stages III and IV. Professional organizations that are so rigidly structured that they provide no opportunities for Stages III and IV among nonmanagers are the poorer for it.

CONCLUSION

What is the value of this way of conceptualizing professional careers in organizations? What implications does it have for managing professional employees?

Edgar Schein pointed out in 1971 that "we do not have readily available concepts for describing the multitude of separate experiences that the individual encounters during the life of his organizational career." We experienced the need for such concepts in trying to wrestle with the problems of obsolescence and performance among professionally trained employees. To explain the differences we found in performance ratings, we especially needed a clearer picture of what Schein calls the organizational definition of a career—"the set of expectations held by individuals inside the organization which guide their decisions about who to move, when, how, and at what speed."

The concept of career stages has provided us with a way of describing that set of expectations. But it is important to note that these expectations were not necessarily a part of the formal organization. In fact, in the organizations we studied it was the informal and often unstated expectations about the critical activities and relationships a person should engage in at each stage that determined both formal and informal rewards. In our view, the study of an organization as a setting in which careers are lived provides both a fruitful lead and a new perspective for understanding organizations.

But our model of career stages has both pragmatic and theoretical implications for those who live in organizations as well as for those who manage them. Individuals need a longitudinal framework within which to form their own career decisions. Managers need a

Figure 3 Percentage of people in each stage holding management and nonmanagement positions in five R & D organizations

Stage	Individual Contributors (%)	Managers (%)	Total (%)
I	100.0	0.0	100
II	98.7	1.3	100
III	65.2	34.8	100
IV	25.9	74.1	100

framework for predicting some of the long-term consequences of short-term career decisions. Managers in several organizations have found it useful to examine the stages of career development in their own organizations as a way of identifying the factors that block or facilitate movement between stages.

Performance Appraisal and Career Development

Too often performance appraisal interviews focus only on the past year or, at best, on plans for the forthcoming year. Rarely do a manager and a subordinate discuss careers, because neither the manager nor the subordinate has a way to talk about career development in terms other than the prospects for promotion. The career stages model can be helpful in guiding such a discussion. A number of managers have found that just discussing the model with individuals helps them to think more clearly about their careers and begin to identify alternatives and strategies for development that they hadn't previously considered.

The concept of stages can help a person think more clearly not only about what he should be doing and learning in his present job but also about what he should do if he wants to advance to another stage. A person who has learned what he needs to do in Stage I can begin to demonstrate his ability to work independ-

dently, develop an expertise that others recognize, and begin to apply that expertise. A person in Stage II may begin to take a new employee under his wing, show him how the system works, teach him some of the finer technical points, and so on. The Stage I person who wants to progress in the organization could ask himself: "Am I reluctant to make decisions on my own?" A person aiming for Stage IV could ask himself whether he is able to think about the needs of the organization as a whole and not just about his own group.

Timing

We aren't saying that anyone can promote himself to Stage IV. We do say that people can begin to do the work of the next stage and thus facilitate the transition to that stage. However, timing is a significant issue. There is a fine line between trying to move too quickly into the next stage and staying in the present stage long enough to obtain a learning base sufficient for subsequent growth. Too many people are so intent on getting into management that they don't establish the technical base they will need when they are called on to direct others.

Finally, and this is important, the individual must be responsible for deciding whether to stay in that organization. Sometimes an individual is capable of moving into Stage III or Stage IV activities and willing to do so, but the opportunities in the present organization are limited. On the other hand, failure to develop the skills and attitudes needed at the next stage could negate the effect of a change of organizations.

Manpower Planning

Although the primary responsibility for career management lies with the individual, the organization can do some things to facilitate career development. To become aware of the problem is the indispensable first step. Many managers are insensitive to the changing level of opportunities in their organizations. One company was having serious problems with

Figure 4 Proportionate distribution of professionals and managers in each stage reported by five R & D organizations

Stage	Proportionate Distribution of Professionals in Each Stage (%)
I	13.4
II	46.2
III	29.3
IV	11.1
	100.0

turnover in its sales force. The company had grown rapidly for ten years, doubling sales every three years. Then growth leveled off to 5 percent a year. However, the district sales managers continued to recruit new salesmen with promises of promotion into management within 18 months and so on. When the promised promotions didn't materialize, the disillusioned salesmen left to go to work for the competition, usually within two or two and one-half years.

An awareness of this problem can come from an analysis of the demographic data. How many employees, engineers, accountants, and managers, for example, does the organization have in each stage? What are the prospects for expansion and for having new positions open up? What is the turnover in each group?

It is also important for managers to share data with their people. Recently 60 upper-level managers in a large organization were asked whether they thought they would be promoted at least one more time before retirement. Fully 80 percent said no, not because they felt they lacked ability but because they felt there were no opportunities. In fact, the organization was planning on having most of them assume higher-level responsibilities.

Dual Ladders

The concept of career stages could help to explain some of the confusion and disillusionment that have arisen around the dual ladder. In attempting to recognize the contributions a nonmanagerial professional can make to an organization, most dual ladder programs have dichotomized the technical and the managerial roles. Often the roles in the technical ladder are described in terms of the lone individual contributor—a super Stage II person.

As we noted earlier, organizations have other roles for their experienced and competent senior people to fill. Stage III people, whether or not they are in management, tend to deal with the outside, train and develop others, and provide direction for important projects or activities. A recognition of the similarities between the activities and relationships of Stage III managers and Stage III nonmanagers could help professionals to recognize that some experience in a management position may be a legitimate form of preparation for a senior technical role, just as a Stage III or IV nonmanager may make the best candidate for a formal management slot.

Job Assignments

All our research indicates that the job assignment is the single most important variable in career development. There are many ways in which this variable can be manipulated. A person who is seen as too narrow can be moved to a new project that forces him to apply his existing skills to new problems. Someone who is finding it difficult to become independent of his mentor can be transferred to a job that facilitates such a transition. A change of job assignment is no panacea, but it can be pivotal in helping people develop their careers.

Finally, organizations need to find ways of loosening their structures, rules, and procedures to make it possible for more people to move through the stages. In most organizations more people combine the ability and desire to do Stage III and IV work than are allowed to do so. Often there are policies or traditions that permit only certain people to deal with customers, suppliers, and so on or that make it difficult for individual contributors to serve as mentors. Some managers are unwilling, for example, to let senior employees serve as mentors to the newcomers in the organization. Sometimes their fear is justified, but more often it prevents the formation of a very productive relationship.

Most organizations and most managers are both unsuccessful and uncreative in managing senior professionals. Organizations that learn to perform that task well will have a considerable competitive advantage.

Organizations need to be more creative in making it possible for people to move both ways through the stages without the fear of a clear or permanent loss of status or prestige. Often the individual and the organization are locked into

motivating an unrewarding relationship. It
needs to become much easier for people like
George Dunlop to make the transition that he
made. As more senior managers set the
example of this type of transition, hopefully it
will become a more acceptable career alternative.

Consciously or unconsciously we all carry
in our heads models to help us think about
careers in organizations. We have concluded
that many of the models being used to make
decisions that affect careers are misleading. In
our view, the longitudinal concept of career
stages can be helpful to both professionals and
managers as they make decisions about their
careers.

Early Career Issues and Concerns

The major task for the early career manager is entry into both the organization and the profession. This process of entry is characterized by two major activities: "joining up" and "breaking in." Every year thousands of college graduates enter American organizations to begin their careers in management. During the first few years of their careers almost half of these young managers will leave their first organization and move on to another organization or go back to school. This high turnover of young managers is a considerable waste of human resources and highlights the importance of the "breaking in" period for organizations and individuals alike.

Once the individual and the organization have selected each other, the two parties must learn to adapt to one another. This process of adaptation will be greatly affected by individual and organizational expectations, as well as by the attempts of the organization to socialize its new members. In the first reading for this section, Kotter explores the nature of individual and organizational expectations in the "joining up" process. The importance of these initial expectations has been highlighted by the notion of the psychological contract. By the use of this term we mean "a series of mutual expectations of which the parties to the relationship may not themselves be even dimly aware but which nonetheless govern their relationship to each other." [1] Kotter describes the importance of matching initial expectations in an effort to maximize performance, creativity, satisfaction, and tenure.

Based upon their expectations, organizations attempt to shape the individual's behavior to satisfy their needs. Schein comments that it is as if the organization were "putting its fingerprints" on people. [2] In a formal sense, however, this process is referred to as socialization. In the next reading Feldman describes the various

[1] H. Levinson, C. R. Price, H. J. Munden, and C. M. Solley, *Men, Management and Mental Health* (Cambridge: Harvard University Press, 1962).

[2] E. H. Schein, "Organizational Socialization and the Profession of Management," *Industrial Management Review*, 9 (1968), pp. 1-15.

aspects of organizational socialization. Schein best summarizes the importance of socialization from both the point of view of the organization and the individual:

> The process is so ubiquitous and we go through it so often during our total career that it is all too easy to overlook it. Yet it is a process which can make or break a career, and which can make or break organizational systems of manpower planning. The speed and effectiveness of socialization determine employee loyalty, commitment, productivity and turnover. The basic stability and effectiveness of organizations therefore depends upon their ability to socialize new members.[3]

There is strong evidence to indicate that the very early employment period is crucial to the development of a healthy individual-organization relationship, for it is in this initial period of interaction that the two sets of expectations come into direct confrontation. In the third reading of this section, Hall examines the careers of new managers in organizational settings. He describes a model of career development which highlights the importance of early job challenge and success as a method of increasing a manager's satisfaction and commitment. The challenge for management is to recognize the potential of young managers and to create organizational opportunities which will utilize rather than destroy the very qualities which make them valuable—education and youthful enthusiasm and idealism.

The next article by Webber continues our examination of the career concerns of young managers, who often react to their careers with great levels of frustration and dissatisfaction. Webber explores the factors which create this frustration and dissatisfaction and offers several useful strategies to help the young manager better "manage" early career experiences.

The last reading in this section stresses the importance of forming a mentor relationship. A mentor is defined not in terms of formal roles (such as boss, teacher, senior colleague), but rather in terms of the nature of the relationship and the functions it serves. The mentor acts as teacher, sponsor, host and guide, exemplar, and counselor. According to Levinson, the mentor's primary function, then, is to foster the young manager's career development.

[3]*Ibid.*

The Psychological Contract:
Managing the Joining-Up Process

John Paul Kotter

A growing number of organizations in recent years have been reporting problems that center around getting the new man, often a recent college graduate, "on board." These problems take on many forms:

• Some organizations have reported as much as a 50 percent turnover rate of new men after their first year of work.
• Recently, some corporations have complained about a generation gap between new men and older managers which was putting a severe strain on their organization.
• Other companies complain about the loss of creativity, innovativeness and energy in their new employees during their first few years (often labeled a "stifling of creativity").
• Managers have often complained about the naiveté of new employees. ("They come in with unrealistic expectations and then get mad when they don't come true!")
• Organizations have reported that it takes some managerial and technical specialists two years or more to really get on board, while others have reported that it takes one-half or one-fourth that time.

This article is concerned with the process of assimilating new employees into an organization, which we call the "joining-up" process. All of the above incidents are symptomatic of

problems in this process. It is the purpose of this article to present research that argues the following points:

1. Early experiences (the joining-up period) have a major effect on an individual's later career in an organization. Specifically, early experiences can significantly affect job satisfaction, employee attitude, productivity level, and turnover.

2. Efficient management of the joining-up process can save an organization a great deal of money by making employees more efficient faster, by increasing job satisfaction, morale and productivity, by decreasing turnover, by increasing the amount of creativity, by decreasing counterproductive conflict and tension, and by increasing the number of truly effective members within the organization.

For an organization that hires twenty-five college graduates with bachelor's degrees each year, the difference between a well-managed and a mismanaged joining-up process is $200,000 a year at a minimum.

3. Due to a complex set of forces most organizations do a poor job of managing the joining-up process. Often because of a problem of measurement, organizations either do not realize this problem exists or do not realize its magnitude.

This article will outline some recent research and present the results. To clarify the implications of the research, two case studies will be presented, followed by a summary and a set of conclusions.

THE RESEARCH

Research was recently undertaken at MIT's Sloan School of Management to explore problems in the joining-up process and to try to understand how it can be better managed.[1] A simple model of the process was constructed and data was gathered with an eight-page questionnaire given to a randomly selected group of Sloan masters graduates and Sloan Fellows. These Sloan masters graduates had completed a two-year masters degree program in management somewhere between 1961 and 1969. Sloan Fellows are managers in their 30s and 40s who had just completed a one-year "masters" program. Ninety responses from middle managers ranging in age from twenty-three to forty-five were eventually used in the data analysis.[2]

At the heart of the model was the concept of the "psychological contract," which was first introduced a decade ago by Chris Argyris[3] and Harry Levenson.[4] As it was defined for this research, the psychological contract is an implicit contract between an individual and his organization which specifies what each expects to give and receive from each other in their relationship.

When an individual joins an organization, he has expectations of what he expects to receive (such as advancement opportunities, salary, status, office space and decor, amount of challenging vs. dull work, and so on) as well as expectations of what he expects to give (such as technical skills, time and energy commitment, communication ability, supervisory skills, loyalty, and so on). The organization also has expectations of what it expects to receive from the new employee, (examples of which are similar to what the employee expects to give) and expectations of what it expects to offer him in return (examples of which are similar to what the employee expects to receive).

These expectations can be the same, or they can be quite different. For example, a young chemical engineer from MIT may expect that he will be given his own office when he goes to work for a company. If the company also expects to give him an office of his own, then there is a "match." If they do not expect to give him his own office, there is a "mismatch." This mismatch can be small (they expect he will share an office with one other person) or large (they expect he won't be given an office, desk, or anything). These four sets of expectations and the matches and mismatches make up the "psychological contract."

This contract is very different from a legal or labor contract. It may have literally thousands of items in it (see Table 1 for an example of some categories used in the research) although the job seeker or new employee may consciously think of only a few. His expectations of the types of technical skills he will give may be very clear, while his expectation of how willing he is to take on company values may be very unclear. Likewise, the organization may have a clearer picture of some expectations than others. These expectations may be explicitly discussed during recruiting or with the first supervisor or they may not. The new recruit may have a deep, clear understanding of some, all or none of the company's expectations and vice versa. Finally, this contract changes as the individual's and the company's expectations alter.

Research Results

The research findings can be summarized in the following points:

1. The first finding confirmed the major research hypothesis that psychological contracts, which are made up primarily of matches in expectations, are related to greater job satisfaction, productivity, and reduced turnover than are other contracts which have more mismatches and less matches. In other words, those people who established a contract that was comprised of more matches in expectations, had a more satisfying and productive first year and remained longer with the

Table 1   Types of Expectations*

(a)

The following list of thirteen items are examples of areas in which an individual has expectations of receiving and an organization has expectations of giving. That is, for each item in this list, the individual will have an expectation about what the organization will offer him or give him in that area. Likewise, the organization has an expectation about what it will offer or give the individual in that area.

1. A sense of meaning or purpose in the job.
2. Personal development opportunities.
3. The amount of interesting work (stimulates curiosity and induces excitement).
4. The challenge in the work.
5. The power and responsibility in the job.
6. Recognition and approval for good work.
7. The status and prestige in the job.
8. The friendliness of the people, the congeniality of the work group.
9. Salary.
10. The amount of structure in the environment (general practices, discipline, regimentation).
11. The amount of security in the job.
12. Advancement opportunities.
13. The amount and frequency of feedback and evaluation.

(b)

The following list of seventeen items are examples of areas in which an individual has expectations of giving and the organization has expectations of receiving. That is, for each item in this list, the individual will have an expectation about what he is willing or able to give or offer the organization in that area. Likewise, the organization has an expectation about what it will receive from the individual in that area.

1. The ability to perform nonsocial job related tasks requiring some degree of technical knowledge and skill.
2. The ability to learn the various aspects of a position while on the job.
3. The ability to discover new methods of performing tasks; the ability to solve novel problems.
4. The ability to present a point of view effectively and convincingly.
5. The ability to work productively with groups of people.
6. The ability to make well-organized, clear presentations both orally and written.
7. The ability to supervise and direct the work of others.
8. The ability to make responsible decisions well without assistance from others.
9. The ability to plan and organize work efforts for oneself or others.
10. The ability to utilize time and energy for the benefit of the company.
11. The ability to accept company demands which conflict with personal prerogatives.
12. Social relationships with other members of the company off the job.
13. Conforming to the folkways of the organization or work group on the job in areas not directly related to job performance.
14. Further education pursued off-company time.
15. Maintaining a good public image of the company.
16. Taking on company values and goals as one's own.
17. The ability to see what should or must be done, and to initiate appropriate activity.

*These twenty-nine types of expectations were adapted from earlier research by Berlew and Hall.[5]

company than those people whose contract had fewer matches.

We have all observed personal examples of this phenomenon in its extreme. A number of the Sloan masters graduates reported that they took their first job with completely unrealistic expectations of how hard it would be to introduce new techniques into their companies. This expectation, although unrealistic, was an important one to each of them initially. They lasted in their first jobs on the average of one year.

The more subtle differences in job satisfaction or productivity resulting from a greater or lesser number of matches in the psychological contract are more difficult to observe. The pattern often looks like this: The contract formed during the joining-up period has mismatches, but neither the employee nor his boss really recognizes them or confronts them. After the first year the employee begins to "feel" those mismatches as disappointments, letdowns, and so on. Since he thinks the company has broken their contract, he reacts by slowly breaking his part of the bargain. He often "digs in" and becomes another moderately productive, uncreative, body.

2.   The concept that showed a measurable relationship to productivity, satisfaction, and turnover was "matching," not getting more or less than was expected. Mismatches that gave more than one expected caused as many problems as those which gave less than one expected. In other words, organizations or individuals who approach the contract trying to get "the most," or "the best" instead of "a fit" or "a match" are missing the boat. Often we don't have strong preferences for something, but we still plan for the future based on what we expect. For example, Warren, a twenty-five year old bachelor working for a West Coast aeronautics firm, expected that he would be transferred East after one year of work. He really didn't care one way or the other, but based on his expectation he made elaborate plans for the move, which, when it didn't occur, left Warren very upset.

The sales department of a moderate sized industrial products firm put on a strong recruiting campaign a few years ago to get the "best men possible for the money." Their strong recruiting effort did succeed in getting a remarkably strong group of new men. Unfortunately, the job did not require the skills many of these young men had. The contracts formed had many large mismatches in them (but mismatches which the company thought were in its "favor"). Within two years the company lost 60 percent of these men and only 10 percent (two men) were doing very well.

3.   It was found that the clearer an individual understood his own expectation on an item, the higher was the probability of a match. Likewise, the clearer an expectation was to the organization, the higher the probability of a match.

It is fairly obvious what is happening in this case. Many times people do not explicitly think of all the areas in which they have expectations. Often a new employee out of college isn't consciously aware of what he wants and needs, or what he is capable and prepared to give. Unfortunately organizations also are not clear as to what they expect (in detail) either. As a result they don't talk about many areas nor pay attention to them. Mismatches can occur by accident, out of neglect.

What is needed then is for the new man, the company, and his boss to carefully consider all areas of expectations in order to overcome the problem of clarity. One of the reasons this hasn't been done in the past is that people have not considered its importance.

4.   If the new man explicitly discussed his expectations with a company representative, the two parties' mutual understanding of the other's expectations increased and so did the probability of matching.

There are a number of reasons why this doesn't happen more frequently. There often appear to be norms surrounding the interview and the initial work period which define some items as not legitimate to talk about. The fact that the new man often feels powerless limits his ability to initiate such a discussion. His supervisor may be overworked and not rewarded for helping the new man and as a result doesn't initiate what could be a complex deep discussion.

These first four points are summarized in model form in Figure 1.

5. It was further discovered that clarity (point 3), discussion (point 5), and even some give and take were not enough to resolve some mismatches, which we called basic. In this situation, an individual and his organization, having clarified and discussed their expectations, find themselves unwilling or unable to find a commonality of expectations in an area which is important to both of them. In some cases, this may mean that the employee should resign, a reality that some people and some organizations don't like to face.

It was also discovered that there were small but statistically significant differences—mismatches—between the expectations of all individuals as a group and all organizations as a group on some items (see Table 2).

As the reader can see, the individuals had higher expectations with respect to the personal development opportunities they would be offered, the amount of interesting work they would be offered, and the amount of meaning or purpose in their work. On the other hand, the organizations had higher expectations toward the amount of security that they would offer the individual. The organizations also had higher expectations of the individual's ability to work with groups, his taking on of organizational values and goals, and his willingness to conform.

Schein, in an earlier article, suggested that basic differences in expectations seemed to be developing between recent college graduates and industry.[7] In particular he reported that college graduates seemed to have higher expectations of advancement opportunities, increased responsibility, and personal growth opportunities. He also reported very different expectations on how to sell ideas and get things

done, how important and practical "theoretical" knowledge was, and how ready the new man was for use. These findings are consistent with the ones reported in Table 2.

It is important then for a particular organization to be sensitive to growing differences in expectations between it and its new men. Resolving these basic differences can be a much more difficult task than resolving the other types of differences. In an extreme case, resolving this problem could require an organization to find a new labor pool or to undergo major internal changes in order to survive on a long-run basis.

6. Finally, for the particular sample used in this study (Sloan School graduates and Sloan Fellows), the nature of the conflict in the process looked something like this: the individual was most interested in exchanging non-people related skills (technical knowledge, drive, writing ability, and so on) for exciting, challenging, meaningful work and development (and advancement) opportunities. The organization, however, expected to give the individual less of that which he expected most, and expected to receive in addition to skills, more on such items as conformity, loyalty, and so on.

In summary, there are a number of general points that result from this research which are not usually found in "conventional wisdom." First, the initial period *is* very important, and as such is worth carefully managing. Second, what you don't know *can* hurt you. A clear understanding of one's own expectations and the other party's will help form better contracts. Third, the key in contract formulation is achieving a match or a fit, *not* getting more, or the best, or whatever. Fourth, if an organization and an individual have one or more very central, basic mismatches, it may be in their best interests to shake hands and part. Finally, if an organization's expectations get too far out of line with its labor pool, it can get into deep trouble.

In order to obtain a better feel for the implications of this research, let us look at a few examples of organizations who have tried to

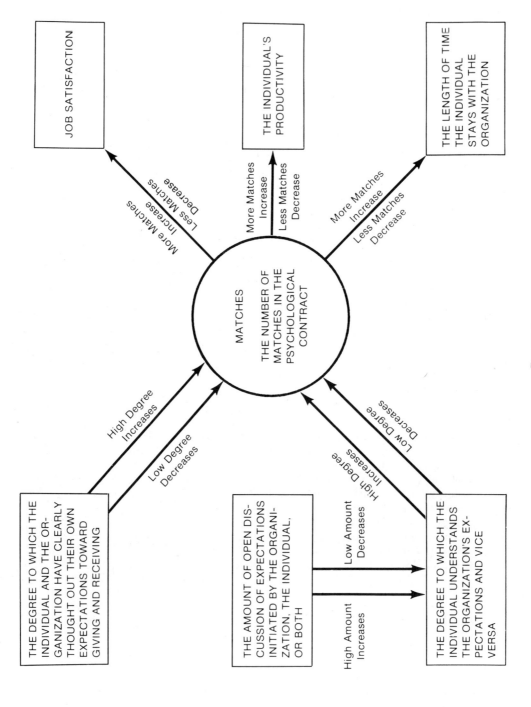

Figure 1

Table 2   Basic Mismatches[6]

Note: All differences are statistically significant at .05. The expectations are listed in decreasing order of statistically significant differences (from .0003 to .048).

Expectation	Mean for Individual[a]	Mean for Organization[b]
1) Personal Development Opportunities	4.54 (individual expects to receive)	4.20 (organization expects to give)[b]
2) Security	2.30 (individual expects to receive)	2.94 (organization expects to give)[b]
3) Taking on Values and Goals	2.80 (individual expects to give)	3.30 (organization expects to receive)[b]
4) Ability to Work with Groups	3.75 (individual expects to give)	4.06 (organization expects to receive)[b]
5) Conforming	2.19 (individual expects to give)	2.53 (organization expects to receive)[b]
6) Interesting Work	4.36 (individual expects to receive)	4.10 (organization expects to give)[b]
7) Sense of Meaning or Purpose	4.24 (individual expects to receive)	3.98 (organization expects to give)[b]

a. As measured on a 1 to 5 scale (1 = not expected, 5 = strongly expected.)
b. As perceived by the respondent.

improve the management of their joining-up process.

Applications: Case Study I

This first case involves a manufacturing plant of a large consumer product company, employing about 300 workers and forty managers. In June, the plant hired three new college engineering graduates as junior managers. For their first three months they participated in a combined program of work and training. A senior manager at the plant was concerned that the plant could do a better job of getting the new employees on board. In particular his concerns were:

• He wanted the new men to get up to speed, to become "socialized" and to learn the plant's norms faster (in general to learn more about the plant, the people, and so on).
• The new men (almost through with training) would be getting their "first boss" soon. He wanted them to explore their expectations and to be prepared for negotiating a psychological contract with their new boss.

• He wanted to receive feedback from the new men on their three month history with the company and to explore better methods for future training programs.
• In addition, he wanted some of the plant's top management to get a feel for what the new college graduates were like, and to explore management's implicit expectations of the new men.
• Finally he wanted to do some team building. He wanted to help the new men feel part of their management team.

To accomplish these goals, four senior managers, three supervisors, and the three trainees were invited to a twelve-hour session, led by an outside consultant, spread out over three days during their shut-down period. Prior to the session the three trainees and three supervisors (who had been with the organization only one to two years) filled out questionnaires on their specific expectations of giving and receiving, and answered how clear each expectation was to them (see Table 1 for such a list of expectations). The senior managers filled out questionnaires on what the company expected to give and receive to each of the new employees. This exercise was designed to help the participants explore explicitly their expectations before the session.

The session began with a "contract setting" exercise for the twelve-hour session. The participants were asked to state explicitly what they expected to give and to receive from this session and the consultant, as the workshop leader, did the same. A contract was then explicitly established among all the participants which included the goals of the session, the roles each person would assume, the schedule we would follow, and so on. This provided the group with a good start for the session and with some real-time experience concerning psychological contracts and contract setting.

The next input was a brief lecture on the joining-up process and the concept of the psychological contract. Following this, the group was divided into three homogeneous groups (new men, supervisors, senior managers) and given time to develop lists of "mismatches." The new men and young supervisors were told to identify mismatches from their own experiences, including the cause. The senior managers were told to develop a list of what mismatches they thought new men often have when they join the company.

It was interesting to note that all three lists were different. The mismatches the new men presently felt were different from those of the one to two year men. The senior managers' list reflected their own experiences and was also different. In a sense the three lists provided a chronological picture of the problems and concerns an employee faced as he grew up in this organization.

The three groups, one at a time, presented their lists, point by point, and the entire group discussed them. This discussion was one of information exchange, exploration and confrontation. Information was candidly exchanged on subjects that were not normally discussed but which were important (performance criteria, dress, hair length, career paths in the company, money, company policy, and so on). Many misunderstandings and misperceptions (on the part of all three groups) were aired and resolved. One of the new men started asking some questions about how to get something done that he had been suppressing for weeks out of a fear of looking stupid. A major conflict that one of the supervisors faced was confronted (he was seriously considering leaving) and, after the session, resolved (he was transferred).

The session ended with some group problem solving on the issue, "what can we do better concerning our joining-up process." They developed several recommendations including the use of similar sessions in the future. The participants' response to the session was enthusiastic and the senior manager who initiated it felt it had accomplished his five goals.

Case Study II

A much larger effort, which is in progress at this writing, involves an R&D division of a giant consumer products company. Some of the top management became concerned about the joining-up process in their division due to a number of factors, including a speech on socialization and joining-up by Ed Schein. They established a task force comprised of a diagonal slice of the organization, an internal organizational development specialist, and an external consultant.

The division contains about 400 people, twenty of whom had been with the company one and one-half years or less. The first task of the group was a diagnostic one, in which information was collected from various sources in and out of the organization. As a part of this effort, almost all of the new employees (two groups of eight) met for a one day session designed to help them examine and articulate their brief experiences with the company. Questionnaires were given to all new people, their bosses, and their boss's bosses. These inputs and others from other divisions, academia, and so on led to a diagnosis of critical variables that could be improved upon.

The most important factor turned out to be the skills of the new man's supervisor. The process was facilitated if the new man's supervisor had skills in the following areas: giving and receiving feedback, articulating expectations and performance criteria, explaining realistically decisions passed down from above, coaching and helping, communicating, understanding new people's problems, and so on. Other important factors included the selection of the first project, the selection of the first environment (including boss, peers, and section), formal and informal training, opportunities for quickly learning about the company and facilities, the clarity of key policies, the reward system, and so forth.

At this writing, the task force is planning and implementing changes in the organization based on their diagnosis and understanding of the joining-up process. The types of changes they have developed can help the reader to see what can be done to improve a joining-up process.

Creation of a training program for a new man's boss.—This program is designed to help him better understand the new man and the joining-up process and to help him develop better skills as a coach.

Creation of a criterion for project selection.—A more careful selection of first projects can speed up a new man's learning.

New formal training activities to replace old ones.—New formal training was created to replace the old based on new employee feedback on inefficiencies, usefulness, and so on.

Explicitly stated division policies.—Unclear policies in some key areas were causing false expectations in important areas. Top management is changing this.

Creation of a joining-up workshop.—This workshop is somewhat similar to the one described in the first case study, except that the new man's boss is present, and there is more emphasis on relationship building and contract setting.

Planning aid for supervisors who expect new man.—A number of devices have been created

to help supervisors plan for their new man's arrival. These include help in setting training objectives, in meeting a wide range of new man needs, and so forth.

Creation of performance criteria.—Vague performance criteria have caused unreal expectations. Supervisors are now creating more explicit, but not mechanistic ones.

This effort, which is still in progress, will take about one and one-half years in total.

SUMMARY AND CONCLUSIONS

Early experiences in an organization can have a great effect on a person's career. The joining-up process, which determines these experiences, must be carefully managed. The quality of the management of the joining-up process will effect two major outcomes: the cost of getting new people on board and keeping them in the firm, and the level of productivity, commitment, innovativeness, and so on of people when they get on board.

Unfortunately in many organizations this process is mismanaged, or not managed at all. The costs of mismanagement are very high.

The concept of the psychological contract has proven to be a useful one in examining the joining-up process. Recent research has shown that if a new person's expectations are out of line with the company's this will show up in low production, low creativity, dissatisfaction, and turnover.

While it is not really useful to propose "cookbook" solutions for better management of the joining-up process beyond the conclusions drawn from the research, the following are key variables in most organizations' joining-up process.

A) Recruiting Effort. Does your recruiting effort allow both the recruitee and your organization to exchange accurate expectations? Does the recruitee get a fairly realistic picture of the challenges and problems in your organization? Do you carefully explore his expectations and try to get the best fits or matches or do you look for "good people"?

B) The First Supervisor. Do the managers who supervise new employees have the skills and knowledge to help create sound psychological contracts? Are they good coaches and teachers? Do they know enough about the organization to help someone else learn? Are they effective members themselves? Do you carefully select and train first supervisors? In many organizations this man is the key variable in this process.

C) Reward and Control System. Do the supervisors of new men perceive that they are being rewarded for efficient and effective management of a new man's joining-up process or do they think they are rewarded only for doing the "real work"?

D) First Job Environment. Does the environment a new man is put into contribute or detract from his getting on board? Does it help reduce his initial anxieties and help make him a part of the group? Will his peers teach him what you want him to learn about his job and the organization? Careful selection of the first environment and activities outside of it (as in Case I) can prove useful.

E) Performance Criteria and Training Objectives. Do the supervisor and the new man know what the reward system is for the new man? Is the performance criteria clear to both? Are training objectives clear to both? In other words, how clear are your expectations of new men?

F) Training. Do the formal and informal training activities achieve the training objectives quickly and effectively or do they waste time, frustrate the new man, teach the wrong things and bore everyone? What assumptions do you make when you design the training activities? Do they come close to meeting the expectations of new men?

G) First Assignment. How is the first assignment or project chosen? Does it provide an opportunity for the new employee to learn, meet people, grow, and so on. Is it clear to the new man why he was given that assignment, what he can get out of it, and what is expected of him?

Obviously this isn't an exhaustive list, and the importance of these items will vary from organization to organization, but it should give the reader a feeling of what can be adjusted for better results.

In the final analysis, the payoff for a particular organization will depend upon its awareness of the importance of this process, and upon the creativity with which it systematically examines its unique situation and derives solutions for better management of this process.

REFERENCES

Based on a Master's Thesis by the author completed at the Sloan School of Management at MIT under the direction of Professors Edgar Schein and Irwin Rubin.

1. See "The Psychological Contract: Expectations and the Joining-Up Process," an unpublished Master's thesis by the author (Sloan, 1970).
2. Data was collected during January and February, 1970.
3. Chris Argyris, *Understanding Organizational Behavior* (Homewood, Ill.: Dorsey Press, 1960).
4. Harry Levenson, *Men, Management & Mental Health*, (Cambridge, Mass.: Harvard University Press, 1962).
5. David E. Berlew, and Douglas T. Hall, "The Socialization of Managers: Effects of Expectations on Performance," *An Administrative Science Quarterly* (September, 1966), pp. 207-223.
6. "The Psychological Contract: Expectations and the Joining-Up Process," an unpublished Master's thesis by the author (Sloan, 1970).
7. Edgar H. Schein, "How to Break in the College Graduate," *Harvard Business Review* (November-December, 1964), pp. 68-76.

A Practical Program for Employee Socialization*

Daniel C. Feldman

What is it about the ways organizations recruit, select, and develop employees that makes some new recruits feel competent and others helpless, makes some feel effective as good organization members and others feel isolated and rejected, makes some workers passive observers and others active contributors to organization success?

These are the basic questions in the study of organizational socialization, the study of the ways by which employees are transformed from total company outsiders to participating and effective corporate members. The success of the socialization process is critical for individuals, because the way their careers are managed by organizations influences both the quality of their work life and the quality of their outside lives. And as the success of organizations becomes increasingly dependent on the commitment of members rather than on traditional control systems, the questions posed here about organizational socialization become increasingly important to organizations as well.

I recently conducted a large-scale study of the socialization process at a community

*This research was part of a doctoral dissertation presented to Yale University Graduate School. The author wishes to thank J. Richard Hackman for helpful comments on this article. Richard Hackman, Clayton Alderfer, and Gerrit Wolf provided valuable assistance during the conduct of the research.

hospital, using as a sample 118 employees—nurses, nurses's aides, radiology technologists, accounting clerks, and tradespeople (plumbers, electricians, and carpenters, for example). I interviewed each employee extensively, and each completed a questionnaire about his or her experiences in entering and adjusting to the organization. This article discusses the highlights of the research, which was addressed primarily to four sets of questions:

1. What happens to individuals as they enter organizations and adjust to new work assignments? What are the indicators of good socialization experiences?

2. What are the results, or consequences, of socialization programs? What aspects of socialization programs most influence these results? What are the differences in outcomes between the socialization experiences of professional, paraprofessional, and nonprofessional workers?

3. What are the specific practices and policies that organizations can follow at each stage of socialization to make the process easier, quicker, and more effective for employees?

4. What are the general implications of this research for the use and design of organizational socialization programs?

We'll consider each of these sets of questions separately.

WHAT HAPPENS TO INDIVIDUALS AS THEY
ENTER ORGANIZATIONS AND ADJUST TO
NEW WORK ASSIGNMENTS? WHAT ARE
THE INDICATORS OF GOOD
SOCIALIZATION EXPERIENCES?

There seem to be three distinct stages that
employees go through as they adjust to new jobs
in organizations.

Stage I: "Getting In"

The socialization process begins even before
employees enter the organization. First of all,
before they actually take jobs and enter the
organization, they try to get a full picture of
what life in the organization is really like.
Second, they try to search for jobs for which
they are "best suited"—in terms of making the
best use of their talents, in terms of working
with people whose company they would enjoy,
or in terms of a variety of other reasons.

There are two indicators that the socialization process is going smoothly for people at this
"getting in" stage. The more positive these
indicators are for individuals, the more likely it
is that the two later stages of socialization will
go smoothly as well. These two indicators are:

1. *Realism.* The more realistically a person
portrays himself to the organization, and the
more realistically the organization portrays
itself to the person, the more likely it is that the
person will be hired for a job for which he is well
suited and that he will receive the type and
amount of training he needs. A study of appointments to West Point, for example, found
that those who received a booklet realistically
portraying life at the military academy were
more likely to accept appointments to the
academy and to survive the first year than were
those who had received no booklet. Similarly,
John Wanous found that realistic job previews
for telephone operators resulted in higher job
satisfaction and greater job survival without
reducing the flow of qualified applicants.

In the community hospital situation, the
behavior of both employees and supervisors
during the selection process in the accounting

department illustrates this relationship. Employees in the accounting department do
mainly clerical work, such as billing, typing,
and keypunching. A very important aspect of
these jobs, however, lies in dealing with
patients and lawyers, often hostile, who are
trying to unravel payment problems or billing
errors. This part of the job is often not
communicated to new employees. Most employees who had not known that their jobs
would entail so much interpersonal conflict
often felt that they had unfortunately taken
clerical jobs much less suited to their abilities
than other, similar jobs available, while those
who had been forewarned about the interpersonal conflict made a better adjustment. On the
other hand, employees are generally made
aware of the fact that the workload is heavy and
that the jobs demand speed. Obviously, realism
works both ways. Employees who either
overestimated their own typing skills—a sin-
cere misconception—or incorrectly pictured
their abilities to their prospective supervisors
were more likely to discover after being hired
that their jobs were too much for them.

The case of Arthur, a relatively new
tradesman in the hospital's engineering department, illustrates the problems that unrealistic
expectations can create. Arthur, a licensed
refrigeration expert, fully expected to be doing
refrigeration repairs. But he was sent to the
electrical shop, where he felt "like I was at a
road with ten forks, not knowing where to turn
or even how to find out how to turn." Three
months after the study, I learned that Arthur
had quit his job after a period of great ill will
with co-workers and supervisors.

2. *Congruence.* It is important, too, that
people have the skills necessary to do the jobs
that organizations need them to perform and
that the jobs the organization provides can satisfy individual needs and preferences. If this
congruence of individual needs and skills with
organizational demands can be achieved, we
can expect greater general satisfaction and
work motivation on the part of individuals and
longer job tenure for new recruits as well.

On the other hand, where the congruence

between job requirements and individual needs is low, great job dissatisfaction is a likely result. Barbara, a nurse's aide, commented, "I don't respect what I'm doing. . . . I have a good mind and I'm not using it." She was overqualified for her job and found coming to work unpleasant: "I don't say, 'Gee, I can't wait to get to work.' This job just has to be tolerated." Nancy, a radiology technologist trained to do sophisticated radiological tests, complained bitterly that she spent most of her time doing routine X-rays. When asked which direction she thought her career would take, she replied, "I didn't spend three years being trained to say, 'Hold it, now breathe,' and I don't expect to spend the next three years saying it, either."

Stage 2: "Breaking In"

During the second stage of the socialization process, the "breaking in" stage, the employee actually enters the organization and attempts to become a participating member of his own work group. There are four major activities of employees at this stage.

First, employees establish new relationships with co-workers and supervisors, both as they perform their jobs and as they relax with others during breaks and lunches. Second, employees learn new tasks that are needed to do their jobs; this involves not only learning new skills, but also becoming acquainted with the operation and maintenance of equipment, learning the bureaucratic procedures associated with their jobs, and so on. Third, new employees clarify their roles in the organization. Since job descriptions are generally expressed in very global terms, employees often insert their own personalities into jobs, putting more emphasis on those tasks they particularly like to perform or feel competent to perform. During the first few weeks and months, employees try to define exactly what tasks they have to do, what the priorities among those tasks are to be, and how they are to allocate their work time among them. Fourth, employees not only evaluate their progress within the organization, but also try to come to some agreement with others in the work group about the overall quality of their work and about specific areas of strength and weakness in job performance.

In this "breaking in" stage, there are four indicators that the socialization process is still running smoothly—indicators that suggest the last stage of socialization will go smoothly as well:

1. Acceptance. The more accepted a new recruit feels, the more he will feel trusted and be trusted by other group members; he will also be more likely to receive evaluative and informal information that will help him both in doing his job and in interacting with other organization members. Both Dornbush, writing about the "union of sympathy" among recruits in a Coast Guard Academy, and Becker, writing about new medical students, indicate that work groups can serve as a defense against oppressive forces in the organization, as a source of emotional support, as a source of possible solutions for work problems, and as a source of referral for appropriate types of behavior.

Feelings of lack of acceptance at work impact heavily on an employee's sense of self-worth: One accounting clerk in the hospital, for example, commented that she "felt like an orphan, hoping someone would take me in," while another clerk reported she spent over $50 per month in long-distance phone calls to talk to friends near her former residence about her present problems with co-workers. Uneasiness at work influences performance as well. For instance, Bruce, a radiology technologist, was experiencing a good deal of difficulty in his relationships with workers: "I've been here two months, and even now I don't feel accepted. . . . I worry about my relationships with other workers all the time. . . . This worry drives out concern for patients, for work, for everything."

2. Competence. Employees need to feel self-confident and skilled, both to bolster self-esteem and to begin a "benign circle of development," writes M. B. Smith. "Launched on the right trajectory, the person is likely to accumulate successes that strengthen the effectiveness of his orientation toward the world, while at the same time he acquires the knowledge and skills that make his further success more probable. . . . Off to a bad start, on the other hand, he soon encounters failures that make him hesitant to try. . . . And he falls increasingly behind his fellows in acquiring the knowledge and skills that are needed for success on those occasions when he does try."

Joan, a billing clerk, was seen as truly competent by her co-workers; assigned the clients whose last names began with the letters O through Z, she was affectionately known as the Wizard of Oz by peers, who constantly turned to her for help. Joan expected to stay in the organization and work her way up the hierarchy. In contrast, Carol, another clerk, reported feeling like "a little nothing, a very little cog in a very big wheel." Although she was unsuccessful in getting through training, her supervisors decided to keep her on after her probationary period. Now both Carol and her supervisors are regretting that decision and both are fearing the impact of termination.

3. Role definition. The more the individual employee can set his own priorities and allocate time the way he would like among the jobs he has to do, the more satisfied the employee will be. When supervisors are responsive to negotiating job descriptions and assignments with employees, employees report feeling more committed to doing high-quality work and having positive feelings about supervisors and co-workers. Moreover, as Edgar Schein points out, it is healthy for individuals to question some of the demands put on them during socialization. When an employee accepts all the behavioral demands and values of supervisors, he "curbs his creativity and thereby moves the organization toward a sterile form of bureaucracy." Organizations should demand that employees accept only those behaviors and values that are crucial to the accomplishment of organizational goals, and should allow employees some freedom to be independent and resourceful.

In the hospital, we see the impact of role definition most clearly in nursing service. Three-year diploma nurses tended to feel that

the mark of a good nurse is the ability to keep on schedule, to handle all patients quickly and efficiently, and to be solicitous of the attending physician's demands. By contrast, four-year degree nurses tended to feel that the mark of quality nursing care is emphasis on the total individual patient, both his physical and his psychological needs, and that the nurse should share more fully in the diagnosis and treatment decisions made on the floor.

The 30 head nurses, too, differed in their philosophy of nursing, with some putting more emphasis on administration of nursing care and others on counseling. Those nurses who shared their head nurse's philosophy of nursing and defined their jobs accordingly also tended to feel more fairly and equitably evaluated on their job performance; those nurses who did not share their head nurse's idealization of the nurse's role—the bulk of the three-year nurses—experienced greater turnover and requested more internal transfers. In fact, most of the four-year diploma nurses request transfers to oncology or geriatrics, where counseling is a more accepted nursing activity and where head nurses with that attitude are more often assigned. As one nurse put it, "Some people put emphasis on patients, others on beds. We all have priorities—some of us are just lucky enough to get supervisors with the same ones!"

4. Congruence of evaluation. Employers and employees should also be able to come to some agreement over the individual employee's performance evaluation and his or her success in the organization. If an employee feels that he is progressing well, and a significant number of his peers agree with his evaluation, then the employee is likely to continue in his work with feelings of satisfaction and self-esteem. If, however, he feels that he has performed well, but others feel he has not, he will continue behaving in inappropriate ways and will be less likely to continue satisfactorily in his job. Unless the individual employee receives feedback soon to correct his perceptions and behaviors and/or gets additional help or training, his long-term prospects in the organization are poor.

Two main factors were most frequently

cited as sources of friction over evaluation. Tony, a radiology technologist, stated that in her department "the standards are set so high that no matter how well you perform, you still feel incompetent." Radiology technologists and nurses also reported that they got feedback only when they performed poorly, never when they performed well. This led one nurse to comment that "even a well-trained pigeon should be positively reinforced more than once every three hundred and sixty-five days." At times this resentment over failure to evaluate fairly or frequently leads to severe supervisor-subordinate interpersonal problems or even to sabotage of the workflow.

Stage 3: "Settling In"

Once an employee has entered an organization and come to some tentative resolution of adjustment problems in his or her own work group, he needs to resolve two types of conflicts. The first are *conflicts between work life and home life.* Work and home can come into conflict over the employee's schedule (for example, both the number of hours worked and when they are scheduled, vacation time, days off), the demands on the employee's family, and the effect of the job on the quality of home life (for example, amount of worry and preoccupation associated with work, demands on the family for emotional support, and so on). The second set of conflicts that the employee needs to deal with are *conflicts between his work group and other work groups in the organization.* Different groups in the organization—other departments or divisions, superiors further up the organization hierarchy, and so on—may have very different expectations of the employee from those his work group has of him.

There are two indicators of a successful "settling in" period:

1. Resolution of outside life conflicts. We have already observed that work life can influence one's outside life in terms of scheduling, demands on an employee's family, and the quality of life possible for an employee outside of work. Employees who do not resolve these conflicts may be forced to leave the

organization at some point in their career or experience emotional withdrawal. These outside life conflicts are more common for women—and they are particularly severe for women with children at home. In the hospital, for example, Irene, a married accounting clerk with two children, reported that an hour before work closed, her mind became "like a pile of leaves blowing across the lawn—I start dwelling on the million errands I have to run for my children, and how I'm going to get them all done." Another employee reported feeling like a split person, "a hassled, grousing housewife masquerading as a chin-up professional nurse."

2. Resolution of conflicting demands. Members of other departments may disagree strongly with a new recruit's definition of his job and may have very different expectations of a new member of the work group. Employees who are continually upset by these work conflicts and who have not developed decision rules to deal with them will need to invest more energy and time in resolving each and every conflict and will therefore have less energy for dealing with their actual task demands. Nurse's aides, in particular, had a hard time dealing with all the conflicts that they experienced as they moved from department to department performing the tasks of nursing service. One aide commented, "In this hospital, everyone passes the crap down to the next lowest level, and we end up getting the most unrefined crap in the place." The aides' supervisors, and the aides themselves, acknowledged that the aides spent almost as much time in fighting with supervisors, fighting with people in other departments, and complaining to others as they spent in doing real work.

For example, nurse's aides do most of the transporting work of the floor—bringing patients down for X-rays, special treatments, and so on. Their supervisors instruct them simply to leave the patient off and come back to the floor to continue their work. X-ray and other departments, however, often demand that the nurse's aide remain with the patient until after the treatment so that the patients are not left hanging around their departments. If the aide leaves without the patient, he or she is reprimanded by auxiliary service; if the aide returns late to the floor, he or she is reprimanded by the head nurse. As a last-ditch attempt to solve the transport problem, nurse's aides met with nursing administrators and made the suggestion (which was accepted) that the aide would stay with the patient if and only if the auxiliary service supervisor obtained permission from the head nurse on the floor.

WHAT ARE THE RESULTS, OR CONSEQUENCES, OF SOCIALIZATION PROGRAMS? WHAT ASPECTS OF SOCIALIZATION PROGRAMS MOST INFLUENCE THESE RESULTS? WHAT ARE THE DIFFERENCES IN OUTCOMES BETWEEN THE SOCIALIZATION EXPERIENCES OF PROFESSIONAL, PARAPROFESSIONAL, AND NONPROFESSIONAL WORKERS?

There are several ways in which we can evaluate the consequences of socialization programs for individuals: general satisfaction of workers, mutual influence, internal work motivation, and job involvement. Let's look at each of these outcomes a little more closely and examine what aspects of the socialization process influence them.

General Satisfaction

J. Richard Hackman and Greg Oldham define general satisfaction as the degree to which an employee is satisfied and happy in his or her work. Two types of organization outcomes are most frequently associated with the level of general employee satisfaction. The first of these outcomes is absenteeism and turnover. Research is convincing that the more satisfied a worker is, the longer he or she will stay on the job and the lower his or her absenteeism will be. The second of these outcomes is job performance. Evidence suggests that general satisfaction may be related, under some but by no means all circumstances, to a moderate increase in job performance.

My study showed four variables to be positively associated with general satisfaction: congruence, role definition, resolution of conflicting demands, and resolution of outside life conflicts.

1. Congruence. Congruence is most strongly correlated with general satisfaction; the better the fit between an individual and his work, the more happy and satisfied he will be with his job situation. Where the fit is not good between the individual and the job—as in the cases of our overqualified nurse's aide and radiology technologist—the consequent dissatisfaction can cause individuals to think of leaving their jobs altogether.

2. Role definition. Role definition and general satisfaction are also positively related. Employees who could largely determine what tasks they would do and how they could allocate their time among those tasks expressed more positive attitudes about the nature of their work and their relationships with other members of their work group. We saw one good example of this relationship with nurses who held the same or different philosophies as their supervisors. In the former case, both the nurse and her superior shared the same definition of the job and general satisfaction was high, while in the latter case, differing job definitions led to conflicts and low satisfaction.

We found another example of this relationship in the engineering department. There are several short-term projects to which the tradespeople in the department may be assigned, ranging in desirability from jobs on a renovation crew to jobs like shoveling snow or cleaning up after a flood. Employees with latitude in accepting or rejecting short-term jobs enjoyed their work more and had more positive feelings about their supervisor.

This latitude in accepting or rejecting short-term jobs often depends on the supervisor's evaluation of the employee. If a supervisor feels particularly positive about an employee, the supervisor may give the worker more opportunities to learn new tasks and skills and may be more willing to let him dump unwanted chores on others. If the supervisor has a low evaluation of the employee, however, he or she may load all the simpler tasks on him or hold him back from doing more challenging tasks until the employee has mastered the tasks already assigned.

Role conflict stemming from demands from different departments serves as a constant irritant to some hospital employees, making the overall quality of the work experience less positive. We see this relationship in our example of the nurse's aides. We also see it frequently among the registered nurses. Hospitals have two hierarchies—a medical hierarchy from the chief of staff down to orderlies, which is responsible for medical care, and an administrative hierarchy from the chief administrator down to first-line supervisors, which is responsible for the operation of the entire hospital facility. The nurse's role is overloaded with responsibilities to both hierarchies: As part of the medical hierarchy, the staff nurse is the only employee allowed to give certain medical treatments and use certain medical equipment, and she is ultimately responsible for the medical services provided by all the staff under her. Simultaneously, as part of the administrative hierarchy, she acts as liaison between floor staff and auxiliary medical personnel, the chief person responsible for record keeping, and the employee responsible for scheduling the floor staff and for requesting and accounting for supplies.

3. Resolution of conflicting work demands. Nurses who are less upset by role conflicts—and such conflicts are inevitable—have come up with some decision rules for handling them and thus are happier in their work situations. Their most common way of learning how to handle these role conflicts is by modeling the behavior of senior nurses on the floor. New nurses are generally not required to deal with external groups their first two weeks at work; during this time they have ample opportunity to learn which conflicts they will face most often and some of the best ways of dealing with them. For instance, a perceptive nurse will learn not to escalate a conflict with another department to a higher level in the organization; if a conflict must be escalated to be solved, that is the job of the head nurse. She may also learn which people in other departments are the most cooperative, so that conflicts can be avoided by requesting out-of-the-ordinary favors when receptive staff will be on duty. Nurses may also learn not to try to settle conflicts on night duty or weekends; there are too few staff members on duty to warrant making issues out of work hangups. If a nurse does not catch on to these rules by herself, generally she is explicitly told about them by her peers or by her head nurse at evaluation time.

4. Resolution of outside life conflicts. The positive relationship of this resolution to satisfaction raises some provocative issues for the role of the organization in the socialization process. The finding suggests that what happens to the employee outside of the workplace does indeed influence his or her satisfaction with the job, much as in the cases of our female accounting clerk and nurse, and that organizations, in fact, have little influence over one major determinant of job satisfaction.

There are some interesting differences between departments on general satisfaction, as shown by comparing registered nurses and tradespeople from the engineering department. See Figure 1.

Nurses rated lower than tradespeople on the four variables related to general satisfaction. While nurses and tradespeople both have jobs that suit their skills and abilities, nurses have a good deal of difficulty in defining their jobs because they have so many different tasks to perform, along with disagreements over assigning priorities to these tasks. Moreover, nurses have the severest role conflicts to handle—at work, managing the conflicting demands of medical and administrative duties and, at home, managing unusual scheduling problems and the effects of patients' problems on them. By contrast, tradespeople have fewer inconsistent demands put on them as they clarify their work roles. They have very little to do with the medical hierarchy at all and can pretty much go about their business without

Figure 1

Tradespeople and nurses on general satisfaction and its correlates

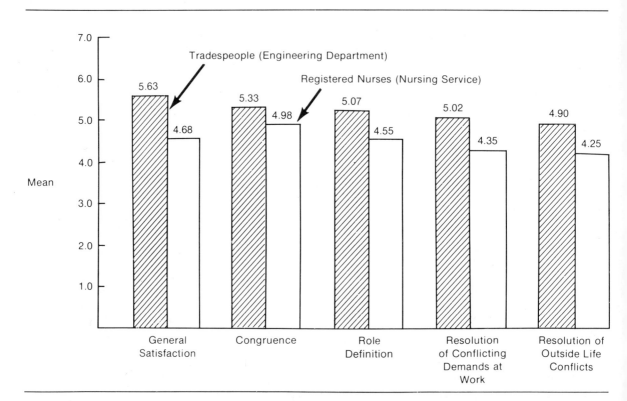

being bothered; rarely, if ever, do tradespeople have to work nights or weekends.

Mutual Influence

Mutual influence refers to the extent to which an employee feels some control or power over the way work is carried out in his or her department. One of the most frequently cited indicators of ineffective socialization is lack of influence. Indeed, John Van Maanen writes that "the socialization process is often deemed unsuccessful if it produces the overconforming member," while Robert Dubin refers to such overconformers as "institutional automatons." Although an employee must generally accept

the legitimacy of influence attempts by the organization as a condition of employment, establishing a legitimate influence on his own part is likely to make him a much more creative and participative member of his group.

Two variables at the "breaking in" stage—competence and congruence—are associated with mutual influence. Employees believe that until such time as they feel on top of their jobs, they would look foolish trying to suggest changes about work-related activities to co-workers or supervisors. Moreover, the employees studied felt that they needed to earn the right to make suggestions, and that the way to do this was to demonstrate competence. Carol, our accounting clerk who felt incompetent at her job, remarked, "Who will listen to my suggestions when I am blasted by my boss at least once a day for a major error?"

And, when employees feel they are evaluated fairly, they feel they have a good chance of getting at least an open hearing from a superior on some suggestions. Joan, "the Wizard of Oz," was seen as competent by supervisors and felt fairly evaluated; as a result, she felt she had some power and control over the way things were done in her unit. By contrast, when employees feel that they are not appreciated or fairly evaluated, they doubt that their supervisors will appreciate and positively evaluate any of their suggestions. For instance, one radiology technologist at the hospital who felt unfairly evaluated also felt that the inequitable evaluation reflected her supervisor's lack of confidence in her and a negative evaluation of her contributions to the radiology group. When asked if she felt she could influence the way work was done in her department, she replied, "You can't make Tuesday Friday."

Most hospital procedures and operating policies are mandated by law or determined at the very top levels of the organization; for these reasons, mutual influence scores across departments are consistently low.

Internal Work Motivation and Job Involvement

Internal work motivation refers to the degree to which an employee is *self*-motivated to perform effectively on the job. At least in the management literature, internal work motivation is cited as a likely outcome of training and development programs, and is most frequently related to job performance—that is, the greater the employee's motivation to work, the higher the quality of that employee's work.

Job involvement refers to the degree to which an employee is personally committed and involved in his work; in other words, the degree to which the total work situation is an important part of his or her life. It is often cited as a necessary condition if the individual is to fully accept the demands placed upon him by members of an organization.

It is important to note that *no* variable in this research is significantly and positively related either to internal work motivation or to job involvement. It is more likely that the *nature of the work itself* rather than the way one is recruited or trained at work makes a difference in increasing the levels of these two variables.

A number of studies, especially those by G. Richard Hackman and Edward Lawler and by Hackman and Greg Oldham, have shown that there are strong relationships between jobs with high "motivating potential scores" and high internal work motivation and job involvement. Five job characteristics contribute to the motivating potential of jobs: variety of skills required to do a job, task identity (the degree to which the job requires completion of a "whole" piece of work), the significance of the job to other people, the amount of freedom and discretion the employee has at work, and the amount of feedback the employee gets from the job itself on how effectively he or she is performing. The three jobs with the highest motivating potential—nurse, radiology technologist, and tradesperson—also have the three highest scores on these two outcomes. All three jobs have high skill variety, task identity, and feedback from the job itself. These jobs involve the use of several different skills; workers do identifiable pieces of work; employees can tell right away—from patients, from films, or from equipment—whether they have performed effectively. In addition, nurses have high task significance and a good deal of autonomy as well.

In jobs with lower motivating potential—accounting clerk, for example, or nurse's aide—employees experience lower job involvement and internal work motivation. Their jobs require fewer skills, allow less autonomy, and are much less significant than the other jobs studied. Accounting clerks do not even have high task identity, because each clerk does only a small piece of work involved in billing a patient or in collecting payments. On internal work motivation, for example, nurses scored 6.03 (out of 7) while accounting clerks scored 5.53; on job involvement, nurses scored 3.57

Figure 2A
Scores for total sample and job categories on internal work motivation

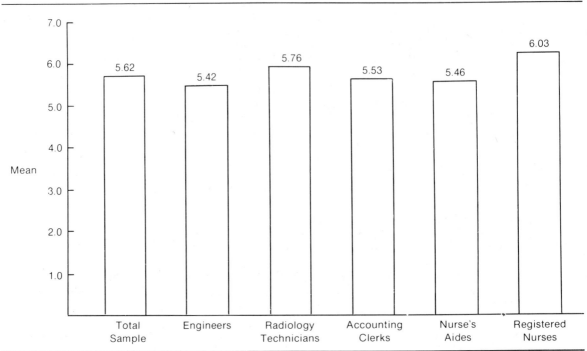

while accounting clerks scored 2.87 (See Figures 2A and 2B).

WHAT ARE THE SPECIFIC PRACTICES AND POLICIES THAT ORGANIZATIONS CAN FOLLOW AT EACH STAGE OF SOCIALIZATION TO MAKE THE PROCESS EASIER, QUICKER, AND MORE EFFECTIVE FOR EMPLOYEES?

The research provided some tentative ideas about ways in which socialization can be made more effective. Let's consider some of these ways.

Stage 1: "Getting In"

Give prospective employees information not only on particular job duties, but also on the work group, promotion and transfer opportunities, and so on. Individuals often fail to get realistic information—many times because it's distorted to give him or her a rosier picture of the job and the organization. But though it is unnecessary to trigger feelings of discontent by relaying to new recruits every negative aspect of every personality or work group, new employees *should* know the types of work they will most frequently be doing, what exceptions to this work pattern are made, how frequently and under what circumstances they are made, and what the general climate of the work group is like as well as something about the pattern of supervision in the work group. Is the particular supervisor relatively authoritarian or does he leave the individual plenty of leeway in the way he or she goes about the job?

Design selection and placement programs that:

1. Make more realistic assumptions about the relationships between personal characteristics and job performance.

2. Consider the needs and desires of job applicants as well as the demands of the organization.

3. Allow for more flexibility and growth in career paths.

We have discussed how important it is for organizations to accurately picture the organization to the individual and to put him in a job for which he is well suited. The literature is conclusive on the positive outcomes that accrue to organizations from such practices. What is not so obvious, and not so well documented, is the fact that there are changes in both individuals and jobs over time, so that having

people tightly fit jobs at one point may not turn out to be the best planning in the long run. There is evidence that people are the way they are precisely because they have spent a good deal of their lives in particular jobs—that they might be different if they were in different job settings. Moreover, a selection system should be flexible enough to deal with changes in the environment. If the technology of job production changes to a more sophisticated skill level, for example, the organization will be stymied if it is fully staffed with people already working at their highest skill level with no aptitude for better performance, no capacity for further learning, and no desire for growth. Organizations need to be more flexible in manpower planning to prevent massive changes in personnel or technology in unstable environments.

Figure 2B

Scores for total sample and job categories on job involvement

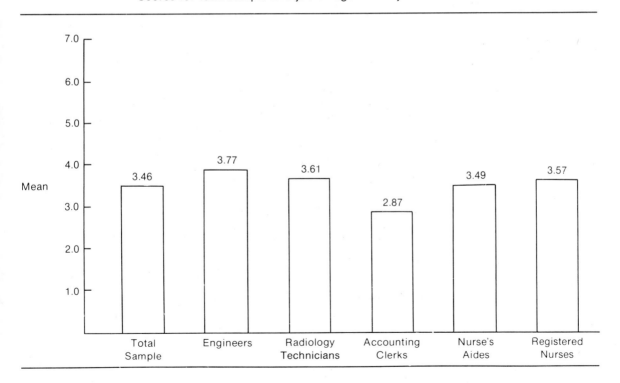

Stage 2: "Breaking In"

Carefully design orientation programs that:

1. Allow opportunities for new recruits to meet the rest of the employees upon, or soon after, their arrival.

2. Choose the key people involved in the orientation for their social skills as well as their technical skills.

3. Give the people in charge of the orientation extra time to spend with new recruits for informal task learning and social talk.

4. Do not put new recruits in the position of having to choose sides or be labeled as a participant in interpersonal or intergroup conflicts.

It is surprising how much impact the first few days in the organization can have on new recruits. When they come into a group and no one introduces them or makes them feel welcome, they start out having bad feelings about the work experience. The choice of people to take charge of orientation is important as well—they need to have social skills as well as technical skills, and they should be given extra time to spend with new recruits. They should also help to buffer new recruits from existing interpersonal conflict, which confuses new employees and keeps them from making friends or trusting others until they can understand the tensions involved.

Structure a training program that:

1. Identifies job-relevant skills and provides training geared to those skills.

2. Provides frequent feedback to employees on how they are performing.

3. Integrates formal training with informal training and orientation programs.

There is an abundance of training literature that conclusively demonstrates the need for job-relevant skill training and for frequent feedback. This research points out, in addition, the need to integrate formal training with informal training and orientation. Many employees reported feeling that until such time as they become friendly with and could trust co-workers, they could not find out information essential to doing their jobs well. In nursing service, for instance, employees felt that some of the most important things to learn about their jobs were the preferences and personalities of the doctors with whom they worked— but only when they were trusted did they receive such information. The average length of time employees reported it took to feel accepted by others was 2.7 months, while the average time it took to feel competent was over twice as long, six months (see Figure 3). Only in radiology, where there is a great deal of hostility between graduates of the hospital's own school of radiology and graduates of other programs, does this relationship not hold.

Provide a performance evaluation system that:

1. Allows face-to-face meetings between employees and supervisors.

2. Has performance criteria that are as objective as possible.

3. Trains supervisors in how to give feedback.

Peter Drucker, George Odiorne, and other management-by-objectives authorities have all stressed the importance of the feedback process and the need for objective performance criteria, the setting of realistic goals, and competent supervisory handling of feedback meetings. My research adds to and reinforces this literature by pointing out the importance of the congruence of evaluation as well as the absolute level of evaluation, and the impact that lack of feedback has on employees.

Use the addition of new work group members as an opportunity to:

1. Reallocate tasks as much along individual preferences as possible.

2. Consider work redesign projects.

It is inevitable that employees will bring particular strengths and weaknesses to their jobs and have strong preferences for some assigned tasks over others. Instead of trying to avoid these individual differences, supervisors should try to reallocate tasks as much along individual preferences as possible and use the

Figure 3

Estimated time to feel competent and time to feel accepted for total sample
and job categories

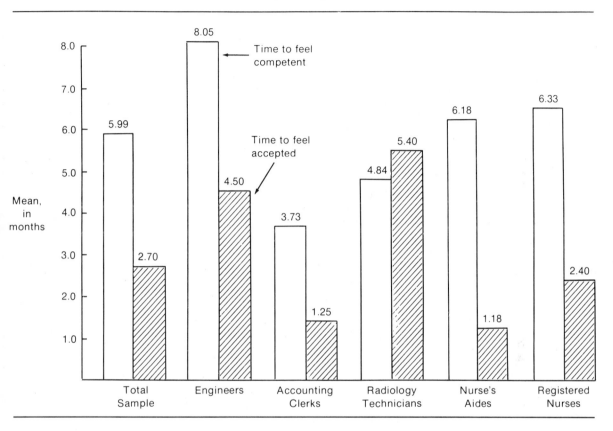

opportunity posed to change the boundaries of group membership in ways that will yield both more efficient and more satisfying group work designs.

Stage 3: "Settling In"

Provide counseling for employees to help them deal with work and home conflicts.

Be as flexible as possible in scheduling work for employees with particularly difficult outside life conflicts and in adjusting the work assignments of employees with particularly bad conflicts at work.

Recognize and deal with structural or interpersonal problems that generate conflicts at work.

This study demonstrated the impact that role conflicts can have on general job satisfaction and turnover among employees. As organizations become more and more complex, and as two-career families and new work patterns become more prominent, we can expect role conflicts to play an even greater part in determining the quality of the work life of employees. It is important for the organization to take as active a part as possible in dealing with role conflicts by providing structural changes in workflow or work assignments and by using social science interventions such as third-party intervention or intergroup conflict resolution wherever they seem appropriate.

WHAT ARE THE GENERAL IMPLICATIONS OF THIS RESEARCH FOR THE USE AND DESIGN OF ORGANIZATIONAL SOCIALIZATION PROGRAMS?

Don't expect too much from socialization programs. A major implication of this research is that socialization programs are not appropriate for achieving some of the results most frequently expected from them. Managers often expect that socialization programs will help them motivate new workers and facilitate employee communication. Unfortunately, none of the variables commonly associated with the socialization process are significantly correlated in this study either with internal work motivation or with employee job involvement. What socialization programs *do* affect are the general satisfaction of workers and their feelings of autonomy and personal influence. These factors are important, because general satisfaction consistently relates to decreased turnover and absenteeism and because mutual influence may increase the number and quality of creative suggestions made by workers. Employers need to consider more carefully just what they want to accomplish in the development of individuals and tailor their programs more carefully to those ends.

Make sure that organizational efforts in the socialization process are continuous. Different organizations and different levels of organizations tend to focus on one phase of socialization as being particularly important, thus underemphasizing the other two phases. The two most common emphases in socialization programs are:

1. Concentration on the attraction and recruitment of workers. This is most frequent in organizations heavily staffed with professional workers—such as hospitals, universities, and law and accounting firms. The levels at which this strategy is most frequently used are the higher levels of the organization, where the cost of hiring the wrong applicant or the implications of choosing the wrong candidate are greatest.

2. Concentration on the training and development of workers. This is most often found in organizations heavily staffed with unskilled or low-skilled labor, such as production and manufacturing companies. The emphasis on socialization is also more common at the lowest levels in an organization (that is, nonsupervisory personnel). The rationale: Since the jobs are unskilled, only minimal effort should be put into recruitment and much more effort into training and developing new employees.

When organizations concentrate only on recruitment and selection, they may prolong the time it takes workers to adjust to their jobs; when organizations concentrate only on training and development, they risk hiring an unnecessarily large percentage of people who are unsuited for the jobs involved and who will be hard to train. To most effectively socialize new employees, organizations must incorporate all three phases of the socialization process into their plans and actions.

Don't depend too heavily on occupational socialization in planning particular socialization programs. Even professional and technical employees have socialization needs beyond what's provided for in a professional or technical school. Workers need to learn how their particular job is practiced in a particular setting. They need to know whether their professional goals and personal needs can be met by a particular organization; they need to know what procedures and tools are used in the particular organization, what skills will be most utilized, and what activities will be required of them most frequently. They need to know not only what will be expected of them in terms of dealing with their co-workers and other work groups in the organization, but also the impact this particular job will have on their outside lives. Organizations need to pay more attention to the variances in workers' behavior that may be attributable to the particular organization's socialization practices rather than merely to the differences between occupations.

Potential for Career Growth

Douglas T. Hall

Most recent discussion of the generation gap has focused on its negative aspects—the conflicts and destructiveness which receive so much attention from the mass media. This paper will examine the impressive potential of energy, ideas, and other resources which lies in the differences between young people in organizations and their older colleagues.

The careers of young people, recent graduates, in organizational settings, will be examined.

We will review what seem to be the desires and the values of new graduates, how they affect the organization, and how the organization in turn affects the new graduates. Despite some strong feelings that managers may have about the way new people are shaking up organizations, the reverse process is still stronger.

We will examine research and theory on careers and identify factors which facilitate success in career development.

We will try to translate the research findings into suggestions for changing organizations to improve the ways careers are managed.

GAP IN VALUES

The concerns of present youth differ from those of previous generations in the following important areas:

1. There is now more concern about basic values, not just different values, but values *per se.*
2. Action is more important. Not only are values more salient, but there is strong emphasis on behaving in accord with one's values. Merely talking about one's values tends to be suspect; values are not trusted unless they are backed by action. The cry is, "Do it!"
3. Personal integrity, honesty, openness, and realness are more important. After the revolution, hypocrisy may be a capital offense!
4. Many of the "new culture" (Slater, 1970) values are humanistic. Today's students are more concerned about personal development, their own intellectual and especially emotional growth, than students were previously. This reflects a movement away from concerns for occupational success and security, away from a vocationally-oriented education form, and toward a greater awareness and pursuit of their own personal definition of a meaningful life and life's work. As Jerry Rubin has put it, "We're not in school to learn how to make a living; we're here to learn how to live!" In terms of Maslow's (1954) need hierarchy, the change is a shift away from security and toward growth. Maslow's theory would explain this shift by saying that since security needs have been largely satisfied for today's youth

Reprinted from *The Personnel Administrator*, May–June 1971, with permission from the American Society for Personnel Administration.

(by their present affluence and lack of experience of an economic depression), they are not concerned about the determinants of future career security—organizational promotions, professional recognition, or a high income. The satisfied security needs are no longer a source of motivation. Present day youth are free to pursue personal growth and meaning more fully.[1]

5. Related to the humanistic and value orientation is a concern for the ultimate social value of one's work. Not only is the intrinsic meaning and challenge of a job important, but also the *consequences* of one's work are more important to youth (as recruiters for large chemical companies realize). Similarly, work involving social service is becoming increasingly important.

6. The definition of legitimate authority is changing. Authority based on age or position is less highly regarded. The authority of one's expertise, personal style, personal convictions, or accomplishments carries much more weight with today's youth. Greater mutual influence is also valued in young people's relationships with authority (Ondrack, 1971). In career terms, this means that young people want more personal control over decisions affecting their lives.

If there is a gap in our society it is probably more accurate to call it a value gap rather than a generation gap. There is probably just as much of a gap in attitudes within the population of college students or people in their twenties as there is between the mode of young people and people twenty years older. And, of course, many "over'30's" hold the values described above. We have to be more specific and talk about values as well as age.

WHAT YOUNG PEOPLE WANT IN WORK

When one translates these new values into a work situation, what do people look for in their work? Most important, perhaps, recent graduates want challenging work—work that is meaningful and ability-stretching to them. Basically they want to have more of a sense of feeling competent in the work they do. Competence, the need to have an impact on one's personal environment, is a critically important human need (White, 1959). This seems especially strong in the present generation of young people.

Another valued feature is a more collaborative relationship with their superiors: they want a lowering of the authority distance between them and the next man up, more opportunities to make their own personal choices, and an organizational climate that is more open and flexible. They also want an opportunity to get more psychologically involved in the work they are doing; they place increasing stress on intrinsic rather than extrinsic rewards for their work. Dissatisfaction about intrinsic work challenge is especially strong in the first year of work (Schein, 1968). There are many complaints about job rotation training programs, in which people are given special projects and are asked to do research on a limited problem. Very often they feel they are unable to get deeply enough into that one project to get a sense of being competent and a feeling that they are really learning something new; it may be a standard project that all new people are assigned to for two or three months, a training assignment that the company does not really take seriously. The new employees may also feel frustrated because they cannot go to the next step and be responsible for action that may grow out of their recommendations.

DIFFICULTIES ENCOUNTERED

Often, however, the talk of wanting challenge and competence seems to be more rhetoric than

---

[1]This need hierarchy also explains the differences between the goals of Black and White activists. The above reasoning applies mainly to White middle class youth. Generally, Black youths have not grown up in such affluence. As a result, White activists tend to repudiate their affluence and focus on humanizing society and facilitating greater personal growth and "internal freedom." Blacks, on the other hand, tend to focus on the specific economic and political forces that are still depriving Black people of basic security.

reality. When one looks at what happens, what the new people actually do, they often seem to avoid precisely what they say they most desire.

There is a tendency to avoid sustained effort on one activity, even though there is much talk about wanting to get really involved in something. If the opportunity exists young people often do not take advantage of it. Related to this, although they talk of personal involvement and growth, one senses that they really do not push themselves to their limits. This is especially frustrating when one knows that these are impressively bright people. Perhaps one reason athletes tend to do well in business is that they are used to developing themselves—setting goals for themselves and getting into the disciplined process of pushing themselves to their limits. Unfortunately, many new recruits are so bright that they can perform fairly well on a minimum amount of effort. Then they tend to become apathetic because they rarely experience success by their own high standards.

Another frequent problem is a difficulty in committing oneself for too long to any one system. Very often, when young people talk about personal searching and discovering themselves, one gets the impression that they are actually avoiding committing themselves to anything permanent. They move from one job to another and from one system to another—whether the system is an organization, a group, or a family relationship.

In spite of their concern for challenge, new people often avoid some of what I see as the true challenges in work—facing up to authoritarian supervisors and trying to work with them, confronting differences, and resolving those differences. As Ondrack (1970) says, among people who score low on authoritarianism there is a tendency to give up on those who score high and say, "Okay, he's rigid, that's his bag. I can't fight it."

There is a tendency to avoid interpersonal conflicts, which is surprising because a lot of students are committed to the idea that there are very strong conflicts and problems existing in society, and that there is a need to use power and confrontation to produce social change. I had one of Yale's Students for a Democratic Society leaders in one of my T-groups, and I wondered what would happen when he became active in the group. "He's really going to blow the lid off," I thought. He was the meekest person in the group. What we, and he, learned was that his way of coping with interpersonal conflicts was to raise them to an institutional level and say, "I can face aggression, I can face conflict, but not a one-to-one basis. I can't face it myself. I've got to be part of some organization like Students for a Democratic Society that gives me the sense of power to confront other organizations."

However, conflict can be one of the most important determinants of challenge in a job. Indeed, some returned Peace Corps volunteers have indicated that business—or work in other types of large organizations—is more challenging than anything they faced in the Peace Corps, because in business there is greater conflict and resistance to their ideas. It is relatively easy, they say, to go to a foreign country where everybody sees them as experts. However, when a person goes to work in business, people resist his ideas; he has to compete and sell his ideas to superiors skeptical of (and perhaps threatened by) the efforts of the young.

Another characteristic of recent graduates is a sense of impatience and confidence often based on moral imperatives that create an appearance of arrogance. These are people who are critical and concerned. They look as if they have all the answers, and this creates a sense of threat for older people in an organization. Unfortunately, it may be an impression that is quite a bit stronger than the young people themselves want to communicate.

A SYNDROME OF UNUSED CAREER POTENTIAL

One unfortunate overall result of these differences between young graduates and older members of organizations is the creation of a syndrome of unused potential, a syndrome which shows up in several different self-reinforcing effects.

Results from a number of different studies (Berlew and Hall, 1966; Schein, 1967; Hall and Lawler, 1969; Campbell, 1968) show clearly that challenge is very important to the way a person's career develops. In a way it is unfortunate that the word *challenge* has become a part of the rhetoric both for students criticizing organizations and for recruiters praising their organizations, because people tend to lose track of just how important it really is. A study of young managers (Berlew and Hall, 1966) followed people at American Telephone & Telegraph for five years and in another company for seven years. Performance was evaluated by their salary scale and ratings from their supervisors and other people, mainly in personnel, who were in a position to evaluate them.

The more challenging a man's job was in his first year with the organization, the more effective and successful he was even five or seven years later.

Unfortunately, the amount of challenge in initial jobs in most organizations is invariably low, despite the fact that it is very important. In a study of R & D organizations, there were only two companies out of twenty-two interviewed in which people described their first jobs as being moderately high or high on challenge (Hall and Lawler, 1969). There was only one company that had a conscious policy of making the first assignments difficult. Most companies felt that they should bring the person along slowly, starting him off on an easy project and cautiously adding more challenge only as the recruit proved his ability at each stage of escalation. This is a strategy to *measure* the person's ability by approaching it from below rather than by *stretching* it through high work goals and high standards of excellence!

A traditional problem is the expensive training which is invested in new employees before they can earn their pay. Increased challenge and less formal training would increase the utilization of new people from the very beginning, benefiting both the individual and the organization.

Another factor found to be related to performance was pressure on the person to do high quality work and to assume a degree of financial responsibility in his work (Hall and Lawler, 1970). In the R & D setting this pressure was often associated with accepting responsibility, getting new projects for the organization, and obtaining outside funding for the work. This may have required direct contact with customers rather than through the supervisor. Organizations in which people felt personal pressure for quality work and attaining the financial goals of the organization were found to be highly effective. But again, we rarely found evidence of quality pressure or evidence of professional people being given financial responsibility in their work.

SELF-ACTUALIZATION SATISFIED LEAST

A further problem was that the most important need for the researchers—self-actualization—was the least satisfied (Hall and Lawler, 1969). Further, we found that the longer researchers worked for an organization, the less important self-fulfillment was to them and the more important security was. Increasing tenure was also related to three significant changes in self-image: the people reported themselves as being less active, less strong, and less independent as tenure increased. The intriguing idea here was that there is theory (Argyris, 1957) that predicts just this kind of human decay with increasing length of service in organizations. Because of the conflict between the needs of growing individuals and the requirements for organizations for tight control and uniformity, people become less concerned about their own growth, and they become less independent, less strong, and less active as they spend more time in the organization.

Another finding (Hall and Lawler, 1969) that surprised the R & D managers in our feedback session with them concerned a communications gap—a disagreement between what the managers were doing and what their subordinates said the managers were doing. We asked everyone if the organization had a regular performance appraisal system and, if so, were the results discussed with the man appraised. In most of the organizations, the directors said, "Sure, we do it every six months."

We talked to the researchers. Not only did they generally report that the appraisals did not take place, but for some we had to explain what a performance appraisal system was!

Because the appraisal system seemed to be there when we talked to the directors and it was not there when we talked to the professionals, we called it the "vanishing performance appraisal." There was little feedback on how people were performing. We know that feedback is important for the learning and self-correction of any kind of system, and this resource was being lost to these R & D systems.

HIGH ASPIRATIONS

Another aspect of the syndrome was a great sense on the part of the recent graduates that their important skills and abilities were not being used. New graduates possess high levels of training when they begin work. Indeed, the definition of education is to bring students to the frontiers of knowledge, the very latest techniques and theories. One purpose of a college or university is to perform the change function in society, and one way it does this is through the people they send out. In this sense, new graduates are societal change agents. They come into the organization with new techniques, and they want to apply them. They find this difficult first because they lack the skills of applying what they know and second, because the organization tends to resist innovation. This difficulty is compounded by the fact that people coming out of college build up a falsely high aspiration level about the extent to which they are going to be using their new skills.

One example of the unrealistic aspiration problem is a man I knew who had just finished his first year at the Harvard Business School. He was seriously hoping to begin as a vice president of finance for a respectably-sized organization. He was convinced that he had the ability to perform the job, and he was going to find it. Although he did not find it, he still felt that he *ought* to be a vice president in charge of finance. That attitude shows through; on the one hand it creates anger on the part of his superiors, and on the other hand it creates a certain amount of threat. In fact, developing this degree of confidence in students is one of the main socializing functions of many business schools.

CREATING CHALLENGE

Another problem is that the new recruit really does not know how to create his own challenge in a job. This is the fault of educational institutions. Very often people are accustomed to being *given* projects and *given* challenging work. They do not know how to take an unstructured and undefined situation and find something important in it, thereby defining the job for themselves. There is a contradiction: they want challenge, and independence, but they don't want to find challenge independently. They want it given to them by someone else. Research has shown that people tend to be rather passive about even major career decisions: the type of organizations they work for, whether they change jobs, and the type of jobs they accept (Roe and Baruch, 1967). Very often they respond to external challenge, demands, or changes more than they do to their own career blueprint. A person does not tend to chart a course for himself and decide that this is the time to make this move, and this is the time to make this other move, and this is how to get from point A to point B. Career choice is not really as much a conscious strategy as one might expect.

SOURCES OF THREAT

Young graduates often threaten their superiors (Schein, 1968) and this threat is probably a major contributor to the syndrome of unused potential. There are different reasons why superiors may be threatened by a new man. For one, training programs are often defined so that the new man is seen as someone special, a "bright young man," or a "crown prince." However, his supervisor may be in a terminal position. He may have worked all his life to reach his position, and now is confronted with a "young kid," who within a year, may be promoted above the position which the supervisors had taken his whole career to attain.

Another cause for threat is that new men are coming in right out of college and may know more about a special area than the superior does. This threat may apply more in technical work than in general management. This threat is compounded when the superior has had to spend a great deal of time doing administrative work which kept him from upgrading his technical knowledge.

High starting salaries cause problems, too. The young man today makes far more than the boss did when he started his career; in fact, the new man's salary probably comes painfully close to what the boss is making right now. Personal styles are also different—the young man is probably more likely to rock the boat, make waves, and create pressure for change. All of these personal threats created by young people can reinforce the syndrome of unused potential and actually make their later experiences less satisfying.

NEGATIVE EFFECT

The overall result of this syndrome is that in the early career years one finds great changes in the man's self-image, attitudes, aspirations and motivation—all generally in a negative direction. He is less optimistic about how he is going to succeed with the organization (Campbell, 1968). He sees himself as having less impact on the organization, and his values tend to conform more to those of the organization (Schein, 1967). Schein's research shows how the values of business students tend to move toward those of authority figures in whatever system they join. Among students in an MBA program, values tend to move toward the values of the faculty and, interestingly, away from those of businessmen. But when the MBA's start working, they move back again toward the

managers' values and away from the faculty's values. Thus, as they become more integrated into their organization, a certain amount of change toward organizational values tends to occur, but one would hope that the new man would not also lose whatever creativity he might bring into the system.

MODEL FOR CAREER GROWTH

If there is some sort of self-perpetuating syndrome causing decay in the new man's self-image and career motivation, it is possible to reverse that process and find a way to increase his motivation and self-image.

One way of thinking about career growth is in terms of analogies with child development. It is generally agreed that the first year of a child's life is a critical period (Bowlby, 1951), and that the first year of a person's work experience seems equally critical (Berlew & Hall, 1966). We also know that there tend to be more changes in attitude and motivation in the career than in specific skills and ability (Campbell, 1968); i.e., post-college career development seems to be more a process of socialization and attitude change than a process of acquiring skill and competence.

If the first year is the critical period in developing attitudes, why not begin by giving the new person the kind of challenging job experience which will have a lasting effect?[2]

[2]Some companies have found that upgrading initial jobs has the unintended consequences of making subsequent jobs seem less exciting and stimulating. However, if the impact of the first job is more enduring than that of later work, the gains of initial challenge will outweigh the problems. What these companies' experiences have shown, however, is the systematic and interactive nature of jobs with careers and organizations: changing a person's job affects his attitude toward his subsequent jobs. To maintain the positive gains from improved initial jobs, the organization should also improve later jobs. Changing such a wide range of jobs, though, very quickly evolves into a full-blown program of organization development. The last section of this paper describes in more detail the connection between career development and organization development.

Every challenge can establish a self-motivated cycle of behavior. Hall and Nougaim (1968) found that young managers who were successful in their organization experienced greater satisfaction of their achievement and self-esteem needs than people who were less successful; also, in all managers there was a marked increase in the need for achievement over time, which seems appropriate for business managers.[3] Achievement is important in a business career, but achievement satisfaction increased only for successful people; it decreased for less successful people. The more successful men also became more involved in their work—they saw work as playing a more important role in their total lives at the end of five years in the organization than they did in their first. It is interesting that the people who were less successful did not become less involved; they stayed about equally involved. This is encouraging, because it may mean that if there is some sort of cycle, it may work more in the positive direction than in the negative. The encouraging thing for the people who are less successful is that they do not seem to decrease their involvement or to "drop out." At some later point they may move into more challenging jobs, experience some sort of success, and then become more involved. Therefore, the problems of unused potential may not be irreversible.

CONDITIONS FOR PSYCHOLOGICAL SUCCESS

When one puts these ideas of success cycles together, one comes close to a concept developed by Kurt Lewin (1936) and applied by Chris Argyris (1964) to organizations, called *psychological success*. In experimental studies where people were working on attaining very specific

[3]A business career is probably one of the best arenas for satisfying a person's achievement needs. Businesses have very concrete goals and one can easily measure his performance. Despite all the negative stereotypes about business careers, one cannot overlook how useful a setting they create for satisfying achievement needs.

tasks, a person would be asked to set a target or goal for himself and try to achieve it. Lewin measured their aspiration levels and then looked at what happened to the aspiration levels and self-esteem after either success or failure. After people were successful they generally tended to raise their level of aspiration and to experience greater self-esteem. The response to failure varied. If the person had an initially high sense of self-esteem, he tended to persist, not to lower his aspirations. The reaction to success also varied. If a person had a history of failure and had succeeded once, he often stopped while he was ahead.

The relationship between a career and the experiment seems clear; the difference is that with the career the time span is the person's entire life rather than a two-hour experimental session. But the similarities seem quite strong. One can get some clues to career growth by looking at the conditions that Lewin found were important to psychological success.

1.   The person had to choose a challenging goal for himself, one that represented a challenging level of aspiration to him.

2.   He had to set his goals independently; it had to be his own goal, not one imposed by somebody else.

3.   The goal must be meaningful to him, central to his image of himself, so that if he succeeded he would see himself in a different light as a more competent person.

4.   He had to attain the goal he sought.

In terms of the psychological success model, then, if people set challenging goals for themselves related to their careers, and if they work independently and attain them, they should experience a sense of success, and they should see themselves in a different light. This success would then lead to self-identity growth. The experience of increased self-esteem may also generalize to their career identity, so that they would be more committed to their careers and be more likely to set additional career goals again at a later time.

This model is shown in Figure 1.

The success model is also similar to

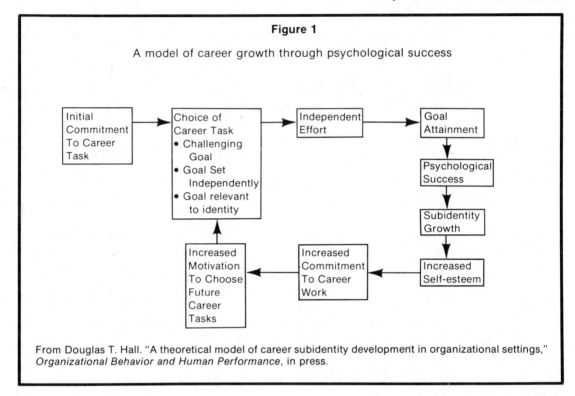

Figure 1

A model of career growth through psychological success

From Douglas T. Hall. "A theoretical model of career subidentity development in organizational settings," *Organizational Behavior and Human Performance*, in press.

McGregor's (1960) description of management by objectives and target setting. McGregor was not talking specifically about a man's career, but it is easy to relate the two. Challenging goals, as used here, are similar to what McGregor talks about as an objective, a concrete measurable target that a man can work for and either attain or not attain over a particular time period. Then later to the extent that the person attains the goal, he becomes more involved in his career and also becomes a more effective member of his organization.

CHANGES NEEDED TO FACILITATE GROWTH

What kind of changes in the organization might be made to facilitate career development? Probably the very first would be changes in jobs. How does one change jobs to get people into a positive success cycle?

THE FIRST ASSIGNMENT

The first step would be to analyze the initial jobs that new people are given in the organization. What happens to a young person when he walks in the door? If that first year is a critical period, when he is especially susceptible to learning new attitudes, what is happening to him during that important time? Is he just absorbing information and not really accomplishing important objectives? Is that time sort of an investment that the company feels required to make in him? Or is the first year a time when the company really expects to challenge him? Does the company have some concrete goals for him to reach?

The ironic fact seems to be that organizations look at the first year as a necessary evil: an investment they have to make in the person, until they can assign him an important project where he can make a valuable contribution. At the same time, the man is impatient for something that has meaning and challenge.

Both the organization and the individual want and need the new person to have challenge and good performance, but for understandable reasons both are frustrated. It is not easy to make jobs more challenging when one gets down to the specifics of the task. It may mean hiring fewer people so the organization can do a better job on the assignments that they are given. One organization found that its turnover was so high that it had to hire 120 men each year in order to have 20 at the end of the year. So it took a gamble and figured that perhaps this attrition was because the first-year jobs were so unchallenging. The next year it hired 30 people and worked hard on upgrading first-year jobs. At the end of the year 25 people were employed and giving far better first-year performances.

Another recommendation related to early challenge is the elimination of job-rotating training programs. The first job ought to be a realistic, permanent assignment and not one seen as special or part of a training program. This generates *job success* rather than a *succession of jobs*. Moving through different short-term jobs means men are observers of different parts of the organization, rather than fully-functioning participants. The term "rotation" literally means "going around in circles." Maybe that is one reason why young employees' self-perceptions tend to go down in the first year. The young person feels that he is not doing anything really worthwhile, that he is just being paid to sit around and observe. If he stays, this is going to have an adverse effect on his self-image—he is being paid a lot for doing little.

THE SUPERVISOR

Another consideration is the superior to whom a new man is assigned. Probably the boss has more impact on the definition of the job than any other factor. Therefore, if management is going to redesign jobs, it must also redesign bosses or train them to deal with a new man.

This was another realization of the previously-mentioned company that tried upgrading first-year jobs. It learned in the first year that it had to work with the bosses as well as new recruits. In the second year it put the supervisors through a long training program before new people came into the organization. Then, as part of the training program for the new people, the company also involved the superiors, so that each recruit and his boss went through the program as a team.

This type of learning helps a superior develop a sense of what we call "supportive autonomy" (Hall and Schneider, 1969), so he can tread the fine line between allowing a man independence (i.e., "sink or swim") on the one hand, and providing assistance with excessive control, on the other hand. The combination of autonomy and the supervisors' availability and willingness to work as a coach when the young person wants help may be the best combination for learning (Hall and Schneider, 1969; Pelz and Andrews, 1966).

PERFORMANCE REVIEW

Supervisors should also learn how to provide performance reviews. This very specific kind of skill is one that supervisors ought to be able to do quite well. If the new employee is left on his own to determine his performance, his conclusion may be based on highly distorted information. It is far better to have the feed back come through formal channels and get it straight rather than have the person get it through indirect and unreliable means, such as the supervisors' manner of saying hello on a certain morning.

An important need for supervisors in this area is to develop skills in confronting interpersonal problems. If the new person is given autonomy, and if the supervisor sees himself as a bit more of a helper than he may have originally, this suggests that some new problems may arise. The new man is going to make mistakes, and he and his supervisor are going to have to learn how to get through these problems and conflicts as a pair. Also, the supervisor has to learn to put on pressure at the appropriate times, when to exercise authority, and when to get tough. It is not only a matter of learning new values and attitudes about supervisory style, it is also a matter of translating these into specific interpersonal skills and knowing how to apply them at various times.

One way of achieving some of the necessary confrontation and problem-solving skills would be through a planned, structured exercise. A group of new employees could meet and draw up a statement describing their attitudes toward the organization, toward their supervisors, and toward their careers. Their supervisors would also meet as a group and draft a similar statement covering their attitudes toward the new men and their ideas of what the views of the new recruit are. These statements would then be used in diagnosing important career and organizational problems. The structured process and the group-level focus may make it less threatening to confront the problems and to work through to solutions than unstructured or one-to-one encounters may be.

THE RECRUIT AND HIS GOALS

A third area of change concerns the organization's long-term plans for the new recruit. Perhaps most important would be the creation of a semi-annual work planning and review program, designed after the work of McGregor (1960) and the General Electric Company.

The purpose of such a program would be to establish collaborative goal-settings and more self-directed careers. However, the organization and the individual must be aware of and avoid the tendency for such programs to "vanish." Such a program should allow for individual differences in administrative and interpersonal skills, which have been found to be related to career success (Campbell, 1968). Its focus should be on developing these skills in terms of specific day-to-day behaviors which can be measured and changed by the person and his supervisor.

Another useful exercise would be for the new recruit and his supervisor to examine the company's goals (or the department's or work group's goals) in relation to the recruit's personal goals and desires. One issue would be the *valence* of the organization's goals to the recruit: can he identify with them? Are they important to him and how can they be made more important? The other issue is their *instrumentality*: does he see his efforts toward the organization's goals as also leading to his own satisfactions? If not, how could this connection be better established?

The organization must be aware of the emotional development taking place in the recruit in his early career years. Organizations, like universities, have tended to see personal growth as being independent of or irrelevant to the "really important" career development changes—new skills, abilities, and knowledge. The bulk of a man's career changes, however, are in the motivational and attitudinal area (Campbell, 1968). Since motivation and attitudes are related to performance and success (Hall, 1971), it is clear that organizations should see these personal changes as relevant to their interests. In particular, one never knows when, how, and what attitudes may be acquired by a new man. The change may result as much from the climate of the organization as from the work itself. Much personal stress may result from the need to achieve, and the relative lack of security in the first year with a new organization. It would also be useful to be alert for turning points which may help mark important career transitions—the first performance appraisal, the first completed project, or a particular transfer or promotion. Certain events may have symbolic value which make them far more important to the recruit than the organization or the supervisor may realize, and it is important to attempt to see the recruit's career as it appears to him.

FAMILY CHANGES

Along with recognizing the career as emotional change and identity development, it is also important to recognize the impact of another important contributor to these changes—the family. Family changes, such as marriage, children, relocation, or the death of a relative often have profound effects on a person's identity, attitudes, and motivation. If these family changes happen to be congruent with career changes, the mutually reinforcing effects could be far more potent than the sum of the separate influences. An example of congruent family and career effects might be the way marriage and a significant promotion could both contribute to increased career involvement and personal responsibility. On the other hand, a problem in a critical family transition could greatly disrupt a person's adjustment to an equally important career change. An example here might be in-law problems in the new marriage and problems with the supervisor in the recent promotion which might both center on the issue of competence in relationships with older people or authority figures. The combination of similar problems around the same issues in two central areas of one's life could greatly compound any feeling of incompetence or low esteem which might result from either problem separately. This interaction of family and career issues is discussed in White (1952), Levinson (1968), and Cox (1970).

THE ORGANIZATION REWARD STRUCTURE

The fourth arena for facilitating career development concerns characteristics of the organization itself. One important activity would be the examination of the organization's reward structure in relation to the new recruit's path-goal profiles. Is the company using rewards that are valued by the new recruit? Also, does the recruit know what kind of behavior leads to these rewards? An example of a mismatch here occurred in R & D labs, where the most common rewards were money (pay raises); however, the scientists did not really understand what they had to do to get a pay raise, and furthermore, there was evidence that intrinsic satisfactions, such as greater challenge or autonomy, meant more to them than money. As a result the

companies were trapped in an upward spiral of salaries with little apparent change in employee satisfaction (Hall and Lawler, 1969). Therefore companies should: 1) attempt to design jobs so that efforts toward company goals also contribute to satisfying employee's needs, and 2) clarify the organization's reward structure so that executives and lower-level employees are in agreement about the kind of performance that is expected and rewarded. Again, an examination of these issues through a structured exercise involving senior managers and recent graduates would probably be fruitful.

Even before the recruit is hired these organizational expectations should be communicated to him, clearly and realistically. College students have become surprisingly accurate at diagnosing inflated or distorted recruiting information, and it usually backfires. This is especially important in view of the great sensitivity and value for openness found in today's students. Indeed, according to Schein (1969), students report that the areas companies stress the most in their recruiting literature are often those about which they are most defensive; therefore, what are promoted as their strongest points often betray their weakest. In the insurance industry, an experiment revealed that recruitment literature stressing both the pros and cons of selling life insurance attracted just as many new agents and resulted in lower turnover among the new employees and the concomitant high costs of training (LIAMA, 1966). Therefore, to get and retain good people, "Tell it like it is."

IMPACT OF PEER GROUP

Another part of the individual's organizational environment with high potential for career impact is his employee peer group. Most of the new member's informal learning is communicated by the peer group (Becker, Geer, Hughes and Strauss, 1961; Becker, Geer, and Strauss, 1969; Hall, 1969). The peer group can also provide important emotional support, coaching, and identification models to help the new recruit manage identity changes, difficult problems, and critical turning points (Hall, 1969; Schein, 1968). Peer group interaction is also associated with reduced turnover (Evan, 1963).

The peer group is often the employee's main emotional link to the organization; often he comes to value the organization only because of his regard for his peers. For example, much of the zeal and bravery of Marine troops is based on their devotion to their buddies rather than a general commitment to Marine Corps values. Therefore, an organization would do well to examine the nature of work group interaction patterns, norms, and values.

If these norms and values run counter to the organization's goals, a serious problem may exist, and an organizational diagnosis might be conducted to determine the probable reasons. If the work group culture is supportive (or perhaps neutral) vis-a-vis organizational goals, it would be useful to create structures which would encourage work-related peer interaction—such as weekly problem-solving sessions, an informal morning coffee break, team projects, or older "coaches" assigned to new men.

The important point here is that because the peer group is a potent force, there is a certain amount of risk attached to utilizing it. A group of employees can very accurately diagnose a "poor" organizational climate and can effectively transmit this awareness and quota-restricting pressures to new members. Thus, the peer group can be either strongly functional or strongly dysfunctional for organizational identification.

CONCLUSION

Perhaps one common element among most of these lever points for facilitating careers is that they have high potential value in either causing or curing problems. There is much in the way of energy and resources in both the new recruit and the organization he enters. In nature, when two systems in different states interact—as in a value gap or an electrical voltage differential—potential energy is available. By applying what we know about organizations and careers to the so-called generation gap, we may develop its potential rather than short circuit it.

REFERENCES

Argyris, C. Integrating the individual and the organization. New York: Wiley, 1964.

Becker, H., Geer, B., Hughes, E., & Strauss. A. Boys in white. Chicago: University of Chicago Press, 1961.

Becker, H., Geer, B., & Strauss, A. Making the grade. Chicago: University of Chicago Press, 1969.

Behavioral Research Service. A comparison of a work planning program with the annual performance appraisal interview approach. Crotonville, N.Y.: General Electric Company, undated.

Berlew, D., & Hall, D. T. The socialization of managers: Effects of expectations on performance. Administrative Science Quarterly, 1966, 11, 207-223.

Bowlby, J. Maternal care and mental health. Geneva: World Health Organization, 1951.

Campbell, R. Career development: The young business manager. In J. R. Hackman (Chm.), Longitudinal approaches to career development. Symposium presented at the American Psychological Association, San Francisco, August 1968.

Cox, R. D. Youth into maturity. New York: Materials for Mental Health Center, 1970.

Evan, W. M. Peer-group interaction and organizational socialization. American Sociological Review, 1963, 28, 436-440.

Hall, D. T. The impact of peer interaction during an academic role transition. Sociology of Education, Spring 1969, 42, 118-140.

Hall, D. T. A theoretical model of career subidentity development in organizational settings. Organizational Behavior and Human Performance, 1970, in press.

Hall, D. T., & Lawler, E. E. III. Unused potential in research and development organizations. Research Management, 1969, 12, 339-354.

Hall, D. T., & Nougaim, K. An examination of

Maslow's need hierarchy in an organizational setting. *Organizational Behavior and Human Performance*, 1968, 3, 12-35.

Hall, D. T., & Schneider, B. Work assignment characteristics and career development in the priesthood. In L. W. Porter (Chm.), Traditional bureaucratic organizations in a changing society. Symposium presented at the American Psychological Association, Washington, D. C., August 1969.

Levinson, D. J. A psychological study of the male mid-life decade. Unpublished research proposal, Department of Psychiatry, Yale University, 1968.

Lewin, K. The psychology of success and failure. *Occupations*, 1936, 14, 926-930.

L.I.A.M.A. *Recruitment, selection, training, and supervision in life insurance.* Hartford: Life Insurance Agency Management Association, 1966.

Maslow, A. *Motivation and personality.* New York: Harper, 1954.

McGregor, D. *The human side of enterprise.* New York: McGraw-Hill, 1960.

Ondrack, D. A. An examination of the generation gap: Attitudes toward authority. *Personnel Administration*, May-June 1971, Vol. 34, pp. 8-17.

Pelz, D. C., & Andrews, F. M. *Scientists in organizations.* New York: Wiley, 1966.

Roe, A., & Baruch, R. Occupational changes in the adult years. *Personnel Administration,* July-August 1967, 30, 26-32.

Schein, E. H. Attitude change during management education: A study of organizational influences on student attitudes. *Administrative Science Quarterly,* 1967, 11, 601-628.

Schein, E. H. The first job dilemma. *Psychology Today*, March 1968, 1, 27-37.

Schein, E. H. Personal change through interpersonal relationships. In W. Bennis, E. Schein, F. Steele, & D. Berlew (Eds.), *International dynamics.* (Rev. ed.) Homewood, Ill.: Dorsey, 1968, 333-369.

Schein, E. H. How graduates scare bosses. *Careers Today*, charter issue, 1968, 89-96.

Schein, E. H. The generation gap: Implications for education and management. Working paper #326-68, Massachusetts Institute of Technology, 1969.

Slater, P. *The pursuit of loneliness: American culture at the breaking point.* Boston: Beacon, 1970.

White, R. W. *Lives in progress.* New York: Holt, Rinehart, and Winston, 1952.

White, R. W. Motivation reconsidered: The concept of competence. *Psychological Review,* 1959, 66, 297-323.

Career Problems of Young Managers

Ross A. Webber

Drawing on interviews with more than one hundred managers, discussions with several hundred more, and published literature, this article examines some of the common difficulties experienced by young specialists and managers and offers some advice on career management. Hopefully, no one is so unlucky as to confront them all, but knowledge forewarned is courage armed.

EARLY FRUSTRATION AND DISSATISFACTION

The early years of one's first permanent job can be difficult. The young college graduate's job expectations often exceed reality, eliciting feelings of underutilization that can result in departure.[1] The causes of this condition rest with the young person, organizational policy, and incompetent first supervisors.

Conflicting expectations. Business school graduates often are trained through cases to think like managers and to solve top-level executive problems. If they enjoyed this perspective in college, they may expect real work to be similar and their actual authority to equal the synthetic

authority in class. But this takes years to achieve, so they frequently experience difficulty in adapting to changed time horizons that accompany the transition from school to work. Many students have been accustomed to almost immediate gratification and to short time spans —this semester, next academic year, a few years to graduation. The passage of time and status changes are clearly signaled by changes in routine and frequent vacations.[2]

A permanent job is quite different. The time horizon is much longer, fewer events mark time passing, and it is a full year until a two-week vacation. Not surprisingly, some young employees attempt to perpetuate the school perspective by changing jobs frequently and taking off on unofficial vacations. However understandable the behavior, older managers perceive it as immature.

These older managers may also be at fault because they don't provide young specialists and managers with sufficient challenge. Large organizations tend to treat newly employed college graduates as all the same and to assign them to boring tasks that could be performed by people with less education. Management argues that young people's expectations are

© 1976 by the Regents of the University of California. Reprinted from *California Management Review*, volume XVIII, number 4, pp. 11 to 33, by permission of the Regents.

unrealistic and they must prove themselves before being assigned more important jobs.[3] But many young people detest being treated as "average" or as a member of a category like everyone else. They want to be considered unique, if not special, because their culture stresses the individual.[4]

Corporate culture, however, emphasizes efficiency in handling large numbers of people identically until individuals have demonstrated their uniqueness. Paradoxically, management's attitudes and policies may promote the very "immature behavior" that is given as the reason for the policies in the first place. Obviously, patience and understanding are needed on both sides.

Before concluding that it is better to work for a small organization, one should realize that situations change. Beginning professional and managerial positions in small businesses are reported to be more challenging and satisfying than similar posts in large firms. Small companies can't afford to train young graduates on unproductive jobs, so they put them to work on important tasks immediately. Nonetheless, five to ten years into careers, the views reverse: middle managers in large organizations report their jobs as more challenging and rewarding than those in small firms, who mention frustration and pressure for conformity. In the large organizations, middle-level jobs apparently carry more autonomy and authority than do similar level positions in small firms where the top can dominate everything.[5]

Incompetent first supervisor. A first boss plays a disproportionate role in a young person's career.[6] The impact of an incompetent first supervisor can be especially unfortunate because the early experience tends to be perpetuated. What operates is a kind of self-fulfilling prophecy. If a superior doesn't expect much of his young subordinates, he doesn't challenge them and many don't perform well.[7] Even worse, if the incompetent supervisor doesn't set high standards for himself, almost everyone's performance deteriorates.[8] The word spreads that other managers don't want people

from the group; the young person can be stuck in a dead end.

Ambitious young specialists and managers want visibility and exposure—opportunity to show higher-level executives how well they can perform and to understand executive problems and objectives. A fearful intermediate supervisor, however, can block such opportunity by relaying all communications himself and not allowing his subordinates to see higher levels. Handing a report to your immediate boss with no opportunity to argue in its favor and never hearing what happens to it can be very disturbing (especially if you discover later that your name on the cover was replaced by your superior's).

Organizations should institute policies to ensure that young specialists and managers enjoy the opportunity to communicate with and be evaluated by several higher executives and not just by their immediate supervisors. And young managers should fight for the right to go along with reports.

Resignation may be the best answer to an untenable position under an incompetent supervisor, but short of this step, understanding the situation may allow an individual to set higher personal standards than the boss does. He or she may be able to perform better than others in a demoralized department—even only slightly better may bring the attention of other executives who are not blind to the difficulty of performing well in that setting. The organization, of course, would be better off if young graduates were assigned mainly to the best supervisors, and many firms do this.

INSENSITIVITY AND PASSIVITY

All human organizations are political. This is neither condemnation nor praise, merely fact. For an organization to be effective, its managers must engage in the politics by which power is directed to problems and solutions implemented. Unfortunately, many young managers are insensitive to or even resentful of the political aspects of organizations.[9] This hurts them personally because they are passive about their careers, and it hurts the organization because it hinders development of power coalitions necessary for effective results.

Insensitivity to political environment. Managers who climb hierarchies rapidly tend to be proteges of successful higher executives.[10] These sponsor-protege linkages move together because members come to respect and trust each other. They personalize organization life and make it more predictable. When a manager has a problem, he prefers to consult someone whom he knows, not just an anonymous occupant of a bureaucratic position. To be sure, the criteria for inclusion in the group are often arbitrary and undemocratic in devotion to old-school tie and proper religion, race, or sex, but they are important nonetheless.

The importance of political relationships to the organization is that they form the power coalitions necessary to make and implement decisions.[11] Very few organizations are autocratically ruled by one omnipotent person; even fewer are pure democracies where the majority dominates. Most require a skillful minority coalition able to lead the majority through competent argument and common action. Without strong coalitions, power remains fractionated, actions are divisive, and the organization drifts willy-nilly.

A common complaint about young business school graduates is that they overemphasize analytical tools and rational decision making to the detriment of human understanding.[12] In spite of their desire to be treated as unique individuals, some observers note, they treat others as objects to be manipulated. Thus, the new graduates apparently are more Machiavellian in their managerial attitudes and more willing to use coercion than are practicing managers.[13] As one corporation vice president puts it, "It takes us a couple of years to show our business school graduates that an organization is composed of people with whom they must develop personal relationships."

Personal passivity. Insensitivity to political environment is frequently accompanied by personal passivity and inadequate probing of the world around the young manager.[14] Such a person fears what he may discover about himself or assumes that virtue guarantees reward, so that good intentions will ensure that people will think he is doing a fine job. One man's experience as committee chairman illustrates such a common career mishap. Dave Seymour was assistant administrative manager of a regional office of a large company. He reported to the regional administrative manager responsible for office operations. Shortly after Dave assumed the post, the regional vice president personally requested that he become chairman of a committee to find ways to improve office efficiency. The committee was composed of various junior managers whom the vice president appointed. Dave accepted the job with alacrity because he saw it as an opportunity to prove his managerial potential.

Unfortunately, two years passed and nothing happened except meetings and collection of hundreds of pages of data and recommendations. None were implemented by district or regional managers. Dave hadn't known what to do; the vice president never inquired and Dave couldn't make up his mind to raise the issue with him. Dave had been flattered to be appointed chairman and figured it was an opportunity to distinguish himself. Months later he found that he had made no impact. Details differ, but the pattern is common.

Dave's first mistake was that he accepted the assignment without analyzing his political position and the attitudes toward change among the executives who would actually implement any improvements. Second, he did not clarify his personal power or the committee's authority. What were they to do? Issue orders directly to managers and try to persuade them to adopt the changes? Or just gather information in case anyone ever asked for it? The third mistake was that Dave did nothing to avoid his fate as time passed. He did not initiate action to modify the political environment or to better define his authority.

When accepting a delegated task, it is important that a subordinate try to clarify the nature of the delegation by asking certain questions.

- After I look into the problem, should I give you all the facts so that you can decide?
- Should I let you know the alternatives available with the advantages and disadvantages of each so you can decide which to select?
- Should I recommend a course of action for your approval?
- Should I select the alternative, let you know what I intend to do and wait for your approval?
- Should I take action, let you know what I did and keep you informed of results?
- Should I take action and communicate with you only if it is unsuccessful?

Dave did not ask these questions of his vice president. Worse, he didn't inform his superior that no changes were being made. No doubt this is one of the most difficult acts in management, but sometimes a subordinate must inform a superior that he (the subordinate) is powerless and that nothing will improve unless the superior acts. At times you must push your boss to make a decision.

It is often easier to drift with the times and hope things will work out for the best, but this is not a recipe for managerial success. The paradox is that the most promising young staff specialists may be the ones who find it easiest to drift. To be in demand is a mark of status and being busy gives a feeling of importance. Consequently, a good young person might allow himself to be dominated by other's desires, to be overcommitted to a narrow specialty, and to remain in a staff position too long. If you think of the organization as a cone, the staff tends to be on the outer surface, while line management is closer to the central power axis.[15] In his or her thirties, a young person may find himself making too much money to accept the pay of a lower line position, which is farther away from the top but has a more direct route to it. Young managers should take time to explore and probe the organizational environment and to understand people's attitudes, develop relationships, and clarify their own positions.

Ignorance of real evaluative criteria. A central rule for managerial success is "please your boss." Unfortunately, what pleases him or her is not always clear so that insensitive and passive young managers don't know the real criteria by which performance is being evaluated. Business is often less structured and more ambiguous than the authoritarian stereotype that many young people bring with them. Of course, managers highly value good performance, as measured by profits, sales, productivity, and so on. Subordinates who occupy positions where results can be easily measured in these terms tend to report greater satisfaction and autonomy in their jobs than those in posts where performance cannot be evaluated quantitatively.[16] People in positions measured only by subjective evaluation tend to be less satisfied and to feel greater pressure for conformity in dress, thought, and action. In the absence of other criteria, these people may be measured by how closely they fit the superior's prejudices rather than by actual results.

Most people are biased by their own successes or failures in making judgments. We like others to be like ourselves, especially successful others because they verify our own correctness. Superiors tend to rate more highly those subordinates who are like them in appearance and managerial style.[17] Hence, hair length, speech habits, and clothes do affect how personnel are evaluated, with some superiors seeing mustaches and mod suits as signs of immaturity and radicalism while others perceive them as showing creativity and vitality.

The same is true for evaluation on the basis of managerial style. However, since the predominant style in the past has been authoritarian, many superiors more highly value subordinate managers who demonstrate authoritarian leadership. Even in the absence of corroborating performance data, authoritarian managers may be more highly rated than those who are participative or abdicative. One study indicated that a "permissive" manager whose division had good performance and much higher morale was rated as having no promotability, while a parallel authoritarian division manager with equal performance and lower morale was cited for excellent potential.[18]

A manager who desires to utilize a less directive style that is ill-suited to his superior's expectation is in a difficult position. If his boss is a hard-driving authoritarian manager, he may expect good subordinate managers to be similar to himself. By asking frequent questions and demanding reports, he makes it difficult for the subordinate to be anything but authoritarian.

A courageous, tough, and independent manager in the middle may serve as a buffer between his superior and his subordinates. By absorbing the pressure coming from above and not passing it on immediately to his people, he allows them enough autonomy to proceed collaboratively. Such leadership requires demonstrable success to survive.

Tension between older and younger managers. Tension between older and younger professionals and managers is very common. It may be exacerbated by individual personalities, but basically it stems from differences in life and career stages. A recently graduate specialist or manager understandably relies on what he or she knows best—academic knowledge. He or she is at least somewhat familiar with statistics, psychology, and economics, and these can be very valuable. Unfortunately, they can also hinder his working relationships with older managers.

Armed with an arsenal of analytical techniques, the young manager looks for problems to which they can be applied. But frequently the problems which the textbook solves are not the important ones. He may even talk to older personnel in the arcane vocabulary of "stochastic variables," "break-even points," and "self-actualizing opportunities." Such talk can be very threatening to an older person to whom it is unfamiliar. He may perceive the younger person as endeavoring to manipulate him.

In some cultures, older persons are automatically respected for age and assumed wisdom, but in the United States the young may respond to the older person's skepticism with veiled contempt. Because the older manager doesn't know the new techniques, the young specialist or manager erroneously infers that he is not as competent or important. But this can

be a career-crippling mistake, because organizational contribution and influence have little to do with technical knowledge. An offended older executive can oppose the younger person's future advancement.

A young person should recognize that some older managers will see him or her as a threat (although the managers will deny it, even to themselves). The threat is not to position, but one of obsolescence and a reminder of human mortality.[19] Tension can arise even when the older person likes the younger. The young specialist should endeavor to show respect for the older, to frame his vocabulary appropriately, and to avoid condescension. As the young person comes to recognize the importance of political influence and intuitive judgment, he can develop the vertical coalitions helpful to both older and younger.

LOYALTY DILEMMAS

Loyalty is a popular but vague concept that is subject to both praise and scorn. There is little doubt, however, that most people in authority value subordinates' loyalty. But what is this quality? Some of the various unspoken views on loyalty that superiors expect of subordinates are: obey me; work hard; be successful whatever it takes; protect me and don't let me look bad; and tell me the truth. All of these concepts of loyalty are partially valid and contribute to organizational effectiveness. Unfortunately, all can also be distorted to the detriment of people and organization.

Loyalty as obedience. The superior can equate loyalty with subordinates doing what they are told. All managers have a right to expect general obedience, but excessive emphasis on it enshrines the "yes man" philosophy as organizational religion. It is understandable that a subordinate's willful disobedience would be construed as disloyalty, but equating loyalty and obedience assumes that authoritarian management is the only valid style while it ignores the possibility that loyalty may sometimes reside in not doing what the boss has ordered because disaster could follow.[20]

Loyalty as effort. Young specialists and managers are rightly expected to work hard in the interest of the organization. Executives are skeptical of the intentions of young people who make a minimal commitment to their work. Yet when effort and hours worked are equated with loyalty, people will put in excessive hours without real effort or contribution. Consider the comments of some young managers in the home office of an insurance company:

"The officers are the first here in the morning and the last to leave at night; they are always here Saturdays and many Sundays."

"They set the pace and, at least implicitly, it is the pace we must accept and follow."

"If you want to get ahead this is the pattern you must accept. Contribution tends to be judged in terms of time spent in the office, not things accomplished."

"If you want to get ahead, you come in on Saturdays regardless of whether it is necessary or not. The cafeteria and offices are sometimes filled with people who just feel they can't afford not to come in on Saturday."

Thus, behavior can become a game to convince others that you are loyal even when it contributes nothing to organizational effectiveness.

Loyalty as success. The superior can see loyalty as synonymous with reliability and successful performance whatever it takes (and don't bother him if it entails shady things he shouldn't know about). It is reasonable to expect honest effort, but this version of loyalty can be tough because it adds a moral criterion to judgment of competence. Thus, not all young managers who miss deadlines are disloyal. The task may simply be impossible within legal or ethical limits. A superior who judges all people and performance from a loyalty perspective will discourage honest communication and encourage illicit managerial practice.

Loyalty as protection. The superior expects the subordinate to protect him and the organization from ridicule or adverse evaluation by others. Subordinates who only follow their superior's instructions to the exact letter *are*

disloyal if they don't exercise common sense and fill obvious gaps. This version of loyalty has particular relevance where the superior is a generalist over specialist subordinates who know more than he does in their areas of expertise. In return for subordinate concern and protection, he implicitly promises to look out for their personal and political interests.

This loyalty concept sometimes includes an injunction to subordinates never to disagree with the superior in public when the boss's boss or outsiders are present. This makes sense, but it can become exaggerated when a sharp distinction is made between "us," to whom we owe loyalty, and "them," to whom we don't. The efforts of coalitions to conceal, contain, or cover up their mistakes reflect this view of loyalty. Violation through "leaks" and overly candid communication with outsiders is one of the most heinous organizational crimes because it threatens the security of the hierarchical system.[21] There is little that managers fear more than subordinates' trying to make them look bad in order to get their positions. Unfortunately, an insecure superior will sometimes attribute this motivation to a young manager when it really doesn't exist.

Loyalty as honesty. This view of loyalty exults truth over harmony. The superior expects the subordinate to warn him of potential failure before the control system picks it up or others find out. This can be particularly hard on a young manager because it tells him to report his own mistakes. To do so is threatening because the bearer of bad tidings is sometimes confused with the tidings. The Turks have an old proverb that warns, "he who delivers bad news should have one foot in the stirrup." Most of us would prefer not to report impending failure in the hope that it will go away or that no news will be interpreted as good news. One of America's most dynamic companies fights this by pushing the dictum, "don't let us be surprised by unpleasant news." Not reporting failure before it produces adverse results is worse than the failure itself.

The dilemma. The young manager's problem is that sometimes he doesn't know what version of loyalty is expected by the organization or superior. He may even discover that a boss entertains several simultaneously contradictory views: that he expects strict obedience, but will be angry if obedience leads to poor performance; or that he interprets mistakes as disloyalty but still expects advance warning of impending failure. Loyalty expectations may violate the young manager's personal values if there is no excuse for failure and the hierarchy must be protected at all costs. Under such unhappy circumstances, the role-conflict-resolution tactics possible include conformity to power or authority, selectively ignoring what he can get away with, attempting to modify the superior's expectations, or departure.

PERSONAL ANXIETY

With time, promotions, and increased rewards, job satisfaction improves for most managers. The daily task becomes more challenging, yet new concerns crop up for many young managers—anxiety about personal integrity, organizational commitment, and dependence on others.

Anxiety about integrity and commitment. People admire different qualities at different stages of life. High school students place high value on independence as they struggle to become adults; college students stress individuality as they endeavor to find their uniqueness; older executives admire decisiveness that would allow them to bear the burdens of high office more easily. Young middle managers especially admire conviction and integrity in the person who remains his own man but believes in what he or she is doing. As they are rewarded by the organization, many persons begin to question the fundamental value of their jobs.[22] As one young brand manager for a major food company put it, "I'm a success, I earn over $20,000 per year, and I get a big kick from my job and seeing the climbing sales chart, but sometimes I wonder if getting 'Colonel Zoom' cereal on every breakfast table is really that important!" (Especially since it is being attacked by nutritional experts as having little food value.)

This questioning can be difficult for a young manager to understand. After years of apprenticeship, he is reaping the rewards of effort—autonomy, discretionary authority, and opportunity to achieve. Job morale is high. But for some it is not enough, because questions nag. "Am I really selling out to the organization?" "Have I forgotten to ask the important question of what I'm contributing to society?" If he or she concludes that the answers are more affirmative than negative, the young manager is faced with a dilemma—what to do?

Open complaint about the organization's activities may cause others to view the complainer as disloyal, hindering present security and future promotability. Associates and superiors will subtly suggest to the displeased young manager that he keep quiet, work his way upward, and then change company policy if he desires to. This is not bad advice, but the young manager might find being an executive so satisfying that he forgets what it was that he wanted to change. He might alleviate his dissonance by changing his personal values to agree with the dominant view. This facilitates total commitment to the organization and promotes the certainty that most of us desire. Such a solution may work for the individual, but it may ultimately harm society.

No entirely satisfactory answer exists for this dilemma. If the organization's mission and policy are in violent disagreement with personal values, the best course is resignation and perhaps a new career.[23] But premature departure can also be a cop-out, a flight from difficult moral choices. If the decision is to stay, the young manager should strive to keep alive his values, to apply them to small matters which he controls, and to remember them when he has the power to affect policy.

Attitudes toward commitment are ambivalent. A sense of certainty about career is desired because it simplifies one's life and stills the restlessness about whether one is in the right place. Nonetheless, many young people also fear commitment because it means closing doors and giving up the pleasant illusion that they can still do anything they wish. Yet maturity means facing reality and deepening interests. Therefore, a central facet of all careers is balancing commitment to the organization with maintaining a sense of independence.[24] Pure rebellion which rejects all organizational values and norms can end only in departure; pure conformity which accepts everything means loss of self. Creative individualism accepts pivotal values and norms, but searches for ways to have individual impact.

The occasion for loss of integrity is often a person's first failure. After a history of success in school and work, a young manager with a weak sense of identity can be overwhelmed by destruction of his illusions that he cannot fail, that he is immune to career crisis, and that he enjoys widespread social support. The current generation of young people may be especially vulnerable in this area because they are the progeny of prosperity. Success has grown, unchecked by fear of economic deprivation.[25]

Anxiety about dependence. One aspect of the struggle for maturity is to declare psychological independence of home and parental authority while identifying oneself as an individual. Dependence on others is difficult to handle shortly after successfully establishing one's independence. Thus, undergraduate students tend to dislike team projects in which their grades can be lowered by others' mistakes. Nonetheless, total independence is impossible in real organizations. Superiors are dependent on subordinates' performance, subordinates are dependent on their superior's judgment and effective representation, and middle managers are dependent in both directions.

All of this dependence can provoke anxiety. For example, many junior military officers have suffered from psychosomatic illness because they bear the responsibility for their unit's safety and performance when they don't have as much experience or technical knowledge as their senior enlisted personnel. They cannot solve their problems by denying their dependence, but these problems can be reduced by learning the technical details of subordinates' duties. In the long run, however, young supervisors must recognize interdependence and strive to facilitate subordinate performance while representing their interests upward.

Most young adults are aware of their fear of being dependent on others, but they usually are not conscious of anxiety about having others dependent on them.[26] As they acquire spouse, family, job status, and community position, they receive increasing demands to give financial, temporal, and emotional support to more and more people and organizations. This sense of others' dependency can be gratifying, but time and energy are limited. Independent and self-reliant managers are sometimes disturbed to discover that they feel dominated by the needs of people dependent on them. If and when the burden becomes too great, they must establish life priorities that balance demands of family, organization, and community in a way that may fully satisfy none, but allows relations to continue with all.[27]

ETHICAL DILEMMAS

Few young people begin their careers with the strategic intention of being unethical as a means to success. And few managers are unethical as a matter of policy. Yet the majority share a problem of determining what is ethical or unethical when faced with unexpected dilemmas.[28] Many people believe that ethical means "what my feelings tell me is right." Unfortunately, feelings are very subjective phenomena, so one person may think that misleading advertising is all right while another believes it is wrong.

Others argue that ethical means religious beliefs or the golden rule, law and common behavior, or what contributes to the most people. Clearly, no single view of ethics is always correct or incorrect. A manager should assess his decisions from a variety of useful perspectives.[29]

Ethics as economic self-interest. When a young manager in a high-technology firm was offered a position by a competitor, his employer sought a court injunction to prevent his moving. On the witness stand it was suggested that there was a matter of loyalty and ethics involved in leaving with the knowledge and expertise he had derived from his employment. The young man's response was, "Loyalty and ethics have their price; as far as I am concerned, my new employer is paying the price." [30]

It is easy to criticize this manager for his ethics and choice of language, but he is expressing faith in the free market system—that scarce resources such as he should flow to the buyer who can utilize them most and who is willing to pay the highest price. Ability to pay theoretically reflects market demand and social interest, so he could best serve society by changing employers for more money. [31] In addition, his position reflects the temporary nature of his demand. Like the athlete, his technical skills are subject to obsolescence and he owes it to himself to gain the most from them while they last. Under this ethic, his only responsibility to his present employer is to give him the opportunity to match the offer.

Not everyone shares this faith in the free market system, however, because ability to pay could reflect raw monopoly power and not consumer wishes. [32] And even those who believe that the market should allocate resources in this way don't all agree that economic self-interest is a good criterion for ethical decisions at the individual level. Most people see no connection between "ethical" and "economic" or "self-interest."

Ethics as law. When asked about kids' buying his pornographic magazines, a publisher and purveyor of "adult" material responded, "What's the matter, don't you like to look at pictures of naked pretty girls and boys? I keep within the law. My magazines aren't meant for kids, but I can't keep them from buying them. That's the government's problem."

For this businessman, law is the criterion for decision making. If society thinks what he is doing is unethical, it is government's responsibility to legislate. In the absence of prohibition, he does what is allowed. Certainly managers bear responsibility as citizens to obey the law. [33]

The young marketing managers in the electrical equipment industry who secretly met to fix prices and allocate markets violated the law, and in their case the law was relatively clear. [34]

Sometimes the law is not clear, though. Even the managers in the electrical conspiracy argued that the law was vague because it required competition and prohibited collusion, yet they believed that cessation of "cooperation" would lead to dominance by the giant firms and decreased competition.

Most people feel that adherence to law is a necessary but insufficient basis for ethics. Behaving legally so you won't be punished is merely being prudent, not ethical. Law imposes demands from outside, while ethics should come from inside. [35] Besides, if law constituted the only behavior limits, government and law enforcement would swell to overwhelming proportions. Big Brother would be everywhere and freedom to do either wrong or right would disappear.

Ethics as religion. If government law is not sufficient, what about higher law? One business executive suggests that there should be no problem knowing what is proper, "If a man follows the Gospel he can't go wrong. Too many managers have let basic religious truth out of their sight. That's our trouble."

Most religions maintain that there are universal moral principles that should guide human behavior[36]—that in almost all times and places, thou shalt not lie, steal, or murder, for example. Thus, advertisements that deceive customers and industrial espionage to discover a competitor's secrets are clearly proscribed by common religious principles. Nonetheless, only a minority of managers think such principles are the basic ethical criteria for their managerial decisions. The problem is that moral principles are often abstract and difficult to apply to specific cases. [37] To be sure, intentional lying is clearly wrong, but most businessmen sincerely believe they must hide information and distort public communication as protection against competitors or unions. And stealing seems wrong, but padding expense accounts or "borrowing" company tools doesn't seem so immoral when the employer knows and seemingly condones it (perhaps this is a form of supplemental compensation). Catholic theology holds that every employer has an obligation to pay at least a "living wage," but determining this is subject to debate. Perhaps it is just unrealistic to expect a guide to conduct developed in the Middle East 2000 years ago to have direct relevance to the complex conditions of modern managers.[38]

Pragmatists argue that religious teachings and the golden rule are not meant to apply to competitive business anyway, that management is more akin to a poker game than to the religious life.[39] If obfuscation and deception are part of the game and everyone knows it, then they are not sinful. Finally, many people subscribe to no religious beliefs and bitterly resent believers' attempts to impose their tenets on everyone. Clearly, religion as an ethical guide is helpful and good, but only to some people some of the time.

Ethics as common behavior. "But everyone does it" has been a popular guide and justification for behavior from time immemorial. Realists argue that if the majority engage in a certain activity, then it must be all right, regardless of what parents or policemen say. The young manager could make his judgments based upon the characteristic behavior of his boss and his organization or industry, not universal rules. Thus, the garment salesman argues that he couldn't possibly follow the strict custom against booze and sex as aids to selling computers. His industry accepts such inducements and buyers expect them, so he feels he couldn't compete without them. Similarly, managers in fiercely competitive industries argue that they can't be as open about costs and policies as a monopoly such as telephone communications.

Every young manager will experience the pressure of others' behavior as determinant of his own.[40] Yet we have a paradox: most agree that others' behavior is not the most elevated criterion for individual decisions yet still maintain that their superior's behavior is the major reason they behave unethically. It is the top that sets the ethical tone in most organizations and this is one of the gravest obligations of high-level executives. Their behavior will be emulated and converted into institutionalized custom by lower managers.[41]

A young person caught in such an unhappy situation pursues one of several courses: he adjusts his personal beliefs and stays happily; he stays, but with a guilty conscience (hopefully to change things when he gains power), or he departs.

Ethics as impact on people. Upon being asked about unethical managers, a former president of General Electric observed that unethical people are not the problem: "What we must fear is the honest businessman who doesn't know what he is doing." Thus, most companies that have polluted the air and despoiled the land did so out of ignorance, not immorality. Knowledge may assist managers in making decisions based upon what is best for the greatest number of people.

This is what schools of business administration and management have striven for—to make management a profession whose primary concern is social contribution, not narrow self-interest.[42] By teaching prospective managers how business, economy, society, and environment interact, the hope is that their graduates will take the broader picture into account when making decisions. No intelligent executive in the last quarter of the twentieth century can really believe that air and water are "free goods" to be used as he or she unilaterally deems most profitable for the firm. Even if the firm doesn't pay for them, his education should have shown him that society does.

No doubt ignorance has occasioned much apparently unethical behavior, and greater professional knowledge should be of great benefit to all. But unfortunately, some professionals who have taken the Hippocratic oath or sworn allegiance to the Constitution cheat clients, defraud the public, and rape the environment. It is naive to expect that education alone is a sufficient guide for ethical behavior. Besides, what contributes to the greatest number of people sometimes means exploitation of the few or even breaking laws. Some executives have violated various business laws in order to protect the jobs of employees on the grounds that no one is hurt by colluding with a competitor, but many would be out of work and collecting unemployment compensation if pure competition existed.

Beware of cynicism. No single ethical criterion is sufficient. The young manager striving to be ethical should do more than depend on economic self-interest, obey the law, observe his religious principles, follow his superior, and obtain the greatest good for the most people. He will have to take all of these into account filtered through his subjective judgment of what is right. In making these judgments, however, he should guard against cynicism.

Many people attribute poorer motivation and more unethical behavior to others than themselves. Young people today seem to be very cynical about business ethics and managers. They tend to believe that practicing managers engage in more unethical behavior than they would and more than the managers themselves think they do. Thus, students attribute such activities as padding expense accounts, stealing trade secrets, and immoral cooperation to managers to a greater extent than the managers anonymously report that they do. Research suggests that the younger the person, the greater his cynicism about managers; the older the manager, however, the greater the optimism about others. Whether this reflects time or "the times" is unknown. Do people become less cynical as they become older and see that everyone isn't as unethical as they had once thought? If so, today's young people might become less cynical as they climb their organizational ladders. Or is today's cynicism actually justified because older managers forget what it is like at lower levels or delude themselves about actual practice?

Nonetheless, excessive cynicism encourages unethical behavior on the grounds that "I'd be a fool not to if everyone else is." Cynicism thus can be self-fulfilling prophecy. More likely, a young manager who believes

everyone does it will discover that they don't and that if he does, his career may be ruined.

ADVICE ON CAREER MANAGEMENT

Advising young people on how to manage their careers is a risky proposition. It depends upon the individual's objectives and his or her definition of success: Climbing to the top? Maintaining integrity? Keeping job and home separate? Happiness? These are not mutually exclusive goals, but they can be competitive.[43]

Assuming that a young manager's objective is to climb to higher managerial ranks, the following suggestions have been offered by various people:[44]

• Remember that good performance that pleases your superiors is the basic foundation of success, but recognize that not all good performance is easily measured. Determine the real criteria by which you are evaluated and be rigorously honest in evaluating your own performance against these criteria.
• Manage your career; be active in influencing decisions, because pure effort is not necessarily rewarded.
• Strive for positions that have high visibility and exposure where you can be a hero observed by higher officials. Check to see that the organization has a formal system of keeping track of young people. Remember that high-risk line jobs tend to offer more visibility than staff positions like corporate planning or personnel, but also that visibility can sometimes be achieved by off-job community activities.
• Develop relations with a mobile senior executive who can be your sponsor. Become a complementary crucial subordinate with different skills than your superior.
• Learn your job as quickly as possible and train a replacement so you can be available to move and broaden your background in different functions.
• Nominate yourself for other positions; modesty is not necessarily a virtue. However, change jobs for more power and influence, not primarily for status or pay. The latter could be a

substitute for real opportunity to make things happen.

• Before taking a position, rigorously assess your strengths and weaknesses, what you like and don't like. Don't accept a promotion if it draws on your weaknesses and entails mainly activities that you don't like.

• Leave at your convenience, but on good terms without parting criticism of the organization. Do not stay under an immobile superior who is not promoted in three to five years.

• Don't be trapped by formal, narrow job descriptions. Move outside them and probe the limits of your influence.

• Accept that responsibility will always somewhat exceed authority and that organizational politics are inevitable. Establish alliances and fight necessary battles, minimizing upward ones to very important issues.

• Get out of management if you can't stand being dependent on others and having them dependent on you.

• Recognize that you will face ethical dilemmas no matter how moral you try to be. No evidence exists that unethical managers are more successful than ethical ones, but it may well be that those who move faster are less socially conscious.[45] Therefore, from time to time you must examine your personal values and question how much you will sacrifice for the organization.

• Don't automatically accept all tales of managerial perversity that you hear. Attributing others' success to unethical behavior is often an excuse for one's own personal inadequacies. Most of all, don't commit an act which you know to be wrong in the hope that your superior will see it as loyalty and reward you for it. Sometimes he will, but he may also sacrifice you when the organization is criticized.

SUMMARY

Frustration and dissatisfaction in young graduates' early careers is widespread because of several factors: their job expectations are unrealistic; they find it difficult to change from school's short-range perspectives to work's long-range view; many employers assign them boring tasks that don't challenge them; and they may begin under an incompetent first supervisor. As a result, turnover from first positions is substantial.

Many young specialists and managers are insensitive to the organization's political aspects so that they needlessly offend older managers and fail to develop alliances necessary to concentrate power on important issues. To compound their problems, some are passive in not asking questions to clarify what is expected of them and what authority they possess. They let their careers drift under the control of others without even knowing the real criteria by which superiors evaluate their performance.

Loyalty presents one of the most difficult dilemmas for many young managers; everyone values it, but its meaning varies. For some superiors loyalty is subordinates doing exactly what they are told. For some it is subordinate success whatever the means. For still others it is subordinates who protect the executives and organization from looking bad. Finally, for a few it is subordinates who communicate honestly what is going on. All of these conceptions of loyalty are partially valid; an organization should value obedience, effectiveness, effort, reliability, and honesty, but all can distort behavior if carried to excess.

With time's passage and achievement, many still young managers experience anxiety about personal integrity, commitment, and dependence. They worry that they are losing track of their personal values while being rewarded for their contributions. They wonder if they are really doing something worthwhile that justifies the doors they have closed and the opportunities passed by. And some feel they are so interdependent with others that they are losing control of their lives.

The occasion for personal anxiety about integrity and commitment is when young managers are faced with ethical dilemmas. Most think they should be guided by personal feelings, but this is extremely subjective and other criteria should also be examined: economics and self-interest, regulations and laws, religious principles, others' customary behavior, and impact on people. All of these criteria can be helpful in making decisions, but none alone is sufficient all the time. In making decisions, however, be wary of cynicism that assumes the worst in everyone else. It can lead to improper and inappropriate behavior.

Career advice includes admonitions to perform well, be active in managing your career, strive for visibility and exposure, develop relations with senior sponsors, learn quickly and train a subordinate, nominate yourself for new positions, rigorously assess your strengths and weaknesses, don't be trapped by narrow job descriptions, recognize that organizational politics are inevitable, and be prepared for ethical dilemmas.

REFERENCES

1. Over 50 percent of all MBA's leave their first employer within five years. J. A. De Pasquale and R. A. Lange, "Job-Hopping and the MBA," *Harvard Business Review* (November-December 1971), p. 4ff. See also, J. A. De Pasquale, *The Young Executive: A Summary of the Career Paths of Young Executives in Business* (New York: MBA Enterprises, Inc., 1970); and G. F. Farris, "A Predictive Study of Turnover," *Personnel Psychology* (1971), pp. 311-328. When a young graduate joins an organization, a "psychological contract" is forged between individual and organization. If the organization doesn't live up to the individual's perception of the contract, he feels offended and leaves. Unfortunately, the specific terms of this implied contract are seldom discussed. J. P. Kotter, "The Psychological Contract: Managing the Joining-up Process," *California Management Review* (Spring 1973), pp. 91-99. The reasons why the relationship is initially vague lie in the implicit bargaining and selling that take place in the attraction and selection process. No one really wants to communicate "truth." See L. W. Porter, E. E. Lawler III, and J. R. Hackman, "Choice Processes: Individuals and Organizations Attracting and Selecting Each Other," in *Behavior in Organizations* (New York: McGraw-Hill, 1975), pp. 131-158.

2. Lawler argues that expectation of immediate gratification means that management should shorten periods between evaluation and award frequent small raises rather than yearly. E. E. Lawler, "Compensating the New Life-style Worker," *Personnel* (1971), pp. 19-25. See also, T. F. Stroh, *Managing the New Generation in Business* (New York: McGraw-Hill, 1971).

3. In general, the younger the managers, the higher the level they expect to reach in their careers. Thus, virtually all are disappointed at some time. M. L. Moore, E. Miller, and J. Fossum, "Predictors of Managerial Career Expectations," *Journal of Applied Psychology* (January 1974), pp. 90-92. Some executives are highly skeptical of MBA's in particular. Here is a portion of a letter written to the editors of *Columbia Journal of World Business* (May-June 1968), p. 5.

"I can't agree completely with Mr. [T. Vincent] Learson's statement (Jan.-Feb. 1968) that the salvation of the business world is the "scientifically trained man that comes from the ranks of the graduate schools." I have found many of these people have no concept of the value of a dollar. They are theorists only and for the most part have no desire to learn the basic fundamentals of the business they are engaged in, but rather consider themselves above finding out the basic principles of the business by experience. They want everyone to hand them experience on a velvet pillow and are too concerned with taking over the presidency of an organization six months after they enter an organization. I do believe the scientifically trained graduate student does have his place in industry, but. . . ."

4. A. G. Athos, "Is the Corporation Next to

Fall?" *Harvard Business Review* (January-February 1970), pp. 49-60. For more on characteristics and expectation of young managers and specialists, see J. Gooding, "The Accelerated Generation Moves into Management," *Fortune* (March 1971), p. 101ff.; and L. B. Ward and A. G. Athos, *Student Expectations of Corporate Life* (Boston: Graduate School of Business Administration, Harvard University, 1972).

5. L. M. Porter, "Where is the Organization Man?" *Harvard Business Review* (November-December 1963), pp. 53-61.

6. J. A. Livingston, "Pygmalion in Management," *Harvard Business Review* (July-August 1969), pp. 81-89.

7. D. E. Berlow and D. T. Hall, "The Socialization of Managers: Effects of Expectations on Performance," *Administrative Science Quarterly* (September 1966), pp. 207-223.

8. In general, a superior's stringent personal standards are associated with higher subordinate performance than lower personal standards. The superior's personal standards also seem to exert more influence on subordinate performance than subordinate's personal standards. The best performance, however, is where both superior and subordinates have high personal standards. J. P. Campbell, M. D. Dunnette, E. E. Lawler, and K. E. Weick, *Managerial Behavior, Performance and Effectiveness* (New York: McGraw-Hill 1970), pp. 447-551.

9. For some case studies of sensitive and insensitive young managers, see W. R. Dill, T. L. Hilton, and W. R. Reitman, *The New Managers* (Englewood Cliffs, N. J.: Prentice-Hall, 1962).

10. E. E. Jennings, *The Mobile Manager: A Study of the New Generation of Top Executives* (Ann Arbor: Graduate School of Business Administration, University of Michigan, 1967). For examples of the critical importance of sponsors or mentors for ambitious females, see Gail Sheehy, *Passages: Predictable Crises of Adult Life* (New York: E. P. Dutton, 1976) and J. Thompson, "Patrons, Rabbis, Mentors—

Whatever You Call Them, Women Need Them, Too" *MBA* (February 1976), p. 26.

11. On the importance of power, McMurry writes:

    "The most important and unyielding necessity of organizational life is not better communications, human relations or employee participation, but power. . . . Without power there can be no authority; without authority there can be no discipline; without discipline there can be difficulty in maintaining order, system and productivity. An executive without power is, therefore, all too often a figurehead—or worse, headless. . . . If the executive owns the business, that fact may ensure his power. If he does not, and sometimes even when he does, his power must be acquired and held by means which are essentially political."—R. N. McMurry, "Power and the Ambitious Executive," *Harvard Business Review* (November-December 1973), p. 140.

12. J. S. Livingston, "Myth of the Well-educated Manager," *Harvard Business Review* (January-February 1971), pp. 79-88. In general, Livingston argues that there is no relation between managerial success and school performance and that schools don't develop important attributes. That "wisdom" is the neglected attribute is maintained by L. Urwick, "What Have the Universities Done for Business Management?" *Management of Personnel Quarterly* (Summer 1967), pp. 35-40.

13. One survey indicates that MBA students express more authoritarian and Machiavellian views than do practicing managers, but that business school professors were more Machiavellian than either! J. P. Siegel, "Machiavellianism, MBA's and Managers: Leadership Correlates and Socialization Effects," *Academy of Management Journal* (September 1973), pp. 404-411. A similar finding is in R. J. Burke, "Effects of Organizational Experience on Managerial Attitudes and Beliefs: A Better Press of Managers," *Journal of Business Research* (Summer 1973), pp. 21-30.

14. D. Moment and D. Fisher, "Managerial

Career Development and the Generational Confrontation," *California Management Review* (Spring 1973), pp. 46-55. See also, D. Moment and D. Fisher, *Autonomy in Organizational Life* (Cambridge: Schenkman, 1975).

15. Three-dimensional cone model of organization from E. H. Schein, "The Individual, The Organization and The Career. A Conceptual Scheme," in D. A. Kolb, I. M. Rubin and J. M. McIntyre, *Organizational Psychology: A Book of Readings* (Englewood Cliffs, N.J.: Prentice-Hall, 1971), pp. 301-316.

16. Porter, op. cit.

17. Campbell et al., op. cit.

18. The study compared three regional managers of different styles—"authoritarian," "permissive," and "recessive" (*laissez-faire*). Objective measurements indicated no difference in regional performance, but higher management consistently rated the authoritarian as most effective and promotable. J. H. Mullen, *Personality and Productivity in Management* (New York: Temple University Publications, Columbia University Press, 1966).

19. H. Levinson, "On Being a Middle-Aged Manager," *Harvard Business Review* (July-August 1969), pp. 51-60.

20. That not obeying may be loyalty is demonstrated by D. Wise in *The Politics of Lying* (New York: Random House, 1973). Newton Minow, appointed head of the Federal Communications Commission by President John F. Kennedy, is quoted as saying that in April 1962, after a story that was highly critical of the President was broadcast on the NBC "Huntley-Brinkley Report," Kennedy called Minow. As Minow recalls the conversation, it went like this:

JFK: "Did you see that goddamn thing in 'Huntley-Brinkley'?"

Minow: "Yes."

JFK: "I thought they were supposed to be our friends. I want you to do something about that."

Minow says he did not do anything, instead calling a Kennedy aide the next morning and asking him to tell the President he was lucky to have an FCC chairman who doesn't do what the President tells him.

21. For a disturbing example of the retribution heaped on a manager who reported his firm's shortcomings to the press, see K. Vandivier, "The Aircraft Brake Scandal," *Harper's Magazine* (April 1972), pp. 45-52.

22. On changing career identities, see D. T. Hall, "A Theoretical Model of Career Subidentity Development in Organizational Settings," *Organizational Behavior and Human Performance* (January 1972), pp. 50-76; and J. F. Veiga, "The Mobile Manager at Mid-Career," *Harvard Business Review* (January-February 1973), p. 115ff.

23. Hirschman suggests that economists will tend to exaggerate the power of leaving while political scientists and sociologists conversely underrate it. A. Hirschman, *Exit, Voice and Loyalty* (Cambridge, Mass.: Harvard University, 1970). On new careers see D. L. Hiestand, *Changing Careers After Thirty-Five* (New York: Columbia University Press, 1971). Connor and Fielder recommend that firms pay for the reeducation of unhappy managers who could then move on to other careers. S. R. Connor and J. S. Fielder, "Rx for Managerial Shelf Sitters," *Harvard Business Review* (November-December 1973), pp. 113-120. See also, R. F. Pearse and B. P. Pelzer, *Self-directed Change for the Mid-career Manager* (New York: Amacom, 1975).

24. A. Zaleznik, G. W. Dalton, L. B. Barnes, and P. Laurin, *Orientation and Conflict in Career* (Boston: Graduate School of Business Administration, Harvard University, 1970). The authors suggest that many people never reconcile this conflict between personal identity and organizational values, yet those in conflict may be more effective than those who are "oriented" toward the organization. See also, E. H. Schein, "Organizational Socialization and the Profession of Management," in Kolb et al., *Organizational Psychology: A Book of*

Readings pp. 1-16. Stoess reports a study indicating that managers are relatively more conforming than the general population. A. E. Stoess, "Conformity Behavior of Managers and Their Wives," *Academy of Management Journal* (September 1973), pp. 433-441.

25. E. E. Jennings, *Executive Success: Stresses, Problems and Adjustments* (New York: Appleton-Century-Crofts, 1967): and E. E. Jennings, *The Executive in Crisis* (East Lansing Graduate School of Business Administration, Michigan State University, 1965).

26. E. Fromm, *The Art of Loving* (New York: Harper & Row, 1956).

27. J. Steiner, "What Price Success," *Harvard Business Review* (March-April 1972), pp. 69-74. For optimistic advice on how open communication between husbands and wives can help to solve many of the conflicts at home caused by an executive's commitment to career, see E. J. Walker, "'Til Business Us Do Part?" *Harvard Business Review* (January-February 1976), pp. 94-101.

28. The conceptions of ethics are from R. Baumhart, *Ethics in Business* (New York: Holt, Rinehart and Winston, 1968). See also S. H. Miller, "The Tangle of Ethics," *Harvard Business Review* (January-February 1960), pp. 59-62; J. W. Towle (ed.), *Ethics and Standards in American Business* (Boston: Houghton Mifflin, 1964); T. M. Garrett, *Business Ethics* (New York: Appleton-Century-Crofts, 1966); C. C. Walton, *Ethos and the Executive* (Englewood Cliffs, N.J.: Prentice-Hall, 1969).

29. G. F. F. Lombard, "Relativism in Organizations," *Harvard Business Review* (March-April 1971), pp. 55-65; J. F. Fletcher, *Situation Ethics* (Philadelphia: Westminster Press, 1966); J. F. Fletcher, *Moral Responsibility: Situation Ethics at Work* (Philadelphia: Westminster Press, 1967).

30. M. S. Baram, "Trade Secrets: What Price Loyalty," *Harvard Business Review* (November-December 1968), pp. 66-74. On various horror stories of managers who supposedly put profits over ethics, see F. J. Cook, *The Corrupted Land* (New York: Macmillan, 1966) and R. L. Heilbroner, et al., *In the Name of Profit* (Garden City, N.Y.: Doubleday, 1972).

31. M. Freedman, *Capitalism and Freedom* (Chicago: University of Chicago Press, 1962). Carr argues that it is dangerous to a manager's career to act purely upon personal beliefs, but he can help his organization if he can show how unethical policies actually harm economic performance. A. Z. Carr, "Can An Executive Afford a Conscience?" *Harvard Business Review* (July-August 1970), pp. 58-64. Thus, Carr is both pessimistic and optimistic—pessimistic that only economics guides business behavior, but optimistic that many dilemmas may be converted to economic terms where economics and public interest correspond. That good ethics is good economics and good business is argued by G. Gilman, "The Ethical Dimension in American Management," *California Management Review* (Fall 1964), pp. 45-52.

32. J. K. Galbraith, *The New Industrial State* (Boston: Houghton Mifflin, 1967).

33. A. Chayes, "The Modern Corporation and Rule of Law," in E. S. Mason (ed.), *The Corporation in Modern Society* (Cambridge, Mass.: Harvard University Press, 1959), p. 25ff.

34. C. C. Walton and F. W. Cleveland, Jr., *Corporations on Trial: The Electrical Cases* (Belmont, Ca.: Wadsworth, 1967).

35. A former chairman of the Chase Manhattan Bank writes about ethical problems:
"Government's response to the problem, characteristically, has been that 'there oughta be a law.' In the first session of this Congress, more than 20,000 bills and resolutions were introduced, 20 percent more than in the first session of the previous Congress. The same approach has been in evidence on the state and local levels. The objective seems to be to hold together our fractured moral structure by wrapping it in endless layers of new laws— a kind of LSD trip by legislation. Yet it

should be clear by now, even to busy lawmakers, that the great lesson to be learned from our attempts to legislate morality is that it can't be done. For morality must come from the heart and the conscience of each individual." George Champion, "Our Moral Deficit," *The MBA* (October 1968), p. 39.

36. H. L. Johnson, "Can the Businessman Apply Christianity?" *Harvard Business Review* (September-October 1957), pp. 68-76; J. W. Clark, *Religion and the Moral Standards of American Businessmen* (Cincinnati: South-Western, 1966).

37. T. F. McMahon, "Moral Responsibility and Business Management," *Social Forces* (December 1963), pp. 5-17.

38. See *Fortune* editorial in response to Pope Paul's encyclical "On the Development of Peoples" (May 1967), p. 115. The editors argue that the Church's view would hinder growth and harm the underdeveloped nations more than a few unethical companies do.

39. A. Z. Carr, "Is Business Bluffing Ethical?" *Harvard Business Review* (January-February 1968), pp. 143-153. In a similar vein, Levitt argues that advertising is like art: it is not reality, but illusion and everyone knows it. Therefore, some distortion is acceptable. T. Levitt, "The Morality of Advertising," *Harvard Business Review* (July-August 1970), pp. 84-92.

40. Baumhart, op. cit.

41. On the difficulties of managers who are confronted with accepting questionable conduct of their superiors, see J. J. Fendrock, "Crisis in Conscience at Quasar," *Harvard Business Review* (March-April 1968), pp. 112-120. For reader response to the situation, see J. J. Fendrock, "Sequel to Quasar Stellar," *Harvard Business Review* (September-October 1968), pp. 14-22.

Ninety-eight percent said it was wrong to keep quiet, but 64 percent admitted they would be tempted to.

42. K. R. Andrews, "Toward Professionalism in Business Management," *Harvard Business Review* (March-April 1969), pp. 49-60. Some are skeptical about whether business schools really affect the ethics of their graduates. An executive observes, "They tend to get the notion up at Harvard that some things are more important than profits. But that doesn't affect them when they come here. They're not really contaminated. They're typical, intelligent, ambitious, greedy, grafting, ordinary American males." Quoted in S. Klaw, "Harvard's Degree in the Higher Materialism," *Esquire* (October 1965), p. 103. Schein argues that educational institutions tend to accept the values of the enterprises they prepare students for. E. H. Schein, "The Problems of Moral Education for the Business Manager," *Industrial Management Review* (Fall 1966), pp. 3-14.

43. On different career perspectives, see H. O. Prudent, "The Upward Mobile, Indifferent and Ambivalent Typology of Managers," *Academy of Management Journal* (September 1973), pp. 454-464.

44. Career advice is summarized in E. E. Jennings, *Routes to the Executive Suite* (New York: McGraw-Hill, 1971). See also, R. H. Buskirk, *Your Career: How to Plan It, Manage It, Change It* (Boston: Cahners, 1976). A summary of books on career planning may be found in K. Feingold, "Information Sources on Life Style/Career Planning," *Harvard Business Review* (January-February), p. 144ff.

45. B. M. Bass and L. D. Eldridge, "Accelerated Managers: Objectives in Twelve Countries," *Industrial Relations* (May 1973), pp. 158-170.

The Mentor Relationship

Daniel J. Levinson

The mentor relationship is one of the most complex, and developmentally important, a man can have in early adulthood. The mentor is ordinarily several years older, a person of greater experience and seniority in the world the young man is entering. No word currently in use is adequate to convey the nature of the relationship we have in mind here. Words such as "counselor" or "guru" suggest the more subtle meanings, but they have other connotations that would be misleading. The term "mentor" is generally used in a much narrower sense, to mean teacher, adviser or sponsor. As we use the term, it means all these things, and more.

The mentoring relationship is often situated in a work setting, and the mentoring functions are taken by a teacher, boss, editor or senior colleague. It may also evolve informally, when the mentor is a friend, neighbor or relative. Mentoring is defined not in terms of formal roles but in terms of the character of the relationship and the functions it serves. A student may receive very little mentoring from his teacher-adviser, and very important mentoring from an older friend or relative. We have to examine a relationship closely to discover the amount and kind of mentoring it provides.

I shall speak of mentors in the male gender. This reflects the current reality: the men in our study had almost exclusively male mentors.

Indeed, they rarely had women friends at all. This is further evidence of the gap between the genders in our society. In principle, a mentor may be either the same gender or cross-gender. A relationship with a female mentor can be an enormously valuable experience for a young man, as I know from my own experience. The increased entry of women into currently male-dominated occupations will have a salutary effect on the development of men as well as women.

There is some evidence that women have even less mentoring, male or female, than men. One of the great problems of women is that female mentors are scarce, especially in the world of work. The few women who might serve as mentors are often too beset by the stresses of survival in a work world dominated by men to provide good mentoring for younger women. Some young women have male teachers or bosses who function as mentors. This cross-gender mentoring can be of great value. Its actual value is often limited by the tendency, frequently operating in both of them, to make her less than she is: to regard her as attractive but not gifted, as a gifted woman whose sexual attractiveness interferes with work and friendship, as an intelligent but impersonal pseudo-male or as a charming little girl who cannot be taken seriously.

What are the various functions of the

mentor? He may act as a *teacher* to enhance the young man's skills and intellectual development. Serving as *sponsor*, he may use his influence to facilitate the young man's entry and advancement. He may be a *host* and *guide*, welcoming the initiate into a new occupational and social world and acquainting him with its values, customs, resources and cast of characters. Through his own virtues, achievements and way of living, the mentor may be an *exemplar* that the protégé can admire and seek to emulate. He may provide *counsel* and moral support in time of stress.

The mentor has another function, and this is developmentally the most crucial one: to support and facilitate the *realization of the Dream*. The true mentor, in the meaning intended here, serves as an analogue in adulthood of the "good enough" parent for the child. He fosters the young adult's development by believing in him, sharing the youthful Dream and giving it his blessing, helping to define the newly emerging self in its newly discovered world, and creating a space in which the young man can work on a reasonably satisfactory life structure that contains the Dream.

The mentor is *not* a parent or crypto-parent. His primary function is to be a transitional figure. In early adulthood, a young man must shift from being a child in relation to parental adults to being an adult in a peer relation with other adults. The mentor represents a mixture of parent and peer; he must be both and not purely either one. If he is entirely a peer, he cannot represent the advanced level toward which the younger man is striving. If he is very parental, it is difficult for both of them to overcome the generational difference and move toward the peer relationship that is the ultimate (though never fully realized) goal of the relationship. The actual parents can serve certain mentoring functions, but they are too closely tied to their offspring's pre-adult development (in both his mind and theirs) to be primary mentor figures.

The mentor who serves these transitional functions is usually older than his protégé by a half-generation, roughly 8 to 15 years. He is experienced as a responsible, admirable older sibling. Age differences much greater or less than this are not common, and they pose special hazards. When the mentor is a full generation older—say twenty years or more—there is a greater risk that the relationship will be symbolized by both in parent-child terms. This tends to activate powerful feelings, such as excessive maternalism or paternalism in the elder, and dependency or Oedipal conflicts in the younger, that interfere with the mentoring function. When the age difference is less than 6 to 8 years, the two are likely to experience each other as peers. They may then be intimate friends or collaborative co-workers, but the mentoring aspects tend to be minimal.

Still, a person twenty or even fifty years older may, if he is in good touch with his own and the other's youthful Dreams, function as a significant mentor figure. And a person the same age or even younger may have important mentoring qualities if he has unusual expertise and understanding, and if both have the maturity to make good use of the mentor's virtues.

In the usual course, a young man initially experiences himself as a novice or apprentice to a more advanced, expert and authoritative adult. As the relationship evolves, he gains a fuller sense of his own authority and his capability for autonomous, responsible action. The balance of giving/receiving becomes more equal. The younger man increasingly has the experience of "I am" as an adult, and their relationship becomes more mutual. This shift serves a crucial developmental function for the young man: it is part of the process by which he transcends the father-son, man-boy division of his childhood. Although he is officially defined as an adult at 18 or 21, and desperately wants to be one, it takes many years to overcome the sense of being a son or a boy in relation to "real" adults. The process extends over the entire novice phase of early adulthood and becomes problematic again in the late thirties (see Chapter 9). Mentors can thus play a significant role throughout early adulthood.

I have described the mentoring relationship in its most developed and constructive form. Of course, relationships vary tremendously in the degree and form of mentoring involved. Mentoring is not a simple, all-or-none matter. A relationship may be remarkably beneficial to the younger person and yet be seriously flawed. For example, a teacher or boss cares for and sponsors a protégé, but is so afraid of being eclipsed that he behaves destructively at crucial moments. A relationship may be very limited and yet have great value in certain respects. Some men have a purely symbolic mentor whom they never meet. Thus, an aspiring young novelist may admire an older writer, devour his books, learn a great deal about his life, and create an idealized internal figure with whom he has a complex relationship.

In a "good enough" mentoring relationship, the young man feels admiration, respect, appreciation, gratitude and love for the mentor. These outweigh but cannot entirely prevent the opposite feelings: resentment, inferiority, envy, intimidation. There is a resonance between them. The elder has qualities of character, expertise and understanding that the younger admires and wants to make parts of himself. The young man is excited and spurred on by the shared sense of his promise. Yet he is also full of self-doubt: Can he ever become all that both of them want him to be? At different times—or even at the same moment—he experiences himself as the inept novice, the fraudulent impostor, the equal colleague and the rising star who will someday soar to heights far beyond those of the mentor.

Mentoring is best understood as a form of love relationship. It is difficult to terminate in a reasonable, civil manner. In this respect, as in others, it is like the intense relationship between parents and grown offspring, or between sexual lovers or spouses.

The mentoring relationship lasts perhaps two or three years on the average, eight to ten years at most. It may end when one man moves, changes jobs or dies. Sometimes it comes to a natural end and, after a cooling-off period, the pair form a warm but modest friendship. It may end totally, with a gradual loss of involvement. Most often, however, an intense mentor relationship ends with strong conflict and bad feelings on both sides. The young man may have powerful feelings of bitterness, rancor, grief, abandonment, liberation and rejuvenation. The sense of resonance is lost. The mentor he formerly loved and admired is now experienced as destructively critical and demanding, or as seeking to make one over in his own image rather than fostering one's individuality and independence. The mentor who only yesterday was regarded as an enabling teacher and friend has become a tyrannical father or smothering mother. The mentor, for his part, finds the young man inexplicably touchy, unreceptive to even the best counsel, irrationally rebellious and ungrateful. By the time they are through, there is generally some validity in each one's criticism of the other.

And so it ends. Much of its value may be realized—as with love relationships generally—after the termination. The conclusion of the main phase does not put an end to the meaning of the relationship. Following the separation, the younger man may take the admired qualities of the mentor more fully into himself. He may become better able to learn from himself, to listen to the voices from within. His personality is enriched as he makes the mentor a more intrinsic part of himself. The internalization of significant figures is a major source of development in adulthood.

Section 4

Mid-Career Issues and Concerns

The mid-life or mid-career years have been coming under increasing scrutiny recently. It seems clear that this period carries with it a peculiar set of pitfalls, predicaments, and opportunities. Schein identifies the following "problem" areas which develop in mid-life.[1] First, many managers report feelings of depression, discouragement, and lack of energy, enthusiasm, or motivation. Second, some feel trapped in organizations or careers from which there is no place to go. Finally, many report numerous family problems and increased pressures for familial involvement.

The problems of mid-career can be better understood by considering the major issues which people face at this time in their lives. The first reading in this section describes the "crisis" of becoming middle-aged. The key to understanding this conflict seems to be in the word "middle," which implies that one is thereafter on a descending path. Levinson thoroughly explores both the personal and organizational implications of being a mid-career manager in today's organizations. He suggests that the mid-career manager undergoes significant changes in health, work style, point of view, family relationships, and personal goals.

Based on the intensive study of forty selected men (ten executives, ten biologists, ten factory workers, and ten novelists), Dan Levinson's article adds insight to our understanding of the mid-life transition. Three major tasks must be accomplished during this phase of adult development: (1) terminating the era of early adulthood; (2) taking the first steps toward the initiation of middle adulthood; and (3) dealing with the polarities that are sources of deep division in life.

The next selection deals with one of the greatest managerial problems during the mid-career years—obsolescence. What do you do with a person who is no longer able

[1] E. H. Schein, *Career Dynamics: Matching Individual and Organization Needs* (Reading, Mass.: Addison-Wesley Publishing Co., 1978).

122

to cope with the increasing complexities of the job? What can you do so the obsolescent executive won't be you? These are questions which Burack attempts to answer in his treatment of this major mid-career concern.

These selections suggest that there are four main issues with which individuals must deal in order to successfully manage their mid-career years. The first issue concerns a self-assessment of progress to date—Dream versus Reality. A manager must determine the degree of congruence between earlier goals, ambitions, and dreams and actual career progress. The second relevant issue for mid-career managers relates to the achievement of balance between work and family involvements. The acceptance of mentoring tasks and activities is another issue of major concern for managers in the mid-career stage. These responsibilities for support, guidance, role model, and coach often create high levels of stress. Finally, since the problems of technical and managerial obsolescence are so great, the mid-career manager must strive to achieve and maintain a strong growth orientation. The appreciation and understanding of these major mid-career activities and issues will enable both the individual and the manager to better cope with the stress of this stage.

On Being a Middle-Aged Manager

Harry Levinson

For most men, attainment of executive rank coincides with the onset of middle age, that vast gulf which begins about 35 and endures until a man has come to terms with himself and his human fate (for no man matures until he has done so). It is the peak time of personal expansion, when a man lives most fully the combined multiple dimensions of his life. He has acquired the wisdom of experience and the perspective of maturity. His activity and productivity are in full flower; his career is well along toward its zenith. He is at the widest range of his travels and his contacts with others. He is firmly embedded in a context of family, society, career, and his own physical performance. His successes are models for emulation; his failures, the object lessons for others. He has become a link from the past to the future, from his family to the outside world, from those for whom he is organizationally responsible to those to whom he owes responsibility. In a word, he has it made.

And need it all come to a harsh and bitter end? *No.*

A man cannot alter his inevitable fate. But he can manage the way he comes to terms with it. If he does so, rather than simply letting events take their course, he can do much to prolong the richness of his life as well as his years.

Sophocles, who lived to be more than 90, wrote *Oedipus Rex* at 75 and *Oedipus et Colonus* at 89. Titian completed his master-piece, "The Battle of Lepanto," at 95; he began work on one of the most famous paintings in the world, "The Descent from the Cross," when he was 97. Benjamin Franklin invented bifocals at 78. Benjamin Duggar, Professor of Plant Physiology and Botanical Economics at the University of Wisconsin, was removed at age 70 by compulsory retirement; he then joined the research staff of Lederle Laboratories and several years later gave mankind Aureomycin. At 90, Pablo Casals still played the cello as no other man ever had. Santayana, the philosopher, wrote his first novel, *The Last Puritan*, at 72. Carl Sandburg wrote *Remembrance Rock* at 70. Freud's activities continued into his 80's.

These men are the exceptions, of course. But the fact that many people can mature creatively indicates that there is indeed hope for all of us who are closer to 35. In this article I propose to examine some of the experiences of middle age and suggest ways of maintaining creative potential.

First, however, permit me a brief qualification. I am not arbitrarily splitting businessmen into under 35 and over 35. That would be unrealistic. The figure 35 is not fixed. It will waver, because I am using it here in the sense of a stage of life, not a birthday.

INDEXES OF HEALTH

Behind the flowering of middle age, a critical physical and psychological turnaround process is occurring. This is reflected in indexes of health. Statistics from Life Extension Examiners indicate that specific symptoms—such as extreme fatigue, indigestion, and chest pains—rise sharply among young executives just moving into top management. Only one third of the symptoms found in the 31- to 40-year-old management group can be traced to an organic cause, the examiners report.[1] They suggest that these problems come about because of both the manner in which the men live and the state of mind in which they work.

PSYCHOLOGICAL FACTORS

While some explanations for this increase in symptoms are no doubt a product of the aging process itself, there are more pressing psychological forces. The British psychoanalyst, Elliott Jaques, contends that a peak in the death rate between 35 and 40 is attributable to the shock which follows the realization that one is inevitably on a descending path.[2] This produces what for most men is a transitory period of depression. Depression increases a person's vulnerability to illness. There is much medical evidence to indicate that physical illness is likely to occur more frequently and more severely in people who feel depressed.

Lee Stockford of the California Institute of Technology reports from a survey of 1,100 men that about 5 out of 6 men in professional and managerial positions undergo a period of frustration in their middle 30's, and that 1 in 6 never fully recovers from it. Stockford attributes the crisis to a different kind of frustration: "This is the critical age—the mid-30's—when a man comes face to face with reality and finds that reality doesn't measure up to his dreams."[3]

A number of factors in executive work life contribute to the intensification of these feelings and the symptoms which result:

Increasing contraction of the hard work period. The average age at which men become company presidents is decreasing. As it does, the age span during which success can be achieved becomes narrower. The competitive pace therefore becomes more intense. It is further intensified by devices such as management by objectives and performance appraisals which give added impetus to the pressures for profit objectives.

Inseparability of life and career patterns. For managerial men in an intensely competitive career pattern, each year is a milepost. Time in job or level is a critical variable. If one does not move on time, he loses out on experience, position, and above all, the reputation for being a star. This means there necessarily must be repetitive subpeaks of anxiety around time dimensions.

Continuous threat of defeat. When both internal and external pressures for achievement are so high, the pain of defeat—always harsh—can be devastating, no matter how well a man seems to take it. Animal research indicates that when males are paired in combat, up to 80% of the defeated ones subsequently die although their physical wounds are rarely severe enough to cause death. We cannot generalize from animals to humans, but we can get some suggestion of the physical cost of the experience of personal defeat. When we turn back to the management pyramid and the choices which have to be made, obviously many men experience defeat, and all must live with the threat.

Increase in dependency. To cope with competition, the executive, despite his misgivings, must depend on specialists whose word he has to accept because of his lack of specialized knowledge. In fact, John Kenneth Galbraith advanced the thesis in *The New Industrial State* that the technical infrastructure of an organization really makes the decisions, leaving only pro forma approval for the executive.[4]

[1] "Clinical Health Age: 30-40," Business Week, March 3, 1956, p. 56.
[2] Elliott Jaques, "Death and the Mid-Life Crisis," *The International Journal of Psychoanalysis,* October 1965, p. 502.
[3] Unpublished.

[4] Boston, Houghton Mifflin Company, 1967.

The specialists have their own concepts, jargon, and motivation which often differ from those of the executive. Every executive wants to make good decisions. He is uneasy about decisions based on data he does not fully understand, gathered by people he does not fully understand, and presented in terms he does not fully understand. He is therefore often left to shudder at the specter of catastrophe beyond his control.

Denial of feelings. Commitment to executive career goals requires self-demand and self-sacrifice, and simultaneously inhibits close, affectionate relationships. One cannot allow himself to get close to those with whom he competes or about whom he must make decisions, or who are likely to make decisions about him. Often he bears a burden of guilt for the decisions he must make about others' careers.[5] No matter how strongly a man wants the achievement goals, he still has some feelings of anger, toward both himself and the organization which demands that sacrifice, for having to give up other desirable life goals. He must hold in tightly these feelings of anger, together with the feelings of affection and guilt, if they are unacceptable to him or in his business culture. Repressed feelings must continuously be controlled, a process which requires hyper-alertness and therefore energy.

Constant state of defensiveness. The pursuit of executive success is like playing the children's game, "King of the Hill." In that game, each boy is vying for the place at the top of the stump, fence, barrel, or even literally, the hill. All the others try to push the incumbent from his summit perch. Unlike the game, in executive life there is no respite. Given this state of affairs, together with the other conditions to which I have just referred, one must be always "at the ready," as the military put it. To be at the ready psychologically means that one's whole body is in a continuing emergency state, with resulting greater internal wear and tear.

[5] See "Management by Guilt" (Chapter 18) in my book *Emotional Health: in the World of Work* (New York, Harper & Row, 1964).

Shift in the prime-of-life concept. Western societies value youth. It is painfully disappointing to have attained a peak life stage at a time in history when that achievement is partially vitiated by worship of youth, when there is no longer as much respect for age or seniority. This is compounded by one's awareness of the decline of his physical capacities. Thus, at the height of a manager's attainment, he is likely to feel also that he has only partly made it, that he has already lost part of what he sought to win. Since only rarely can one have youth and achievement at the same time, there is something anticlimactic about middle-age success.

SUBTLE CHANGES

The issues having to do with health are only one facet of the middle-aging process. There are also subtle, but highly significant, changes in (1) work style, (2) point of view, (3) family relationships, and (4) personal goals. Let us look at each of these in turn.

1. Work Style

Both the mode and the content of the work of creative men differ in early adulthood, or the pre-35 stage, from that of mature adulthood, or the post-35 stage. Jaques pointed this out when he observed:

> The creativity of the 20's and early 30's tends to be a hot-from-the-fire creativity. It is intense and spontaneous, and comes out ready-made. . . . Most of the work seems to go on unconsciously. The conscious production is rapid, the pace of creation often being dictated by the limits of the artist's capacity physically to record the words or music he is expressing. . . . By contrast, the creativity of the late 30's and after is sculptured creativity. The inspiration may be hot and intense. The unconscious work is no less than before. But there is a big step between the first effusion of inspiration and the finished creative product. The inspiration itself may come more slowly. Even if there are sudden bursts of inspiration they are only the beginning of the work process.[6]

[6] Jaques, op. cit., p. 503.

Jaques adds that the inspiration for the older man is followed by a period of forming and fashioning the product, working and reworking the material, and acting and reacting to what has been formed. This is an experience which may go on for a period of years. The content of work changes, too, from a lyrical or descriptive content to one that is tragic and philosophical, followed by one that is serene. Jaques recalls that Shakespeare wrote his early historical plays and comedies before he was 35, his tragedies afterward.

Contrary to popular misconception, creativity does not cease at an early age. It is true that creative men have made major contributions before 40, but it is equally true that those who demonstrated such creativity continued to produce for many years thereafter. In fact, both in the arts and in the sciences, the highest output is in the 40's.

Executives have many of the same kinds of experiences as artists and scientists. Executives report the greatest self-confidence at 40. Though their instrumentality is the organization, younger and older men do different creative work with organizations. The younger man is more impulsive, flashy, and star-like with ideas; the older man is more often concerned with building and forming an organization. A conspicuous example is the hard-hitting company founder who, to the surprise of his organization, becomes less concerned with making money and more preoccupied with leaving an enduring company. Suddenly, he is talking about management development.

2. Point of View

Concurrent with the shift in work style or orientation is a shift in point of view. This occurs in political and social thinking as well as in business. It is a commonplace that most people become more conservative as they grow older. It is an unspoken commonplace that they are more bored.

True, many activities are intrinsically boring and become more so with repetition, but others no longer hold interest when one's point of view has changed.

Disillusionment. Some of the boredom results from disillusionment. Early idealism, the tendency toward action, and the conviction of the innate goodness in people are in part a denial of the inevitable. Young people in effect say, "The world can be rosy. I'll help make it that way. People can be good to each other if only someone will show them how or remove the conditions which cause their frustration."

But in mid-life it becomes clear that people are not always good to each other; that removing the conditions of frustration does not always lead to good, friendly, loving behavior; and that people have a capacity for being ugly and self-destructive as well as good. One evidence for the denial of disillusionment is the effort in so many companies to keep things "nice and quiet." Such companies are characterized by the inability to accept conflict as given and conflict resolution as a major part of the executive's job.

Obsolescence. Another factor in change in point of view has to do with the feeling of becoming increasingly obsolescent. The middle-ager feels himself to be in a world apart from the young—emotionally, socially, and occupationally. This is covered today by the cliché "generation gap." But there is something real to the distance because there is a tendency to feel that one cannot keep up with the world no matter how fast he runs. Thus the sense of incompetence, even helplessness, is magnified. Some of this is reflected in an attitude that middle-aged executives often take.

For example, I once addressed the 125 members of the upper management group of a large company. When I finished, I asked them to consider three questions in the discussion groups into which they were going to divide themselves:

1. Of what I had said, what was most relevant to their business?
2. Of what was most relevant, what order of priority ought to be established?
3. Once priority was established, who was to do what about the issues?

They handled the first question well when they reported back; none had difficulty specifying the relevant. They had a little more difficulty with the second. None touched the third; it was as if they felt they were not capable of taking the action with which they had been charged.

Vocational choice. This incident might be excused on a number of bases if it were not for other unrelated or corroborative evidence which reflects a third dimension in our consideration of change in point of view. Harvard psychologist Anne Roe did a series of studies on vocational choice in the adult years. In one study she was trying to find out how people make decisions about selecting jobs.

"The most impressive thing about these interviews," she reports, "was how few of our subjects thought of themselves as considering alternatives and making decisions based on thoughtful examination of the situation.... They seemed not to recognize their role as chooser or their responsibility for choices. It was, indeed, this last aspect we found most depressing. Even among the executives, we find stress on contingencies and external influences more often than not."[7]

Pain of rivalry. The sense of being more distant from the sources of change, from the more impulsive agents of change, and of not being a chooser of one's fate spawns feelings of helplessness and inadequacy. This sense of remoteness is further magnified, as I have already noted, by feelings of rivalry. For boys, playing "King of the Hill" may be fun. For men, the greater the stakes and the more intense the motivation to hold one's place, the more threatening the rivals become. Yet, in the midst of this competitive environment, one is required to prepare his rivals to succeed him and ultimately to give way. The very name of the game is "Prepare Your Successor."

I recall a particular corporate situation in which the president had to decide who was to be executive vice president. When he made his choice, some of his subordinates were surprised because, they said, the man he picked was the hottest competitor for the president's job and

usually such men were sabotaged. The surprising part of the event, as far as I was concerned, was not the choice, but the fact that the subordinates themselves had so clearly seen what tends to happen to rivals for the executive suite. It is indeed difficult to tolerate a subordinate when the executive senses himself to be, in any respect, on a downward trail while the subordinate is obviously still on his way up and just as obviously is demanding his place in the corporate sun.

This phenomenon is one of the great undiscussed dilemmas of the managerial role. Repeatedly, in seminars on psychological aspects of management, cases refer to executives who cannot develop others, particularly men that have nothing to fear, in the sense that their future security is assured and they still have upward avenues open to them. What is not seen, let alone understood, in such cases is the terrible pain of rivalry in middle age in a competitive business context that places a premium on youth. This paragraph from Budd Schulberg's *Life* review of *Thalberg: Life and Legend* captures the rivalry issue in one pointed vignette:

> There was to be a dramatic coda to the Irving Thalberg Story: the inevitable power struggle between the benevolent but jealous L.B. Mayer and the protégé he 'loved like a son.' Bitter was the conflict between Father and Son fighting over the studio's Holy Ghost. They fought over artistic decisions. They fought over separation of authorities. They fought over their division of the spoils, merely a symbol of power, for by now both were multi-millionaires. It was as if the old, tough, crafty beachmaster L.B. was determined to drive off the young, frail but stubborn challenger who dared ask Mayer for an equal piece of the billion-dollar action.[8]

In this case, the rivalry was evident in open conflict. It could be with men at that level and in that culture. However, in most cases, if the rivalry does not go on unconsciously, it is carefully disguised and rationalized. Executives are reluctant to admit such feelings even to themselves. Therefore, much of the rivalry is unconscious. The parties are less aware of why

[7]Anne Roe and Rhoda Baruch, "Occupational Changes in the Adult Years," *Personnel Administration,* July-August 1967, p. 32.

[8]*Life*, February 28, 1969, p. 6.

they are quarreling, or perhaps they are more aware of the fact that they never seem to settle their quarrels. Every executive can test such feelings in his own experience by reviewing how he felt when a successor took his place, even though he himself moved up, particularly when that successor changed some of his cherished innovations.

Thus it is difficult for each of us to see the unconscious battle he wages with subordinates, now wanting them to succeed, now damned if they will. Subordinates, however unable they are to see this phenomenon in themselves, can usually see it quite clearly in the behavior of the boss. But then there are few upward performance appraisals to help make such behavior conscious, and the behavior itself indicates to the subordinate that the rival would do well to keep his mouth shut.

Dose of anger. The change in point of view which throws such problems into relief and intensifies fear (though rarely do executives speak of fear) is compounded further by a significant dose of anger. It is easy to observe the anger of the middle-aged executive toward today's youth—who have more money, more opportunity, and more sex than was available yesterday. There is anger, too, that the youngsters are free to "do their thing" while today's executives, pressed by the experiences of the depression and the constraints of their positions, sometimes find it hard to do what they really want to do.

The anger with youth is most often expressed as resentment because "they want to start at the top" or "they aren't willing to wait their turn or get experience" or "they only want young ones around here now." It is further reflected in such simultaneously pejorative and admiring descriptive nouns as "whiz kids," "jets," and "stars." These mixed-feeling phrases bespeak self-criticism and betrayal.

Every time the middle-aged manager uses such a phrase, he seems also to be saying that he has not done as well or that he has been undercut. He who had to learn how to size up the market from firsthand contact with customers finds that knowledge now useless, replaced by a computer model constructed by a man who never canvassed a customer. He who thought business to be "practical" and "hardheaded" now finds that he must go back to school, become more intellectual, think ahead conceptually, or he is lost. The kids have outflanked him. They have it so good, handed to them on a platter, at his expense.

Older generations have always complained that the youth not only are unappreciative of their efforts, but take for granted what they have struggled so hard to achieve. Nevertheless, management has never taken seriously the impact of such feelings on executive behavior. The result is an expensive loss of talent as it becomes apparent to young people that managements promise them far more than companies deliver.

I am certain in my own mind that it is the combination of rivalry and anger which makes it so difficult to create challenging ways to use young people in management. (Certainly it is not the dearth of problems to be tackled.) That in turn accounts for much of the astronomical turnover of young college graduates in their first years in a company and also for much of their subsequent disillusionment with managerial careers.

3. Family Relationships

The same narrowing which occurs in the cycle of achievement in business has also been taking place within the family. People are marrying at earlier ages, children are being born earlier in the marriage and therefore leaving their parents earlier. In turn, the parents live alone with each other longer (according to latest census figures, an average of 16 years). This poses several problems which come to a head in middle life. By this point in time one usually has lost both his parents. Though he may have been independent for many years, nevertheless for the first time he feels psychologically alone.

Because an executive can less readily establish close friendships at work, and his mobility makes it difficult for him to sustain them in his off-work relationships, he tends to have greater attachment to his children. He therefore suffers greater loss when they leave home, and he usually does not compensate for these losses any more than he actively compensates for the loss of old friendships through death and distance.

His heavy commitment to his career and his wife's to the children tend to separate them from each other—a problem which is obscured while their joint focus in on the children. When the children leave home, he is left with the same conscious reasons for which he married her as the basis for the marriage (attractiveness, charm, liveliness) and often the same unconscious ones (a substitute for mother, anything but like mother, a guaranteed nonequal, and other, similarly unflattering, reasons).

But she is no longer the young girl he married. She has aged, too, and may no longer be her ideal sylph-like self of twenty years before. If, in addition, his unconscious reasons for marrying her are now no longer as important as they were earlier, there is little left for the marriage unless the couple has worked out another basis for mutual usefulness.

Meanwhile, for most couples there has been a general decrease in satisfaction with each other, less intimacy, a decline in frequency of sexual intercourse, and fewer shared activities. Wives become more preoccupied with their husbands' health because age compels them to unconsciously rehearse for widowhood. Husbands sense this concern and the reasons (which sometimes include a wish for widowhood) for it, and withdraw even more. This is part of what increases the sense of loneliness mentioned earlier, in the context of the need for greater closeness. These factors contribute to the relatively new phenomenon of the "twenty-year" divorce peak.

4. Personal Goals

Up to approximately age 45, creative executive effort is largely self-centered. That is, one is concerned with his achievement and his personal needs. After age 45, he turns gradually to matters outside himself. As psychologist Else Frenkel-Brunswik has shown, he becomes more concerned with ideals and causes, derived from religious or parental values.[9] He also becomes more concerned with finding purpose in life.

For example, a young executive, a "jet" in his company, became a subsidiary president early. And while in that role he became involved in resolving racial problems in his community. Although still president, and likely to be promoted to head the whole corporation, his heart is now in the resolution of community problems. Similarly, another executive has retired early to become involved in conservation. Still others leave business for politics, and not a few have become Episcopal priests.

As part of this change (which goes on unconsciously), there are periods of restlessness and discomfort. There appears to be a peak in travel between the ages of 45 and 50, and also a transitory period of loneliness as one leaves old, long-standing moorings and seeks others.

The restlessness and discomfort have another source. When the middle-aged manager is shifting his direction, he must necessarily use psychological energy for that task. As a consequence, it is more difficult to keep ancient, repressed conflicts under control. This is particularly true when the manager has managed to keep certain conflicts in check by promising himself he would one day deal with them. As he begins to feel that time is running out and that he has not delivered on his promises to himself, he begins to experience intense internal frustration and pressure. Sometimes he will try to hide such conflicts under a contemporary slogan like "identity crisis."

Not long ago, a 42-year-old executive told me that despite his age, his professional engineering training, and his good position, he was still having an identity problem. He said he really did not know what he wanted to do or be. A few questions quickly revealed that he would prefer to be in his own business. However, the moment we touched that topic, he was full of excuses and wanted to turn away from it. He did

[9]"Adjustments and Reorientation in the Course of the Life Span," in *Middle Age and Aging*, edited by Bernice L. Neugarten (Chicago, The University of Chicago Press, 1968), p. 81.

indeed know what he wanted to do; he was simply afraid to face it. He wanted to be independent but he could not break away from the security of his company. He had maintained the fantasy that he might some day, but as the passing years made that less likely, his conflict increased in intensity.

Most men will come nowhere near doing all they want to do with their lives. All of us have some degree of difficulty and frustration as a result. We become even more angry with ourselves when the prospect arises that time will run out before we have sampled, let alone savored, much of what there is in the world. But most of us subtly turn our efforts to meeting those ideal requirements.

The important point in all this is that, as psychologist Charlotte Buhler points out, it relates directly to survival.[10] The evidence indicates that a person's assessment as to whether he did or did not reach fulfillment has more to do with his old-age adjustment than literal loss of physical capacities and insecurity. Put another way, if a man has met his own standards and expectations reasonably well, he adapts more successfully to the aging process. If not, the converse holds: while experiencing the debilitation of aging, he is also simultaneously angry with himself for not having done what he should have. Anger with self is the feeling of depression. We have already noted the implications of depression for physical illness.

SIGNIFICANT IMPLICATIONS

Up to this point, we have been looking at the critical physical and psychological symptoms of the aging process. Now let us turn to the personal and organizational implications in all this.

Facing the Crisis

First, all of us must face up to the fact that there is such an event in men's lives as middle-age

crisis. It is commonplace; it need not be hidden or apologized for. It frequently takes the form of depressive feelings and psychosomatic symptoms as well as increased irritability and discontent, followed by declining interest in and efforts toward mastering the world.

There is a premature tendency to give in to fate, to feel that one can have no choice about what happens to him, and, in effect, to resign oneself to the vagaries of chance. This period is essentially a mourning experience: regret, sorrow, anger, disappointment for something which has been lost—one's precious youth—and with it the illusion of omnipotence and immortality. It is necessary to be free to talk about the loss, the pain, and the regret, and even to shed a tear, literally or figuratively. We do indeed die a bit each day; we have a right to be shaken by the realization when we can no longer deny it.

When a middle-aged manager begins to experience such feelings, and particularly if they begin to interfere with his work or his enjoyment of life, he should talk to someone else about them, preferably a good counselor. This kind of mourning is far better than increasing the intense pace of running in an effort to escape reality. In the process of talking, the wise man reworks his life experiences and his feelings until he is all mourned out and no longer afraid of being mortal.

When a manager can take his own life transitions and his feelings about them seriously, he has the makings of maturity. In the course of making wine, after the grapes are pressed, the resulting liquid is left to age. In a sense, it continues to work. In the process of aging, it acquires body, color, and bouquet—in short, its character.

Like wine, people who work over their feelings about the aging process acquire a certain character with age. They deepen their awareness of themselves and others. They see the world in sharper perspective and with greater tolerance. They acquire wisdom. They love more, exploit less. They accept their own imperfection and therefore their own contributions. As Jaques has put it, "The successful outcome of mature creative work lies thus in constructive resignation both to the imperfections of men and to shortcomings in one's work. It is this constructive resignation which then imparts serenity to life and work."[11]

The middle-aged manager who fails to take himself, his crises, and his feelings seriously keeps running, intensifies his exploitation of others, or gives up to exist on a plateau. Some managers bury themselves more deeply in their work, some run after their lost youth with vain cosmetic efforts, others by chasing women, and still others by pursuing more power. A man's failure to mature in this sense then becomes a disease that afflicts his organization. He loses his people, his grasp of the realities of his life, and can only look back on the way it used to be as the ideal.

The executive who denies his age in these ways also denies himself the opportunity to prepare for what is to come, following some of the suggestions I shall discuss in the next section. He who continues to deny and to run will ultimately have to face emptiness when he can no longer do either and must still live with himself. The wise man will come to terms with reality early: he will take seriously the fact that his time is limited.

Taking Constructive Action

Second, a man must act. Only he who acts on his own behalf is the master of himself and his environment. Too many people accept what is for what will be. They most often say, "I can't do anything about it." What they really mean is that they won't do anything. Check your own experience. How often do you mean "won't" when you say "can't"? Much of psychotherapeutic effort is directed to helping people see how they have trapped themselves this way. There are indeed alternatives in most situations. Our traps are largely self-made.

There are a number of fruitful avenues for action in both personal and business life. In personal terms, the most important efforts are the renegotiation of the marriage and the negotiation of new friendships. Husband and wife might wisely talk out their accumulated differences, their disappointments and mutual

frustrations as well as their wishes and aspirations. As they redefine their marriage contract, they clarify for themselves their interdependence or lack of it. If they remain silent with each other or attack in their frustration, they run the danger of falling apart in their anger at the expense of their need for each other.

In social terms, the executive must make a formal effort to find and cultivate new friends with a particular emphasis on developing companionship. We know from studies of concentration camp survivors and of the process of aging that those who have companions cope most effectively with the traumas of life. Those who do not almost literally die of their loneliness. As a man becomes less self-centered, he can devote more energy to cultivating others. When he individualizes and cultivates the next person, he creates the conditions for others' recognition of him as a person.

In public terms, the executive must become future oriented, but this time in conceptions that go beyond himself and his job. He invests himself in the future when he becomes actively involved in some on-going activity of social value which has enduring purpose. Hundreds of schools, colleges, hospitals, and community projects—most of them obscure—await the capable man who gives a damn and wants that damn to matter. Most executives need not look more than a few blocks beyond their offices for such opportunities.

In business terms, the executive should recognize that at this point in time he ideally should be exercising a different kind of leadership and dealing with different organization problems. In middle age, the stage Erik Erikson has called "the period of generativity,"[12] if he opts for wisdom, he becomes an organizational resource for the development of others. His wisdom and judgment give body to the creative efforts of younger men. They help turn impulse into reality, and then to shape and reshape it into a thousand useful products and services. They offer those characteristics in an executive to be admired and emulated. He shifts from

[11]Jaques, op. cit., p. 505.

[12]*Childhood and Society* (New York, W. W. Norton & Company, Inc., 1964), p. 13.

quarterback to coach, from day-to-day operations to long-range planning. He becomes more consciously concerned with what he is going to leave behind.

Organizing for Renaissance

Third, organizations must take the middle-age period seriously in their thinking, planning, and programming. I know of no organization—business, university, church, or hospital—which does. No one knows how much effectiveness is lost.

If one of the needs for coping with middle-age stress is the opportunity to talk about it, then part of every supervisory and appraisal counseling should be devoted to some of the issues and concerns of this state. Company physicians or medical examining centers should provide time for the patient to talk with the doctor about the psychological aspects of his age and his life. Sessions devoted to examining how groups are working together should, if they are middle-aged groups, have this topic on the agenda. Company educational programs should inform both men and their wives about this period and its unique pressures. Personnel counselors should give explicit attention to this issue in their discussions.

Obviously, there should be a different slant to executive or managerial training programs for men over 35 than for those under 35. Pre-35 programs should be geared to keeping the younger men "loose." They should be encouraged to bubble, to tackle old problems afresh. This is not the time to indoctrinate men with rules and procedures, but rather to stimulate them toward their own horizons. Training challenges should be around tasks requiring sparkle, flashes of insight, and impulsive action.

Developmental programs for men over 35 should be concentrated largely on refreshment, keeping up, and conceptualization of problems and the organization. Tasks and problems requiring reorganization, reformulation, refining, and restructuring are tasks for men whose psychological time it is to rework. Brilliant innovative departures are unlikely to come from such men, except as they are the fruition of a lifetime of ferment, as was the *aggiornamento* of Pope John XXIII.

For them, instead, more attention should be given to frequent respites from daily organizational chores to get new views, to examine and digest them in work groups, and to think of their application to organizational problems and issues. When they move toward the future, they are likely to go in protected steps, like the man crawling on ice who pushes a plank before him. Pushing them hard to be free of the plank will tend to paralyze them into inaction. Rather, training programs should specifically include small experimental attempts to apply new skills and views with minimum risk.

Much of managerial training for these men should be focused on how to rear younger men. This means not only emphasis on coaching, counseling, teaching, and supporting, but also time and opportunity to talk about their feelings of rivalry and disappointment, to ventilate their anger at the young men who have it so good—the whole world at their feet and no place to go but up. Finally, it should include the opportunity for them to recognize, understand, and accept their uniquely human role. Instead of rejecting the younger men, they can then more comfortably place their bets and cheer their favorites on. In the youngsters' winning, they, too, can win.

For the executive, his subordinates, and the company, middle age can truly be a renaissance.

The Mid-life Transition

Daniel J. Levinson

The late thirties mark the culmination of early adulthood. At around forty a man can make some judgment regarding his relative success or failure in meeting the goals he set himself in the enterprise of Becoming One's Own Man. Success here means that the enterprise has flourished: he has achieved the desired position on his "ladder"; he has been affirmed within his occupational and social world; he is becoming a senior member of that world with all the rewards and responsibilities seniority brings.

Often a man looks forward to a key event that in his mind carries the ultimate message of his affirmation by society. This "culminating event" takes on a magical quality in his private fantasy. If it goes the right way, he will know that he has truly succeeded and is assured of a happy future. A poor outcome, on the other hand, will mean that he has failed in a profound sense, that not only his work but he as a person has been found wanting and without value.

When a man experiences a developmental crisis in the late thirties, it stems from the overwhelming feeling that he cannot accomplish the tasks of Becoming One's Own Man: he cannot advance sufficiently on his chosen ladder; cannot gain the affirmation, independence and seniority he wants; cannot be his own man in the terms defined by his current life structure. Whatever the degree of his success or failure—no matter whether he is advancing brilliantly or in the depths of crisis—as long as a man is concerned primarily with these ques-

tions he has not yet emerged from the period of Becoming One's Own Man.

At around 40, a new period gets under way. The Mid-life Transition ordinarily has its onset at age 40 or 41 and lasts about five years. For the fifteen men in our sample who completed this period, the average age at termination was 45.5, the range 44 to 47. We doubt that a true Mid-life Transition can begin before age 38 or after 43.

The Mid-life Transition is a bridge between early adulthood and middle adulthood. As in all transitions, a man must come to terms with the past and prepare for the future. Three major tasks must be worked on.

- One task is to terminate the era of early adulthood. He has to review his life in this era and reappraise what he has done with it.
- A second task is to take his first steps toward the initiation of middle adulthood. Although he is not yet ready to start building a new life structure, he can begin to modify the negative elements of the present structure and to test new choices.
- A third task is to deal with the polarities that are sources of deep division in his life. Let us consider the three tasks in turn.

REAPPRAISING THE PAST

The initial focus in the Mid-life Transition is on the past. The major task is to reappraise the life structure of the Settling Down period, within the broader perspective of early adulthood as a whole and even of preadulthood. A man's review of the past goes on in the shadow of the future. His need to reconsider the past arises in part from a heightened awareness of his mortality and a desire to use the remaining time more wisely. Past and future coexist in the present, but he suffers from the corrosive doubt that they can be joined.

Now the life structure itself comes into question and cannot be taken for granted. It becomes important to ask: What have I done with my life? What do I really get from and give to my wife, children, friends, work, community—and self? What is it I truly want for myself and others? What are my central values and how are they reflected in my life? What are my greatest talents and how am I using (or wasting) them? What have I done with my early Dream and what do I want with it now? Can I live in a way that combines my current desires, values and talents? How satisfactory is my present life structure—how suitable for the self, how viable in the world—and how shall I change it to provide a better basis for the future?

As he attempts to reappraise his life, a man discovers how much it has been based on illusions, and he is faced with the task of *de-illusionment*. By this expression I mean a reduction of illusions, a recognition that long-held assumptions and beliefs about self and world are not true. This process merits special attention because illusions play so vital a role in our lives throughout the life cycle.

The profound human ambivalence toward illusion is reflected in our everyday language. On the one hand, illusion has a negative connotation. It is associated with magic, sleight of hand, enchantment, errors of perception and belief. In a culture highly committed to science, technology and rationality, illusion is generally regarded as inappropriate or even dangerous. The word itself derives from the Latin ludere, to play. While playful illusions can be accepted as part of the imaginative world of childhood, an adult is expected to be more realistic, practical, down to earth. The loss of illusions is thus a desirable and normal result of maturity.

On the other hand, our culture recognizes that illusions have their value even in adult life and that giving them up is often painful. We enjoy magic as a game of illusion. We use the term "disillusionment" to refer to a painful process through which a person is stripped of his most cherished beliefs and values. To be disillusioned is not merely to have lost one's illusions, it is to become cynical, estranged, "unable to believe in anything." This is one possible outcome of the loss of illusions, but not the only one.

To identify the broader process which is so important in the Mid-life Transition, I use the term "de-illusionment." The process of losing or reducing illusions involves diverse feelings—disappointment, joy, relief, bitterness, grief, wonder, freedom—and has diverse outcomes. A man may feel bereft and have the experience of suffering an irreparable loss. He may also feel liberated, free to develop more flexible values and to admire others in a more genuine, less idealizing way.

Illusions can be tremendously harmful; but they can also inspire works of great nobility and accomplishment. They play a crucial, helpful and hurtful part in the lives of most persons during early adulthood. Some reduction in illusions is now appropriate and beneficial, but it is neither possible nor desirable to overcome *all* illusions in the Mid-life Transition or even by the end of middle adulthood. Illusion continues to have its place—a mixed blessing, or a mixed curse—all through the life cycle. The best way to avoid illusions is not to want anything very much. And that is hardly a prescription for a full life.

Early adulthood provides a fertile ground for illusions. Individual capabilities and drives are at their peak. A man must "believe in" himself—even in the face of reality, if need be—and in significant persons, groups and ideologies, so that he can shape a course toward a better life for himself and others, according to his lights. "Good enough" development in early adulthood means that he has aspirations, makes commitments to persons and enterprises, and strives with some enthusiasm and discipline toward valued goals.

MODIFYING THE LIFE STRUCTURE

As the Mid-life Transition proceeds, the emphasis gradually shifts from past to future. A man must make choices that will modify the existing life structure and provide the central elements for a new one. He must begin planning for the next phase. As he makes a commitment to these choices and embarks upon a new pattern of existence, the transition is over and a new period—Entering Middle Adulthood—begins.

Some men make significant changes in the *external* aspects of the life structure during the Mid-life Transition. The more drastic changes involve divorce, remarriage, major shifts in occupation and life style, marked decline in level of functioning, notable progress in creativity or in upward social mobility.

Other men make fewer and less visible external changes. They tend to "stay put" during the Mid-life Transition, remaining in the same marriage and family, the same surroundings, occupation and even work place. If we look more closely, however, we find that important though less obvious changes have occurred. A man's marital relationship is different, for better or worse. His children are growing up and family life is taking new forms. His parents have died or have become more dependent, and this has considerable impact upon his role as son and family member. Even if he is in the same work place, the character of his work has been altered as a result of changes in technology, in organizational structure or in him. Seemingly small promotions or demotions have greatly affected his work activities, his position in the work world, and the personal meaning of work for him. Finally, he has been influenced by changes in the nation and the world, such as war, depression and social movements of all kinds. These changes affect everyone in some way, but the effects are mediated by a man's age and period of development.

The Mid-life Transition also brings significant changes in the *internal* aspects of a man's life structure. He works on various developmental issues that have special urgency at mid-life. He may change appreciably in social outlook, in personal values, in what he wants to give the world, in what he wants to be for himself. The inner changes may be highly conscious and openly expressed, or subtle and hidden. They may come out in dramatic external changes. Even if the changes merely color the fabric of his life without grossly altering it, they give it a substantially different meaning.

A primary task of the Mid-life Transition is to modify the life structure of the thirties and to create the basis for a new structure appropriate to middle adulthood. The final test of the developmental work done here, as in all transition periods, is the satisfactoriness of the life structure emerging from it. Whatever the nature of the developmental work done, and however modest or profound the structural changes wrought, the individual's life in the mid-forties will differ in crucial respects from that in the late thirties. In Chapter 16 we shall examine more closely the changes occurring in various elements of the life structure.

THE INDIVIDUATION PROCESS

Throughout the life cycle, but especially in the key transition periods such as infancy, pubescence and the Mid-life Transition, the developmental process of *individuation* is going on. This term refers to the changes in a person's relationship to himself and to the external world. The infant, leaving his mother's womb, must gain some idea of his separate existence. He must decide where he stops and where the world begins. He must separate himself from his mother, yet maintain a tie to her. He must form a sense of "reality" that allows him to accept his surroundings as having an independent existence not necessarily subject to his control. The child's world gradually expands to include his family, neighborhood and friends; and his self becomes more complex through his relationships with other persons and institutions.

These changes are part of the individuation process. In successive periods of development, as this process goes on, the person forms a clearer boundary between self and world. He forms a stronger sense of who he is and what he wants, and a more realistic, sophisticated view of the world: what it is like, what it offers him and demands from him. Greater individuation allows him to be more separate from the world, to be more independent and self-generating. But it also gives him the confidence and understanding to have more intense attachments in the world and to feel more fully a part of it.

Every developmental transition, as I have said, involves termination and initiation: the termination of an existing life structure and the initiation of a new one. In order to accomplish this, a person must reappraise and modify the existing life structure. This is a challenging and difficult job; it would perhaps be impossible if individuation were not simultaneously playing a role. In a transition period, individuation is the underlying process that links termination and initiation. It prepares the inner ground, laying an internal basis on which the past can be partially given up and the future begun.

In the Early Adult Transition, a boy-man begins his novitiate in the adult world and takes an important step in the individuation process. He must loosen his ties to the pre-adult world and the pre-adult self. Depending in large part on how well individuation goes at this time, he forms a valued adult identity and becomes capable of living with a greater degree of autonomy. He has more responsibility for himself and others and gains competence in his various social roles.

At best, however, a man in his mid-twenties is but a step beyond adolescence. His pre-adult self, with its ties to parents and the pre-adult world, operates with great force throughout early adulthood. Although some developmental gains may be made in the Age Thirty Transition, he will not be much more individuated in the late thirties than he was at 25. After the Early Adult Transition, the next great opportunity for developmental work on individuation is the Mid-life Transition. In this period, a man must modify the early adult self (including, as it does, the baggage of unresolved problems from childhood and adolescence) and the life structure of the late thirties. Greater

individuation is needed if he is to form a life structure more appropriate for middle adulthood.

What are the most significant changes to be made in mid-life individuation? Most investigators emphasize a single facet of the process. Erikson gives primary emphasis to Generativity *vs.* Stagnation as a stage of ego development in the middle years. According to Jaques, the central issue at mid-life is coming to terms with one's own mortality: a man must learn now, more deeply than was possible before, that his own death is inevitable and that he and others are capable of great destructiveness. In her biographical study of Goya, Martha Wolfenstein proposes that the reworking of destructiveness was the basic process in his transformation, during his forties, from an excellent court painter to an artist able to deal with the universals of human tragedy. Bernice Neugarten identifies the basic mid-life change as a growing "interiority": turning inward to the self, decreasing the emphasis on assertiveness and mastery of the environment, enjoying the process of living more than the attainment of specific goals.

Jung first proposed the distinction between the first and the second half of life, with the years around forty as the meridian. He showed that a new effort at individuation begins at mid-life and continues through the remaining years. Unlike many later writers who adopted his term but not his complex understanding of its meaning, he distinguished many facets of the individuation process.

Steering a course somewhere between the single-factor emphasis of some investigators and the tremendously complex approach of Jung, we shall discuss four tasks of mid-life individuation. For a given individual some of these may be more problematic or more conspicuous than others, but all of them are present and all must be considered in a general understanding of adult development. Each task requires a man to confront and reintegrate a polarity—that is, a pair of tendencies or states that are usually experienced as polar opposites, as if a person must be one or the other and cannot be both. As he becomes more individuated in middle adulthood, a man partially overcomes the divisions and integrates the polarities.

FOUR TASKS OF MID-LIFE INDIVIDUATION

The four polarities whose resolution is the principal task of mid-life individuation are: (1) Young/Old; (2) Destruction/Creation; (3) Masculine/Feminine; and (4) Attachment/Separateness.

Each of these pairs forms a polarity in the sense that the two terms represent opposing tendencies or conditions. Superficially, it would appear that a person has to be one or the other and cannot be both. In actuality, however, the paired tendencies are not mutually exclusive. Both sides of each polarity coexist within every self. At mid-life a man feels young in many respects, but he also has a sense of being old. He feels older than the youth, but not ready to join the generation defined as "middle-aged." He feels alternately young, old and "in-between." His developmental task is to make sense of this condition of in-between and to become Young/Old in a new way, different from that of early adulthood.

The Destruction/Creation polarity presents similar problems of conflict and reintegration. The Mid-life Transition activates a man's concerns with death and destruction. He experiences more fully his own mortality and the actual or impending death of others. He becomes more aware of the many ways in which other persons, even his loved ones, have acted destructively toward him (with malice or, often, with good intentions). What is perhaps worse, he realizes that he has done irrevocably hurtful things to his parents, lovers, wife, children, friends, rivals (again, with what may have been the worst or the best of intentions). At the same time, he has a strong desire to become more creative: to create products that have value for himself and others, to participate in collective enterprises that advance human welfare, to contribute more fully to the coming generations in society. In middle adulthood a man can come to know, more than ever before, that powerful

forces of destructiveness and of creativity coexist in the human soul—in my soul!—and can integrate them in new ways.

Likewise, every man at mid-life must come more fully to terms with the coexistence of masculine and feminine parts of the self. And he must integrate his powerful need for attachment to others with his antithetical but equally important need for separateness.

All of these polarities exist during the entire life cycle. They can never be fully resolved or transcended, though some utopian thinkers have held out this promise and some great religious prophets have been seen by others (though rarely by themselves) as having done so. They are not specific to the Mid-life Transition, but they operate here with special force.

Every developmental transition presents the opportunity and the necessity of moving toward a new integration of each polarity. To the extent that a man does this, he creates a firmer basis for his life in the ensuing phase. To the extent that he fails, he forms inner contradictions that will be reflected in the flaws of his next life structure. It is human both to succeed and to fail in these tasks: even as we resolve old conflicts and reach new integrations, we also create the contradictions that will in time stimulate further change and development.

The individuation process and the integration of polarities are ultimately internal and must be carried out within the person. I want to emphasize, however, that a polarity is not solely an inner matter. It is part of a man's life. The opposing tendencies exist both within the self and in the external world. As individuation progresses, a person not only becomes internally more differentiated and complex; he also develops more effective boundaries that link him to the external world and enable him to transact with it more fully. Moreover, the factors that influence how he deals with a polarity are external as well as internal. The splitting of young and old or of masculine and feminine occurs in our culture and social institutions as well as in each individual personality. We can understand a man's struggles to reintegrate a polarity only if we place these struggles within the context of his life and take account of both self and world. Developmental work on the four polarities will be discussed further in Chapters 14 and 15.

THE MID-LIFE TRANSITION AS DEVELOPMENTAL CRISIS

Some men do very little questioning or searching during the Mid-life Transition. Their lives in this period show a good deal of stability and continuity. They are apparently untroubled by difficult questions regarding the meaning, value and direction of their lives. They may be working on such questions unconsciously, with results that will become evident in later periods. If not, they will pay the price in a later developmental crisis or in a progressive withering of the self and a life structure minimally connected to the self.

Other men in their early forties are aware of going through important changes, and know that the character of their lives will be appreciably different. They attempt to understand the nature of these changes, to come to terms with the griefs and losses, and to make use of the possibilities for growing and enriching their lives. For them, however, the process is not a highly painful one. They are in a manageable transition rather than in a crisis.

But for the great majority of men—about 80 percent of our subjects—this period evokes tumultuous struggles within the self and with the external world. Their Mid-life Transition is a time of moderate or severe crisis. Every aspect of their lives comes into question, and they are horrified by much that is revealed. They are full of recriminations against themselves and others. They cannot go on as before, but need time to choose a new path or modify the old one.

Because a man in this crisis is often somewhat irrational, others may regard him as "upset" or "sick." In most cases, he is not. The man himself and those who care about him should recognize that he is in a normal developmental period and is working on normal mid-life tasks. The desire to question and modify his life stems from the most healthy part of the self.

The doubting and searching are appropriate to this period; the real question is how best to make use of them. The problem is compounded by the fact that the process of reappraisal activates unconscious conflicts—the unconscious baggage carried forward from hard times in the past which hinders the effort to change. The pathology is not in the desire to improve one's life but in the obstacles to pursuing this aim. It is the pathological anxiety and guilt, the dependencies, animosities and vanities of earlier years, that keep a man from examining the real issues at mid-life. They make it difficult for him to modify an oppressive life structure.

A profound reappraisal of this kind cannot be a cool, intellectual process. It must involve emotional turmoil, despair, the sense of not knowing where to turn or of being stagnant and unable to move at all. A man in this state often makes false starts. He tentatively tests a variety of new choices, not only out of confusion or impulsiveness but, equally, out of a need to explore, to see what is possible, to find out how it feels to engage in a particular love relationship, occupation or solitary pursuit. Every genuine reappraisal must be agonizing, because it challenges the illusions and vested interests on which the existing structure is based.

The life structure of the thirties was initiated and stabilized by powerful forces in the person and his environment. These forces continue to make their claim for preserving the status quo. A man who attempts a radical critique of his life at 40 will be up against the parts of himself that have a strong investment in the present structure. He will often be opposed by other persons and institutions—his wife, children, boss, parents, colleagues, the occupational system in which he works, the implicit web of social conformity—that seek to maintain order and prevent change. With luck, he will also receive support from himself and from others for the effort to examine and improve his life.

Why do we go through this painful process? Why should a crisis so often be our lot at mid-life? In Chapter 2 I noted several sources of difficulty stemming from the era shift between early and middle adulthood. Moreover, we need developmental transitions in adulthood partly because no life structure can permit the living out of all aspects of the self. To create a life structure I must make choices and set priorities. In making a choice I select one option and reject many others. Committing myself to a structure, I try over a span of time to enhance my life within it, to realize its potential, to bear the responsibilities and tolerate the costs it entails.

Every life structure necessarily gives high priority to certain aspects of the self and neglects or minimizes other aspects. This is as true of the Settling Down structure of the thirties as of all others. In the Mid-life Transition these neglected parts of the self urgently seek expression. A man experiences them as "other voices in other rooms" (in Truman Capote's evocative phrase). Internal voices that have been muted for years now clamor to be heard. At times they are heard as a vague whispering, the content unclear but the tone indicating grief over lost opportunities, outrage over betrayal by others, or guilt over betrayal by oneself. At other times they come through as a thunderous roar, the content all too clear, stating names and times and places and demanding that something be done to right the balance. A man hears the voice of an identity prematurely rejected; of a love lost or not pursued; of a valued interest or relationship given up in acquiescence to parental or other authority; of an internal figure who wants to be an athlete or nomad or artist, to marry for love or remain a bachelor, to get rich or enter the clergy or live a sensual carefree life—possibilities set aside earlier to become what he now is. During the Mid-life Transition he must learn to listen more attentively to these voices and decide consciously what part he will give them in his life.

Meeting the Threat of Managerial Obsolescence

Elmer H. Burack

Managerial obsolescence evolves with a growing discrepancy between the manager's expertise and the changing demands of jobs and work structures. Technological change is a primary causal factor in managerial obsolescence, and should therefore be a key point of departure for coping efforts.

For example, technological changes in manufacturing involve production processes, materials, products and procedures including information systems. The managerial groups which are most vulnerable to obsolescence are the technical support staff groups reinforcing line management in such functions as production, quality control, maintenance and industrial engineering. However, line managers and administrators also may be threatened. The rapid transformations brought about in organizational systems by technical changes have a major impact on managerial personnel.[1] Skills acquired through years of experience can quickly become outmoded, and managers may be faced with demotion, separation, loss of status and damaged self-image.[2]

Each new technological advance threatens the relevance of pre-existing managerial knowledge and experience. For example, the introduction of computers[3] has its impact on decision-making, with judgment and experience being displaced by systems analyses.[4] In fact, managerial skills and knowledge display the same vulnerability to obsolescence as does equipment.[5] Improvements in manufacturing processes, products and materials give rise to stresses which often challenge the competence of managers and technical support groups.[6] Nevertheless, in our study of forty-four companies, the commitment of resources to plant and product strategies was not matched by comparable strategies for the conservation of manpower resources.

Our research experience with computer related changes in non-manufacturing situations differed in technical specifics yet gave rise to similar redefinition of jobs and organizational responses.

IMPLICATIONS FOR POLICY-MAKING

Business management must reckon with the need for managerial upgrading as well as recruitment of new skills.[7] Thus, more attention must be given to individual development and retraining which will entail special costs.[8] Yet all too often the interests of policy-makers in encouraging the maintenance of job relevance are not supported by budgetary programs. Nothing signals company interest quite as fast as budget lines for educational or self-development programs.

Technological change with its attendant implications for obsolescence is importantly related to corporate policy-making. Management, especially top management, has a key role in initiating technical changes as well as in responding to them. Figure 1 illustrates the managerial roles in forming and implementing change policy. The organizational environment is the matrix within which a wide range of factors operate to shape and diffuse change. Recognizing the interplay between environment, policy and technological change is the first step in controlling obsolescence.

Top level planning traditionally has focused on the economic and physical rather than the manpower aspects of change. However, it is the responsibility of the company decision-makers to anticipate future change in terms of the company's financial, technical and personnel resources and to chart their significance to manpower policy.[9] The chief executive, senior officers and board of directors are key instru-

ments; they must become intimately involved in the policies that launch change and must understand the implications of change for all levels of management. The decisions of these policy-makers determine the technological posture of the organization, affecting conceptual and analytical approaches and realigning experience and educational needs. They also play important roles in timing specific activities and even in generating future obsolescence problems. Accordingly, their understanding of their role in policy matters is crucial in coping with managerial obsolescence.

The specifics of technological change are fashioned by such agents of change as process engineers, facility planners, industrial engineers, and programmers who often operate on the basis of cost/benefit analyses and other objective criteria. Other organizational functionaries—personnel officers and manpower planners—who might be called "manpower translators of change," typically play secondary roles. Detailed projections of internal manpower needs for skill inventories, audits and development programs are generally lacking in

Figure 1 Policy Processes and the Implementation of Change

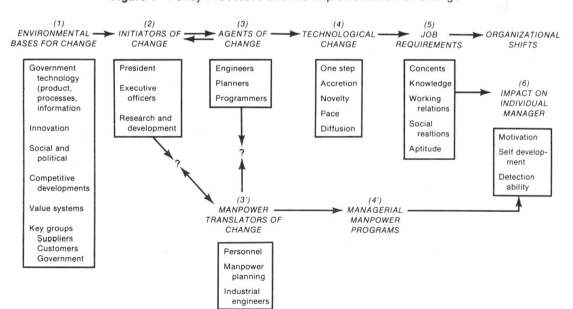

organizations. Research reveals on all too common preoccupation with demographic analyses, focusing on numbers and locations but lacking insight into the other manpower requirements. Thus, there is a failure to recognize or anticipate those forces creating the various dimensions of obsolescence.[10] Consequently, organizational and individual efforts to cope with change tend to be defensive responses rather than rationally planned offensives.

CHANGE AND THE DECISION-MAKER

Problem solvers and decision-makers (for example, R & D, planners, engineers/programmers) in an organization set the pattern of managerial competency and adaptability. Obsolescence is most likely to occur when the requirements of planning, problem solving and administration are beyond the skills or adaptability of these groups.[11] However, demands on these individuals must be viewed within the framework of the company's total decision-making system, including the division of responsibility[12] for problem solving among all levels of authority and between operating and support personnel.[13] The pressures which develop are very often uneven. In some circumstances, modest re-allocations of responsibilities can help to relieve otherwise difficult situations. For example, in one of the manufacturing units included in our research, a modest reorganization of a production manager's subordinates and staff (re-assigning some staff units) permitted him to continue effective activities by confining his efforts to more specific operational matters. Since both his age and circumstances worked against a major redevelopment program, the solution proved acceptable to the company and manager.

CHANGE BY ACCRETION VS. ONE-STEP CHANGE

Gradual changes in work systems have cumulative effects which make the detection of obsolescence difficult. Individuals may respond by withdrawal from the work situation, poor performance or open conflict. The manager may postpone remedial measures until mounting stresses produce unavoidable manpower problems. Even with enough time to develop the necessary inputs of education or experience, individual apathy combined with lack of policy-maker awareness and support for constructive manpower developmental programs may abort remedial measures. Under these circumstances, updating efforts are likely to be ill constructed crash programs which are essentially defensive.

One-step change programs pose different detection and adjustment problems. The warning signals are clearer in such obvious changes as building a new plant or adding new production lines and processes.[14] When major one-step (technological) changes are made, personnel functionaries are likely to be aware of the upcoming changes. However, too often those concerned with manpower planning do not participate in planning change, or their participation is severly limited.

Managerial adaptability to change is affected by four categories of factors:

- organizational climate and support;
- age and attitude toward change;
- education and career development paths; and
- professional experience and knowledge base.

These points are briefly discussed in the following section.

CHANGE AND THE ORGANIZATIONAL CLIMATE

An organizational climate which is supportive of managerial adaptability to change implies cooperation among superiors, subordinates and colleagues in structuring attacks on obsolescence, including definition of problems and proposals for solutions. The quality and integrity of the supportive climate will profoundly affect the organization's total ability to meet the threat of managerial obsolescence. The basis of a supportive climate is the organization's policy framework which sets the tone for manpower approaches and procedures. There is a need for corporate value systems which encourage and reward individual development.

Age and attitude toward change. Individuals react uniquely to the changing demands of advanced systems. Age works against adaptability, bringing physical limitations, temperamental rigidity and community and family conflicts. A large segment of the managerial and scientific work force has reached an age once considered "prime," but now often described as "over the top." Managers may be anxious to preserve the status quo when customary tastes or habits are threatened.[15] The need to give "meaning to the roles of those displaceable by computers" or various alibis can encourage resistance to change.[16]

Education and career development paths. The new technologies require more advanced levels of formal and technical education posing new threats for managers in both operating and support functions. Reliance on experience in the face of rapid changes in work and information systems and management techniques is a significant source of managerial obsolescence.[17] It has been estimated that the half-life of the schooling of technical men may be as low as ten years[18] and the steady pressure of change will continue to shorten this life span. A manager's specific job requirements, the quality of coaching by supervisors and colleagues together with shifts in the corporate job structure further affect his obsolescence potential.

At some point in time, changing job needs threaten the individual's know-how. Tension, gradual lowering of job performance and morale, conflict and inability to provide creative answers are some of the symptoms of incipient obsolescence.

The point in time when a job threat is likely to emerge depends upon such factors as the manager's level and scope of responsibility; whether his role is an operating or supporting one; the quality and number of the staff elements available for support; and, the type of change (accretion or one-step). Consequently, the concept of half-life obsolescence potential requires modification when it is used as a managerial tool. Specific curves can be constructed, for example, for high change areas and half-life approximated by comparing the literature of a field at different points in time and gauging the rate at which topics, tools and concepts are being introduced or eliminated.

Professional experience and knowledge base. Supervisors and managers, as well as the professional supporting staff are susceptible to obsolescence in varying degrees. They differ in practical experience and levels of formal education, both of which influence the capacity for self-development. The experience oriented individual tends to be greatly influenced by cues from the company environment—both motivational incentives and behavioral cues from the organization's value system.[19] Operating managers and many supporting staff members with varying formal educational credentials may approach self-development in quite another manner. Men with more formal education are likely to develop the learning habit: the prevalence of achievers among the educated is higher. Moreover, a professionally oriented manager may be influenced by his colleagues, inside and outside the organization. There are greater pressures for the professional to broaden his knowledge base to keep up with emerging job needs,[20] although he may prove unresponsive to these needs.

OBSOLESCENCE DETECTION PROCEDURES AND COPING MECHANISMS

Efforts to build functioning detection systems and appropriate coping mechanisms will have to start with a broad understanding of the factors creating obsolescence and their impact on policy, processes and manpower planning. From these basic insights, the role of the manpower functionaries takes shape—they will be specialists in observing and anticipating changes both in technology and in the organization's social system and will rationalize interactions between managers and their supervisors so that appropriate appraisal, counseling and coaching can take place. Forced updating may be employed and individuals may be reassigned to encourage flexibility or to broaden experience. Efforts may also include active encouragement for self-development tailored to individual needs, utilizing tuition reimbursement and where indicated, time off for special classes.

Detection. Top management's policy on training and development should encompass the strategic possibilities for the development of human resources to support long-range company objectives. Thus, it is necessary to replace short-run response-type action with a more deliberate view of future job needs in both quantitative and qualitative terms. The final effect of such policy would be to approximate individual needs for education and development and to coordinate programs of education with guided job experiences in a career planning approach. Appraisal routines and assessment/opportunity centers are two effective techniques which can be used in mapping out career plans.

a. **Appraisal routines.** Procedures for appraising performance or, "management-by-objectives," can be useful in career planning where professionals provide instruction and guidance for those assuming the appraiser's role. It is especially important that a non-hostile environment be created which will permit frank discussion between boss and subordinate. The appraiser must understand the manpower implications of change and be able to relate them to current performance. Considerable skill in human relations is necessary to the success of these routines.

b. **Assessment/opportunity centers.** Although still innovative in design, these centers permit systematic approaches to judging individual potential and needs. The emphasis is on diagnosing capabilities, determining areas of need based on job requirements, and mapping out a developmental

program for growth and improved performance at the individual level. The center formalizes a procedure where personnel specialists and trained line managers are brought together as a panel reflecting a wide range of knowledge and skill for gauging individual performance potential and needs.

Personnel officials and resident manpower talent within assessment/opportunity centers can spearhead self-detection approaches. One such approach is the preparation of self-administered "quizzes" in collaboration with various field experts. By highlighting recent gains in special fields at periodic intervals, members of functional units are alerted to new developments. The hidden agenda (for the individual) underlying these quizzes and releases is to suggest important new directions of development in particular fields. Although some specific learning is inherent in this approach, the main thrust is to raise questions and encourage inquiry.

The role of supervisors is crucial to obsolescence detection and the support of individual self-development. A supervisor is in a position to detect obsolescence potential among his subordinates since his work involves constant contact with those in his organizational unit. At the same time, the supervisors' comprehension of job demands and working relationship with subordinates are key elements in establishing a supportive climate for continuing self-development. Supervisory training should:

a. develop sensitivity to the features of change and the broader aspects of a job's educational and experience underpinnings;

b. lead to an understanding of the symptoms of obsolescence; and

c. establish a supervisor/subordinate relationship based on trust and mutual exchange which permits thoughtful guidance, accommodation, and support.

Furthermore, since the supervisor serves as a model of expected behavior, his continuing self-development provides an important example for subordinates.

The annual medical examination is another approach to obsolescence detection which has been given too little attention. Increasing numbers of firms are making an annual medical check-up an important routine for maintaining the well-being of its invaluable manpower resources. Although the examination has concentrated on physical well-being, it is obvious that an individual's psychological state has a direct bearing on his physical health. Tension, conflict and frustration may well be viewed within a larger framework which includes job obsolescence as a potent source of psychological and physical stress.

Detection and coping efforts must be incorporated in support systems (reward, information, and so on), such as that based on the computer. Manpower information systems should provide for periodic detection audits, contacts with job incumbents, and the dissemination of information on opportunities and challenges which may be better suited to an individual's capabilities, including vacancies and new jobs and upcoming educational and training opportunities.

Detection audits deserve special attention. Not only do they measure the dimensions of the obsolescence threat, but they also provide unique opportunities for matching education, experience and personality with job requirements. A computer-based approach to such audits incorporating the full range of factors involved in change, can back up a detection system and make possible analyses which include the man, the job and technical change. The assessment/opportunity center previously described can serve as a central point for supporting these audits.

In order to maximize the usefulness of detection audits, it will be necessary to involve the manpower translators of change in all phases of planning. The first requisite is an inventory of current manpower resources and a forecast of upcoming needs. Both are dependent on a solid personnel data base which is too often lacking. Such procedures call for an awareness of the current responsibilities of managers and how they will be affected by upcoming changes. Analytical models for such forecasting are just beginning to develop. However, they promise

broader usefulness and greater precision. Awareness of the crucial importance of such forecasting is much more important than preoccupation with the technical details of specific models.

Coping. A number of approaches are at hand for companies seeking to launch or extend practical programs for dealing with obsolescence of human resources: capitalizing on in-house technologies such as the computer; enlightened tuition programming; "learning leaves-of-absence" or "company sabbaticals"; in-house conferences and imaginative uses of company library facilities for "activating the company's knowledge base." Of course, budgetary support is superior to empty pronouncements.

Extending in-house technology. Existing computer technology is used mainly for routine information processing and problem solving with little attention directed to its potential in education. A few companies have taken steps to utilize the computer for various business games and exercises in management institutes. One of the companies studied utilizes the results of a series of exercises as a major item in promotability. The same company, a large electronics manufacturer, also brings in various field personnel such as salesmen for periodic updating sessions with the computer/outputs as the principal learning vehicle.

Programmed instruction is another in-house technology which can be used to support self-detection efforts and to permit self-paced instruction under *non-threatening* circumstances. A large insurance firm apprises company personnel of the availability of various tapes which can be checked out for home use. Other than a simple "out" record, no permanent record is kept of the check-out transactions.

Library facilities. The learning center concept is closely allied with company library facilities. The ability to tap this resource for self-development can significantly improve management's coping efforts. Enlarging abstract services, improving data retrieval through greater use of tapes, for example, and availability of computer terminals represent some approaches to increasing the value of the company library. The availability of these resources must, of course, be communicated to all appropriate organization members. This "center" notion is a clear signal from the organization that continuing education and self-development is important for all.

Tuition programming. Perhaps the key point here is that the money "give-away" must stop and be replaced by an approach which reflects a unity of organization objectives, manpower objectives, career development and individual need. Accomplishments are severely restricted where tuition support is viewed as inherently good or a necessary fringe benefit. For example, in a large consumer goods manufacturing company with six divisions, program participation was highly variable, ranging from 2.0 percent in one division to 12.0 percent in another. Discussions with both company officials and participants provided little evidence of a tuition policy, much less an enlightened, comprehensive program bringing together company needs and individual development.

Sabbaticals. The company "sabbatical" is of recent origin and warrants the close scrutiny of manpower officials. Some organizations, divisions or departments are likely to remain squarely in the change areas, thus the length of time required for managing change cuts the time available for self-preparation. Some firms have already made annual management institutes part of a continuing program for combating obsolescence. Few, however, have realized the need for extended learning time wherein special educational or degree programs can be pursued.

The most difficult challenge of all is the need to develop a philosophy of management which will actively support efforts to detect and combat managerial obsolescence on an organizationwide basis. Routine dissemination of information on proposed changes and their probable effects on individual managers is essential, but only a first step in creating support for and participation in development programs. Substantial, even unprecedented, changes in company policies and official attitudes may be required—work hours may need reorganizing, coaching efforts and other programs may have to be instituted. Most managers will need active encouragement to participate in development programs. They are often blind to upcoming changes and their probable impact on jobs, and are unaware of their own deficiencies and of what is needed to overcome them. It is only through a well thought out procedure for identifying job needs, and for evaluating and training managerial skills, that a program for preventing obsolescence can succeed. Such a program requires the full and informed support of top management.

SUMMARY

The central thesis of this article is that technological change is the point of departure for appraising and coping with managerial obsolescence. However, too often complacency and lack of know-how characterize managerial manpower planning and implementation. Managing change—including change in managerial responses—is a responsibility of top management. The roles of leadership and policy making in the management of change are poorly understood although commitment to managing change is essential to the maintenance of organizational health. Lack of such commitment will be reflected in inadequate obsolescence detection and ineffective coping devices.

To avoid reliance on inadequate defensive tactics—overlooking, for example, the potential of promotable, non-college personnel and ignoring the half-life factor in managerial skills—it will be necessary to strengthen detection procedures and encourage greater participation by manpower translators of change. Such participation is especially important in the early stages of policy making where the first critical decisions concerning technological and organizational changes are made. When the manpower translators are "in on the ground floor," the quality of change management will be materially improved.

Lack of far-reaching manpower planning at the top management level can create such costly confusion and short-sighted decisions as: 1. tuition grants without backup support in rule changes; 2. lack of meaningful career planning for individual managers; 3. neglect of manpower audits and skill inventories; 4. failure to hire personnel skilled in handling manpower programs or handicapping them with inadequate data; and 5. assigning low priorities to manpower planning.

The positive approach herein described for attacking managerial obsolescence (including broad program proposals)[21] is more easily described than implemented. However, a balanced manpower development program will surely include mid-career and continuing educational opportunities, formal as well as informal. It will also call for increased realism in viewing job needs, present and future, with careful reexamination of the upgrade potential of present employees as well as hiring standards. It will explore the newer techniques for overcoming individual shortcomings.

Such positive managerial manpower operations clearly require continuous and sophisticated attention to forecasting manpower needs, monitoring changes in terms of their impact on managers, and alerting individuals to opportunities as well as the hazards of technical change.

If managerial obsolescence is to be minimized, continuing education must become a corporate concern rather than a spare time, individual activity. The key to successful handling of the obsolescence problem is organizational commitment to the management of change and an understanding at top levels of the critical interplay between manpower policies and the other dimensions of policy making. Without such commitment and understanding, there can be neither realistic audits of manpower needs nor adequately staffed and financed programs for detecting and coping with obsolescence. The challenges posed by technical change can only be met through supportive relationships and structured programs that use the full resources of the organization to combat the problems of managerial obsolescence.

REFERENCES

The core material for this paper was derived from the research findings of three field studies: Elmer H. Burack and Thomas J. McNichols, Management and Automation, *a study sponsored by the U.S. Department of Labor, Manpower Administration, Office of Manpower, Automation and Training (June, 1968); a study undertaken by the writer and Bernard H. Baum, portions of which appeared in* "Information Technology" Academy of Management Journal *(Sept., 1969); and a series of continuing studies of technological change directed by the writer at Illinois Institute of Technology—findings emerging from the IIT studies are cited elsewhere in the paper.*

The writer gratefully acknowledges the contributions of Professors L. Richard Hoffman (University of Chicago) and Thomas L. Calero (Illinois Institute of Technology).

1. Elmer H. Burack, "The Impact of the Computer on Business Management," *The Business Quarterly* (Spring, 1966).
2. See Robert Dubin *et al., Leadership and Productivity* (San Francisco: Chandler Publishing Co., 1965).
3. Rodney H. Brody, "Computers in Top-Level Decision Making," *Harvard Business Review* (July/August, 1967), pp. 67-76.
4. Joan Woodward, *Management and Technology* (London: Her Majesty's Stationary Office, 1965).
5. Leon C. Megginson, *Personnel, A Behavioral Approach to Administration* (Homewood, Ill.: Richard D. Irwin, Inc., 1967), p. 139.
6. Burack and McNichols, *op. cit.*
7. Based on a study made by the Carnegie Institute of Technology, "The Rising Crisis

in Skills, More Jobs Than Skills," *Steel* (September 7, 1964), p. 58.

8. Louis Carrels, "Eight Steps to Better Training," *Nation's Business* (March, 1961), p. 40.

9. For a positive approach to forecasting these manpower implications see Peter E. Haase "Technological Change and Manpower Forecasts," *Industrial Relations* (May, 1966), pp. 59-71.

10. Based on Elmer H. Burack and Thomas J. McNichols, *op. cit.;* also, an earlier series of studies reported in Elmer H. Burack, "Industrial Management in Advanced Production Systems, Some Theoretical Concepts and Preliminary Findings," *Administrative Science Quarterly* (December, 1967).

11. James R. Bright, *Research Development and Technological Innovation* (Homewood: Richard D. Irwin, 1964), pp. 130-134.

12. Developed by J. A. Raffaele, "Automation and the Coming Infusion of Power in Industry," *Personnel* (May-June, 1962), pp. 32-33; and Megginson, *op.cit.,* p. 135.

13. Walter Buckingham, "The Human Side of Automation," Keith Davis and William G. Scott, eds., *Readings in Human Relations* (New York: McGraw-Hill, 1966).

14. See Warren Bennis, *Changing Organizations* (New York: McGraw-Hill, 1966); and

Elmer H. Burack, "Technology and Supervisory Functions: A Preliminary View," *Human Organization* (Winter, 1967), pp. 256-264.

15. Bright, *loc. cit.*

16. Donald N. Michael, "Some Long Range Implications of Computer Technology for Human Behavior in Organization," *The American Behavioral Scientist* (April, 1966), p. 29.

17. Based on a recent survey of employers by the U.S. Department of Labor, Office of Manpower, Automation, and Training, "Formal Occupational Training of Adult Workers," Manpower and Automation Research Monograph No. 2 (Washington, D.C., U.S. Government Printing Office, December, 1964).

18. Suggested in a panel on manpower and obsolescence at the 32nd Annual Midwestern Conference, Industrial Relations Association, University of Chicago (October, 1967).

19. Alvin Gouldner, "Patterns of Industrial Bureaucracy" (Glencoe: Free Press, 1954).

20. See John W. Gardner, *Self-Renewal* (New York: Harper & Row, 1964).

21. Robert E. Cassidy, "Manpower Planning: A Co-ordinated Approach," *Personnel* (September, 1963), p. 35.

Section 5

Late-Career Issues and Concerns

Many problems of late career are extensions of those identified for mid-career managers. Thus, recognition of one's mortality, fear of obsolescence, tensions derived from changing relationships with one's children, spouse, subordinates, and so on, and anxiety resulting from the realization of increasingly limited opportunities are relevant issues. The challenges for the manager of a late-career employee is to maintain a proactive growth and involvement orientation during this phase of the employee's worklife.

"Nonpromotables" or "shelf sitters" pose a particular problem for managers. These are the mid- or late-career employees who have been designated, officially or unofficially, as unworthy of consideration for promotion. The first selection in this section suggests a rather innovative approach to solving the problems posed by shelf sitters. This new approach is based on encouraging managers to anticipate and prepare for second careers. After encouraging and, in fact, paying for second career training, a company is in a better position to promote early retirement for this group of surplus employees.

There is some evidence to suggest that managers are too hasty in identifying "shelf sitters." Managerial judgments regarding the performance capabilities of older workers are influenced by several age stereotypes which bias decisions about the promotability or developmental opportunities for late-career workers. Common stereotypical views of older workers are that they:

- Are less capable of responding creatively and innovatively
- Are inflexible and resistant to change
- Are unable to deal with crisis situations
- Show little interest in keeping up with the latest technology
- Exhibit increasing nervousness and anxiousness
- Suffer from declining mental alertness

These age stereotypes determine many managerial actions and decisions related to late-career employees which serve to reduce their opportunities for continued growth. For example, there is a tendency to avoid investments in the continued development and retraining of older workers. Similarly, fewer attempts are made to provide performance feedback. In addition, the probability of promotion is somewhat lower for older employees than for identically qualified younger workers. The second selection in this section serves to dispel some of the myths about older workers by summarizing much of the relevant research findings about age and performance. These findings suggest that managers may be involved in yet another "Self-Fulfilling Prophecy." When workers are denied opportunities for growth and development there are declines in motivation and effective contribution. This serves to confirm managerial judgments about nonpromotability and further strengthens age stereotypes.

The recent amendments to the Age Discrimination in Employment Act have extended mandatory retirement age from 65 to 70. Such a change will greatly increase the number of late-career workers in organizations. This fact alone suggests that managers need to be more aware of the career needs of these workers.

Rx for Managerial "Shelf Sitters"

Samuel R. Connor
John S. Fielden

Harry Allen is 49 years old, married, with three children and all the outward signs of the successful business executive. For 18 years, Harry has happily and successfully pursued his career with the ABC Corporation. Shortly after his service in the Korean War, he joined the company, full of good potential and high aspirations. His career growth has been better than most. He arrived 2 years ago at the "launching pad," that level of the organization from which the most qualified men enter the ranks of top management. Although Harry realized throughout his career that only a few would actually reach the top, he was confident that he could compete and would eventually make it.

Last week, Harry's dream ended abruptly. He was passed over in favor of a younger man for the vice presidency. He remembered similar occasions when this had happened—usually it was a matter of two or three years before the passed-over manager was moved laterally, or "put on the shelf." For Harry the prospect was grim.

Harry Allen's situation is not unique. During the past two decades the problem of the "accumulating management resource," as it is often referred to in management jargon—"shelf sitter" is the more colloquial label—has grown to serious proportions. Some knowledgeable observers we know estimate the number of shelf sitters in large industrial corporations to be three to five times as great as it was in the early 1950's. As U.S. industrial corporations have grown more complex, the number of middle managers has increased faster than has either the worker or the top-management population.

Because of this increased growth, it is easy to understand why competition for proportionately fewer top jobs has increased. The unavoidable result has been arrested career development for many thousands of managers. As corporate growth continues, more and more of them will face Harry Allen's situation at younger and younger ages.

LET'S TAKE A FRESH APPROACH

In our opinion, nothing short of a highly innovative and daring approach is going to solve this problem. We shall outline such an approach, first giving a brief overview of it, then turning to a few questions of operation, cost, and practicality. We shall not try to spell out the mechanics of the program in detail, even though we have given them considerable thought in discussions with various people. For one thing, the mechanics of funding and administration would vary from company to company. More important, our purpose here is to describe a *concept* for the many executives in U.S. industry who are concerned about the Harry Allens in their midst.

"Green Stamps" System

The new approach has two aspects. First, it is a system of encouraging all a company's younger managers to anticipate and to prepare for *second careers* in *other* organizations and fields, the preparation to be paid for by the company. Second, as a result of encouraging and paying for second-career training, a company can in better conscience force early retirement (or demotion) on those managers who have been passed over twice and hence are "surplus."

Part of our plan resembles the armed services' solution to their surplus officer problems. In other respects it is more novel. We envisage the corporation giving managers educational credits based on their length of service in lower and middle management. These credits can be thought of as "educational green stamps." In concept they are like the green stamps a customer gets with purchases of gasoline, food, and other products that, when accumulated to a certain point, entitle him to a product of his choice in another line of merchandise.

In a way, the message of this article is simple; in another way, it is profound. We are attacking as outmoded in modern corporations the notion of "one company, one career, retirement at 65." If the surplus manager problem is to be dealt with in business, as it has been in the military, then managers must expect, as officers do, to run a reasonable risk of being declared surplus at an age young enough to begin a second career.

The outdated one-company, one-career notion permeates management education programs in business. If a company is going to spend stockholders' money on educating its managers, the reasoning goes, then managers should be educated to do a better job of doing

what they are already paid to do for the company. That reasoning explains why almost every corporate education program pays tuition costs only for courses of study that promise a direct benefit to the manager in doing today's, or at most, tomorrow's job in the company.

What is wrong with such a system? It prepares a manager for continuing his career in the same company, but he may not be allowed to utilize his training. In that case, the company has wasted its money. A system of this kind is injurious to the individual, to his company, and to the nation. The man or woman in middle management wants to be upwardly mobile. He or she knows that is how the game must be played. Yet the pyramidal structure dictates that the organization must reject more individuals than it promotes. Management's intent is survival of the fittest.

However, *seldom today are the rejects truly rejected.* Instead, they are shelved—and their salaries go on and on. The vast majority of top executives simply do not have the stomach for casting out the deadwood! Oh, they do it occasionally, but for all practical purposes there is as much tenure in corporate life as there is in the academic world.

A green stamps approach would, in our opinion, cope effectively with both the impracticality and the inhumanity of the present system.

FACING THE REALITIES

Before looking at the operation of an educational green stamps program, let us fix in mind some realities of management in a typical medium-sized or large company. For this purpose, let us go back to the case of Harry Allen mentioned at the start of this article and explore his situation. What are his alternatives? What are the likely costs for the company?

Harry, at 49, has been passed over. He knows that he has one strike on him in a game of, at most, two strikes. The options open to him at this point are these:

- He can hang in there and hope he makes the next promotion. But that may be two or three years away. At that time, if he is passed over again, he may be too old to find another comparable job.
- He can quit the company now and move to hopefully greener pastures before the "jig is up" and he is past 50. But this move may only postpone the inevitable, unless he is very fortunate. He knows that unless he performs extremely well in a new job, the second company probably will not give him different opportunities. In fact, not feeling responsible for a short-time employee, the second company could well kick him out on the street rather than put him on the shelf.

Neither of these possibilities is very appealing to Harry. After a few difficult weeks of turning the two alternatives over in his mind, he selects the first one and stays with the company. At least, he rationalizes, he's assured of a job.

Now let us push the calendar ahead three years. Harry is again considered for a promotion and once more is passed over. What happens then? Put on the shelf at age 52, he has little opportunity to exercise power or creativity, and he can get few psychic rewards. As a result, he becomes sour, despite himself. Perhaps he drinks too much, plays more golf, bitches. He remembers his days as a productive manager at a lower level. As for the company, it keeps paying his salary of, let us say, $40,000. Even assuming no raises (although, in most cases, he will receive some cost-of-living increases), it will be giving him more than *half a million dollars* (13 × $40,000) before he retires! For this generous amount, Harry contributes only neutrally or perhaps negatively. Both Harry and his managerial associates anxiously await the magic year 65 of his life.

Inadequate Remedies

Since, in fact, few long-service managers are ever fired outright by U.S. corporations, remedies have been sought for the situation portrayed by Harry Allen.

One approach is to package a special "deal" to sweeten forced early retirement. Sometimes the man is given double his normal severance pay or allowed to remain on salary for up to four years if he will only get out at, say, age 56 and agree to early retirement at 60. But this is a band-aid approach—hardly a sound or thoughtful solution.

The most widespread approach is the establishment of optional early retirement plans. During the past 15 years, retirement ages have dropped from 65 to 55. Unfortunately, early retirement plans are *optional* for the individual and, hence, flabby answers to the problem. The philosophy of early retirement is to enable the manager who has been passed over (or who is tired of his present career) to turn his energies to other interests—at no cost to the company. The idea *sounds* great. The hitch is that only a small number (between 5% and 10%) of those qualifying for early retirement are financially secure enough to afford this alternative. As a result, they duck the issue and refuse early retirement.

Here is why: Benefits received at age 65 are likely to provide about 40% to 45% of a man's salary. Retirement benefits at age 55 provide only about 20% to 25% of his salary. A man at age 55 may well have financial commitments that 20% to 25% of his salary simply cannot satisfy.

No wonder that early retirement plans are given no teeth. Probably motivated by such thoughts as "There but for the grace of God go I," most top corporate executives carry the shelf sitter at or near his highest salary until the person himself is motivated to want out.

UNDOING THE PETER PRINCIPLE

What top management must be willing to do is to pay the necessary price to get the marginal or surplus manager out of his present position. It must keep the Peter Principle from operating. It must be willing either to (a) demote the shelf sitter or (b) force his early retirement into a second career that he has prepared for *at com-*

pany expense. This need is the justification of the green stamps approach.

Demotion is not inhumane. In a competitive environment, a man should rationally expect to be paid only in accord with his abilities—and this should apply to downward movement in a company just as it does to upward. By demoting a man to a level where he performs in a satisfactory fashion, one reverses the Peter Principle, even possibly restoring a man's self-respect and increasing his psychic income.

Demotion or forced early retirement are the choices under the green stamps approach. The option of being financially well-rewarded while sitting on the shelf is removed. Either one works for the corporation at a salary dictated by the job done, or one gets out—only now the getting out is dignified by being customary as well as educationally and financially practical.

Would such a policy injure a company's recruiting success? We fail to see why it would. Those who have great ability and who continue to grow can still make it to the top. In fact, the company's image might well improve as a result of telling recruits the obvious truth—that not all are guaranteed a spot at the top, but the company believes in realistically giving *all* managers a chance to hedge their career bets and prepare for second careers.

As far as demotion goes, this stark fact should serve as a deterrent only to those who lack confidence in themselves and who at an early age fancy a career as a corporate shelf sitter. And what company would regret losing applicants such as these? Moreover, would not the best young recruits applaud a corporation whose policy rigorously clears out executive deadwood from the path of the upwardly mobile junior manager?

MAKING THE PLAN WORK

To make the new plan work, the first requirement is for surplus managers to be so designated promptly. We suggest that this designation be made when a manager has been nominated for a promotion and then passed over two successive times.

Second, eligibility for early retirement must be limited to managers who have accumulated, let us say, 45 age and service credits, with one credit for each year of age and one for each year of service in the company, with a minimum of 10 service credits required. The figure 45 is admittedly arbitrary; management can alter it to fit the circumstances.

Third, the organization must provide educational benefits that encourage employees to prepare for second careers; it would thus take the curse off forced early retirement. These benefits would be in the form of the educational green stamps mentioned earlier. They would replace all other tuition-refund and voluntary education programs for managers sponsored by the company.

The value of a stamp would be the prevailing cost of a graduate-level semester course credit—about $100 today. A manager would start earning green stamps when he or she begins employment with the company and would earn 5 of them each year for 10 years. This would provide a maximum of 50 stamps for each manager. One could not start redeeming the stamps, however, until after the fifth year of employment in the company. The purpose of this restriction would be to limit redemption to managers who have made a commitment to the company. Other restrictions that should be put on the stamps are these:

• They should be usable only for bona fide education programs recognized by the state or other educational authorities. But such courses of study would not have to be related to the employee's present job.
• Although they could be accumulated, they would have to be used before retirement.
• They would not be transferable into cash or other compensation.

Managers with 10 or more years of service, like Harry Allen, would be entitled to $5,000 worth of educational benefits. We believe that this amount (or even the minimum $2,500) would be sufficient to help anyone prepare for a second career.

Preparation and training would depend entirely on the individual and the career area he or she chooses. Facilities for training and preparation are available today in all parts of the country. Seldom could lack of educational opportunities be used as an excuse for not entering a new career.

COST OF PROGRAM

What would an educational green stamp program cost a company? The answer would be determined by two factors:

1. The number of managers using their stamps.
2. The average extent of use.

Let us assume a corporation with 2,000 managerial employees. Theoretically, each of the 2,000 will have accumulated a $5,000 education credit after 10 years of service. But not all of them will be redeeming their stamps at one time—and many of them never at all. Others are not yet eligible. If we assume that at any time only half, or 1,000 managers, are redeeming the credits and that the credits are being redeemed at the rate of $1,000 (10 graduate credits) per year, the total cost to the company will be $1 million per year.

This is a gross cost. As offsets to it we must consider the cost of shelving many managers. We should also consider the savings accruing from a policy of demotion in rank and salary of some of the management surplus. Also we should take into account reimbursements from the government for certain types of job-related education.

Informal estimates and unpublished company reports indicate that the size of the shelf-sitter problem could be between 6% and 12% of the management population. If we conservatively assume a 6% rate and apply this to our example of a 2,000-man management population, we have a surplus of 120 managers. The annual cost of this surplus is as high as $3.6 million (assuming an annual average salary of $30,000, but not taking into account the costs of fringe benefits). If only half of this surplus of 120 managers is reduced by the green stamp program, we are well ahead—the $1 million program cost produces a $1.8 million reduction in surplus manager cost.

There would, of course, be some expense connected with the counseling and placement services needed to make the new program work, but this cost should be only slightly, if at all, greater than the cost of administering current educational job-related programs.

Additional Incentives

To help the plan work, there should also be a certain amount of financial security to accompany the second-career venture. Separation pay should be paid following a prescribed corporate guide. Bear in mind that since 45 service credits (10 of them for service) are necessary for early retirement, most managers would have put in 15 to 20 years of service. Separation pay would range from six months' to a year's salary or more. Also, medical and life insurance benefits could be continued for 2 years, after which the individual could be given a conversion option.

For individuals who plan to enter their own business, low-interest loans could be made available, as is already done in some companies today. The amount would be determined on the same basis as any other business loan. Lastly, the individual should have the option of either receiving a lump-sum retirement payment immediately or deferring retirement payment until he or she is age 55 or 60, whatever is the normal time for the company to begin payments.

HOW REALISTIC?

Is the whole idea of a second career idealistic? Is it unrealistic to expect many managers to start over again at 45 or 50?

Starting over means a reduction in income. It means giving up one's present standard of living—the five-bedroom house, country-club membership, private-school education for the remaining children, and so on. The financial problems of starting a second career are indisputable. On the other hand, preparation for a second career is insurance against the possibility of becoming a shelf sitter, which in most cases is far more tragic than the financial inconvenience of starting over. A second career is the alternative to becoming a "corporate vegetable."

Let us go back to Harry Allen once more. Suppose Harry's company has had a green stamp plan in force for some years. How would Harry feel after being passed over for the second time and being declared surplus? Undoubtedly not so hurt as he was in the earlier description, if we assume that a man of Harry's caliber would have been prudent enough to forgo some golf, some TV viewing, and some evenings with his family in order to cash in his educational green stamps.

Some executives find it difficult to believe that the Harry Allens of business are so prudent and self-motivated. If they are right, then management should establish these policies:

1. Notify a manager when he has been passed over for a significant promotion for the first time. (All too often today, being passed over is kept a secret from the manager.)

2. Instruct the manager to meet with a green stamps counselor, who reviews the situation with him and reminds him that he had better cash in his green stamps quickly, if he has not already done so. The counselor should make it clear that the screening process for future promotion will take place whether the manager has prepared himself or not. "Why gamble?" should be the theme of the meeting.

Such meetings would impress on Harry that his company encourages second-career preparation for all managers and does not regard such actions as disloyal. From the adviser he would learn of prospective areas of future employment. For example, if the conference were taking place today, he would learn that there are immediate openings for managers in hous-

ing programs and in health administration, for teachers in junior colleges, and for managers and specialists in all sorts of federal, state, and local government jobs. True, the salaries are not so high in these jobs, but Harry knows that, if he does have to retire early, he can count on his pension or separation benefits to bolster his finances.

He may also learn of opportunities for starting new businesses and of low-interest loans available from the company. He knows that one option of his early retirement pension allows for lump-sum payments which could tide him over the start-up period in a new business.

Retirement Payments

How much early retirement money would Harry Allen receive? Let us go back to our assumptions at the beginning of this article. Harry is 49, his present salary is $35,000, and he has 18 years of service with the company.

First, Harry is entitled to separation pay. A reasonable calculation is one week of salary for each six months of service, that is:

1. $\dfrac{\$35,000}{52 \text{ weeks}}$ = $673/week
2. 18 years = 36 six-month periods
             = 36 weeks' separation pay
3. 36 × $673 = $24,228

Next, Harry can calculate his retirement benefit. He finds that in 18 years he has earned a total income of $400,000. Retirement benefit formulas naturally vary from company to company, but if the ABC Corporation's formula is like that used by many other companies, Harry will find that he is entitled to $6,300 annually, starting at age 65, for the remainder of his life.

For early retirement, however, this amount would be paid for only the next 10 years. Or, if he desires, Harry has the option of receiving a lump-sum payment of $63,000 (the 10-year payment) less the accrued interest, or about $48,000. If he took this option, he would receive about $72,000 on leaving the company (that is, the sum of $24,228 separation pay + $48,000 lump-sum retirement).

This is a reasonable amount for Harry to have to help him over his first few years of a second career. Any other income-bearing plans such as Harry's own personal investments and savings or a company plan would, of course, add to his overall financial security.

CONCLUSION

If Harry Allen is passed over eventually, after he has completed retraining for a second career, he will not be the same man of our opening example. He can take early retirement and start in on a new career, hopefully one offering satisfaction and dignity. Or he can brace himself for probable demotion to the level where his performance once again is satisfactory or better.

In either case, the chances are strong that, while he may be disappointed not to get the promotion, he will not be bitter at the company or his associates. As for the senior executives who made the decision to pass him over, they will not have to feel guilty about it. They did not do Harry Allen in.

Dealing with the Aging Work Force

Jeffrey Sonnenfeld

The extension of mandatory retirement to age 70, signed into U.S. law last April, has caught most organizations off-guard and has surfaced latent fears about the general age drift in the work force. Management experts and journalists over the last year or so have become quite vocal in their prophecies about the changing complexion of the work force.

We used to hear predictions about the "greening of America." Now we hear references to impending problems resulting from the "graying of America," as the country belatedly awakens to the composite effects of demographic trends, improvements in life expectancy, and changes in social legislation. Executives are being warned to anticipate changes in employee performance and attitudes, performance appraisals, retirement incentives, training programs, blocked career paths, union insurance pensions, and affirmative action goals, among other worrisome issues.

Business managers have been the target of superficial and conflicting admonitions appearing in the press. As the chief executive of a leading paper company recently complained to me, "At first we were interested in the warnings. Now, they all say the same things. We hear all the fire alarms being sounded, but no one suggests where we should send the engines."

The needs of a very different work force overshadow many of the other issues of the 1980s for which managers must prepare their organizations. Just as other organizational activities must adapt to a changing environment, human resource planning dictates a major overhaul in recruitment, development, job structure, incentives, and performance appraisal. Thus management attention should now be focused on specific problems in mid- and late-career planning.

It is hard enough to comprehend the individual aging process without at the same time assessing the effects of an entire population growing older. If Congress and President Carter had not extended the work years, leaders of America's organizations would still have had to face troublesome human resource changes.

As a consequence of the 43 million babies born in the years immediately following World War II, a middle-aged bulge is forming and eventually the 35- to 45-year-old age group will increase by 80%. By the year 2030, this group will be crossing the infamous bridge to 65,

Jeffrey Sonnenfeld, "Dealing with the Aging Work Force," *Harvard Business Review*, November-December 1978, Copyright © 1978 by the President and Fellows of Harvard College; all rights reserved.

increasing the relative size of that population from 12% of all Americans to 17%, a jump from 31 million to 52 million people.[1]

Some labor analysts point out that even those Department of Labor statistics are conservative, for likely changes downward in the mortality rate due to advanced medical treatment are not reflected in the predictions. Today, the average life expectancy is about age 73, which is 10 years longer than the years of life expected at birth in the 1950s.

On examining the rate of this change, one sees that the size of the preretirement population, between the ages of 62 and 64, will not be affected dramatically until the year 2000. Until that time, this group will expand at an annual rate of 7.6% above 1975 figures. Between 2000 and 2010, however, it will grow by 48%. For one to assume, however, that there are at least 22 years before major problems arise would be incorrect. This population bulge will be moving through several critical career phases before reaching the preretirement years.

One should pause and reflect on how, in just the next ten years, the population bulge will be lodged in the "mid-life crisis" age. This added strain will magnify the traditional work and nonwork problems associated with the sense of limited opportunity at that age. Even sooner, the decline in youth population, which is currently causing the consolidation of secondary schools, will shift the balance of power and the approach in company recruitment.

As a consequence, a dwindling young work force will make it more difficult to fill entry-level positions. Already there are predictions about shortages in blue-collar occupations by the mid-1980s.[2] It is not at all too soon for managers to start investigating their company demographics.

On top of the foregoing, the recent legislation on extending mandatory retirement further heightens the concern about job performance in the later years. Sooner than even the advocates of this legislation dreamed, business managers find themselves faced with contemplating the implications of long-tenured senior employees.

The immediate impact of this legislation depends, of course, on how older workers respond to the opportunity to remain on the job. Many companies are looking at the well-publicized trend toward earlier retirement, and concluding that this trend will counteract the effects of extended tenure possibilities. Labor force participation rates are dropping for workers age 55 and older and for those age 60 and over.

A retirement expert on the National Industrial Conference Board, a business research organization, said, "People want to retire while they are still young and healthy enough to enjoy the activities of their choice."[3] Another Conference Board researcher reported that these younger retirees are interested in education, in traveling, and in spending more and more money on themselves.[4]

Also, Victor M. Zin, director of Employee Benefits at General Motors, commented, "There used to be a stigma to going out. He was over the hill, but now it's a looked-for status. Those retirement parties, they used to be sad affairs. They are darn happy affairs now. The peer pressure is for early retirement."[5]

Research suggests, however, that such a trend reflects worker income, education, job conditions, and retirement security. Dissatisfied workers and those with better pension plans seem to be more likely to opt out earlier. The experience of Sears, Roebuck and Polaroid, and several insurance companies which have already introduced flexible retirement, shows that at least 50% of those workers reaching age 65 remain on the job. In contrast, only 7% of auto workers take advantage of the opportunity to continue past age 65.

Gerontologists also do not support an early retirement trend. They cite the greater political activity of older Americans, the increasing average age of nursing home occupants, and a 1974 Harris Poll survey of retirees over 65 who claimed they would still work if they had not been forced out.[6] Such a reversed trend might be strengthened as age 65 becomes early retirement and workers see extended career opportunities.

MID-CAREER CONSIDERATIONS

With the projection of middle-aged workers shortly comprising a large part of the work force, and with greater numbers of older people a certainty later on, executives have good reason to be interested in relationships between age and performance.

Important age and performance considerations are manifest in younger workers well before they ever become established members of the "gray work force." In looking across the occupations of those in their mid-30s to mid-40s, one sees career drops in performance and morale, along with higher rates of turnover. There has also traditionally been higher mobility in these mid-life years as well.

Longitudinal career studies tracking people over ten-year intervals for the past three decades show that, despite growing barriers to employment in certain occupations, there has been an outstanding peak in job mobility for those in their mid-30s to mid-40s. This mobility may vary somewhat across occupations because of exceptionally high turnover rates in some jobs such as sales and service.

Candidates for second careers tend to be in their 40s and report a perceived discrepancy between personal aspirations and current opportunities for achievement and promotion. This gap widens as the opportunity for advancement decreases and results in major career frustration.

Occupational Stagnation

A survey of over one thousand middle-aged men in managerial and professional positions found that five out of every six respondents endured a period of severe frustration and trauma which began in their early 30s. Work performance, emotional stability, and physical health were seriously affected. The study also found that one out of every six middle-aged workers never fully recovered from traumatic realizations that their sense of eternal youth had been replaced by physical deterioration and greater sensitivity to the inevitability of death. The loss of spirit led to lowered goals and diminished self-expectations.

Psychologist Erik Erikson first brought academic attention to this mid-career crisis, characterizing it as the locus of a conflict between feelings of "generativity versus stagnation."[7] The middle-aged worker senses that new starts in life are coming to an end.

Gerontologist Bernice Neugarten, reporting on her research that indicated a new perspective on "time" appears in the mid-to-late 30s, commented:

"Life is restructured in terms of time-left-to-live rather than time-since-birth. Not only the reversal in directionality, but the awareness that time is finite is a particularly conspicuous feature of middle age. Thus 'you hear so much about deaths that seem premature—that's one of the changes that come over you over the years. Young fellows never give it a thought....' The recognition that there is 'only so much time left' was a frequent theme ... those things don't quite penetrate when you're in your 20s and you think that life is all ahead of you."[8]

Harvard psychiatrist George E. Vaillant likens this period to the stresses of adolescence and rebellion against authority and structure. His original clinical research tracks people through 40 years of life, and provides a valuable in-depth analysis of adult development. Vaillant feels that, by 40, people "put aside the preconceptions and the narrow establishment aims of their 30s and begin once again to feel gangly and uncertain about themselves. But always, such transitional periods in life provide a means of seizing one more change and finding a new solution to instinctive or interpersonal needs."[9]

From his clinical studies of people progressing through their middle years, Yale psychologist Daniel Levinson argues, "This is not an extended adolescence, but a highly formative, evolving phase of adult life." He found that, while a smooth transition is indeed possible, more often dramatic chaos is likely to characterize mid-life transition. One's former life structure (e.g., occupation, marital life) suddenly seems inappropriate and new choices must be made.

According to Levinson, "If these choices are congruent with his dreams, values, talents, and possibilities, they provide the basis for a relatively satisfactory life structure. If the choices are poorly made and the new structure seriously flawed, however, he will pay a heavy price in the next period."[10]

Regardless of the causes of this stressful period, several events in society indicate that the symptoms will soon spread in epidemic proportions:

First, those persons reaching the mid-career period in the next ten years will have achieved far higher educational levels and associated higher aspirations than ever experienced by this group previously. By 1980, one out of four workers will have a college degree.

Second, the pattern of occupational growth suggests increasingly insufficient opportunities for advancement in a narrower occupational hierarchy. Unfavorable predictions of future needs through 1985 by the Bureau of Labor Statistics confirm the cause for distress. Professional positions will remain scarce, and the expanded demands of the 1960s for engineers, scientists, and teachers, which influenced so many young people to undertake higher education, will remain history. Clerical, sales, service, and operative workers are expected to be in demand.

Third, the size of the postwar baby boom means intense competition for whatever opportunities do exist. This competitiveness is due to the bulk of the population being at the same career point rather than being more evenly distributed.

Finally, the new legislation on mandatory retirement threatens to further limit opportunities for advancement.

Organizations should prepare now for the inevitable frustrations of career stagnation in the middle years. Already there are individual and organized complaints from those who say that somehow society has cheated them. After investing valuable years in expensive higher education, following glowing promises held out by society, graduates are entering a stagnant labor market. In many cases, academic degrees have become excess baggage to those recipients who are forced to enter the labor market at inappropriate levels.

Many research studies have warned about the growing expectations for self-fulfillment in work. Poor physical health, mental maladjustment, and social disenchantment are consequences of status confict.

Some social analysts have suggested that anarchistic tendencies of the terrorists in Italy and other parts of Europe are expressions of rage against betrayal by the social order. The fury that burned college buildings in this country in the last decade may strike again in the coming decade, as that generation reacts in frustration to limited opportunities and a sense of defeat.

Stereotyped Perception

One of the fears of businessmen is that they will no longer be able to ease out older workers. Much of the initial reaction to the recognition of a graying work force has been to try to figure out new ways of "weeding out the deadwood." Pension inducements, less generous and "more realistic" performance appraisals, and other rationalizations for eliminating older, less desirable workers are being developed.

Who should be the target of those designs? Columnist William L. Safire has echoed the fears of many businessmen who link age to performance:

". . . old people get older and usually less productive, and they ought to retire so that business can be better managed and more economically served. We should treat the elderly with respect which does not require treating them as if they were not old. If politicians start inventing 'rights' that cut down productivity, they infringe on the consumer's right to a product at the lowest cost . . ."[11]

THE LATER YEARS

It is important to explore how much factual evidence there is to support the stereotyping and the prejudices that link age with senility, incompetence, and lack of worth in the labor market. Age 65 was an arbitrarily selected cutoff age used by New Deal planners who looked back historically to Bismark's social welfare system in nineteenth century Germany.

Certainly, one does not have to look hard to find the elderly among the greatest contributors to current society. The list is long of older citizens who have made major contributions in all fields including the arts, industry, science, and government, and who continue to be worthy and inspiring members of our society.

Age-related Change

Physiological changes are most pronounced and most identified with old age, but vary markedly in degree between individuals of the same age. It is not clear what changes are actually a result of aging and what can be attributed to life-styles. Researchers indicate, however, that after age 50 life-style becomes a less influential factor in physiological change than aging itself.

Among age-related changes are declines in the sensory processes, particularly vision, failures in the immunity system that lead to cardiovascular and kidney problems, and degenerative diseases such as rheumatoid arthritis. While 85% of those workers over 65 suffer from chronic diseases, these are not sudden afflictions. Hence 75% of those 60 to 64 years old suffer from these diseases, many of which can be controlled by modern medical treatment. The major effects of these diseases are loss of strength in fighting off invaders and loss of mobility.

Reaction time seems to be affected by the increase in random brain activity, or "neural noise," which distracts the brain from responding to the proper neural signals. A fall in the signal-to-noise ratio would lead to a slower performance and increased likelihood of error. To correct for this possibility of error, performance is delayed to permit time to gain greater certainty. Research on cognitive abilities shows that older people are more scrupulous in the use of decision criteria before responding or forming associations required for decision making. Older people are less likely to use mnemonic or "bridging" mechanisms to link similar concepts. They require a 75% chance of

certainty before committing themselves, while younger people will take far greater risks.[12]

When time pressure is not a relevant factor, the performance of older people tends to be as good, if not better, than that of younger people. In self-paced tests and in self-paced learning situations, older people do not have to make speed versus accuracy trade-offs and, consequently, their performance is higher.

Learning is also inhibited by the delayed signal-to-noise ratio since it interferes with memory. Most of the learning difficulties of older people stem from acquisition and recall rather than from retention. This relates to the two-step process of memory involving an initial introduction and a later retention period. That is, older people have a harder time holding information in short-term memory, awaiting long-term storage, due to neural noise. This is the same sort of problem older people have with recall.

However, once the information reaches long-term storage, it can be retained. The process of inputting the information, and retrieving it, can become blocked for intervals of time. Cognition is perhaps the most important difficulty of older workers and relates to problem solving, decision making, and general learning ability. Training in appropriate mental techniques can overcome many of these short-term memory blockages.

Similarly, intelligence tests often have age biases built in with the inherent speed versus accuracy trade-off. Recent researchers have tried to avoid such a bias and have found problem solving, number facility, and verbal comprehension to be unaffected by age. The ability to find and apply general rules to problem solving are more related to an individual's flexibility and education than to age.

Work Attitude

Research studies on all sectors of the American work force have found that age and job satisfaction seemed to bear positive relationships, but it has become apparent that it is hard to consider job satisfaction without considering what aspects of the work experience are important to the individual.[13] Organizations must carefully consider the type of satisfaction which they are measuring, and try to determine how both the more productive and less productive workers in different age groups vary. Perhaps the types of incentives built into a company's rewards package may encourage the less productive, rather than the more productive, older workers to remain with the company.

Along the same line, increasing monetary benefits but not expanding opportunities for job variety would be a serious mistake if the desired workers are more interested in personal growth and achievement than in financial incentives. Mastery and achievement are closely related to job satisfaction. As such, the need for mastery, or recognized accomplishment, becomes increasingly important.

Thus sudden change in job structure and social networks can be threatening to older workers. Their niche in society is defined largely by their contribution in the work place. The job presents friendship, routine, a sense of worth, and identity. Obsolescence and job change are major fears of older workers.

Job Performance

In reviewing studies of performance by occupation for different age groups, it is important to be aware of biases built into the performance appraisals themselves. On top of this, cross-sectional studies of different age groups are also viewing different individuals. It is quite possible that selection factors in older populations explain much of the difference between older and younger populations. In other words, the older workers staying on the job may be different somehow in their skills or interests in that they have managed to remain on the same job.

Looking first at *managers*, one once again sees the manifestation of the tendency toward caution with age. Victor H. Vroom and Bernd Pahl found a relationship between age and risk taking and also between age and the value placed on risk.[14] They studied 1,484 managers, age 22 to 58, from 200 corporations and used a choice-dilemma questionnaire. It seemed that the older managers were less willing to take

risks and had a lower estimate of the value of risk in general.

These findings are supported by another study on determinants of managerial information processing and decision-making performance; 79 male first-line managers with ages ranging from 23 to 57 years (a median of 40 years) were measured by the Personnel Decision Simulation Questionnaire.[15] Older decision makers tended to take longer to reach decisions even when the influence of prior decision-making experience was removed.

However, the older managers were better able to accurately appraise the value of the new information. Hesitancy about risk taking was also supported in this study; older decision makers were less confident in their decisions.

Another study focusing on task-oriented groups also found that older group members once again sought to minimize risk by seeking more reliable direction.[16] Younger members were more willing to shift authority within the group and to make better use of the experience of others. In this way, younger members of the group were more flexible and more tolerant.

Studies of professionals generally concentrate on *scientists* and *engineers*. Perhaps this is because their output is so easy to measure (e.g., publications, patents). Such studies have found bimodal distributions of innovativeness as a function of age. That is to say, there were two peaks of productivity separated by ten-year intervals in research laboratories compared with development laboratories. The first peak in research laboratories occurred by age 40, and the second peak did not appear until age 50. In the development laboratories, the first peak occurred around age 45 to 50, and the second appeared around age 55 to 60.[17] These studies tracked contribution longitudinally over a person's career.

Wider studies of scholarship and artistic contribution revealed a similar first peak at about age 40 and a second peak in the late 50s. Looking more broadly at productivity, it is clear that creative activity was lowest for the 21- to 50-year old group and generally increased with age.[18] It is also a fact, however, that younger scholars and scientists have a more difficult time achieving recognition in the journal networks than do their senior colleagues.

Older people seem to have achieved superior standing among *sales workers* as well and to have remained higher performers. Reports from insurance companies, auto dealers, and large department stores suggest that age is an asset, if a factor at all, in performance.

In a large study of sales clerks in two major Canadian department stores, performance improved with age and experience, the actual peak performance of the sales clerks being about age 55.[19] In several organizations, particularly high technology companies, however, morale plummeted corresponding to length of service. These latter organizations may have used sales as a traditional entry position for managerial development. Those employees remaining on the job over ten years began to perceive frustration in their personal goals of managerial advancement.

Age has had surprisingly little effect on *manual workers*. In several studies, performance seemed to remain fully steady through age 50, peaking slightly in the 30s. The decline in productivity in the 50s never seemed to drop more than 10% from peak performance. Attendance was not significantly affected, and the separation rate (quits, layoffs, discharges) was high for those under age 25 and very low for those over 45.[20]

These findings may not only indicate greater reliability among older workers, but also suggest that those who have remained on the job are, in some way, the most competent. Such a sorting out of abilities may not take place equally well across all industries. While tenure among factory workers within industries is reduced with age, absenteeism rates in heavy industry and construction do increase with age. This may be a more evident consequence of mismatches between job demands and physical abilities.

Finally, the high variation of manual labor performance within age groups, compared with the variation between age groups, suggests that individual differences are much more important than age group differences. The need to evaluate potential on an individual basis, and

not by age group, has been convincingly established in these studies.

Considerable variation within age groups is found in studies on *clerical workers* as well. A study of 6,000 government and private industry office workers found no significant difference in output by age. Older workers had a steadier rate of work and were equally accurate. Researchers in many studies found that older clerical workers, both male and female, generally had attendance records equal to that of other workers, as well as lower rates of turnover.[21]

Corporate Experience

Many well-publicized reports identify particular companies in various parts of the country which have never adopted mandatory retirement policies yet have continued to be profitable and efficient with workers well into their 70s and 80s. For example, Thomas Greenwood, president of Globe Dye works in Philadelphia, who has retained workers hired by his grandfather, commented, "As long as a man can produce, he can keep his job."[22] The 87-year-old president of Ferle, Inc., a small company owned by General Foods, which employs workers whose average age is 71, commented, "Older people are steadier, accustomed to the working discipline."[23] Sales workers at Macy's department stores in New York have never had to conform to a mandatory retirement age, and have demonstrated no apparent decline in performance attributable directly to age.

Banker's Life and Casualty Company proudly points to its tradition of open-ended employment, retaining top executives, clerks, and secretaries through their late 60s, 70s, and 80s. Of the 3,500 workers in Banker's home office, 3.5% are over 65 years of age. Some have been regular members of the Banker's work force, while others have come after being forced into retirement from other companies. The company reports that older workers show more wisdom, are more helpful and thorough, and perform their duties with fewer personality clashes. Studies on absenteeism at Banker's Life and Casualty show that those over 65 have impressive attendance records.

Large companies that have changed to flexible retirement plans in recent years have had similar satisfactory performance reports. U.S. Steel has permitted more than 153,000 nonoffice employees to continue working as long as they can maintain satisfactory levels of performance and can pass medical examinations.

Polaroid has found that those employees who choose to remain on the job after age 65 tend to be better performers. Company retirement spokesman, Joe Perkins, explained, "If you like to work, you're usually a good worker." He added that attendance is also exemplary as older workers" . . . often apologize for having missed work one day, three years ago because of a cold. There is a fantastic social aspect as people look forward to coming to work." No one is shifted between jobs at Polaroid unless the worker requests a change. Even among older workers whose jobs entail heavy physical demands high performance is maintained.

Performance Appraisal

Generally the companies just mentioned have not had to deal with older workers who remain on the job despite poor performance. There is no guarantee that workers will always be able or willing to perform well, and to relinquish their jobs when they are no longer capable of fulfilling the job requirements. Even if both the company and the individual want to continue their relationship, it is not always possible to effectively match an employee's skills with the company's job opportunities.

This need to identify differences between more and less productive older workers is a difficult distinction to make with current performance measurement techniques. The process must be objective, consistent, and based on criteria that are uniformly applied and which will endure court challenges. Arthur C. Prine, Jr., vice president of R.R. Donnelley & Sons Company, recently explained, "As soon as you pick and choose, you'll scar a lot of people when they are most sensitive. I just dread the thought of calling someone and saying, 'You've worked for forty-five years and have done a wonderful

job, but you've been slipping and you must retire.'"[24]

Instead of carrying less productive older workers near retirement on the payroll, employers may begin to weed them out earlier in an effort to deter age-discrimination charges. Richard R. Shinn, president of Metropolitan Life, forecasts that "employers are going to make decisions earlier in careers if it appears that someone is going to be a problem as time goes on."[25]

Thus predictions of future performance will be important criteria in performance appraisal. Even the use of formal standard evaluations does not eliminate age bias or avoid self-fulfilling prophecies which prejudice the evaluation process.

Such a bias was shown in a recent poll of managers. A 1977 questionnaire of HBR readers concluded that "age stereotypes clearly influence managerial decisions."[26] HBR readers perceived older workers as more rigid and resistant to change and thus recommended transferring them out rather than helping them overcome a problem. The respondents preferred to retain but not retrain obsolete older employees and showed a tendency to withhold promotions from older workers compared with identically qualified younger workers.

Part of this discrimination problem is that many companies consider an employee's potential to be an important element in his evaluation. As mentioned in the section on basic abilities, chronological age never has been a valid means of measuring a worker's potential and now is illegal under the Age Discrimination Employment Act. The strength of various faculties may slightly correlate with age in certain regards, but there is no categorical proof that age has an effect on capabilities. Individuals vary greatly, and useful measures of potential must recognize such differences.

One of the best known functional measures was the GULHEMP system designed by Leon F. Koyl, physician from DeHaviland Aircraft.[27] This system had two dimensions, the first being a physical-mental profile and the second a job-demand profile. Workers were examined on seven factors of general physique, upper extremities, lower extremities, hearing, eye sight, mental features, and personality attributes. These individual factors were plotted on a graph and superimposed on similarly graphed job task profiles. Individuals were then viewed in relation to the job profiles available. While successful in its pilot experience, this federally supported project was not seen as a high priority government expenditure. Thus the project in functional age measurement was terminated.

Functional measures, however, are not the answer to the performance appraisal question. While they can provide the quantifiable "expert" criteria companies might need for age-discrimination suits, their strength lies in largely assessing the potentials of physical labor. The sensitive areas in performance appraisal are evaluations of the more nebulous factors.

Ratings of "mental abilities" and "personality attributes," which were the poorest factors on the GULHEMP scale, are the most sensitive areas in the appraisal process, and the only truly relevant dimensions in most white collar and managerial jobs. Some consulting firms have been assessing the important elements of successful job performance, appraising corporate personnel, and establishing appropriate organizational recruitment and development programs.

WHAT MANAGERS CAN DO

How can companies resolve the kinds of frustration expressed at the beginning of this article by the chief executive of the paper company? Where can they send the fire engines? It is far easier to read about social trends than to perceive ways of preparing for them. It is clear that America's work force is graying. Older workers will tend toward caution, will experience far greater levels of frustration, and will show signs of age individually at very different rates.

However, companies are not fated for stodginess. In this section let us look at six priorities for managers to consider in preparing for the impending dramatic change in their own internal environments:

1. *Age profile*
It has been demonstrated that age per se does not necessarily indicate anything significant about worker performance. Instead, executives should look at the age distribution across jobs in the organization, as compared with performance measures, to see what career paths might conceivably open in the organizations in the future and what past performance measures have indicated about those holding these positions.

2. *Job performance requirements*
Companies should then more precisely define the types of abilities and skills needed for various posts. A clear understanding of job specifications for all levels of the organization is necessary to plan for proper employee selection, job design, and avoidance of age-discrimination suits. For example, jobs may be designed for self-pacing, may require periodic updating, or may necessitate staffing by people with certain relevant physical strengths.

Several companies have looked at the skills needed in various jobs from the chief executive down to reenlisted older and even retired workers who have the needed experience and judgment. For example, as Robert P. Ewing, president of Banker's Life and Casualty, stated, "Our company sets performance standards for each job and these standards are the criteria for employment. Age doesn't count. Getting the job done does."

Such an approach requires careful assessment of needed job competence where traits, motives, knowledge, and skills are all evaluated. When this information is considered in relation to the magnitude and direction of planned company growth, future manpower needs can be predicted. Obsolete job positions can be forecast and workers retrained in advance. Necessary experience cannot be gained overnight, and development programs should be coordinated with precise company manpower needs.

3. *Performance appraisal*
Corresponding with improved job analyses, companies must improve their analyses of individual performance as well. Age biases are reflected in both the evaluation format and the

attitudes of managers. Management development programs should be aware of the need to correct these biases. Both Banker's Life and Polaroid have teams that audit the appraisals of older workers to check for unfair evaluations. These units have also been used to redress general age prejudice in the work place.

Companies need a realistic understanding of current work force capabilities for effective human resource planning. A company cannot adjust its development, selection, and job training strategies appropriately without knowing the current strengths and weaknesses of its workers. Additionally, potential courtroom challenges on staffing and reward procedures necessitate evidence of solid decision criteria.

4. *Work force interest surveys*

Once management acquires a clearer vision of the company's human resource needs, and what basic abilities its workers have, it must then determine what the current workers want. If management decides that it wants to selectively encourage certain types of workers to continue with the organization while encouraging turnover of other types, it must next determine what effects different incentives will have on each group.

In addition, management must be well aware of workers' desires and values so that it can anticipate and prepare for morale drops. Understanding work force aspirations is essential in reducing the harmful organizational and personal consequences of mid-career plateauing. For example, companies might offer counseling programs to those who frequently but unsuccessfully seek job changes, or might consider making alterations in the prevailing company culture and in the norms which link competence and mobility.

5. *Education and counseling*

Management may discover that its workers are also confronted with a variety of concerns regarding the direction of their lives after terminating current employment. Counseling on retirement and second-career development are becoming increasingly common to assist workers in adjusting to the major social disengagement following retirement.

IBM now offers tuition rebates for courses on any topic of interest to workers within three years of retirement, and continuing into retirement. Subject matter need not have any relation to one's job and many workers include courses in preparation for second careers (learning new skills, professions, and small business management).

Counseling is also important to address problems of the work force which remains on the job. Career planning to avoid mid-career plateauing, and training programs to reduce obsolescence, must be developed by each company. The educational programs must reflect the special learning needs of older workers. Self-paced learning, for example, is often highly effective. Older workers can learn new tricks, but they need to be taught differently.

6. *Job structure*

A better understanding of basic job requirements and employee abilities and interests may indicate a need to restructure jobs. Such restructuring cannot be done, however, until management knows what the core job tasks are in the organization and what types of changes should be instituted. Alternatives to traditional work patterns should be explored jointly with the work force. Some union leaders have expressed reservations about part-time workers whom they fear may threaten the power of organized labor. Management, too, wonders about its ability to manage part-time workers. Some part-time workers have found that they "lack clout and responsibility" in their jobs in small companies.

Management may have more flexibility than anticipated in changing conditions like work pace, the length or timing of the work day, leaves of absence, and challenges on the job. With a tightened reward structure for older workers, satisfaction with the job may shift increasingly to intrinsic features of one's current job.

America's work force is aging, but America's organizations are not doomed to hardening of the arteries. Older workers still have much to offer but organizations must look at certain policies to ensure that their human resources continue to be most effectively used.

Organizations must be alert to changing work force needs and flexible in responding to meet those needs.

REFERENCES

1. U.S. Bureau of the Census, "Current Population Reports," Series P-25, No. 61, *"Projections of the Population of the United States, 1975 to 2050"* (Washington, D.C.: U.S. Government Printing Office, 1975).
2. Neal H. Rosenthal, "The United States Economy in 1985: Projected Changes in Occupations," *Monthly Labor Review,* December 1973, p. 18.
3. Jerry Flint, "Early Retirement Is Growing in U.S.," *New York Times,* July 10, 1977.
4. Jerry Flint, "Businessmen Fear Problems from Later Age for Retirement," *New York Times*, October 2, 1977.
5. Ibid.
6. "The Graying of America," *Newsweek*, February 28, 1977, p. 50.
7. Erik Erikson, *Childhood and Society* (New York: Norton, 1963).
8. Bernice Neugarten, *Middle Age and Aging* (Chicago: University of Chicago Press, 1968), p. 97.
9. George E. Vaillant, *Adaptation to Life* (Boston: Little Brown, 1977), p. 193.
10. Daniel J. Levinson, "The Mid-Life Transition: A Period in Adult Psychosocial Development," *Psychiatry*, 40, 1977, p. 104.
11. William L. Safire, "The Codgerdoggle," *New York Times*, September 3, 1977, p. 29.
12. For an example of research on cognitive abilities, see A.T. Welford, "Thirty Years of Psychological Research on Age and Work," *Journal of Occupational Psychology*, 49, 1976, p. 129.
13. See, for example, John W. Hunt and Peter N. Saul, "The Relationship of Age, Tenure, and Job Satisfaction in Males and Females," *Academy of Management Journal,* 20, 1975, p. 690; also, Bonnie Carroll, "Job Satisfaction," *Industrial Gerontology*, 4, Winter 1970.
14. Victor H. Vroom and Bernd Pahl, "Age and Risk Taking Among Managers," *Journal of Applied Psychology*, 12, 1971, p. 22.
15. Ronald N. Taylor, "Age and Experience as Determinants of Managerial Information Processing and Decision Making Performance," *Academy of Management Journal,* 18, 1975, p. 602.
16. Ross A. Webber, "The Relation of Group Performance to Age of Members in Homogeneous Groups," *Academy of Management Journal*, 17, 1974, p. 570.
17. Ronald C. Pelz, "The Creative Years in Research Environments," Industrial and Electrical Engineering, Transaction of the Professional Technical Group on Engineering Management, 1964, EM-11, p. 23, as referenced in L.W. Porter, *"Summary of the Literature on Personnel Obsolescence,"* Conference on Personnel Obsolescence, Dallas, Stanford Research Institute and Texas Instruments, June 21-23, 1966.
18. Wayne Dennis, "Creative Productivity Between the Ages of 20 and 80 Years," *Journal of Gerontology*, 21, 1966, p. 1.
19. *"Age and Performance in Retail Trades,"* Ottawa, Canadian Department of Labor, 1959, as referenced in Carol H. Kelleher and Daniel A. Quirk, "Age Functional Capacity and Work: An Annotated Bibliography," *Industrial Gerontology,* 19, 1973, p. 80.
20. U.S. Department of Labor, *The Older American Worker*, Report to the Secretary of Labor, title 5, sec. 715 of the Civil Rights Act of 1964 (Washington, D.C.: U.S. Government Printing Office, June 1965).
21. See, for example, U.S. Department of Labor, Bureau of Labor Statistics, *Comparative Job Performance by Age: Office Workers,* Bulletin No. 1273 (Washington, D.C.: U.S. Government Printing Office, 1960); and U.S. Department of Labor, Bureau of Labor Statistics, *Comparative Performance by Age: Large Plants in the Men's Footwear and Household Furniture Industries,* Bulletin No. 1223 (Washington, D.C.: U.S. Government Printing Office, 1957).
22. J.L. Moore, "Unretiring Workers, to These

Employees, The Boss is a Kid," *Wall Street Journal,* December 7, 1977.

23. S. Terry Atlas and Michael Rees, "Old Folks at Work," *Newsweek,* September 26, 1977, p. 64.

24. Irwin Ross, "Retirement at Seventy a New Trauma for Management," *Fortune,* May 8, 1978, p. 108.

25. Ibid.

26. Benson Rosen and Thomas H. Jerdee, "Too Old or Not Too Old," HBR November-December 1977, p. 105.

27. Leon F. Koyl and Pamela M. Hanson, *Age, Physical Ability and Work Potential* (New York: National Council on the Aging, 1969).

Section 6

The Meaning of Success

Success has been a dominant theme in our efforts to better understand managerial career issues; however, in many respects, we know very little about the meaning of success itself. For the most part we have assumed a very specific, achievement-oriented definition. Thus, success means rising to the top of the organization as quickly as possible. Since success is probably a very personal concept, it is naive for us to assume such a universal, limited meaning.

In the first reading in this section, Tarnowieski challenges our preconceived notions of success. He presents the results of his research on the changing success ethic and concludes that the American manager's idea of success is a very personal one. It is not always related to achievement and advancement in the organization. For many, success means peace of mind, harmony, and balance in one's personal and professional life; and job satisfaction, or self-actualization. The results suggest that we cannot accept a global or universal model of success, but instead must strive for greater understanding and acceptance of diverse success orientations.

Not only do we need to expand our definition of success, but we also need to consider some of the dysfunctional consequences of the traditional success orientation. Overinvolvement, overcommitment, and stress are but a few of the possible consequences of this achievement-oriented success norm. In the second selection Steiner begins to consider the "costs" of success. He identifies interpersonal problems, physical ailments, and on-the-job difficulties as the result of the tension which often accompanies the rise in economic, professional, and social status.

Toward a New Definition of Success

Dale Tarnowieski

For some people, success is a way of life and not a goal.
—D. Tarnowieski

What is success? This is a question that each man must answer for himself. No blanket definition of success is possible. In fact, a number of businessmen participating in this study believe success to be an individual phenomenon which defies definition altogether.

Each survey respondent was given an opportunity to define success in his own terms. About 55 percent of the responding executives did so, and their individual definitions have been grouped by similarity under the several generalized definitions listed in Exhibit 28.

More than a third of the responding businessmen define success in terms of the *achievement* of either specified or unspecified goals. Here, the emphasis is almost always on achievement, accomplishment, or reward rather than on the goals themselves. Where specific goals are referred to, they are varied: personal, career- or family-related, altruistic, simplistic or complex, and very often an aggregate. The fact that so many respondents equate success with the sense of personal satisfaction derived from

achievement is not surprising. In the broad American historical experience, achievement is a traditional and dominant theme. The drive to achieve has always been a fundamental American characteristic, and these survey results suggest that it is very likely to continue to greatly influence the American idea of success.

These definitions are representative of those grouped under *achievement*:

- Success is being inwardly satisfied with one's outward performance.
- Success is being satisfied with what you have done with your life.
- Success is that feeling of satisfaction deep down inside oneself with a goal achieved, a task at last accomplished, a job well done.

As can be seen in the exhibit, about one in every eight respondents defines success in terms that suggest a basic understanding of the concepts with which the research and writings of the late Abraham Maslow are concerned. Many

173

Exhibit 28 1,548 businessmen define success in their own terms*

Success defined in terms of . . .	No. of Respon- dents
1. Achievement of goals	535
2. Self-actualization	192
3. Harmony among personal, profes- sional, family, and social objectives	181
4. Making a contribution to a greater good	121
5. Happiness or peace of mind	115
6. Greater job satisfaction	98
7. Self-respect and the respect of others	49
8. Enjoyment in doing or in being	39
9. Job and financial security	38
10. Honesty and personal integrity	37
11. Spiritual growth	19
12. Family	11
13. Authority over others	5
14. Other	97**
Total	1,548

*Groupings were made from their written responses to an unstructured question.
**26 respondents suggested that success is an individ- ual phenomenon which cannot be defined.

respondents refer specifically to Maslow's concept of self-actualization. Other respondents refer to Maslow by name. For the 192 businessmen whose personal definitions of success have been grouped under self-actualization, success is largely synonymous with maximum self-realization, with self-discovery, with progressive self-development toward what Maslow termed "full humanness," an increased understanding of "one's own deep nature."

One respondent defines success as simply "growth toward 'self-actualization'"; another, as that state of being one arrives at "when 'actual' is the same as 'potential.'" An examination of the nearly 200 individual definitions provided by the respondents in the "self-actualization" category reveals that for most of these businessmen the rewards in life are principally derived from increased self-awareness—knowledge of themselves and their capabilities, and the application of that knowledge wherever the conditions of experience allow. One respondent

put it this way: "Success is growth. With few exceptions, nature takes care of the body—a boy will physically grow into a man. But each man, by himself, through his own initiative, must nurture his own intellect and nourish his own soul."

For 181 businessmen success means *harmony*—harmony among their various personal, professional, and social aspirations. For these respondents, success is balance—a harmonious balance among objectives. It seems to be very important to these respondents that their various goals, in whatever realms of experience, are compatible, each with the other.

Only about one percent of the businessmen reporting define success in essentially spiritual or religious terms. Of those who do, three out of every four are between the ages of 30 and 49. No respondent under 30—and only one businessman 60 years of age or older—framed his personal definition of success around religious or spiritual concepts.

It is interesting to note that while respondents 39 years of age or younger account for only 32 percent of the total survey sample, nearly 44 percent of all businessmen who think of success in terms of "happiness," "peace of mind," or "enjoyment in 'doing' or in 'being'" are under 40. It is older respondents (over 40 years of age), for the most part, who define success in terms of "self-actualization." Most of these businessmen are employed in top- or executive-level management, while middle- and supervisory-level managers are more apt to equate success with happiness, peace of mind, or enjoyment.

Relatively few respondents define success in terms of the long American tradition of rugged individualism. Few define success solely in terms of the development of *character*. Few definitions suggest that material well-being is the *summum bonum* in life, and only five respondents say that "authority" (authority over others) is an important measure of success. That so few equate authority with success is somewhat surprising, considering the substantial number of survey respondents who say that enhanced occupational status and authority is for them a primary life objective.

One observer with many years of both business and academic experience believes that "the minute rating for 'authority' suggests an unwillingness on the part of many businessmen to admit to the primacy of the power drive, chiefly because such an admission is no longer respectable or socially acceptable. A close examination of businessmen in action will reveal many more than these survey results suggest whose overall behavior is predominantly power-oriented."

A second observer with a background in education and research believes that the definitions of success provided by the AMA survey respondents indicate that success is, for most people, something personally determined and individually felt. "How success is defined by the individual in today's society, is increasingly determined by personal circumstance, private values, and knowledge of one's inherent or acquired capabilities. But when we talk about success, we are really talking, for the most part, about values. If the individual definitions of success provided by the businessmen surveyed are honest definitions, they tell us, by their variety, that the whole area of human values, like human beings themselves, is a highly complex, yet relative, subject."

A third observer believes that the results show that success is largely a psychological experience. "Success is a personal thing, an individualized phenomenon. Each man must decide for himself what success means to him, and then pursue his understanding in his own way. Few seem to define success in quantitative terms. Success is something inwardly *felt* according to most people in the survey."

A New York City clergyman who believes that a profound philosophical revolution is in the making in America and in other highly industrialized and technology-based societies offered this assessment after reviewing much of the AMA survey data:

I believe that the survey results confirm what I have sensed for some years now: more and more people—and I'm not just talking about young people, by the way—are beginning to more greatly value the richness, or the potential richness, of human experience and the rewards inherent in a social reality in which genuine opportunities for self-expression are nearly limitless. This is an encouraging sign for our society.

In recent times, we have anesthetized the human spirit, the human "will," to a far greater extent than the vanity resulting from our material accomplishments will allow most of us to admit. In the workplace, we call it *dehumanization*; in society at large, we call it *alienation*. It doesn't really matter what we call it, though. What is important to know is that when we rob men of their "will," their spirit, we take from them *life* itself. But self-preservation is the most powerful of all human instincts. If we do not hasten to return to the mass of men their *life,* they will take it back, and the consequences of their action, I fear, will be more tragic for our society than anything I can describe.

Sad but true, we know a thousand times more about industrial processes, for example, than we know about the essential nature, the inner workings, of man. But so many of the leaders of our society find it impossible to admit to themselves that men could perform such wonders, such technological marvels as are representative of our time, and know so little about themselves. But people everywhere are beginning to sense that something is terribly wrong and terribly out of balance in our society; they are beginning to insist that the needed changes be made—and change will come whether forced or voluntary.

A number of business leaders who examined the AMA survey data are troubled by the level of discontent with organizational life suggested by the responses of some status subgroups—middle and supervisory management personnel, in particular. One San Diego personnel executive's comments are representative of their concern. He cited the following passage from Roger M. D'Aprix's recent book *Struggle for Identity—The Silent Revolution Against Corporate Conformity.* D'Aprix contends that the vital task for organizational management in responding to changing employee values will be

. . . to inject meaning back into our work and to do so in supportive communities of people. It will require reordering of priorities. It will require retraining of managers. It will require new and dramatic modes of organization. Most of all, it will require the management of the organization to lead and to feel in ways that heretofore have been alien except in a few enlightened and progressive organizations. . . . It will require the individual to take on added responsibility for his own growth and to stand on his own two feet as a free and dignified person. It will also require him to renew his trust in people and his willingness to relate to others as an autonomous and real individual. And it will require him to make and sustain contact with other people in communities of common interest and concern. Finally, it will require a new tolerance on his part, a willingness to listen to and to try to comprehend the needs and aspirations of others. All in all, it will require nothing short of revolutionary change.[1]

The San Diego personnel executive believes that

people have worked for organizations too long; it is time for organizations to go to work for people. This will mean that most organizations will have to change their attitudes toward people, to stop looking at them through rose-tinted glasses that distort reality, to stop observing them through the eyes of wishes, fear, and preconceived notions that cause them to invent rather than to observe. Modern, complex, bureaucratic organizations are going to have to come to terms with the spirit of cooperation which is fast replacing competitiveness as the way in which increasing numbers of people want to get things done. If people are to feel like they're getting anywhere—getting anything accomplished for themselves or with respect to organizational objectives—the organizations for which they work are going to have to create an atmosphere in which all employees feel that everything humanly possible is being done to provide them every opportunity to expand their horizons—within their professional field, within their companies or organizations, and within the greater society. Our society has become too integrated for organizations to continue to believe that they can limit their concerns and interests to what happens between eight in the morning and five at night.

The personnel manager explained how organizations can enhance their *own* opportunities for success:

By doing nothing different from what I've just described. That is to say that the organization will enhance its own opportunities for success . . . will help itself most by helping its employees more. It will enhance its own well-being by helping the individuals that make up the organization to realize their full potential as managers, clerks, production employees, board chairmen, members of the bowling team, husbands, wives, young adults, part- or full-time students, doers, thinkers, and so on—you know, the "whole man."

What can the individual do to maximize his own opportunities for personal and professional growth? "The individual must begin to insist, as a matter of principle," the personnel executive emphasized, "that his employer provide him those opportunities."

A promotional brochure published last winter by The Personnel Association of Toronto, Inc., contained this brief statement about changing worker attitudes and values:

The raw, rugged, self-assertive individualism of employees driven by the need to maintain their existence and expecting to be managed in an authoritarian-submissive way is a value system which is changing. Employees are developing values encompassing awe, humility, integration, unity, simplicity and (a new) perception of reality. Insisting upon receiving trust and respect, these employees take their work seriously; yet they may be wrapped up in what they personally want to do. Such employees must be managed by "acceptance management"—taking them as they are without subordinating them to the organization.[2]

A review of the business literature provides many descriptions of the characteristics of organizations in which enlightened management is at work. An excellent description of the kind of corporate climate in which individuals may hope to maximize their growth opportunities was presented at Princeton University in 1961 by C. H. Greenewalt, then president of E. I. du Pont de Nemours & Company, Inc.:

The organizational process through which common men perform uncommon deeds cannot endure in the face of anything that deprives individuals of dignity, of belief in their own importance, of opportunity to test their powers of initiative, of experiencing the heartwarming spark of achievement.

The highest possible premium must be placed on fresh and original ideas untrammeled by traditional thinking. On this there must be no inhibiting restrictions. Organizations exist and prosper only by giving free reign to men's minds and spirit in a climate of achievement moderated by the practice of good manners. Both of these environmental conditions must somehow be preserved, but there is a stout and significant difference between observance of simple amenities and coercion or subservience; between conformity with codes of behavior designed to facilitate social intercourse and individual surrender to uniformity of thought.[3]

In an article for the March-April 1971 *Harvard Business Review,* James Lee suggests a number of the characteristics of the kind of progressive organization that Greenewalt is talking about. The trend in such organizations, in Lee's opinion, is

Toward
- More autonomy for individuals in institutional settings.
- Greater demand for information affecting autonomy, health and security, and increased ability to get this information.
- Wider participation in institutional planning and decision making.

- Greater dependence upon individual's judgment in institutional task performances.
- More widespread recognition of the potential power of the nonmanager to effect institutional goal attainment.
- More self-evaluation consistent with the implicit disciplines of the task.
- More response to the law of the situation.
- More organic organizational structures.

Away from
- Elitism (blood, class, or technical).
- Mechanistic organizational structures.
- Sacredness of management rights and institutional policies and procedures.
- Formal discipline based upon position authority.[4]

The AMA survey results strongly suggest that substantial numbers of businessmen would welcome the more organic, less mechanistic organizational environment that Greenewalt, Lee, and others envision. If enough of the new values which seem to be emerging in American society take hold in a commonplace manner, progressive organizations—both business and institutional—will be compelled to move away from elitism and rigidity of methods and structure and toward the establishment of an organizational climate that is more natural, more spontaneous, more organic—and not just on paper, but in practice. Many organizations will have to significantly change the ways in which they think and act, and those that do will be those that sense the direction in which human progress is moving.

What Price Success?

Jerome Steiner

Ever since Prometheus defied the gods of Olympus and dared to give the fire of intellect and knowledge to mankind, it has been acknowledged that a successful man's achievements are often won at the expense of his personal life.

The ulcer, our twentieth-century version of the vulture that daily disemboweled Prometheus in punishment for his daring achievement, is only one of the many symptoms of modern man who has lost touch with himself. As today's business managers move into top executive positions, they become increasingly prone to interpersonal problems which are reflected in alcohol ingestion, marital instability, sexual maladjustment, and physical complaints that sometimes lead them fruitlessly from doctor to doctor.

The executive may also develop on-the-job difficulties that increasingly separate him from those very subordinates with whom he was recently in competition and whom he must learn to trust and rely on. Moreover, he often becomes the object of increased demands for leadership and direction from social organizations which he originally joined for relaxation and companionship, or out of loyalty to personal ideals. At home, he may find that he has lost the art of contented leisure, communication with his wife and children, and a sure knowledge of the functional capacity of his physical being.

Certainly not all top executives enter a state of personal identity crisis when they achieve business success; and some develop only minor stresses, never recognizing the reasons for their discomfort and lowered efficiency. But all of these symptoms reflect the increase in tension that parallels a rise in social, economic, and business position.

The following is a brief history of a successful businessman whose name is fictitious, but whose personal identity crisis was real. His problems are not uncommon and may help us in understanding areas of stress and their effect on an executive's life and work.

THE CASE OF MR. BROWN

At age 45, Frank Brown is a self-made man. Although he has no academic degrees or special training, Brown was recently promoted to the vice presidency of a medium-sized manufacturing company. He is known as an assertive man who makes friends easily and is very active in community affairs (secretary of his lodge, president of his church group, Citizen of the Year in his town). He is married, has a son who was recently married and a daughter in college.

Despite many physical complaints, Brown is in good condition, other than being slightly overweight. His complaints include "gall bladder" attacks (no physiological basis was found for these), "allergic" irritation of the eyes, lower back pain, and insomnia. He was referred to a psychiatrist after his intestinal discomforts were unrelieved by medical treatment.

Critical History

After being discharged from the Army, Brown obtained a supervisory position in a large West Coast city. He married soon after and was sent to a branch office in the Midwest. He worked his way through staff positions and was eventually asked to set up an office in another city.

The family relocated and their first child was born. After spending five years in the new city, Brown accepted a more lucrative job, and the family moved again. He remained in this position for several years, having little difficulty in organizing and running a small office while he and his wife became involved in community activities and extensive entertaining. A second child was born.

Brown then accepted a job organizing an office for a new company, and his business responsibilities increased to include the hiring of staff and the supervision of middle-management personnel. He had little contact with lower-echelon personnel in the organization thereafter, but was well liked by the "management team." It was during this period that Mrs. Brown developed a number of psychosomatic complaints and the children began to manifest behavioral disorders necessitating referral to a child-guidance clinic.

The growth of the corporation resulted in management moving to another city. Mrs. Brown resented this move, but accepted it. After several years Brown began to feel that his outside activities were somehow not pleasing; he no longer looked forward to lodge and church meetings. His wife became active in various organizations, but the couple had few activities in common other than those involving Brown's business associates.

As his responsibility grew, Brown found that he had to spend increasing amounts of time "checking" his subordinates and ensuring

the smooth operation of his branch of the organization. His social life began to be restricted to business contacts, and even his occasional golf games were with people he knew in the business world. He became briefly depressed, but he was not aware of feeling this emotion predominantly.

Mrs. Brown suffered a more severe depression, consulted several psychiatrists, and began to take tranquilizing and antidepressant medication. The couple's sexual life dwindled and eventually stopped. It was during this time that Brown was referred to the psychiatrist. In addition to his physical problems, he complained that his wife did not understand him and had little sympathy for his discomfort. He also felt that he could no longer communicate with his children.

Now, at times of business expansion and business activity, Brown's depression is relieved and he is unaware of any difficulties. His physical complaints remain, however, and his secretary has taken the role of "nurse." The marital adjustment of his son has not been good, his daughter has been involved in numerous antisocial and rebellious activities, and his wife has become a regular psychiatric patient.

WHY DOES SUCCESS GO SOUR?

While Brown's problems did not develop overnight, his identity crisis occurred, unfortunately, at a period in life known to physicians as "involution"—the time in the life cycle (usually the early forties) when the body no longer responds as it once did to the dictates of the will. The speed of thinking is slowed, the memory is not as keen, and the physical machinery begins to break down.

Involution of the body is a crisis in itself because the involutional person, like the adolescent, must learn to know and accept a changed set of physical traits that he calls "himself." While these changes take place in everyone reaching middle age, an executive's upward mobility often imposes particular stresses, on both himself and his family, that can exacerbate the situation and lead to personal crisis. These stresses are particularly felt on the job, at home, and in social life.

On the Job

Until he is promoted to upper management, an individual usually has the personal goal of achieving high position. Once he arrives, however, he can no longer depend on this familiar goal in planning for the future. As he advances, pressure increases for a shift of focus from his own growth and development to that of the corporation or the industry as a whole. He is increasingly pushed to identify himself with the business rather than his own future—a change in goal direction that, in itself, can cause a crisis in identity.

A person's relationship with his colleagues also changes dramatically once he has reached top management. For example, one of the factors involved in success is competitive striving with one's peers; yet the nature of competition changes as an individual nears the apex of the organizational pyramid. To be sure, competition as a way of life continues as he learns to identify with the corporation and compete for *its* well-being, but he can no longer experience the intense face-to-face rivalry by which he once knew himself and identified his place in the company's structure.

Furthermore, he becomes more dependent on former peers. As was seen in Mr. Brown's progression, the corporate structure increasingly isolated him from those with whom he had originally been in close touch (often the very people he challenged when striving for the goal of promotion, but now subordinates on whom he must depend for information and assistance). Thus an executive who prides himself on his independence and ability to shift the organizational structure so he can rise through it suddenly finds himself relying on the entire organization beneath him, and he must cope with the stress of this increasingly dependent position.

At Home

Some of the qualities that facilitate an executive's achievements (e.g., the ability to seize opportunities, adjust to new situations, and concentrate energies) place additional burdens on his home life. Members of his family have often moved from community to community, from church to church, and from school to school. His wife may have sublimated her own needs in furthering her husband's career, taking second place to his advancement.

Resentment builds up over the years. The wife frequently turns to her children or to activities outside the home for satisfaction of her own needs; and now that her husband needs support, she is not so willing to give it. She must also face the changes in her physical identity and often makes her own difficulties part of her husband's burden of problems.

Moreover, the executive's continuous, intensive upward struggle absorbs some of the emotional investment that he might have had in his children; and his preoccupation with business and frequent absences from home often contribute to his alienation from family members. When the children leave home, his primary role as "parent" shifts back to that of "husband." The changed man and the changed woman must get to know each other again without the interposition of children and family affairs. But instead of the potentially comforting and giving situation he would hope to find at home, the executive often encounters an isolation not unlike the isolation that he increasingly senses at work.

In Social Life

As an individual attains corporate eminence, he can no longer simply be a member of a church or club. He is now expected to act as a pillar of the community, as one who is primarily responsible for the support and success of its various organizations. Where demands had previously been made for his participation, they are now made for his leadership.

In his social and community life, as in his

business life, he finds himself at the top of the pyramid, subjected to the demands and complaints of groups under his guidance. Where he might have expected to get gratification for his own unconscious dependent longings, he is beset with requests for service and money, resentment for nonparticipation, and blame for failures.

BROWN'S DISTRESS

Depression at the time of involution generally results from a sense of loss in various converging areas—loss of a certain degree of physical strength and stamina, separation from children who have left home, and various changes of identity. Furthermore, a man and his wife often grow apart during the years of his business pursuits, and, as in Brown's case, an intensification of their relationship to help compensate for the losses may no longer be possible.

Consequently, the executive who prides himself on being self-sufficient and independent may attempt to solve his problems on his own. The "solutions," however, often take the form of increased alcohol ingestion, tranquilizers, the development of psychosomatic illnesses, and searches for peace and "giving" outside his family (perhaps with a mistress). The applause of a crowd at a testimonial dinner and pictures in the newspaper substitute for a real sense of appreciation from those to whom he feels closest.

Danger Signals

It is often not easy for a family to recognize and admit that occupational mobility of the father/husband is having adverse effects on the home. The danger signals often occur when an executive's business success and social position make them increasingly difficult to understand.

In the Brown family, for example, the increased behavioral disturbances of the children and Mrs. Brown's visits to physicians and psychiatrists were not connected by the couple, or

by their doctors, to Brown's problems. Both the family and the various medical specialists appear to have accepted as necessities the continual moving and Brown's position of "giver." His attention and involvement became increasingly directed to outside affairs; and his achievements reduced the family members' feelings that they could be justifiably angry and critical.

The downward spiral. Eventually, a vicious circle is set up in which the executive's need for business and social success becomes greater in order to compensate for the reduced amount of dependency gratification being supplied by family and subordinates. The result is further intensification of the family's problems, so that it is less able to meet the needs of its members. Ventilation of feeling is frustrated at home by lack of communication, and at work by the demands of the executive's position. His business world and social clubs are unable to fully compensate, and his efficiency is decreased because of his symptoms.

Thus, Brown's decreased functional capacity, increased interpersonal problems, and personal anxieties prevented him from enjoying the success which he had struggled so long to achieve and from sharing this success with his family.

PREVENTING IDENTITY CRISES

How might an executive be assisted in overcoming these obstacles that prevent him from reaping all the rewards earned by his long years of sacrifice and struggle? How can he adapt happily to his accomplishments and share them meaningfully with others? There are a number of ways these goals can be reached.

As in most situations, prevention of the problems rather than treatment of them after their development is the most effective and simplest method of control. If one becomes aware of the dynamics of his own needs and the needs of his family prior to reaching the top echelon, identity crises can be avoided.

Young executives, for example, can benefit

from an understanding of human needs before they are personally confronted with the crises outlined in this article. This can be achieved through company-sponsored training progams and sensitivity groups or, even earlier, by attention to family dynamics in graduate schools of business administration.

If an executive who is already established spots any of the previously mentioned danger signals in his household, this should be an indication that he must become involved in the exploration and treatment of family difficulties. And assessing these difficulties in terms of his ambitions and career plans should be one of his first concerns—the avoidance of crisis may well involve significant choices and compromises. The executive should consider these important questions:

• What effects are my career pursuits having on my family?
• How important is my home life?
• How far do I really want to go in business?
• What role does my family play in decisions I make that affect them?

And these questions should be asked not just unilaterally, but with the help and consultation of the executive's family. His wife should be encouraged to participate in career discussions; his children should have the opportunity to express their feelings about impending moves, his business involvements, and so on.

Ultimately, the efficient and functioning executive is one who is able to make choices and evaluate the risk to himself and to his ambition with an adult acceptance of the fact that he cannot have his cake and eat it. If he does this, it is unlikely that he will come to a time in life where he must face either (a) the regret of never having reached the top of the pyramid while having a happy home or (b) the regret of having achieved business success in a setting of domestic unhappiness. The ability to weigh and compute behavioral consequences that helped push him upward should also help him find an alternate route upward when choice is "forced." The rational man does not always take the path of least resistance.

Coping Mechanisms

Men are not perfect and danger signals are often missed. For the executive already entangled in an identity crisis, there are numerous avenues of assistance. The opening phase of any form of help, however, involves the executive's own awakening to his problems. This recognition may, in some cases, be sufficient in itself to effect positive changes.

Acknowledging personal problems is often difficult for an executive who has always relied on his independence and self-sufficiency. For such a man to acknowledge that he has a problem he cannot solve alone is a big first step toward improvement. People have a natural resistance to painful self-knowledge and develop, over their lifetimes, characteristic ways of defending themselves from such knowledge and the attendant discomfort. The process of self-discovery, of learning who we really are rather than who we think we are, can arouse the deepest anxiety, and nothing but one's own desire to change constitutes adequate motivation to overcome it.

Depth-therapy. Those individuals who feel they are in serious difficulty should consider undertaking depth-therapy with a qualified physician. From the point of view of a physician, increased interpersonal problems and personal anxieties, which are the usual presenting symptoms of a person in a crisis such as I have described, are not just blocks to desirable experiences; they constitute psychopathology in need of treatment. Blocks cannot really be dissolved without reaching and probing defenses which have often been long embedded in a person's life style.

A physician is familiar with life-and-death issues, and is trained in the responsibility for carrying through whatever he opens. And, while the term "life-and-death issues" may sound like an exaggeration, it actually is not. There are real dangers involved in dealing with identity crises and real dangers in lifting the lid off the mechanism of a functioning human being. A physician relies heavily on his education and background to enable him to constantly evaluate emotional processes as they take place.

Group experiences. For the executive who decides not to undertake depth-therapy, or does not consider himself in need of such treatment, a group experience focused on the problems of the rise to the top can be an enlightening intellectual experience. It could mean a reawakening to alternative values that allow an individual to appreciate again the sensation of his natural self as well as the family he has often forgotten during his career climb.

The experience of sharing problems with executives in similar situations can also lead to a reduction of the feeling of isolation inherent in "top of the pyramid" status. It may revive those satisfying emotions which the executive once knew in immediate, face-to-face contact with his peers.

There is a plethora of organizations offering sensitivity training, encounter groups, therapy groups, psychodrama groups, T-groups, and so on. Industries have now formed their own groups. But care should be exercised in choosing one. Many of these groups offer a form of experience which changes the participant very little, while allowing him to think that he is "doing something about his problems." Others, however, constitute a commitment to an experience that goes to the heart of the matter; these are concerned with neither miracles nor "as if," *ersatz* emotionality.

CONCLUSION

Those qualities which have enabled an executive to succeed in business often serve him ill at the end of his climb. Unfortunately, as was explained earlier, this end occurs during his involution. The difficulties inherent in these converging stress factors might be minimized if progress and business achievement were seen as family affairs and not a "fact" or "gift" brought home to the family. Just as wife and home formed part of the support in making achievement, so they must continue to function after achievement. Consideration of family affairs during the affairs of business might well preserve the family as a going concern that can reward its head when he has greater need from it and is less the object of its demands.

One cannot climb a mountain, however, without the danger of falling off. Any executive who has made it to the top has lived intimately with this very image. Whether, at the summit, he finds himself above the clouds, confronted by a breathtaking panorama of the world below him, or in a precarious windy niche, or with yet another mountain in his path, depends not so much on what mountain he climbed as on who he is and how he got there. If he can adapt happily to his accomplishment, he will reap all the rewards that his long years of struggle sowed. But if it overwhelms him, and, true to his character, he plunges, brave and solitary, into a more lonely struggle than any he has yet attempted, it is possible that ultimately success may not seem worth the price he has paid.

Section 7

Special Career Issues for Women and Minorities

Increasing numbers of women and minority managers are entering organizations. Managers must become more responsive to the special problems and issues related to the career advancement and development of these individuals. Epstein identifies some of the barriers to upward mobility which women encounter in the organizations. They include such things as the lack of female role models, the lack of a critical mass, exclusion from the informal network, societal stereotyping, and the like.

Kanter describes the "plight" of the token woman. Among the many pressures placed on such managers is the burden of being both the symbol and spokesperson of *all* womanhood. Although Kanter's article specifically refers to women, the issue of tokenism is just as relevant for minority managers and should be considered with this in mind.

In addition to the pressures of tokenism, minority managers must deal with other career pressures. Sarachek describes the results of intensive interviews with sixteen black managers. The concerns expressed by these managers are similar to the barriers identified earlier by Epstein—informal exclusion, lack of sponsorship, and stereotypes.

The entrance of women and minorities into the managerial ranks of organizations is nothing new. It has been an important social priority for well over a decade; however, the primary focus has been upon how members of these minority groups are selected and enter the organization. One might say that these were first-order concerns of equal employment. It is now time to identify some of the second-order priorities and concerns for women and minorities. These are the issues affecting advancement and the identification of a career future. These topics are discussed in this section.

Institutional Barriers: What Keeps Women Out of the Executive Suite?

Cynthia Fuchs Epstein

A movie of some years ago called *Barbarella* had a haunting scene in which the heroine, marooned in a wasteland, sees in the distance a horde of automated dolls, lovely, wide-eyed, long-haired dolls, the kind little girls have long cherished. But as Barbarella moves close to these creatures, she is dismayed and terrified to see that their mouths open and shut like those of puppets, emitting shrill sounds and revealing teeth that are steel traps, sharp and pointed.

This to me seems to symbolize current reality. Whether women ask for equality softly or firmly, the male gatekeepers, and some established women as well, often hear only shrill and piercing sounds. Requests are heard as demands. Demands seem to imply violence. This response is by no means universal but it predominates. It prolongs the resistance to women's participation in spheres long dominated by men, and reflects the continued cultural conflict between the norms specifying womanly or ladylike behavior and the norms specifying competent business and professional behavior.

Both our perceptions of behavior and our expectations as to proper behavior shape present conditions. Women newcomers to business and the professions still face age-old prejudices and cultural biases that define their roles and their potential contributions. These stereotypes intrude on their social and business relations with men and make assimilation difficult.[1]

Of primary importance are those informal structures of interaction in the business and professional world that affect and are affected by women's behavior. Informal behavior is institutionalized at least as thoroughly as the formal modes of interaction depicted on organizational charts, and it is probably more important to analyze informal interaction. The closer one gets to the top, the more commonly are decision-making judgments and rewards determined by subjective criteria; "understandings" rather than rules govern behavior, and personal qualifications are judged against a range of attributes not immediately relevant functionally to the job at hand. These factors have always been important, but they may become even more important as legal strictures forbid the exclusion of women and others once rejected categorically.

A. TRENDS IN THE STATUS OF WOMEN

Before considering the informal modes of institutional exclusion of women, we may review women's position, cross-culturally over the years, as it bears on these issues.

Perhaps the factor that best determines what may be women's work is not the nature of the work performed nor the burden it may create mentally or physically, but rather the symbolic significance of the work and whether or not it is considered important, honorable, and desirable. The greater the social desirability of a type of work, the less likely it is that women are identified with it. All societies seem to prefer *men* in the jobs most valued. Even where women constitute a majority among personnel of an occupation, such as in school-teaching, librarianship, or textile work, men seem to have a disproportionately greater chance to be in the top administration of the field. This is true even in Soviet medicine, where men, although a minority of the profession, hold the top professorships and hospital administration posts.[2] In all cultures, women are at best tolerated in the most desired fields, and the few found there are regarded as having special and idiosyncratic traits that justify the anomaly.[3] This rationalizing impedes women's integration into top jobs even when few formal obstacles exist.

Although today we assume widespread changes in the position of women, there have probably been fewer significant changes than media publicity indicates. The 1970 census showed percentage increases for women in male-dominated professions and occupations not unlike those of the previous two decades. Women lawyers rose from 2.4 percent of the profession in 1940 to 3.5 percent in 1960 and 4.9 percent in 1970, a minimal increase in light of the enormous emphasis on women's liberation during the sixties. In medicine women moved from 6.5 percent of their profession in 1960 to 9.3 percent in 1970, but women were only 8.5 percent of all medical students that same year.[4] Presumably those percentages have increased since the 1970 census.

But some of the statistics point the other way. In manufacturing industries the percentage of managers dropped from 7.1 percent women in 1960 to 6.3 percent in 1970.[5] This was below the 6.4 percent listed in 1950, when the status of women was relatively lower than during the previous two decades and when the proportion of women dropped in all career-oriented spheres of life. It was a period characterized by Jessie Bernard as the time of the "motherhood mania."

There are few reliable statistics about women's opportunities for promotion in publishing, banking, commerce, or the public utilities. When the statistics are at hand, it will then be necessary to look beyond the new titles to the actual roles being filled.[6] Visibility is a central problem for women in business and the other male-dominated professional activities. Certain jobs are less visible than others, and those in the former don't get as much credit as they would otherwise. Women tend to get the jobs that are actually and symbolically less visible—*actually*, because they do not have contact with clients and with the market, and *symbolically*, because the jobs they have are not defined as crucial.

One further complication is that even where women are given higher-level administrative jobs, these do not lead to top-management posts, but rather are on ancillary routes that may be dead ends. A woman may be called a vice president or special assistant to the president, but be assigned to administrate an affirmative action plan or asked to recruit women personnel. Such activity is rarely viewed as more than peripheral to the goals of the firm and is unlikely to lead to the top. Today the diverging of women to alternative routes may occur at a higher level than before, but the ultimate consequences are the same.

1. Characteristics of Women in Top Management

There are still so few women executives that certain tantalizing questions must go unanswered: e.g., Are there "self-made" women in the same sense that some men are seen as self-made? A study attempted by the Harvard Business School in the late sixties had to be abandoned for lack of sufficient subjects. In 1966 the British Political and Economic Planning organization (PEP) sponsored a study of women in managerial jobs in government service, the British Broadcasting Corporation, and two large companies. The team of researchers, headed by Michael Fogarty and Rhona and Robert Rapoport, reported on their work in two volumes published in 1971 called *Women in Top Jobs* and *Sex, Career and Family*.[7] They found that women who rose to the top of these organizations did so largely because of chance, the wartime diversion of manpower, or the death of a relative. It was clear that the women who assumed directorship roles under these conditions would not have sought them, nor been offered them, under normal circumstances.

In the United States in 1971 Margaret Hennig[8] studied twenty-five women presidents and vice presidents of medium-to-large nationally recognized business firms, out of a specially selected sample of one hundred women who then held such posts. Most were widows or daughters of men who had led these firms or women who had other ties with a man in command. *Fortune*, in an article on the ten top-paid women in the United States, reported a similar situation that serves to underline the importance of affectional or kinship ties in determining women's success.[9]

Why should this be so? In a world where the door is barred to women, only a few get in totally uninvited, most of them because of special circumstances. Friendship and kinship provide an alternative opportunity structure, paralleling a system of protégéship by which men gain entrance to the inner circles. As intimates of the mighty, women have access to the information *any* aspirant needs to mount the ladder of success. But the route of marriage or friendship has never been a true alternative opportunity structure. It is a testament to the subtle skills of the gatekeepers that the underlying disapproval elicited by this kind of alternative route serves as a social control mechanism to ensure that women, already denied recourse to the male strategem, cannot truly succeed by the only strategem open to them.[10]

For women, the costs of using a particularistic route are high and the profits are always contingent. Positions won by being tied to one man are nontransferable. Until a woman has

proven herself, she is in a poor bargaining position for title or money. Her competence is always under scrutiny, and many women can prove their talent only after the death of a husband, if they succeed to his position.

2. Mechanisms of Exclusion

Not only is competition keen for the pinnacles, but active mechanisms thin the ranks of the competitors. Women, like other groups who have potential talent and ability, have been kept out of the pool of eligibles in science, law, and other male-dominated professions. A certain evenness of resistance to the inclusion of women is apparent in these spheres long dominated by men. Women have not had access to the same reward structure that men have, and this is as much a cause of their low participation and productivity in the professions as is the discrimination that bars them.[11]

In some ways the exclusion of women may have been more effective than the barring of other groups because women, unlike the other groups, have had an initial acculturation to values of the ruling elites. They have grown up with men, learned their manners, been educated in their schools, and been exposed to the same circuitry of contacts. But the Radcliffe sisters of Harvard brothers and their other Ivy League counterparts, classes of 1940, 1950, and 1960 (which produced the heads of our corporations, the rulers of our country), somehow were tracked into careers, not usually called careers, as adjuncts to their husbands.

Careers in corporate and government life have typically been so demanding that men have needed able wives to entertain, soothe, make contacts, and offer ballast. Most top careers, in fact, have been cooperative efforts, but husbands hold the titles and power and their wives serve as statusless, unpaid partners.[12] As corporations institutionalized the twelve-hour day for their executives and developed a set of expectations that a man's family be at the call of the corporation, both the single man and the man whose wife who has an independent life have been hampered in the climb to power. The woman executive is likewise handicapped. Given the norms of family life in America, she could hardly be expected to make the same demands on her husband that the husband can make on his wife.

When it was inconceivable for women to be on the same path as men, alternative routes to the top were suggested. As secretaries or gal Fridays, serving men, supposedly they would learn the ropes. Actually some did, and realized too late that it was not know-how alone that would give them promotions; it was knowledge acquired in specified settings and according to certain rules. Women who insisted they be given the same chances as men were seen as immodest and pushy, lacking in the very qualities of charm and grace that made women nice to have around. The female recruit entered the world of work with a built-in bias, with a different set of experiences, without a peer group, to face a situation where she would be damned if she did and damned if she didn't perform well. The British study of women directors indicated that colleagues saw them as "dragons" if they were authoritative, or as "nice mice" if they were mild in demeanor.

3. Problems of Identification

Some of the structures within the occupations are becoming more clearly recognized today as being instrumental in making women feel uncomfortable and unwanted.

The business world has for a long time considered women executives to be such a rarity that clients and colleagues could only react with surprise or disbelief. Most men assumed that any woman at a business meeting was a secretary. A woman executive often had to announce who she was, had no implicit status, and had difficulty exerting authority. Imagine a male executive who could *always* expect to be mistaken for the salesman or the filing clerk, and would have to identify himself and hope he would be treated with respect. Men in positions of authority expect that others will know their power. In fact, they know that the more power they have, the less they need to announce it. Lesser men can lean on the image of power,

emulating the model member of upper corporation management in classic gray flannel suit with vest, and assume an air of detached authority. For women there has been no comparable model.

Ironically, as types of authority loosen and the male executive tends to be more approachable and informal, women may face greater ambiguity in defining their roles than before. One may call the boss "Bill" rather than "Mr. Jones" and still not upset the power structure, because it is clear who stands in authority. But calling the boss "Jane" rather than "Ms. Hastings" may easily produce a patronizing and comradely ambience in which lines of power, difficult to read swiftly between men and women in the clearest of circumstances, are misunderstood.

B. CONSEQUENCES OF THE NUMBERS OF WOMEN IN TOP POSITIONS

We must also consider the relevance of numbers and ratios in interaction. When women in management are few in number, they feel excluded and often become estranged. They say they are not really considered to be part of the organization in a true membership sense, but interlopers. Women's minority position in management is institutionalized by rules guaranteeing a tiny quota. When there is only one woman in the executive suite, it is awkward for her; she has no peer group, no referent for her behavior.[13] And it is awkward for her male colleagues, who perceive her as a lone intruder to their all-male bastion. It is essential to create a critical mass in management, a large enough proportion of women to make their presence a matter of course rather than a phenomenon.

1. Informal Interaction

Numbers and ratios are significant in establishing the all-important norms of informal social interaction, a process that is of utmost importance in top-management circles. Consider the key informal contacts made over lunch, or the easy camaraderie of the bar. A male colleague might feel awkward asking a woman business associate to have a drink, and vice versa. One man to one woman suggests an overture to a specifically social relationship, and the combination of three men and one woman may seem awkward to the woman who might feel like an intruder on their "man talk"; but if there were four men and two women, or three men, then the informal social relations intertwined with business would not have a sexual overtone. In other contexts where no arbitrary rules limit the normal exchanges between men and women, work proceeds smoothly. The mere presence of women does not disrupt the structure, and the men don't feel diminished.

The consequences of a social pattern that distinguishes between men and women in terms of membership, dining rooms, dining tables, or mere access may be more injurious then the degradation suffered by those who are wholly excluded. When women cannot mingle easily with men as colleagues in the informal settings where business gets done, they cannot become fully prepared to exercise influence. When women expect and are given full participation in the formal and informal structures of their occupations at every level, including the top one, they can be included as equals and be let in on the silent rules of the game along with the males.

2. The Reward-Punishment System

With this model of membership a woman would be prepared to make a contribution on her own. She would have to become, as they say, her own "man." She would have to know that her performance will face the same tests as those of men and that on the same criteria she will succeed or fail. This model would not shelter or hide women in invisible positions. It would convince them that if they contribute, they will rise in rank and increase in visibility and be paid and respected accordingly; if they fail, it is not because they are women but because their performance has been found wanting. And as they rise, the standards will become higher, as

with men. When men are clearly at the top, the driving motivation for them ceases to be the expectation of greater rewards—more money or even more rank—but the need (gradually internalized over time) to *continue to achieve*. Few women have so far been exposed to this conditioning.

3. Processes in the Creation of Criteria for Competence

We are concerned about the way in which business roles are institutionalized so that only *certain* people are seen as appropriate partners in normal interaction. Denial of access to the structure in which competence is created has perpetuated the exclusion of women from top posts. Those who are not admitted or who are not *admissible* to inner circles are denied what is perhaps the most crucial learning of their trade. This is most obvious in the case of professions. Top surgeons learn their special skills not when they are in medical school, but when they are selected to be residents with the finest physicians in their specialty. Top lawyers start as apprentices to the senior partners in the large firms. The process is comparable in business, where most skills are not objectively learned but are rather the product of intelligence, diplomacy, know-how, and "know-who." Information about who is the best producer of an item and what kind of pricing is possible is passed on to protégés, who are also introduced to top people.

Our social conditioning encourages us to think of persons of only a certain age or sex or race as being able to understand tasks or to carry them out. Women have not been thought of as business executives, and younger men too have often been discriminated against, simply because they seemed too young to hold a job of responsibility and did not fit the mold. Discrimination is not always directed at the *classic* underdog, but it works against any group that does not fit the stereotype. We may not pity the young man because we expect he will *ultimately* get the position for which he might be fit now. We think he is too young partially because we know that older people do not like to be commanded by the young. But he is also handicapped by our stereotypes about how many years a person should devote to each stage of his career. These expectations are defined by how it has always been done. We also have views about the amount of time any particular task ought to take and how long the workday ought to be for a "committed" person. On all sides we are encumbered by expectations that are operationalized as coercive rules. They are rationalized as logical, but a closer look shows that they are based on unchallenged assumptions and reflect the status quo. These assumptions typically favor the class of persons in command and make others seem to be the "wrong" persons for the job, whoever they are and whatever the job may be.

4. Style, Self, and the Aura of Competence

We must be concerned about the difficulty of objective evaluation of competence. Psychological and sociological studies make clear the impact of "labeling," the process by which a person is called competent or incompetent, appropriate or inappropriate, good or bad. The label defines the self-image that in turn shapes the behavior. A person who is seen as a "go-getter" likely to succeed will work harder than the person who is perceived as inept and unable to accomplish a goal or a dream.

The more we study people who are ostensibly "self-made," the more we see that what really made them is not only their idiosyncratic set of talents but also the framework in which they lived, the opportunities available to them, and the role of persons important in their lives in the formation of a self-image that facilitated career attainments.

Gatekeepers are often so committed to stereotypes that they are incapable of seeing talent or emerging competence because the package in which it is presented is so unexpected. If we do not listen to the brilliant woman because we don't expect bright ideas to come in a female form, we won't hear her contributions. And when, after a while, she falls silent because no one listens, the initial stereotype is confirmed

and reinforced.[14] There are, of course, exceptions to this pattern, but again our stereotypes get in the way.

Women in politics say that because Bella Abzug is aggressive and forthright in her personal style, her congressional colleagues find it embarrassing to interact with her and they try to avoid her as much as possible. It is clear that many male politicians assume an aggressive personal style that is not only tolerated but defined as consistent with leadership. The woman, however, is caught in a morass of conflicting expectations and may be damned whatever style she chooses.

An increase in the numbers of women in male settings will doubtless change current attitudes that accept a greater range of styles for men than for women. Then any one woman's personal style would be less attributable to all women, and each would be accepted as an individual, as is any man. Enough women would be visible at one time to make clear the lack of homogeneity. This has already been demonstrated to some degree in formerly male bastions, such as business and law schools, that now admit substantial percentages of women students. Male students and teachers are accepting women and judging them according to the same standards as men. Men in business and professions do not necessarily intend to discriminate. We all tend to define what we see most often as normal. The world in which they work is mostly male, and that is the most comfortable and natural way for them. Probably few are even aware that women are excluded or made to feel unwanted, although in certain cases the possibility of bad intentions cannot be ignored.

Exclusionary consequences can flow from good motives as well as bad. Some men really do think they are helping a woman by being sensitive to her family responsibilities and not asking her to do the extra work that might be just what she needs to prove her talents and perhaps get a promotion. This paternalism deprives women of the right to decide independently and thereby to learn. No single answer will fit all women, and each must choose her own priorities in life and be free to act accordingly.

5. Culture and the Structure of Motivation

What is unique about the situation of women today is that almost everyone is to blame, including women themselves, who have joined the conspiracy by accepting the idea that they must monitor their ambitions and goals in terms of what everybody else expects of them— including their husbands, children, fathers, or bosses. Our culture expects and encourages women to hold back, not to "go for broke": not to sacrifice family savings or the immediate comfort of the family in service of long-range goals. But this is exactly what is expected of a man who is an entrepreneur or struggling professional. Clearly, motivational structures are not alike for men and women.[15]

While both his private and professional lives combine to encourage the man to put his best into his work, and promise him rewards for doing so, the woman's private life—the home and community—tends to undermine her work goals, presenting challenges to her right to work and outright hostility. Community values will often condemn her career goals as antisocial and an abandonment of husband and children. In her professional life, her colleagues often question her ability and the extent and depth of her commitment. On the basis of an incomplete assessment of her own accomplishments she may form a negative self-image that she then extends, somewhat defensively, to characterize women more generally. These women often stifle their desire for self-fulfillment or deflect it in other directions, some of them destructive to the husbands and children through whom they try to live vicariously.

C. CHANGE AND RESISTANCE TO CHANGE IN THE STATUS OF WOMEN

Things can change, and there is evidence that they are changing. My findings[16] in studying women in elite positions in business and the professions show that the old homily "Nothing succeeds like success" is well grounded in fact. It is a self-fulfilling prophecy not unlike the labeling discussed above. Yet I believe that the idea of opening the doors to women somehow, whether for traditional, cultural, or psycholog-ical reasons, seems a basic threat that will always stand in the way of truly equal opportunities in management for both sexes.

These fears are not groundless; they stem from women's obvious potential. It is certainly true that women, who constitute such a large proportion of the educated, could take over quite a few men's jobs tomorrow if they were so inclined and if they were given the opportunity. Yet it must be possible to devise work structures in which we can upgrade *all* jobs, provide reward incentives for all, and define competition from the bottom to the top in terms of sheer creative talent, ambition, and drive.

The search continues for specific structural solutions to these problems. These cannot succeed without a simultaneous concern with the attitudes that are created early in life in the home and in school, for changing attitudes and changing structure go hand in hand. We may change work conditions more easily than attitudes, but no situation is hopeless. The large law firms that have employed women and have even made them senior partners find that clients accept the judgment of the firm as to who will serve them well. Further, no firm has reported suffering a financial loss or a diminution of prestige for doing so.

At General Motors, once directives were handed down from top management to expedite the affirmative action program demanded by the government, GM's middle managers not only went along, but often found good reasons for changing the old practices. Everyone, it seems, became interested in the success of the plan.

The American Telephone and Telegraph Company now has a vice president who is mobilizing a task force of bright managers to rethink job sequences, job criteria, and job segmentation. They are going beyond the thinking lodged in commonplace notions about how things have been done. Of course, such innovations will have many consequences beyond simply assimilating women.

Women have generally been deprived of the charisma of the halo effect of title and rank. When officers of business concerns give women the same deference as well as accoutrements of office given men, women will be more at ease in assuming command. When firms back women executives with the expectations that they will do well and let their subordinates know it, women will measure up to these expectations. But the institution must feel it has a stake in the person and vice versa. Job commitment and high performance cannot develop when women sense that the promises held out to them are empty, or tokens intended primarily to pacify the demands of EEOC. Women have long permitted themselves to accept a bad bargain, but today more and more they are insisting on a fair price, the market price, for their services.

NOTES

I would like to acknowledge the invisible structure of the reasoning in this paper which, in part, relies on a number of concepts developed by Robert K. Merton in *Social Theory and Social Structure* (Chicago, Ill.: Free Press, 1957). Among those which I immediately identify are those of the power of relative and absolute numbers in the dynamics of social groups; the emergence of a notion of deviance on the part of those whose status sets are inconsistent with the pattern most frequently seen; the unintended consequences of intent; and the self-fulfilling prophecy. Similarly, I am indebted to the perspective offered by Erving Goffman on the presentation of the self.

1. Lawrence C. Hackamack and Alan B. Solid, "The Woman Executive: There Is Still Ample Room for Progress," *Business Horizons*, April 1972, pp. 89-93; and Benson Rosen and Thomas H. Jerdee, "Sex Stereotyping in the Executive Suite," *Harvard Business Review*, March-April 1973, pp. 45-58.
2. Norton T. Dodge, *Women in the Soviet Economy*, Baltimore: Johns Hopkins, 1966.
3. Eleanor Brantley Schwartz, "The Sex Barrier in Business," *Atlanta Economic Reveiw*, June 1971, p. 6.
4. "The Economic Role of Women," *Economic Report of the President*, Washington, D.C., 1973.
5. Ibid., p. 101.
6. Burton G. Malkiel and Judith A. Malkiel,

"Male-Female Pay Differentials in Professional Employment," *American Economic Review*, September 1973, pp. 693-705.
7. Michael Fogarty, Rhona Rapoport, and Robert Rapoport, *Women in Top Jobs: Four Studies in Achievement* and *Sex, Career and Family*, prepared jointly by Political and Economic Planning (PEP) and the Tavistock Institute, London: G. Allen, 1971.
8. Margaret Marie Hennig, "Career Development for Women Executives," unpublished doctoral dissertation, Harvard University, Cambridge, Mass., 1971.
9. Wyndham Robertson, "Ten Highest Ranking Women in Big Business," *Fortune*, April 1973, pp. 80-89.
10. Cynthia Fuchs Epstein, "Bringing Women In: Rewards, Punishments, and the Structure of Achievement," *Annals of the New York Academy of Sciences,* March 1973, pp. 62-70.
11. Cynthia Fuchs Epstein, "Structuring Success for Women: Guidelines for Gatekeepers," *Journal of the National Association of Women Deans and Counselors*, Fall 1973, pp. 34-42.
12. Cynthia Fuchs Epstein, "Law Partners and Marital Partners: Strains and Solutions in the Dual-Career Family Enterprise," *Human Relations*, December 1971, pp. 549-564.
13. Eleanor Brantley Schwartz and James J. Rago, Jr., "Beyond Tokenism: Women as True Corporate Peers: Can Organization Cope with Male Executives Who Resist Working with Women as Peers?" *Business Horizons*, December 1973, pp. 69-76.
14. Matina Horner, "Toward an Understanding of Achievement Related Conflicts in Women," *Journal of Social Issues,* 1972, pp. 157-176.
15. Cynthia Fuchs Epstein, *Women's Place: Options and Limits in Professional Careers*, Berkeley: University of California Press, 1970.
16. Cynthia Fuchs Epstein, "Encountering the Male Establishment: Sex-Status Limits on Women's Careers in the Professions," *American Journal of Sociology*, May 1970, pp. 965-982.

Climbing the Pyramid Alone

Rosabeth Moss Kanter

Some of our competition, like ourselves, have women sales people in the field. It's interesting that when you go in to see a purchasing agent, what he has to say about the woman salesperson. It's always what kind of body she had, or how good-looking she is. They don't tell you how good-looking your competitors are if they're males, but I've never heard about a woman's technical competence or what kind of a sales person she was—only what her body was like.

—an Indsco salesman

Although more women than ever before are moving into management positions in American business, many of them are still virtually "token" women: so few in number and unusual in the business setting that they have the added job of being symbols of all womanhood, rather than making it on their own as individuals. Even so, many people think the token woman is the lucky one, the one who "made it" into a position of power in a world which is still, especially in the upper ranks, almost exclusively a male preserve.

However, in my research in industry, including the large company I shall call Industrial Supply Corporation, I found that the "luck" of the token woman is, at best, mixed. Women in the upper ranks at Indsco worked under a number of disadvantages that their male colleagues never had to deal with—unless they were black.

The difficulties they faced in doing their jobs well and having their performance rewarded stemmed from a single fact—one so obvious it at first seems an unlikely explanation: sheer numbers. The upper-level women at Indsco almost inevitably found themselves *alone* among male peers. Their numerical rarity created continual problems for them as individuals—problems which tend to reinforce a male executive's stereotypes about "what women are like," and which prevent more women from rising in the corporate hierarchy.

In my view, the "plight" of the token woman has less to do with female psychology or physiology, women's expectations of their work, conflicts of having career and family, early socialization as a female—or any of the other favored explanations of journalists and academics—than it has to do simply with numbers. Token women feel and act as tokens in any situation feel and act, because there are so few of them: they are on constant display, never allowed to forget for very long that they are "special cases." What happens to these women is strikingly similar to the fate of lone blacks among whites, older people among younger

Excerpted from Chapter 7 and 8 of *Men and Women of the Corporation*, by Rosabeth Moss Kanter, © 1977 by Rosabeth Moss Kanter, Basic Books, Inc., Publishers, New York.

people, the rare men in a women's group—whenever people are cast in the role of "token."

Indsco's upper-level women, for example, especially those in sales, were highly visible simply because of their rarity. In the sales force, where a peer culture and informal relations were most strongly entrenched, everyone knew about the women. They were the subjects of conversation, questioning, gossip, and careful scrutiny. Their names came up at meetings, and they were often used as examples. Men traveling to regional offices would bring back the latest news about the women there along with other gossip.

In non-sales areas, too, the women developed well-known names, and their reputations often preceded them when they went to another office to do a piece of work. One woman swore in an elevator in an Atlanta hotel while going out to have drinks with her colleagues, and it was known all over Chicago a few days later that she was a "radical."

Some women were even told by their managers that they were watched more closely than their male counterparts. Sometimes the manager intended to be helpful—to let the woman know that he would be right there behind her. But the net effect was the same as that of all the other high-visibility phenomena: the token woman typically worked under different—and more stressful—conditions than men doing the same jobs.

The upper-level women became public creatures. It was difficult for them to do anything in training programs, on their jobs, or even at informal social affairs that would not attract public notice. Their publicity proved a double-edged sword: it provided the advantage of getting attention but at the same time it made privacy and anonymity impossible. As one saleswoman reported, "I've been at sales meetings where all the trainees were going up to the managers—'Hi, Mr. So-and-So'—trying to make that impression, wearing a strawberry tie, whatever. Whereas there were three of us [women] in a group of 50, and all we had to do was walk in and everyone recognized us."

Many would have preferred to be less noticeable: "If it seems good to be noticed," one

said, "wait until you make your first major mistake." Another complained, "I don't have as much freedom of behavior as men do; I can't be as independent."

On some occasions, tokens were deliberately thrust into the limelight and displayed as showpieces, sometimes in ways that violated their sense of personal dignity. One of Indsco's most senior women attended a luncheon at a large downtown hotel under protest. She was given no information about the nature of the event; she was told only that the chairman of the board wanted her there. On the day of the luncheon—a "surprise" held to honor five outstanding businesswomen—a corsage arrived at her office, followed by a vice president to escort her. So she went, and found she was there as Indsco's "prize woman," symbolizing the strides women had made in business. (Although she had been with Indsco 26 years, she had only recently been given two assistants, and thus managerial responsibilities.)

Pictures were taken for the employee newsletter and a few days later she received an inscribed paperweight as a memento. She told the story a few weeks after with visible embarrassment about "being taken on a date—it was more like a senior prom than like a business event." And she said she resented being singled out "just for being a woman at Indsco, not for any real achievement." Yet she had to go, and she had to appear gracious and grateful: the reaction of tokens to their notice was also noticed.

Many of the token women seemed to have developed the capacity—often observed among marginal or subordinate peoples—to project a public persona that hid inner feelings. Although some junior management men at Indsco were quite open about their lack of commitment to the company and their dissatisfaction with aspects of its style, the women felt they could not afford to voice any negative sentiments. They had to play by a different set of rules. One Indsco woman said, 'I know the company's a rumor factory. You must be careful how you conduct yourself and what you say to whom. I saw how one woman in the office was discussed endlessly, and I decided it would be better to keep my personal life and personal affairs separate." Because of the glare of publicity they were forced into the position of keeping secrets and carefully contriving a public performance. They could not afford to stumble.

Indsco's token women were seen by their peers only *as women*: this loaded all of their acts with extra symbolic consequences, and gave them the burden of representing their gender, not just themselves. Some of them were told outright that how they performed could affect the prospects of other women in the company. Every act tended to be seen as an example of "how women perform." In one case a woman in sales went to her manager to discuss the handling of a customer who was behaving seductively. The manager jumped to the conclusion that the woman must have led him on.

Regardless of their expertise or interest, women were often asked to provide a meeting with "the woman's point of view" or to explain to a manager why he was having certain problems with "his women." Some women seized this chance to be a symbol as a way of being included in particular gatherings or task forces; in effect, they embraced their tokenism. "Even if you don't want *me* personally," they seemed to be telling the men, "you can want me as a symbol." But, if they did they would always be left with a feeling of uncertainty about the grounds for their inclusion; they were failing to distinguish themselves as individuals.

It wasn't only the men at Indsco who regarded the token women as symbols—as representatives of their gender rather than as individuals. Upper-level women were scrutinized by women on lower levels, who considered a token's actions as having implications for their own careers. One woman manager who was passed over for a promotion in her department was the subject of considerable discussion by other women, who felt she should have pushed to get the opening and should have complained when she didn't.

Life in the limelight, and the knowledge that their actions and decisions were interpreted symbolically—as "the way women be-

have"—naturally placed an added burden of self-consciousness on Indsco's token women, and sometimes affected the decisions they made. Even decisions about what to wear and whom to sit with at lunch became more than casual. One executive woman deliberately wore pants one day as she walked through an office— not her own—of female clerks supervised by a man who wanted them to wear dresses; she noted that a few women cautiously began to wear pants occasionally. She also decided to let it be known that she was leaving at four p.m. for ballet lessons once a week, arguing that the men at her level did the same thing to play golf, but also knowing that ballet was going to have a very different meaning from golf. Her act was a gesture performed with an audience in mind as much as an expression of preference.

Although the token doesn't have to work to have her presence noticed, she does have to work—harder than her male counterparts—to have her *achievements* noticed. What she *does* tends to be eclipsed by what she *is*. In the sales force, women found that their technical abilities were likely to be eclipsed by their physical appearance, and thus felt additional pressure to perform. Both male peers and customers tended to forget any information women provided about their experiences and credentials, while remembering such secondary attributes as style of dress.

Token women were also aware of another performance pressure: not to make the dominant males look bad. When a token woman does well enough to "show up" a male peer, it cannot be kept a secret, since all eyes are on the token, and it is therefore more difficult to avoid public humiliation of the male. Paradoxically, while the tokens felt that they had to do better than anyone else in order to be seen as competent, they also felt, in some cases, that their successes would not be rewarded, and should be kept to themselves. They needed to toe the fine line between doing just well enough and too well.

A number of men were concerned that women would jump ahead of them, and they made their resentments known. One unwittingly revealed a central principle in the competition when he said, "It's okay for women to have these jobs, as long as they don't go zooming by *me*." Managers, in general, agreed that there was backlash if women seemed to advance too fast. Sometimes, by way of retaliation, male colleagues would abandon a "too successful" woman the first time she ran into problems.

How do tokens survive the enormous amount of scrutiny they receive? Scarce women in large organizations seem to have a choice of three survival strategies, each with its inherent dangers. First, they can overachieve and carefully construct a public performance that minimizes the likelihood of backlash. Second, they can try to turn their high visibility and "specialness" to their advantage. Finally, they can try to find ways of becoming socially invisible.

To succeed with the first strategy, the token woman must be exceptionally competent and able to perform well under close observation. But she must also have the political sensitivity and skill to maintain a delicate balance: always doing well but not doing well enough to generate peer resentment. This combination of competence at the job and political dexterity can take years to acquire. Young women just out of college had the greatest difficulty in succeeding in male domains like the Indsco sales force, and were responsible for much of the high turnover among women in sales. On the other hand, women who were slightly older than their male peers, had strong technical backgrounds, and had previous experience as token women among male peers, tended to manage this strategy more successfully. Their success was likely to increase the prospects for hiring more women in the future: their skills worked both for themselves and, symbolically, for other women.

The second strategy, accepting one's visibility as a token and trading on it, was especially risky because of the weight peer acceptance carried at Indsco. The few women who flaunted their "differentness" had the sponsorship of one of the company's top managers. Nonetheless, the strategy was dangerous because of shifting power alliances at the top, the need to secure peer cooperation to get their jobs done, and the likelihood that some resentful peers would eventually reach the top.

This strategy also made it less likely that more women would be hired at Indsco. The women who used it were less likely to succeed themselves; they also had a stake in maintaining their place in the spotlight, and so tended to be overcritical of female job candidates and to subtly undercut women peers.

The third strategy—invisibility—was more often chosen by the older generation of corporate women, who predated the women's movement and had, years ago, accommodated themselves to token status. To become "socially invisible," involved a number of tactics: dressing to minimize their sexual attributes, so as to blend into the predominant male culture; avoiding public events and staying away from meetings or keeping silent at them; avoiding conflicts, risks, and controversial situations. They made few attempts to make their achievements known or to get credit for their own contributions to problem-solving or other organizational tasks.

So, although they succeeded in blending into the background and not generating resentment, they did so at the cost of limited recognition of their competence.

The performance pressures on people in token positions generate a set of attitudes and behaviors that appear sex-linked, in the case of women, but can be understood better as situational responses, true of any person in a token role. Perhaps what has been called "fear of success in women" is really the token woman's *fear of visibility* because of the likelihood of retaliation. The token must often choose between trying to limit visibility—and being overlooked—or taking advantage of publicity—and being labeled a "troublemaker."

The token woman's difficulties don't stop with the pressures and dilemma that accompany her high visibility in the mostly-male corporate hierarchy. The token woman also shares the problems of any foreigner attempting to operate in an alien culture.

Token women do not share the same unspoken understandings that male executives share as members of the "male culture." For smooth interaction, groups require both discretion (the ability to put statements in their proper perspective) and a shared vocabulary of attitudes (the ability to take feelings and sentiments for granted) so that they can avoid the time-consuming process of translation. At best, group members are likely to be uncomfortable and uncertain when the group is "invaded."

Ironically, token women were thus instruments for underlining rather than undermining the majority male culture. At Indsco, this phenomenon operated most clearly on occasions that brought together people from many parts of the organization who did not know each other well—at training programs and at dinners and cocktail parties during meetings. Here, the camaraderie of men, as in other work and social settings, was based in part on tales of sexual adventures, ability in "hunting" and "capturing" women, and off-color jokes. Other themes involved work prowess and sports, especially golf and fishing. The capacity for and enjoyment of drinking provided the context.

These themes were dramatized and acted out more fervently in the presence of token women than when only men were present. When the men were alone they were just as likely to talk shop or discuss domestic subjects e.g., a house one of them was building.

The token women reported examples of "testing" to see how they would respond to the "male" culture. They said many sexual innuendos or displays of locker-room humor were put on for their benefit, especially by the younger men. (The older men tended to parade business successes.) One woman was a team leader at a workshop (and the only woman) when her team decided to use as its slogan, "The shit of the week," looking to her for a reaction. By raising the issue and forcing her to choose not to participate, the men in the group created an occasion for uniting against her as an outsider and asserting male solidarity. Such behavior served to isolate the women and make them uncomfortable at those very moments when, ironically, people were supposed to be relaxing and having fun.

On more formal occasions, as in meetings, men often interrupted themselves to apologize to a token woman for "male" expressions—swearing, for instance, or sports metaphors:

"Do you know what 'an end run' is, dear?"—thus putting the token in her place, an interloper who took up the group's time. Men's questions or apologies represented a way of asking whether the old or expected cultural rules were still operative—can we still swear? toss a football? use technical jargon? go drinking? tell "in" jokes? By posing these questions overtly, men set the terms under which token women could enter the relationship.

Most women did not want to make a fuss, especially about issues they considered trivial, and irrelevant to their job status, like saying "goddamn" or having doors opened for them. They quickly agreed that things should proceed as they would if women were not present, and they felt embarrassment about stopping the flow of the conversation. None wanted to be a "wet blanket." Thus, saleswomen were often in the odd position of reassuring peers and customers that they could go ahead and do something in the women's presence—like swearing—that the women themselves would *not* be permitted to do. They listened to dirty jokes, for example, but reported they would not dare tell one themselves.

In some cases, men did not want to have token women around all the time; they had secrets to preserve or simly did not know how far they could trust the women, especially those who didn't seem to play by all the rules. The result was sometimes "quarantine"—keeping tokens away from some occasions. Men held informal pre-meeting meetings. They rarely discussed certain topics in the presence of their women peers: admissions of low commitment to the company or concerns about job performance, ways of getting around formal rules, political plotting for mutual advantage, strategies for impressing certain corporate executives.

Women also tended to be excluded from the networks by which informal training and socialization occurred and the politics behind the formal system were exposed. In a few cases, women trainees didn't get direct criticism in time to improve their performance. They didn't even know their work wasn't considered up to par until told to find jobs in other divisions. Toward the upper levels of the corporation, the tendency for peer groups to "quarantine" women was reinforced by men-only social establishments. One senior personnel administrator, committed to placing more women in top executive jobs, was concerned about whether they could overcome the limitations of being excluded from informal exchanges at male clubs.

In contrast, the men also sought reassurance that the token women would not turn against them or use information to harm the group. This was a quite rational concern on occasion. With government pressures and public interest mounting, Indsco women were often asked to speak to classes or women's groups or to testify before investigating committees. One woman was called in by her manager before her testimony at hearings on discrimination against women in business; he wanted to hear her testimony in advance and have censorship rights. She refused, but then made only very general and bland statements at the hearing anyway.

Male peers sought reassurance about embarrassing as well as damaging disclosures. They feared that tokens would find some of the things the men naturally did silly or ridiculous and would insult them where they felt vulnerable. The men also wanted to know that the tokens would not use their inside information to make the men look bad to other women. The joking remarks Indsco men made when they saw women colleagues occasionally eating lunch with the secretaries—"What do you 'girls' find so interesting to talk about?"—revealed some of their concerns.

There were three ways token women at Indsco could demonstrate loyalty and qualify for a closer relationship with the dominants. First, they could let slide (or even participate in) statements prejudicial to other women. They could allow themselves to be viewed as "exceptions" to the "general rule" that women have a variety of undesirable or unsuitable characteristics. (It is an irony of the token situation that women could be treated as both representatives of their type and exceptions to it, sometimes by the same people.)

Token women could also demonstrate loyalty by allowing themselves and women in general to provide a source of humor for the group. At meetings and training sessions, women were occasionally the subjects of ridicule or joking remarks about their incompetence. Some of the women who were insulted by such innuendos found it easier to appear to agree than to start an argument. When a woman objected, the men denied any hostility or unfriendly intention, instead accusing the woman, by inference, of "lacking a sense of humor."

Thirdly, tokens could demonstrate their gratitude for being included by not criticizing their situation or pressing for any more advantage. One major taboo area involved complaints about the job or requests for promotion. The women were supposed to be grateful for getting as far as they had (when other women clearly had not) and thus expected to bury dissatisfaction and aspirations.

There was a tendency to encapsulate executive-level women by defining special slots for them. Once women began to occupy certain jobs—e.g., positions in personnel, benefits, equal opportunity, and affirmative action offices—these jobs gradually came to be defined as "women's slots." Many women, who would otherwise have been interested in the growth and challenge these jobs offered, said they wouldn't touch such a position: "The label makes it a dead end."

At Indsco, tokens were often misperceived at first; they were assumed to be occupying a *usual female* position rather than their *unusual* (for a woman) job. In the office, they were often taken for secretaries; on sales trips, especially when they traveled with a male colleague, they were often taken for wives or mistresses; with customers, they were first assumed to be temporarily substituting for a man who was the "real" salesperson; with a male peer at meetings, they were seen as the assistant; when entertaining customers, they were thought to be the wife or date. Mistaken first impressions can be corrected, although they give the token the extra burden of untangling awkward exchanges and establishing accurate and appropriate role relations. But even when others knew that the women were not secretaries, there was still a tendency within the organization to treat them like secretaries, or make secretary-like demands on them.

In other ways, too, Indsco women were treated in stereotyped fashion by their peers and managers. One asked for a promotion and talked about looking for a better job. Her manager's first assumption was that she did not feel "loved" and that it was his fault for failing to give love to a woman. But what *she* really wanted was more challenge and more money.

The situation of the token women at Indsco was stressful. They were always on display; they were always being tested; they were alternately excluded from the all-male culture of their peers and, when they proved their loyalty, included in it without being able to feel comfortable. Even the best strategy they designed to cope with their anomalous position was likely to have some inner repercussions—ranging from inhibition of self-expression to feelings of inadequacy.

It has been hypothesized that one of the "lethal" aspects of the male role—that literally kills men off at an early age—is the inhibition of self-disclosure. Although a certain amount of masking of personal feelings is, of course, part of the culture in large organizations, this was even more the case for token women. In addition, as women in a culture that defined "maleness" as the norm, they could never be fully themselves or completely natural.

But their peculiar situation was not automatically determined by the fact that they were women. Instead, I believe, it came from the numbers involved, the fact that there were so few of them. When we see women having problems succeeding in management, we shouldn't ask what's wrong with the women and how women can be improved, but rather how the situation—tokenism or powerlessness or organizational loneliness—is preventing them from showing their strengths.

What is the solution? It is simultaneously simply and controversial: *more women.* All the training programs in the world cannot guarantee outstanding or even competent job performance if the organizational situation itself creates handicaps. Women will make fine managers—as good as men—and without the need for special attention, when companies hire and promote enough of them. Until that is accomplished, organizations can try to minimize the handicapping effects of scarcity by bringing in several women at once, by giving women visibility for their job accomplishments rather than their unusualness, and by clustering women rather than giving every group its token.

Numerical goals are objectionable to some companies, but I argue that they will utimately benefit organizations as well as women. It seems clear that relative numbers can strongly affect a person's fate in a work situation and either limit her contribution through tokenism or expand it in a more balanced peer group. In this light the problem resides in the *system*, not in the sex characteristics of the individual. To make a change, therefore, requires action at the *system-level*, that is, in organizational strategy. Otherwise, tokenism will continue to be only a self-perpetuating illusion of progress.

Career Concerns of Black Managers

Bernard Sarachek

If career development is to be handled equitably throughout an organization, higher management must become aware of the special problems and motivations of minority employees who have stepped onto the managerial ladder.

During the last decade, minority employees have been slowly moving up into managerial positions; they have, as some whites declare, "come a long way." In their own view, however, for the most part they have not come far enough, and the climbing of the ladder is made more difficult by the fact that there is still a gap in understanding between blacks and whites.

What are the major career concerns of blacks who aspire to, or have recently attained, managerial positions in industrial settings? This is a question to which higher management (both black and white) must give serious thought if career development is to be handled equitably throughout the organization. In an effort to find some answers to this question, I interviewed 16 black managers—15 male, one female—in two large plants of a national corporation.

In one plant, blacks accounted for less than 3 percent of the work force, while in the other, they were in the majority. In both plants, company efforts to move blacks into management were relatively recent: The 16 interviewees comprised nearly the entire black manage-

rial contingent. The interviewees came from rural Southern and urban Northern settings, from broken homes and stable families, from farm families as well as working-class and small-business families, and from predominantly white neighborhoods and predominantly black ones. Considering the small sample, then, the diversity of backgrounds was impressive.

Each interviewee was encouraged to describe any aspect of his personal history, attitudes, or concerns that he might choose. The responses revealed three principal areas of concern: (1) class consciousness; (2) maintenance of racial identity; and (3) the need for a personal sponsor in higher management. They also revealed some significant tendencies in the higher management of this particular corporation. In many cases, I feel, it would be most enlightening to quote the interviewees directly; they will be identified as subjects A, B, C, and so on.

A MATTER OF CLASS

Most interviewees displayed a keen awareness of clear-cut class barriers and differential class treatment. For instance, A said:

> The closest I can remember to a real anger was three years ago when the company put out a

circular telling everyone that the only reason they didn't have any Negro supervisors was that they had none in their employ prepared to be managers. How could they tell? Unless you were white, had a college degree or previous management experience, upper management would turn you down for promotion, and the supervisors knew that. It makes a supervisor look bad every time he recommends anyone who is turned down.

Even a college degree was no assurance that one could leap the hurdle into a middle-class job. Several interviewees completed their college degrees only to experience the sort of response reported here by B:

I asked my supervisor several times to move me into the chemical lab. He said there was no chem lab. Later he started telling me that only people with Ph.D.s and M.A.s and years of experience worked in the chem lab. Then when I finished college I brought my diploma in and showed it around. My foreman said, "Congratulations, that's great," and then he started laying out the work for the day. . . . It was like telling me, "All right, that's fine, now get back to work." . . . I finally got so frustrated I wrote my own letter to Personnel. I told them that if I couldn't get a job more suited to my talents, then I'd leave. . . . I was interviewed by Personnel and picked up by the chemistry lab. I was lucky. But if I hadn't taken a desperate chance, I might never have moved over the line.

There were many statements similar to that of C:

When they made me a supervisor, I was amazed. Oh, I'm better than any supervisor I ever had, but I never expected to become one. But, you know, it's funny. For years I didn't feel resentful. Then, when I finally was promoted to supervision, it dawned on me that I should have been promoted long ago. Now I am resentful. At my age, the best I can hope for is promotion to maybe one higher level of management. It isn't fair that I don't have the same chance to move up as far as a young white boy just graduating from college.

The movement across class lines into management involves some readjustments in val-ues, rituals, and behavior. Several interviewees expressed cynicism with company etiquette. D noted that the telling of a joke, usually an ethnic joke, was a "kind of ticket of admission" to management meetings, and added that "There's a lot of backslapping and forced phony friendship at these meetings. . . . I go along with it . . . to prove that I'm a regular guy." E said, "It doesn't pay to talk too openly when you're in management," and A was particularly proud that he could control his anger. In fact, there was an almost universal concern for controlling anger and consciously prethinking one's statements. Such control often exacted a toll from the individual: He might have to blow off steam at home.

Other comments reflected interviewees' concern about proper conduct. Some referred to the importance of dressing in an appropriate managerial style, being skilled in the arts of social etiquette, developing a proper command of the English language, and being able to communicate without employing curse words.

Almost all interviewees emphasized the importance of a college education—not just for getting promoted, but for learning to be a better manager. (The university, after all, is a predominantly white middle-class milieu.)

THE ETHNIC QUESTION

Although questions of ethnic identity and class identity fuse at many points, they are distinct. Class concerns focus around one's awareness of barriers to upward economic mobility, while ethnic identity has to do with preserving one's racial reference group.

The black who chooses to cling to an ethnic identity is in a precarious position. If the reference-group identity he seeks is retain lacks suitable definition in his mind, how can he be sure he is not going too far, sacrificing his loyalties and identity, when he makes necessary accommodations to the outside society? A Jewish-American can outwardly attempt to look and act "like everyone else" but still not question the fact that he is Jewish. The black who tries to look and act like everyone else finds

himself asking whether he is risking his "identity."

External pressure on the interviewees to
clarify their black identities was substantial.
Frequently, their children had more militant
feelings about ethnic identity than they did,
and several interviewees mentioned having
experienced distrust on the part of some of their
black subordinates. They spoke of "being
tested" by these subordinates to see whether
they had abandoned their black identity in
order to conform to management's expectations.

One way to handle the black identity question is to reject such identity. Interestingly, the
only two interviewees to choose this course were
the highest-ranking ones. F, who is very light-
skinned, divorced his black wife shortly after
moving into supervision, and subsequently
married a white woman. He had this to say:

> I never really ran into discrimination before I
> started working for this company. . . . This
> created a real identity crisis for me. I spent a lot
> of years thinking it through until I finally
> discovered that . . . I'm an individual. . . .
> [Earlier] I just accepted it as part of the system
> that blacks don't get promoted into super-
> vision, so I found my challenge outside . . .
> racing cars and chasing women . . . I don't see
> any sense facing realities on the job all day
> long and then facing more off the job. . . . I'm a
> man who thrives on competition. The payoffs
> for being a successful competitor are freedom
> and money. I like both. A vice-presidency is
> only a couple more levels up for me, and I think
> that job would give me the challenge and
> freedom I crave. . . . I've plotted out just what I
> have to do and how long it should take me to get
> there.

F's enormous drive may be explained by
much more than the way he chose to resolve his
identity crisis. However, if a person rejects
group identities and loyalties, he can be very
much alone and vulnerable. Conversely, one
who idealizes his own ego cannot easily incorporate a group identity as part of that ego. In a
world in which discrimination against blacks is
real and black hostility toward those who reject
their black identity is also real, a potential

threat to ego exists. Aggressive competition is a
means of testing and proving the strength of
one's ego.

A also tended to idealize his ego, placing
"self" as something to be revered and protected.
He said:

> I have no interest in movements and organi-
> zations. I think of myself as an individual, not
> as a classification, like Negro or Afro-Ameri-
> can. I have run into a few other supervisors who
> resented me because I'm Negro. I don't let
> discrimination stand in my way. . . . Now my
> reputation goes before me.

Other interviewees had developed highly
personalized ideologies. The most elaborate
ideologized vision of the world was described by
G:

> Whites and blacks can't trust each other. . . .
> In our world—as it is—it's better that whites
> and blacks are separate. It's part of the sys-
> tem. . . . Even the government can't buck the
> system. . . . Believe me, it's an effort to main-
> tain my integrity, moving up in management
> and at the same time being black. . . . The way
> I do it is to live strictly by the rules. That way
> you're safe. . . . I love to read because I learn a
> lot about how people behave. I particularly
> enjoy books of intrigue. . . . You may be sur-
> prised to hear what I'm going to say, but the
> higher you go in management, the more ac-
> cepting they are of blacks, because they operate
> by method, not emotion. . . . Management needs
> blacks to supervise blacks. I know the only
> reason I'm here is that I can understand and
> talk with other blacks.

In G's ideology, he has no control over his
world and no responsibility for it. He is a cog in
the machinery of "the system," and the only
realm for freedom is underground, living by
intrigue while outwardly conforming to the
rules of the game.

The interviewees who generated such ideologies all had one thing in common: they were
groping for explanations of personal crisis—in
their home lives or on the job.

THE JOB AS A MISSION

One can affirm one's black identity while moving up a white-dominated hierarchy if his job enables him to further the interests of his fellow blacks. The company offered many opportunities for accomplishing this synthesis: It maintained a program for recruiting and training underprivileged workers and actively recruited high school graduates from inner-city areas. In addition, an individual could actively serve his fellow blacks by working in certain personnel-related jobs, including interviewing and hiring, review of disciplinary charges brought by employees, and job improvement training. H, a supervisor in a training program for the underprivileged, had this to say:

> Many trainees identify me as "Uncle Tom" and the "cabin nigger" but I don't let it get to me because I understand the circumstances. They've never had an opportunity to trust a supervisor before. Frankly, if they close down this training shop, there's a real question in my mind as to whether I'd want to stay on with the company. I want to work with people and help them.

With one exception, all the interviewees who had held positions that allowed them to synthesize the job and a sense of mission spoke of their experiences in these positions with pride and satisfaction similar to H's. That one exception, A, said he "was a little disappointed" when the company made him head of supervisors for the training shop for the underprivileged. This reaction seems consistent with the fact that A was one of the interviewees who chose to ignore racial identity and affirm their individuality.

Several interviewees were organizationally active in the black community. Three of them had sought advancement to greater status, power, and respect in the community when routes to promotion within the company had been blocked; now these men were advancing both within the company and outside. One said he had no difficulty in maintaining his dual managerial role; the other two said they had been thinking about the need to make a career

choice between the company and their outside organizations. Of the 16 interviewees, the three with dual roles showed the most ardent feelings about their moral obligations to the black community. J said, "I get a lot of satisfaction out of being a pioneer."

THE SPONSOR

Several interviewees mentioned the importance of having had the informal aid and sponsorship of higher-status white managers. (That the sponsors were white reflected the fact that the interviewees were the first blacks to be moved into management.) These interviewees mentioned several areas in which the sponsors provided services that went beyond teaching them the job of supervision:

There were a number of incidents in which proven or suspected discrimination obstructed the black managers' abilities to perform their jobs, and some higher-level manager's aid was sought to break these obstructions. Sponsors also frequently "broke trail" for the interviewees by spreading their reputations through the organization; brought interviewees to the attention of higher management when promotion opportunities arose; and publicly acclaimed the interviewees at supervisory meetings, lunches, and informal gatherings.

Sponsors often were not direct superiors of the interviewees, but rather managers who had previously been their superiors. In any case, these informal relationships not only built loyalties between interviewees and their sponsors, but also reinforced the interviewees' feelings of trust, optimism, and loyalty toward the company.

IMPLICATIONS FOR MANAGEMENT

The interviews at this company suggest how important it is for top management to discover ways by which managerial talents can be recognized and developed within the firm. This firm has a national reputation for progressive management techniques; yet for years it had failed to identify the existing managerial talent within its own blue-collar work force. Then, through ignorance and indifference, it had failed to provide the necessary promotion incentives to these blue-collar workers. Other, less forward-thinking organizations are undoubtedly in even worse positions.

The data drawn from the interviews also indicate that a job of human engineering may be necessary if a company wants to draw forth the fullest potential of minority members moving into management. At an early point in their managerial or white-collar careers, those who have the greatest personal need to affirm their minority identity can be aided by being rotated through the sorts of positions that would allow them to combine a sense of company commitment with a sense of community commitment. Those who choose to strongly assert their individuality rather than their minority identities may not need or want such an opportunity.

Finally, the comments of the interviewees suggest the desirability of formally or informally building into the managerial system a process of sponsorship for minority members newly arrived in management. The aim of such sponsorship should not be to create a climate of favoritism, of course, but to aid the new manager in adapting to an unfamiliar role and in dealing with various attitudes on the part of his or her co-workers.

Section **8**

Individual Strategies for Career Management

Management scholars and practitioners alike have recognized the importance of planning, organizing, directing, and controlling activities in order to better assure organizational effectiveness. Few managers transfer and systematically apply these skills to their own careers. Yet these same planning and organizing skills are required to promote individual career effectiveness. This section deals with decision-making and planning activities related to careers.

Managers are constantly having to make decisions about their careers: Accept a transfer? Accept a promotion? Look for a new job? Start a second career? In the first selection Janis and Wheeler develop a framework and a process for better understanding career choices. They identify several ways to make decisions and suggest a procedure to assure better decision-making.

The second selection deals with a subject that is having an increasingly important impact on career decision-making—dual-career couples. With the increase of professional and managerial women in the work force, the incidence of dual-career couples can only become more and more widespread. The Halls address four main issues: (1) the conflicts of dual-career couples; (2) the impact on organizations; (3) managing two careers; and (4) company responses to dual-career couples.

A variety of strategies for individual career planning are identified in the third reading. Several strategies for goal setting, action planning, and problem solving career issues are described. Primarily career planning focuses on the individual's wants, skills, and desires for the future. As suggested in the figure[1] below, an individual's career plans work best when combined with the information provided through the organizational career planning system.

[1]From Elmer H. Burack, "Why All of the Confusion About Career Planning?" *Human Resource Management* (Summer 1977), pp. 21-23.

Organization Career Planning	Individual Career Planning
• future needs • career ladders • assessment of individual potential • connecting organizational need/ opportunity with individual need/desire • coordination and audit of career system	• self-awareness abilities and interests • planning goals: life and work • planning to achieve goals • alternatives, internal and external to organization • career ladders, internal and external to organization

Thinking Clearly About Career Choices

Irving Janis
Dan Wheeler

"Years ago I made a bad mistake, and now I'm paying for it: I'm trapped in this job."

"I should have found out how this firm was run before taking their offer. I had other good prospects at the time."

"They led me down the garden path, and I was damn fool enough to be taken in."

When 81 middle-level executives of a large industrial organization were interviewed for a study of career satisfaction several years ago, a sizable number said they were disgusted with their jobs. In confidence, they complained about petty rules and dull routines that interfered with getting their work done, obstacles to being promoted, long hours that were ruining their home lives, and the disruptions caused by repeated reorganizations. Listening carefully to their complaints, the investigators also heard something else: the men's regrets at their own miscalculations when they first decided to come to work for the company. A few (like those quoted above) candidly admitted that they should have found out much more about what it would really be like to work there before accepting the job.

We have heard comparable complaints from lawyers, physicians, public administrators, and technical specialists. Why do so many intelligent, well-educated people make poor career choices they sooner or later regret? Why do so many fail to correct their mistakes, despite opportunities to reshape their careers?

When people confront a complex problem of trying to satisfy many different objectives and foresee the consequences of various alternatives, they often come up against the limitations of their mental capabilities. Misjudgments also stem from pressures to conform and other social constraints. Above all, the stress of making crucial choices, with serious consequences that one might later regret, sometimes itself impairs critical judgment.

Psychological studies suggest that most people tend to short-circuit the essential stages of search and appraisal when they become aware of possible undesirable consequences of their choices. Even the most mature and the best educated can deceive themselves into believing they have complete information after brief contact with a so-called expert and perhaps a few informal discussions with friends.

Whenever a decision entails serious, life-long consequences, it pays to use sound decision-making procedures. People *can* make sound decisions, and new psychological theories and findings can help them. Some of the approaches we will discuss can be carried out on one's own. Others may require the help of a career counselor or personal adviser. Even people who are highly experienced at making decisions can benefit from a bit of guidance if they are choosing a career, changing jobs, moving to a different city, or whatever.

Consider the following dilemma: You are offered an excellent position in a large organization that is much better than any alternative offer. It will make more use of your training and skills and offers better pay, better working conditions, and greater opportunities for advancement. But the organization is having some financial difficulties that sooner or later could require drastic budget cuts, which could result in the elimination of a large number of jobs, including the one you are being offered. For a decision of this kind, there are *two* risky scenarios to worry about: one is dramatic and obvious, while the other is more subtle and might not receive as much attention as it deserves.

Scenario 1. Recognizing a unique opportunity, you decide to accept the offer. You work hard, you are successful, and you are rapidly promoted, just as you had been led to expect. But after a few years, your worst fears come true. You are laid off, along with hundreds of others, and you suddenly find you are unable to find an acceptable opening in your field in a tight job market. This is what actually happened to thousands of professional engineers and executives when the aerospace industry underwent cutbacks during the early 1970s. And something similar is happening right now to thousands of men and women who have just obtained their Ph.D. degrees and are trying to get jobs in college teaching.

Scenario 2. Recognizing the risks posed by Scenario 1, you decide to play it safe by refusing the offer. Instead, you accept an inferior posi-

tion, with less opportunity for career development, in a financially untroubled organization that everyone says will be going strong long after you reach retirement age. But suppose Scenario 1 does not materialize and you regret the sacrifice you made for the sake of job security? Your work in the safe organization turns out to be no better than could be expected—dull, routine, very little opportunity to make use of your skills or develop your potentialities, and no real hope of promotion. As the years go by, you learn that people in your occupation who took jobs in the more attractive company are comparatively well satisfied and the most talented ones are being rapidly promoted. In short, you have to live not only with a blighted career, but also with the realization that you have failed to grasp your one great career opportunity.

Though the different consequences of such decisions may seem quite obvious, many people overlook some of the risks that could lead to unpleasant outcomes. Sometimes they are simply unwilling to think about such painful things. In the case described above, the most attractive alternative required the calculated risk of a relatively sudden, dramatic disaster, whereas the calculated risk for not choosing that alternative was a long, drawn-out tragedy that could be just as bad or worse. Our choices are often structured in just that way.

What is the advantage of working out these gloomy scenarios? If we don't, we may not know what kind of information we need on the possible consequences of our choices. If we ignore the threat of a drastic budget cut, for instance, we're not likely to seek inside information that will enable us to estimate the likelihood that such a cut will occur. Even if no such information can be obtained, there are advantages to becoming keenly aware of all the things that can go wrong after a decision is made. We can then keep our losses to a minimum by making *contingency plans.*

Studies of occupational choices by economist Eli Ginzberg and others indicate that many people never make a deliberate decision at all. They move from one job to another in haphazard fashion, accepting any new offer that seems better than their current position, without systematically weighing the pros and cons. Even people who are in skilled occupations sometimes find themselves slipping into a career they might not want by taking one small step after another. A person hears about an opportunity to obtain specialized training that sounds as if it could be useful, signs up for it, and then accepts the first job that comes along that makes some use of that training.

Conflict over a career decision usually begins when a man or woman is confronted by some challenging new information. Such a "challenge" may take the form of an opportunity or a threat, an offer of another job that has many attractive features, perhaps, or a report that his or her company may go out of business. Only when people believe that the risks involved in the decision are serious—and that they can find a satisfactory solution—do they actively and thoroughly examine the alternatives. In their recent book, *Decision-Making*, Irving Janis and Leon Mann identify serious flaws in the way many people make decisions and four coping patterns:

Complacency.   People who ignore challenging information about the choices they must make are demonstrating complacency. A typical challenge that people who work in large organizations sometimes choose to ignore is the threat of losing their status and some of their special prerogatives as a result of a reorganization. When complacency is the dominant pattern, people do not believe the risks are serious. They take the attitude that it won't happen, or, even if it does, "It won't affect me."

Complacency also occurs when the challenging information is accepted and the person acknowledges there are risks in continuing with what he's doing—but sees no risks in choosing a new course of action. This type of complacency is shown by men and women who immediately accept an offer of what appears to be a better job with more opportunity for advancement without spending any time or effort to find out what they might be letting themselves in for.

Of course, complacency is entirely appropriate for many decisions, especially when nothing much is at stake. It is justified whenever there are no serious risks from failing to make the best choice among alternatives or when there is no reason to believe dire warnings of disaster.

Defensive avoidance.   When people confronted with a decision believe there is a danger but don't believe that they can find an acceptable solution, they are engaging in what we call defensive avoidance. They may be upset on one level, but manage to remain calm by resorting to wishful thinking, which enables them to deny the seriousness of the threat. The specific patterns of denial can vary considerably. Sometimes it is much like the reaction of people who ignore danger signals from their bodies. For example, there are many who do not do anything about swellings, even though they know such symptoms could be cancer. They try not to think about their symptoms, and they stay away from their physicians and others who could tell them what the symptoms may mean.

Middle-level executives may be reacting in essentially the same defensive way when they fail to think about the implications of a series of minor complaints about their work from superiors. Policy-makers engage in defensive avoidance when they are intent on developing rationalizations for a particular course of action—without examining alternative courses. Some political writers argue that this was the flaw of "the best and the brightest" who were making policy in Washington during the Vietnam war. The most common strategies of defensive avoidance are (1) rationalization ("It can't happen to me"), (2) procrastination ("Nothing needs to be done about it now. I can take care of it later"), and (3) buck-passing ("I am not the one who needs to do something about it; let George do it").

People engaging in defensive avoidance often appear outwardly calm. They are even able to hide the stress from their own awareness. Only when people are forced to deal with some aspect of the threatening situation does the anxiety appear.

Hypervigilance. When people are faced with an immediate threat and believe that there is not enough time to find a solution, they may become hypervigilant. In its most extreme form, hypervigilance is referred to as panic. When hypervigilance is the dominant pattern, people search frantically for a way out of the dilemma and seize upon hastily contrived solutions. They are likely to overlook the full range of consequences of their choice—as well as other viable alternatives. People who are in a panic or near-panic state sometimes show signs of cognitive constriction, such as a reduction in immediate memory span and simplistic thinking. Fortunately, panic is not a very common response.

When a man or woman realizes that the deadline for accepting an offer is approaching and is keenly aware of the risks and consequences of the choices, he or she may display all the symptoms of acute emotional stress. Such a person is likely to fail to make effective use of the limited time available and to choose on the basis of grossly inadequate search and appraisal. Similarly, when people are heavily in debt and lose their jobs, they may get into near-panic states in their attempts to find another one immediately. In their excited state, they may accept the first offer that comes along, but they may also fail to notice subtle signs of trouble ahead that they would normally take seriously.

Vigilance. Vigilant decision-making occurs when anyone faced with a crucial choice believes that (1) the threat is serious, (2) they can find a solution, and (3) there is enough time. When these conditions are met, people conduct an effective search for alternatives and carefully evaluate those alternatives.

Further, they evaluate the information in a relatively *unbiased* way. They also work out contingency plans in case one or another of the risks materializes. In contrast, those who display complacency, defensive avoidance, or hypervigilance are unprepared for even minor setbacks. They develop strong feelings of regret and are much less likely to stick to their decision, even though changing may be quite costly in terms of time, money, and reputation.

Several procedures have been developed to encourage the vigilant coping pattern. They are most applicable at the point that a person is approaching an irrevocable commitment, but has not yet started to carry out the decision. One of these is the balance-sheet procedure, an exercise that requires a person to answer questions about potential risks as well as gains that he or she had not previously contemplated. The procedure involves classifying the expected consequences for each alternative course of action into four main categories: (1) utilitarian gains or losses for self, (2) utilitarian gains or losses for significant others, (3) self-approval or -disapproval, and (4) approval or disapproval from significant others. The decision-maker fills out for each alternative a balance-sheet grid, which describes the positive anticipations and negative anticipations expected from each of the four categories.

One executive who filled out such a balance sheet was thinking about whether to leave his position as a production manager in a large manufacturing plant (see box on page 214). He listed a number of "negative anticipations," from long hours and constant time pressures to "stupid" demands made by the top managers, to his own irritability at home as a consequence of job problems. Nevertheless, this man decided to stay where he was. Why? Because of the weight he gave to the positive entries in the nonutilitarian categories—his pride in his role as leader of a competent team, his sense of welcome responsibility for their high morale, his warm, friendly relationship with the others, whom he did not want to let down by leaving. He felt that his friendship with his immediate superior was especially rewarding and that together the two of them could save their team from the negligence and stupidity of the firm's top managers. All the negative aspects of the job did, however, affect this executive's contingency plans: he was determined to find a position in another firm if the men in his unit were scattered in a planned reorganization.

Studies with Yale College seniors suggest that the balance sheet is a feasible way of stimulating people to become aware of major gaps in their information about decisions. In *Decision-Making*, Janis and Mann illustrate with the following example how this procedure can be something quite different from a coldly intellectual exercise:

"One senior who originally was planning to go to a graduate business school for training to become an executive in his father's Wall Street firm was surprised at first when he discovered that the cells in the balance-sheet grid pertaining to self-approval or -disapproval were almost completely empty. After looking over the standard list of items to be considered in those categories, he was stimulated to write down several ways in which his career as a broker would fail to meet his ethical ideals or satisfy his desire to help improve the quality of life for people in his community. As he thought about these neglected considerations, he became worried and depressed. Then, while filling out the cells of the balance-sheet grid for his second choice—going to law school—he began to brighten up a bit. Eventually he became glowingly enthusiastic when he hit upon the notion that instead of becoming a Wall Street lawyer he might better meet his objectives by being trained for a career in a legal aid clinic or in public-interest law. Finally, his mood became more sober, but with some residual elation, as he conscientiously listed the serious drawbacks (parental disapproval, relatively low income, poor prospects for travel abroad, etc.) of the new career plan he had conceived. Afterward he thanked the interviewer for making him realize he had been on the wrong track and for helping him arrive at his new career plan, which, in fact, he had worked out entirely by himself in response to the open-ended nature of the balance-sheet procedure."

What works for Yale seniors may not, of course, work for other kinds of people. However, three large field experiments have shown that it can work with other populations as well. The tests were done on high-school seniors trying to decide where to go to college and two groups of adults deciding whether or not to diet and attend an early-morning exercise class for health reasons. Those who were asked to fill out balance sheets in making their choices were more likely to adhere to their decision and had fewer regrets afterward than those who did not use the balance sheets.

Why is it beneficial to go through the laborious procedure of filling out a balance sheet? First of all, as in the case of contrasting outcome scenarios, such a procedure counteracts complacency and promotes vigilance. Second, it makes the decision-maker realize the need for contingency plans—figuring out what to do if one or another of the unfavorable consequences listed in the minus columns were to materialize. Third, it helps one to make a more comprehensive appraisal of the alternatives. By seeing all the entries, the decision-maker can start thinking about possible trade-offs, concentrate on the major differences among alternatives, and think about the degrees of importance of crucial pros and cons.

Another procedure designed to promote vigilance is stress inoculation, which is appropriate shortly after a decision is made but before it is carried out. Under this approach, a person is given vivid descriptions of what it will be like to experience the expected negative consequences of the chosen course. Such a method not only makes him or her more aware of the probable difficulties and losses to be expected, but also promotes a certain amount of inner preparation that reduces the likelihood that the person will feel helpless and demoralized if temporary or long-range setbacks occur. We would expect stress-inoculation procedures to be effective for any decision that entails severe short-term losses before substantial long-term gains are attained. The decision to become a lawyer or a physician, for example, entails many long years of training and apprenticeship before attaining professional status and the rewards that go with it. Irving Janis's studies of surgery patients tend to confirm the benefits of stress inoculation. Patients who received information about the unpleasant consequences of their operations were less likely to overreact emotionally to setbacks and adversities after making their decisions (although the data are correlational—that is, other possible explanations for the patients' improved attitudes are not ruled out). Supporting evidence was subsequently obtained by other investigators in controlled field experiments with hospitalized patients.

A Manager's Balance Sheet

The grid lays out the pros and cons of one alternative facing a production manager at a large manufacturing plant who is contemplating a job change: whether or not to remain in his present position. Balance sheets would be filled out for all other alternatives as well—for example, whether to seek a lateral transfer within the company. (The information comes from *Decision-Making*, by Irving Janis and Leon Mann.)

	Positive Anticipations	Negative Anticipations
Tangible gains and losses for *self*	1. Satisfactory pay. 2. Plenty of opportunities to use my skills and competencies. 3. For the present, my status in the organization is okay (but it won't be for long if I am not promoted in the next year).	1. Long hours. 2. Constant time pressures—deadlines too short. 3. Unpleasant paper work. 4. Poor prospects for advancement to a higher-level position. 5. Repeated reorganizations make my work chaotic. 6. Constant disruption from high turnover of other executives I deal with.
Tangible gains and losses for *others*	1. Adequate income for family. 2. Wife and children get special privileges because of my position in the firm.	1. Not enough time free to spend with my family. 2. Wife often has to put up with my irritability when I come home after bad days at work.
Self-approval or self-disapproval	1. This position allows me to make full use of my potentialities. 2. Proud of my achievements. 3. Proud of the competent team I have shaped up. 4. Sense of meaningful accomplishment when I see the products for which we are responsible.	1. Sometimes feel I'm a fool to continue putting up with the unreasonable deadlines and other stupid demands made by the top managers.
Social approval or disapproval	1. Approval of men on my team who look up to me as their leader and who are good friends. 2. Approval of my superior who is a friend and wants me to stay.	1. Very slight skeptical reaction of my wife—she asks me if I might be better off in a different firm. 2. A friend in another firm who has been wanting to wangle something for me will be disappointed.

Does the same sort of thing happen when a person is choosing a job or making plans to retire? The answer is yes. Evidence from a dozen or so field experiments shows that stress inoculation can dampen postdecisional stress and minimize the tendency to reverse the decision when setbacks are encountered. A number of studies indicate that new employees who are given realistic preparatory information when offered the job, or immediately after they accept it, are more likely to stay with the organization.

Where can people go to obtain stress inoculation when they are about to start a new job or make some other important life decision? If they try to do it on their own, they should seek as much information as possible about the job, preferably from someone who knows the inside story and can give a vivid account of what is in store for them, along with some realistic re-assurances that counteract feelings of helpless-ness and hopelessness. It may be very difficult to find a good informant. In such a case, a professional counselor can be helpful if he or she is trained as a decision counselor.

The term "decision counseling" refers to the collaboration of a consultant and client in diagnosing and improving the quality of the person's decisions. This type of counseling can be quite nondirective: the counselor refrains from giving advice about which course of action is best. Instead, he tries to help clients make the fullest possible use of their own resources and reach decisions consistent with their own val-ues. The counselor may be somewhat directive, however, in suggesting where to go for perti-nent information, how to take account of knowl-edge about alternative courses of action, how to find out if deadlines are real or can be nego-tiated, what risks might require preparing con-tingency plans, and the like.

Although there are, as yet, few people who specialize in decision counseling, all these meth-ods may be employed by psychotherapists, career counselors, social workers, and other clinicians who deal with people at a time when they are making important personal decisions. The proposed interventions, which usually re-quire only one or two hours of counseling, obviously cannot be expected to transform per-sons with neurotic disorders who have chronic difficulties in arriving at decisions. Such per-sons require therapy far beyond the scope of decision counseling. But for people who occa-sionally display the defective coping patterns that are in everyone's repertoire, a session or two with a skilled counselor might bring about a marked improvement in the quality of the clients' decisions.

For example, if the client appears to be in a state of acute conflict and is losing hope of finding a good solution, the counselor can try to prevent defensive avoidance. He can start by asking whether there are relatives, friends, or acquaintances who know something about the problem, who might convey new perspectives. When a counselor senses that a client's rational

capabilities are blocked by wishful thinking or rationalizations, he may try to stimulate a full exploration of the pros and cons by asking him to develop a balance sheet. But this alone may not be enough.

With a new type of role-playing technique, called outcome psychodrama, the counselor can attempt to counteract defensive avoidance and stimulate vigilance. The client is asked to par-ticipate in a scenario that requires him to project himself into the future and to improvise a vivid retrospective account of what has hap-pened as a consequence of choosing one or another alternative. The procedure is repeated as many times as necessary to explore the potential risks and consequences of each choice. The counselor refrains from mentioning any specific consequences, leaving it up to the cli-ent's imagination to improvise the specific loss-es (or gains) that might result.

Outcome psychodrama was first used by Janis with clients who came to a family-service clinic with serious marital problems and were undecided about a divorce. Since the technique appeared to be helpful to them, Janis also tried it with male seniors at Yale who were deciding what to do after graduation. Each student was given a framework for constructing psychodra-matic scenarios for each of his leading alterna-tives. He was told to imagine that it was a year after graduation, that things were going "very badly—worse than you thought they would," and that he was having a heart-to-heart talk with a close friend. A supplementary psycho-drama was also tried out for favorable-outcome scenarios.

In most cases, new considerations emerged during the unfavorable-outcome psychodrama that affected the students' evaluation of the alternatives. Some of them were so impressed they changed their preferences. One senior, for example, came up with a number of negative outcomes when he played the role of a lawyer, his first choice of career, going through a postdecisional crisis. He felt the work involved "dull routines," the "stifling of all creativity," and a variety of ethical problems. As a result, he announced that he was inclined to pursue his second choice, a teaching career.

So far only a small amount of research has been done on the effectiveness of outcome psychodrama. What we have learned from recent research suggests it could have a detrimental effect in the early stages of decision-making: if the experience is an intense one, the client may lose hope of finding an adequate solution to his dilemma. It may be quite beneficial, however, in the later stages; especially if a person is about to make a drastic change without having worked out contingency plans. Counselors who try the outcome-psychodrama procedure should obviously use it with caution, and perhaps only in the later stages of decision-making.

While some interventions are not uniformly successful, there is impressive evidence that new self-help procedures and decision counseling, based on the theoretical model of coping patterns, are effective in many cases. There is good reason to be optimistic about the prospects of improving the quality of decisions that profoundly affect our lives. By helping people arrive at an accurate blueprint not only of the favorable and unfavorable consequences of what they decide, but also of the resources at their disposal, the decision counselor can help them build self-confidence, avoid biases and mental blocks, and develop realistic expectations of the future.

Dual Careers—How Do Couples and Companies Cope with the Problems?

Francine S. Hall
Douglas T. Hall

Two years ago, a personnel vice-president for one of the world's largest international banks was asked, "What does your bank do about dual-career couples?" "Nothing," was the reply. "That's their problem."

A few months later a female officer in this bank with the potential to go all the way to the top married a male officer with whom she had lived for several years. The bank had a nepotism rule that forbade two people in the same family to be officers, and this young, highly valued couple was in clear violation of this policy. (Ironically, as long as they were living together, everything was fine so far as the bank was concerned.) Therefore, one of them had to leave. But whom? The couple decided the woman (who was the more highly rated of the pair) should go. But the bank had been under suit by a women's group for sex discrimination in higher management positions, and the loss of this woman was costly indeed. As a result of this policy, the bank's nepotism rule was relaxed to permit relatives to be officers, so long as one would not be in a supervisory relationship over the other.

For reasons such as this, today the question of who is responsible for dealing with dual careers elicits a different response from that of the personnel vice-president above. Most firms, uncertain about *what* to do, still know they have to do something about employees in dual-career families. As one executive put it, "We're losing some damn good people!"

Increasing numbers of two-career couples have changed the composition, values, and mobility patterns of the workforce. (By "two-career couple" we mean a couple, either married or living together, who are both employed.) The consequence of dual-career couples is that traditional personnel policies and practices are no longer adequate to meet the changing needs and problems presented by many employees.

In this paper we will attempt to show how companies can begin to deal with these needs and problems. We will address four issues:

1. What are the typical characteristics and conflicts of couples at different life/career stages?

2. What is the impact of career couples on the organization?

3. What are the necessary ingredients for managing two careers?

4. How can companies develop an effective strategy for dealing with the two-career couple?

Much of our learning to date comes from group interviews and workshops during the last two years with more than 300 people from Chicago, New York, and Washington.

Where couple careers conflict, the loss is not always the one you might expect. In a Chicago bank a rising young man resigned after the birth of a first child so his wife could resume *her* highly successful career. Since bank policy did not allow him to take a leave of absence, the bank had to let him go.

Among employees remaining with their companies there are other problems. At the management level one of the biggest problems presented by the two-career couple is refusal to relocate. The traditional pattern of corporate advancement through mobility is facing greater resistance than ever before. According to a study conducted by the New York firm of Gilbert Tweed Associates, one in three executives can't or won't relocate because it would interfere with the careers or studies of their spouses.

At lower levels the issues are different but no less problematic. Scheduling, overtime, and transferring people to different shifts often meet with similar resistance. Behind the resistance we find conflicts with the spouse's job and the demands of managing two careers while sharing home and family roles.

WHY THE TREND?

Behind the increase in dual-career couples are two social phenomena: a rapid increase in the number of (married) women in the workforce and a shift in values. People are moving away from the traditional success ethic and toward a "quality of life" ethic. Two incomes may be an economic necessity for many couples, but it is also the key to liberation and new life/career choices.

According to the latest statistics, more than half of all mothers with children under the age of three are in the workforce. Based on labor department statistics, we find that 57.7 percent of all working women are married and living with employed spouses. This represents more than 46 million employed men and women (out of 98 million people in the American workforce) who are part of two-career couples.

Indeed, the economic significance of the two-career couple is reflected in Peter Drucker's claim that working wives are the reason consumers aren't "behaving" properly. (During the last few "recessionlike" years, while unemployment and economic uncertainty were high, spending on luxury items such as Cadillac Sevilles, chartered vacation travel, and large homes hit record levels.) Drucker explains this economic paradox as follows (*Wall Street Journal*, December 1, 1976):

> The husband is still considered the breadwinner, and his income is used for normal household purposes. The wife's income averages 60% of the husband's, and is used for "extras." Her money provides the margin for a bigger house, the luxury car, the expensive vacation. But the household spending pattern, based on the husband's income, remains sensitive to consumer confidence and to expectations about job security and income.

Most demographers agree that the influx of women into the workforce can be attributed to at least three forces: economic necessity; search for personal fulfillment outside the home; and technological improvements in the kitchen as well as the bedroom. With the annual rate of inflation for the basic necessities of food, shelter, energy, and health 44 percent greater than the rate of inflation for nonnecessities, a second income is essential in many homes. Women who once worked only until the couple could save a down payment or have a baby now continue working to meet mortgage payments and clothe the kids.

For many other couples, however, the end is not money but professional growth, advancement, and recognition. Meeting these goals takes a heavy commitment of time and energy, and organizational demands may conflict with home/work and personal/family roles.

For some couples, the combined income derived from two working partners brings the security that allows them to pursue what Douglas Hall refers to as the "protean career," a career directed by the person rather than the company and whose driving force is self-fulfillment. Traditionally, in the "organizational career," career tracks, moves, and choices were dictated by corporate needs, opportunities, and policies. Today, many people are exercising more personal choice in making career decisions. They may turn down a promotion or resign from a job that is unsatisfying or incongruent with personal goals and family member needs. For some people, it represents an opportunity to get off the treadmill. For others, it offers the choice of never getting on.

Whether a couple is motivated by economic need or personal and professional fulfillment, organizations are preparing for a new breed of employee. We find this employee to be one who faces conflicts with which he/she is usually unprepared to cope.

The personal issues faced by the dual-career couple, however, are not separate from the career issues each faces as a member of an organization. Our research has found that personal and company concerns interact on how the organization can and will function in the future. Corporate efforts to select, recruit, develop, train, relocate, and promote are all directly affected. To understand how organizations can cope with these problems, let us first consider some typical two-career couples. We are finding that the issues raised by dual careers are different from couples in different career stages. Therefore, we will examine some couples who are representative of their respective career stages.

EARLY CAREER STAGES

Profile I. A Couple at Entry

Anne and Mark never thought much about getting a job. The key to a successful career seemed to be getting an M.B.A. After a year into their program at Northwestern they decided to get married—and panic! Alone, each knew he/she had tremendous potential on the job market and could pick the best offer from among many. As a couple, they wondered if they would be a liability to each other and to a company. They dreaded facing corporate recruiters and wondered if they would ever find jobs together.

However, Anne and Mark were not alone. When they realized that other couples in the program were equally concerned and unprepared, they organized a problem-solving session and "brainstormed" a number of practical ideas. Since Anne's major was more specialized and Mark's (accounting) gave him great mobility, their strategy was to go where her opportunities were the best, knowing that he would be able to locate almost anywhere. They eventually had several good options to choose from and are now off to a good start with major companies.

Profile II. Advancing Careers

Bob and Barbara brought us a different problem. After finishing their degrees, both landed jobs with firms headquartered in the Southwest. He is in a management training program with an oil company. She holds a staff position in the personnel department of a large national service organization. Given that dual-career couples are a relatively recent phenomenon, problems at early career stages tend to catch them unprepared. They have to worry about each of them entering the job market and about conflicts that arise as they follow their separate career paths. They have been in their jobs for a year. Today, Barbara is pregnant and Bob faces the prospect of a field assignment lasting at least a year. "Barb plans to continue her career," he told us. "Her career is very important to her. It's important to me. She shouldn't *have* to give it up."

Barb's chances to advance in her company are good if she stays in the city they live in now, but Bob knows his advancement is tied to moving through a variety of assignments in different locations. Had he and Barb planned how they would handle this? Had he talked to anyone in his company about his concerns? The answer to both questions was "No!" He was worried that his concern about their two careers would be interpreted as a lack of personal ambition and an unwillingness to make personal sacrifices for his own career.

Common characteristics. Although these two couples are at slightly different career stages, they share many similarities. They also share the characteristics of many professional couples we have counseled who are in early career stages. What are these early career characteristics? Typically, these characteristics often include:

1. *Similar career stage needs.* For both partners, the need to develop skills and contacts and gain broad experience in the firm often means traveling, relocations, long hours, and a high degree of job involvement. For each the job is top priority.

2. *Conflicting career path alternatives.* The best opportunity for each, in terms of advancing his/her career, may mean locating or moving in different directions geographically.

3. *High degree of commitment to career goals.* Both partners usually have a drive to make it. Because of this, they understand the other's commitment to career. That doesn't lessen the intensity of their own commitment, however.

4. *Lack of preparation.* Most couples seem to possess little information about managing two careers or what lies ahead if they plan to have a family. Many have no plans and haven't thought through what they will do if faced with a conflict, a crisis, or a baby.

5. *Lack of experience in conflict resolution.* For many people, the conflict over a first job or relocation is their first experience in working on problems together. Their problem-solving skills may be rigid, and they often perceive the situation in terms of "my career versus yours."

6. *Fear or reluctance to approach the company.* Many couples are afraid to discuss their problems with a boss or superior in the firm for fear it will reflect negatively on them and their chances. They tend to see company policies as rigid (whether or not they actually are) and to accept corporate alternatives as "givens" without testing their assumptions.

7. *Personal flexibility.* When pushed, most young couples seem willing to explore life alternatives that fall out of the traditional way of managing a family or marriage. Living apart, long-distance commuting, "taking turns," and so on, are viewed as viable, if not always desirable, ways of taking care of both partners' needs over time.

MID-CAREER STAGES

What about the couple at mid-career? Its crises are no less acute, just different.

Profile III. Established Versus Delayed Career Needs

Jerry and Pat decided to follow his career opportunities, since his degree put him in a visible and high-demand position. After a couple of moves, during which she took jobs out of her field, they had a baby and settled into a city they both loved. He was a rising young star, and she was still trying to patch together odd jobs. When the organization he had left offered both of them jobs in their fields, his present employer panicked. Even though Jerry wanted to stay where he was, the job offer also had a new twist—*spouse bargaining.* Turning down the offer would mean turning off his wife's chances to pursue a career in her field at last. According to Jerry, it was "Pat's turn."

Unlike the couples described above, however, Jerry and Pat went to his employer with the problem, a clear set of goals, and an acceptable solution—helping Pat to find a position in the area. His employer, not wanting to lose him, was relieved to be asked to help—and did. He contacted several local organizations and put Pat in touch with employers who were able to use her skills on a part-time basis. In the end, Pat had two local offers, and the couple stayed. Interviewing them later, we found that Pat felt an increased loyalty to Jerry's employer because of his efforts.

Profile IV. Two Established Careers and a Family

For Mary and John the problem was different. As assistant regional commissioner of a government bureau, she was comfortably settled with three children and a successful husband. But their career problems, according to her, went "way back." He had left a job in one location to join her and get married, then went back to school. Along the way, she had turned down offers in the auto industry as well as a commissioner's job because the location wouldn't offer John much opportunity in his field. As Mary put it, "If the place had no opportunities for him, I wouldn't even consider it." Meanwhile, he regularly turned down jobs in small towns that wouldn't be near the large cities that might offer her a government transfer. When he returned to school again to work on an M.B.A. he jokingly told her, "Now you're grounded for two years."

A year later she was approached about a commissionership in Washington. They agreed that she should pursue the opportunity, and she eventually got the offer. John had told his wife that he would be willing to stay to finish his program and then join her later. When she got the offer, "He went into a tailspin. He thought it was the end of the marriage—that I'd get all caught up in my job in Washington and lose touch with the family." Mary turned down the Washington job. Now that John has finished his M.B.A., he is looking for a new position, and Mary has again responded to opportunities elsewhere. She laughed at this point in the interview. "This time . . . whoever gets there first, wins."

Profile V. Multiple Careers

Ron's family problem was not two careers but several. When presented with the opportunity

to move up and back to the Detroit headquarters of his auto firm, he turned it down. Not only was his wife happily settled, but his two remaining children at home were pursuing successful careers at local schools. One, a high school student, was the local drama star at a school with one of the finest programs in the country. Rather than sacrifice his family's careers, he compromised his own. Two years later, the company came back with the same offer. By this time, his son was graduating and going to college. Ron and his wife were ready to accept the move and, as she put it, "become corporate gypsies one more time."

For couples like these, mid-career also means mid-life. It is a time when family concerns take priority over one's own career. Corporations find themselves on a collision course, running head on into the established needs of spouses and children.

Common characteristics. What are the typical traits of the mid-career couple? Our interviews have developed the following profile:

1. *Career stage needs conflict with life family needs.* In most cases, there are more than two people to think about. A spouse's career may be established beyond the point of mobility and relocation is viewed as traumatic.

2. *Alternative career paths viewed as viable.* Mid-career couples are more likely to ignore the typical career-path alternatives where they conflict, and to view saying no or forgoing one's own needs as legitimate. The company's expectations are not always central; the family's needs are.

3. *Clear couple and family goals and priorities.* People seem to have developed a sense of what is important in life and what isn't. Their goals have crystallized, and factors such as location may be as important as salary. Decisions and plans seem to be made within the parameters of family/couple goals rather than in terms of individual opportunities.

4. *Commitment to the unit.* Couples at this point seem to view themselves as a "unit" or a family. Their careers are no longer individual pursuits but are seen as a "package" or a col-

lective, interactive arrangement. The individual is no longer committed to his/her own career alone. The commitment is now to the family.

5. *Better prepared to plan and cope.* Couples at mid-career have more experience in solving problems, planning together, and making decisions. They also possess more information about themselves, their values, their needs, their organizations, and their career options in general. They usually have fairly well-developed coping mechanisms and ways of handling conflicts.

6. *Less reluctant to approach company.* They are likely to share career concerns with the company and to approach people in the firm in an attempt to find a solution. They feel established within the company and do not see their personal or family career conflicts as a reflection on them as valuable employees.

7. *Acceptance of family as "given," career as flexible.* Career constraints are now viewed as manageable (perhaps because they are more willing to compromise). Children and established-spouse career needs are often viewed as fixed. Thus, at mid-career, personal flexibility seems to decrease while career decision flexibility increases. People are more willing to compromise themselves and the company, less willing to compromise their family.

In the examples we have given, all the couples have had viable career options backed by a strong relationship. Many of the couples we have worked with, however, present a different pattern. Take Donald and Marge, for example.

Profile VI. Mid-Career Crises Versus Spouse Career Needs

After many years in Washington, Donald found himself out of a job. Marge, on the other hand, had finally established herself as a successful photographer with a strong local following. For Donald, the options were elsewhere. He accepted a position in the South, planning for Marge and the children to follow if it worked out. The job didn't turn out to be what he expected, and he realized that local living ar-

rangements wouldn't be acceptable for his family. He quit.

When we met Donald, he was still unemployed and the couple was trying to figure out what he should do and where his many years of service in the government would be marketable. They had agreed that a large eastern city was what they wanted. For Donald, now in his 40s, the options were not opening up. But for Marge, who had followed him around the world for many years, if she was going to have a career, it was now or never.

Donald is typical of many men faced with the necessity or desire to change jobs, career fields, and companies. Often we find that the husband's mid-career crisis coincides with the wife's reentry into the labor market. Like the early career couples, they face competing career-path needs. In most cases, however, the couple is characterized by years of "giving" on the part of the wife.

Now liberated from caring for children and realizing an awareness of their own needs, many women are unwilling to compromise—one more time. Thus we find couples on the verge of a divorce after 20 years of marriage when faced with the prospect of managing two careers for the first time at mid-life. Their old relationship, built around meeting the needs of the husband's career, cannot accommodate the wife's needs too. She either gives up on the marriage or gives up on her needs and bows out as "the little woman behind the successful man."

In one humorous incident we witnessed, a wife sent printed announcements to the guests who would be attending an annual reception given by her husband. The purpose? To tell them that after years of standing at his side in the receiving line she would *not* be there this year. She was proud to announce that they were getting a divorce and that she didn't have to hostess one more reception for *his* business.

While this may seem extreme, it highlights just one of the changes that working women have made on the career-related activities of spouses. Social entertaining is down, particularly at home, while the need to pitch in and help out at home is increasing. Men who used to excuse themselves from a meeting to get to a community fund-raising dinner are now leaving the office to cook dinner.

For some couples, the crisis arises because the husband cannot accommodate to his wife's new work role. This was the case with Karen. As part of a blue collar family, she found that her promotion to supervisor in a manufacturing plant was more than her husband could take. He didn't mind the fact that she could run and repair machines weighing several tons. It was when he found his wife having to go back to the plant at odd hours to deal with a problem or going out for a beer "with the boys" that their marriage faced a crisis and, ultimately, a divorce. As some companies are finding, women are willing and eager to accept nontraditional roles; their husbands are not.

INGREDIENTS FOR MANAGING TWO CAREERS

How do couples and corporations cope? In our interviews we have been able to identify several factors that contribute to the successful management of two careers. Many of our findings reinforce the importance of career competencies in what Donald Super calls "vocational maturity," the "readiness to cope effectively with the developmental tasks of one's life stage in relation to other people in the same life stage." What he is saying is that different life and career stages are accompanied by different conflicts, tasks, and decisions. The couple has to be able to meet these and to deal with them at each stage. Mature coping varies with life and career stage. In particular, there seem to be four critical factors in successful dual-career relationships, as identified by Rhona and Robert Rapoport in their study of British couples. Let us consider each in turn: mutual commitment to both careers; flexibility; coping mechanisms; and energy and time management.

Mutual Commitment to Both Careers

Couples who are able to sustain their relationships and their careers are people who share a mutual commitment to work and to the other's need and right to pursue a career. Ben, for example, likes to brag that his wife is a stockbroker. According to Sally, "He is very proud of the fact and enjoys pulling me into his business contacts. I enhance his position at work."

In many cases, the couple's self-concept is built around themselves as a working team. Sid and Cathy are an example. "Sid is eager to introduce me to his clients and business associates. His career is enhanced by our husband-wife team, which is unheard of in our business. Sid like to use the phrase, 'Two heads are better than one.'" The partner's career is often viewed as an integral part of that partner as a person. Thus we find successful two-career couples much more likely to refer to each other by name—rather than as "my husband" or "my wife"—and to identify or define each other in terms of what he/she does.

On the corporate side, commitment to a spouse's career is a new phenomenon. Although we have not measured corporate commitment to date, we find evidence that companies who are committed to helping couples resolve career conflicts have generally benefited. According to one personnel executive, "If we commit ourselves to helping them, we can usually count on two people who will be highly committed to staying with our organization. Not only do we keep good people, but a positive attitude toward the company is reinforced."

Flexibility

Two types of flexibility seem to be associated with successful career couples—personal flexibility and flexibility in the job. On the personal side, we find that the willingness and ability to shift gears, revise plans, try new ways of doing things, and consider alternatives all lead to greater adaptability to coping with couple problems.

The flexibility the job provides, however, is equally and oftentimes more important, with a payoff to both the career and the relationship. Many of the couples we interviewed had at least one spouse with a high-autonomy job. Libby and Sam are a good example. When he finished his tour of duty in the army, she, a nurse, took a job with a VA hospital to support him while he went to school. Both knew he could accept a job almost anywhere and she could follow. After he graduated, he accepted a position with a well-known hotel chain. She was easily able to transfer to the local VA hospital. Both know that this may be the first of many such moves, but that he can stay with the chain and she can pursue her own career without leaving the VA system.

To the corporate recruiter, a flexible spouse is viewed as a definite asset. One recruiter we know beamed recently about the gold mine he had found: a top-notch woman M.B.A. with a C.P.A. spouse ". . . who is willing to hang his shingle anywhere."

For couples like these, flexibility removes the potential conflict between career-path choices. Autonomy within the job itself, however, has other advantages that contribute to coping with home/job conflicts. Thus the hourly employee who is bound to a set schedule and a time clock may have to call in sick when his children have a school holiday. Professors (in high-autonomy positions) bring their kids to the office.

Coping Mechanisms

For the viable career couple, coping mechanisms are essential. Interestingly, we have found that no single type of coping or coping mechanism is necessarily better than another. The important thing is that the couple has worked out some means of coping with various conflicting demands. In our own case, two careers and two children presented the need to cope with child care. At different times we have used part-time help, live-in help, and day-care centers. All have worked well, depending on the age of the children and the demands of our career schedules in relation to each other. The outside help, however, was the necessary mechanism. After a while, we referred to the babysitter or day-care center as "the glue in our lives."

One couple we know, both staff writers for major publications, drew up a premarital con-

tract stating that they would cope with transfer by "taking turns." When the wife was offered a move to New York she turned it down because she didn't like the city. Is it his turn now? They aren't sure. Realizing that their contract didn't specify things like that, they are now renegotiating their agreement. We asked if they would recommend a contract and they laughed—all too aware that specific conflicts are difficult to anticipate and resolve in advance. "The contract doesn't define the marriage," she replied. "It's the relationship that defines a contract."

Contracts aside, the process of working together on resolving conflicts seems to be the key. For most two-career couples, a relationship that revolves around cooperation and collaboration seems to produce both coping mechanisms and satisfaction with the arrangement. One couple we know appeared for a while to have a rather lopsided arrangement when it came to sharing domestic roles. Queried about this, the wife quickly defended her husband's contributions to the two-career marriage. She provided more domestic support, but she was quick to point out that he gave her much more emotional support. He acted as the sounding board for working through frustrations at the office. This was as necessary a coping mechanism in their two-career lives as getting the laundry done.

In one research study we found that people tend to use three distinct styles of coping with conflicts between different roles. The first, which we called *role redefinition,* involves negotiating with your role senders to change the role and make it more compatible with other responsibilities and interests. Some ways of restructuring your roles include:

• Simply agreeing with role senders that you will not be able to engage in certain activities. (For example, in our community, a hotbed of volunteerism, we are both known as "spot-jobbers." We will accept specific, one-shot volunteer jobs, but we will not accept continuing positions.)
• Enlisting assistance in role activities from other family members or from people outside the family (for example, cleaning or babysitting help).

- Engaging in collaborative problem solving with role senders (boss, spouse, children).
- Integrating careers by working with the spouse or working in related fields (so that the two careers become more like one). Lotte Bailyn refers to this method of coping as "linking up."

Not surprisingly, these activities, which in effect reduce role conflicts by stopping them where they originate—in the environment—are associated with high levels of satisfaction and happiness in the people we studied. They are proactive, collaborative responses to role conflicts, and integrate the careers:

> Most important to me has been the rewarding experience of working with my husband. Observing him in his executive capacity, besides as a father and husband, I have come to understand him and appreciate him even more. (I also understand why his business trips are necessary and why he is working so late. . . .)

The second style of coping was *personal reorientation*, changing one's own attitudes about various roles and doing what was personally seen as most important. Some examples are:

- Establishing priorities. ("A child with a high fever takes precedence over school obligations. A child with sniffles does not. A very important social engagement—especially one that is business related—precedes the tennis.")
- Partitioning and separating roles. Devoting full attention to a given role when in it and not thinking about other roles (for example, "not bringing my work home, so home can be devoted to family and their needs").
- Ignoring or overlooking less important role expectations (for example, dusting).
- Rotating attention from one role to another as demands arise. Letting one role slide a bit if another needs more attention at the time.
- Seeing self-fulfillment and personal interests as a valid source of role demands. ("I chose leisure occupations to balance responsibilities—piano and organ playing, singing for release from being tied down when children are small.")

This style of coping means changing yourself rather than the family or work environment, although personal reorientation may be a necessary step to take before you can accomplish real role redefinition; you need to be relatively unconflicted about what you expect of yourself before you can change other people's expectations of you. Personal reorientation was not significantly related to satisfaction and happiness.

A third style of response to role demands is what we called *reactive role behavior*. This approach involved implicitly accepting all role demands as given and finding ways to meet them. Examples are:

- Planning, scheduling, and organizing better.
- Working harder to meet all role demands. (As one expert on women's roles and role conflict said in frustration, "After years of research, I've concluded that the only answer to a career and a family is, learn to get by on less sleep!")
- Using no conscious strategy. Let problems take care of themselves. This reactive behavior, in contrast to role redefinition, is a passive response to role conflict. Not surprisingly, people who used this style reported very low levels of satisfaction and happiness.

Most companies today are less prepared to cope than couples are. Their experiences with career couples are only beginning to accumulate and the rigidity of company policies frequently makes it impossible to react with speed. In some companies the response to couple conflicts can be classified as either "noncoping" or "control." In one energy company, for example, noncoping has resulted in losing good people to competitors. Saddled with a policy that states employees are to be fired if they turn down a transfer and an average rate of 15 moves in a person's career, personnel administrators admit that the company isn't prepared for the two-career couple. They are now rethinking the wisdom of the policy and the necessity for frequent moves.

The control syndrome reflects just the opposite approach. Rather than relax or reverse policies, some companies are making new ones in anticipation of conflicts— usually conflicts of interest. Thus couples may be required to sign a statement that they will not discuss or divulge business information at home, lest the spouse use it to his/her employer's advantage.

Energy and Time Management

Two factors related to effective coping are the amount of energy a couple is willing to expend to "make it work" and the ways in which the couple handles time. In most cases, we find that people view working on the relationship and managing their respective roles as a legitimate and, in fact, top-priority task. Television watching may be forgone in favor of time spent together talking about how to get through the next week. Cocktails and after-dinner coffee become times for problem solving rather than idle chitchat. The laundry gets folded over the 11 o'clock news, and the spaghetti sauce may be stirred during a phone call to the baby-sitter.

Most working couples "pare their lives," finding time only for essential activities that are of top priority. One husband we talked to recently pointed up the value of time and the fact that he rarely has any to himself after putting in a workday, doing the shopping, coaching his daughter's ball team, and meeting a heavy schedule of work-related social obligations, a requirement in his job. "My family asked me what I wanted for Christmas," he told us. "And I told them that the thing I wanted more than anything else was just a day to myself with no one—absolutely no one—making any demands of me."

Career Competencies

Developing career competencies is as important to managing two careers as the characteristics of the relationship or the job are. The basic skills required for managing one career seem even more important when managing two.

Self-assessment. Most vocational and career counselors agree that getting in touch with yourself—your strengths, weaknesses, and values—is the first step in managing a career.

Among couples, we find that the ability to sort out values and to assess where they are and what they have (or don't have) going differentiates many floundering couples from those who succeed.

Many corporations invest huge amounts of money in managerial assessment centers and psychological testing facilities. Rarely in the past have companies helped people assess their career values in relation to their spouses.

Getting vocational information. We find the need for information about career demands and opportunities is critical, especially at early career stages. Young people frequently accept jobs on the basis of very little information about what will be expected of them in the future, what the typical pattern of movement in the organization is, or what alternatives might be open if they can't or won't follow the typical track.

Goal setting. As we noted earlier in our examples, mature couples typically have clearly defined goals; younger couples do not. Yet, in terms of managing two careers and resolving conflicts, it behooves both the company and the couple to identify career goals clearly. In our illustration of Bob and Barbara, she knew exactly where she wanted to go. She wanted to remain in her staff function in the short run and move up in the personnel department.

Was Bob's goal as clear-cut? He wanted to stay with the company and ultimately wind up settled back in corporate headquarters. Between the couple stood the possibility of several field assignments. "What are the company's goals?" we asked, "What is the purpose of the field assignment?" Bill described the assignment in multipurpose terms: to provide experience with a technical plant facility and its people, to develop contacts in the field that would prove useful later in sales, and to gain supervisory experience. We asked why the assignment had to be a year in the field. "Well," he replied, "it probably takes five to six months to get to know a plant and besides, that's the way it has always been done."

The interview intrigued us. The case was a

classic example of couple and companies assuming they are in a win/lose situation. Either Bob and others like him take the assignment while the spouse gives up her job, or she keeps her job and keeps him at home, affecting his career mobility within his firm.

To get around the conflict, both the couple and the company need to focus first on their goals and second on alternative strategies for reaching them. Are the company's goals really incompatible with those of the employee and the employee's spouse? Does the situation have to be viewed in either/or terms?

When we presented the problem to a class of M.B.A.s, they seized on the opportunity to find a solution and began to redesign the training program as well as the couple's (temporary) lifestyle. The "give" had to be on both sides. Bob and Barb didn't have to be together seven days a week to be happy or successful, they concluded. But neither did the company need Bob warming a chair in Oklahoma for the next 360 days to develop his potential to move up.

What we wound up with was a list of alternatives ranging from a fleet of Lear jets transporting company couples to a system of team management in the field that would allow couples to work staggered schedules alternating between the plant and headquarters. Both we and the class concluded that the key was to find an alternative that fit the goals of the people and the training program. All too often, couples and corporations try to work within a single, fixed alternative rather than try to generate new ways to get themselves or their people where they need to be.

Planning.   The fourth competency is planning, preferably in advance. Sue and Mike are typical of the successful couple. "We try to foresee any major problems or decisions and discuss them early in the game. Everything else falls into place on a day-to-day basis."

Young couples, we find, may not plan. "How will you and Barb react," we asked Bob, "when the assignment finally comes?" "I don't know," he replied. We suggested that he and Barb begin to plan now, to prepare for the inevitable. We strongly suggest planning to the

M.B.A.s with whom we work. One of the strengths of planning, we find, is that couples, in developing alternatives for handling their problems, generate solutions for the company as well.

To prepare entry-level employees, we have our students generate a list of all the questions they fear (about their two-career status) from a recruiter. Then we ask them to generate a list of concerns—questions they want to ask to elicit more information about the job in relation to their own couple conflicts. Last, we have them practice ways to raise these issues themselves during the interview. What we find is that the interviewee's planning also benefits the recruiter. Because the recruiter often cannot ask certain questions, he/she is relieved to have the applicant bring the couple's situation out into the open. Both parties wind up with valid information and do not have to act on (often false) assumptions.

Problem solving.   The final skill that couples and companies need is problem solving—developing and exploring many alternative means for getting around couple conflicts. To be effective at this, we find, both sides have to suspend judgment, stop making assumptions, and think flexibly.

In the seminars we run, we find that the *ability* to engage in problem solving is not the issue. Faced with the necessity, most people can brainstorm an endless list of solutions. The issue is that many couples and corporations don't turn their creative thinking to developing alternative ways of meeting the couple problem. When a situation arises, they aren't prepared to cope.

THE IMPACT OF COUPLE CONFLICTS ON ORGANIZATIONS

What does all this mean for companies? To find an answer, we surveyed 35 organizations based in Chicago. In our interviews, we found at least ten different ways in which couples impact on the personnel function of organizations:

1. *Recruiting.* Recruiters are becoming increasingly sensitive to the role of the spouse in career decisions. They are seeking ways to identify the people who are part of career couples and who have a high likelihood of accepting an offer and staying with the company.

2. *Scheduling.* The need for flexibility has made scheduling and schedule changes more of a problem. Scheduling vacation time and work hours is also affected as more employees seek "off" time to coincide with children's school schedules and day-care center hours.

3. *Transfers and relocation.* This is probably the area of greatest impact and poses the biggest problem for large companies. Refusal to relocate may mean the company must dip into the pool and send less qualified people into a new assignment. Those who refuse to relocate may be fired or quit, entailing high replacement and training costs.

4. *Promotions.* Many couples are less eager for promotion opportunities, regardless of whether they involve a geographic move or not. Many two-career people have aspirations for more free time, less work pressure, and fewer responsibilities. With two incomes the pay differentials may not compensate sufficiently to make promotions worthwhile.

5. *Travel.* People are less willing or able to travel in two-career couples where family demands are high. People seem to "burn out" faster in high-travel occupations such as public accounting, sales, and consulting.

6. *Benefits.* The need for benefit program revision is growing. Both men and women are seeking maternity leaves or leaves without pay to accommodate spouse and family demands. Life insurance has become more important as people accommodate to a standard of living based on two incomes. "Personal days" are another benefit that couples seek and use with greater frequency.

7. *Conflicts of interest.* Employees with spouses in the same professions—such as advertising, banking, accounting, consulting, law, or publishing—or working for competing firms may represent a potential liability or security risk. In the same firm, one spouse may have information that is not normally available to the part of the organization in which the other spouse works. Corporate policies dealing with these conflicts have not yet been developed in most companies.

8. *Career development.* The most significant change that couples have had on career programs is in the area of "career pathing," or the design of developmental tracks through which to move people. This is closely linked to the relocation effect. Many firms are finding the need to redesign training programs with limited geographic mobility in mind.

9. *Deadwood.* The combination of resistance to relocation, lower aspirations, unwillingness to travel, and other drawbacks of this kind presents a potential problem of deadwood among high-potential recruits who would otherwise develop and advance.

10. *Career bargaining.* A newly emerging trend is for couples to bargain for considerations that result directly from the career of the spouse. Examples are assurances of being sent to a particular location, assistance in finding a new position for the spouse, and subsidies until the spouse obtains a position.

Overall, we find that all the changes reflect the need for more flexibility among couples and companies. Rigid policies are giving way to case-by-case exceptions, which are bound to give way in time to major shifts in policies as more couples enter the workforce.

Developing a Company Strategy

How can companies cope with the issues raised by the dual-career couple? The most effective way, we find, is to help the couple to cope. An effective program should have the following characteristics:

- Flexible career development tracks and experiences.
- Skill development in coping with conflict and life/career management.
- Spouse involvement in career planning, decision making, and problem solving.
- Support services for career couples.

What are the components of an effective program? The following seem to be the most important.

Dual-career audit.   When we surveyed Chicago area administrators recently, the number one suggestion was to "recognize the problem." Often, this is only done after a potential problem turns into a crisis. How can you identify the company's couple needs? The most direct way is through an employee survey, preferably one that is built into the regular career audit. What should you be looking for? Here are some sample areas to cover:

- How many employees are presently in a two-career situation and how many probably will be in the next few years?
- How many people interviewed on campus for starting positions are part of two-career families?
- How does your employee population break down in terms of life/career stage, organization level, location, and function? In other words, where are your dual-career employees?
- What conflicts do they have or may they have if they remain?
- How do they perceive company policy, career tracks, support, and opportunities in relation to their own careers?
- In what areas are they most and least competent to manage careers?

Special recruiting techniques.   Three techniques should be considered. The first is the *preselection job preview for couples.* By giving both partners a realistic picture of the company, the job, and the typical career advancement track in terms of hours, travel, and so on, the program helps eliminate potentially bad couple/company fits. The second technique is *dual recruiting*—seeking husband-wife teams at the hiring end. The third technique is *couple counseling and orientation* immediately after selection but before placement. The company would help the couple to identify potential conflicts and begin to plan their coping mechanisms.

Many personnel departments are beginning to identify potential placement possibilities for spouses outside of their organizations. Thus, in recruiting one person, they may informally try, at least, to help the spouse find a job by making names of employers in the area available or by circulating the spouse's résumé to friends in the personnel departments of other companies. Few companies actually promise to find the spouse a job, but there is an increase in informal efforts to help.

Revision of career development and transfer policies.   The first step is to identify the goals of your career development program. Next, examine those goals against existing programs and policies, noting problem areas that may conflict with couple careers. Relocation is the most common problem. Consider whether the goals of the program can be achieved without geographical transfer. The following alternatives may be possible:

- Can field experience be simulated in local training through cases, simulations, or the use of videotaping or other devices?
- Can familiarity with certain facilities, products, and processes be learned in new ways (such as temporary assignments; say, two or three months)?
- Can shorter workweeks or staggered schedules be set up to allow couples to commute more easily?
- Can more training moves and tracks be developed within limited geographical areas?
- What are some of the ways company contacts can be developed without relocation?

In most cases, both training programs and career tracks are based on historical patterns and both are rarely subjected to critical examination. People are developed on the basis of how long it has taken other people to move up or the typical jobs other people have moved through on their way up. A new approach, instituted at Sears, Roebuck, has identified career tracks based on a skills analysis. What skills does a person need to advance? How long does it take to acquire these? In what range of positions can these skills be developed?

Revision of nepotism policies. In many major firms, former nepotism rules are being changed to allow companies to hire spouses. Typically, the policy is that relatives may be employed by the company, but persons may not supervise a relative or be involved in his/her salary, performance, or promotion evaluations.

Assistance for couples in career management. The packaged career materials on the market today, although good in many cases, are geared to individual career planning. In our seminars, we have found that couple planning is critical, even if the focus in on one partner's career. (This is also true, we find, in the single-career family.) Even if one spouse is not in the work-force, he/she may be planning to go back to school or reenter the job market. These decisions are not independent of the working spouse. Similarly, decisions one working spouse may have to make with regard to advancement in the firm could be affected by his/her spouse's career opportunities.

The part of the career management process for which corporate help is critical is in providing information to the couple to help them assess their opportunities, choices, potential conflicts, and developmental needs. The company cannot set goals for the couple, but it can provide programs to help couples develop their career competencies and acquire the information they need. Thus the company's role is helping people to learn the *process* of managing two careers by providing seminars, workshops, and training materials. Although the use of seminars is fairly new, at least one insurance company in Boston has begun to underwrite employee participation in the belief that help in managing the conflicts between work and family will enable employees to perform better.

There are several other ways the company can assist couples with career management:

1. *Developing family and spouse opportunities for company involvement.* Many working couples find that their empathy and willingness to compromise increase with their understanding of the partner's or parent's job and job-related responsibilities. One company sponsors days when family members are invited to "work along-side" a parent to see firsthand what the job involves. Others have used films to orient families to what the company and the parent do. Company-sponsored social events often provide an opportunity for family members to meet co-workers and develop supportive relationships. One major oil company found it difficult to transfer personnel to Saudi Arabia and keep them there. After instituting orientation sessions for husband and wife and asking them to decide *together* whether to accept the transfer, there was a great reduction in the number of people who returned before completing their tour of duty.

2. *Training couples in career coping and problem solving.* Over the past year we have developed several programs for developing couple skills in career coping and problem solving. One, for example, helps couples understand career and life roles and the various techniques for managing role conflict. Another revolves around typical two-career decisions and problems. Using cases, we have been able to help couples anticipate some of the problems they will encounter and then plan a strategy for solving these problems. The more skills the couple has, the less of a problem the dual-career situation creates for the company.

3. *Setting up support structures for transfers and relocation.* Where it is necessary to transfer and relocate personnel, the availability of special services and support may make the difference between whether the target employee accepts or not and be a contributing factor in how quickly the spouse and family adjust. Some of the services helpful to two-career families are:

• Helping to find the spouse a job.
• Locating day-care or child-care arrangements.
• Assisting in selling and buying homes.

• Assisting in getting advance information about the new community during a transfer and helping the couple to become integrated into the community.

• Helping couples to develop strategies for planning and coping with transfers in advance (before either one has been offered a transfer). Specialized relocation companies (for example, Relo and the Relocation Council) are already providing these services on a consulting basis to corporations. The Union Oil Company has reported several cases of successful relocation for couples within their firm. In some of these, one spouse was promoted and the administrative services department helped find an opening in the corporation for the other. In one case, the company granted a leave of absence to an employee to search for a job after her spouse was transferred. For the most part, these success stories reflect a case-by-case approach.

4. *Providing local support services.* In addition to those already mentioned, the two biggest day-to-day needs of the dual-career family still seem to be flexibility and child/home-care services. We do not necessarily advocate company-sponsored day-care centers, but company clout can be wielded in many communities to advance the needs of working parents and their children. Lunch programs, after-school centers and sport programs, and facilities for children of working parents on school holidays are all needs many communities have yet to meet.

5. *Providing couple counseling.* At many points in the process of goal setting, planning, and problem solving, couples need a third party to help them sort out their priorities and resolve conflicts. There are many people who can be used to provide this help, ranging from in-house counselors to outside resource people who are available in your area.

Training of supervisors in career counseling skills. Probably the best source of counsel— if not for the couple, then at least for the employee—is the skilled supervisor. Unfortunately, most supervisors have little training in career management, the areas of working parents (especially women), and conflict resolution. Yet they are the ones most directly affected on a day-to-day basis with the conflicts that work/home roles present to an employee.

What can you do to train supervisors?

• Provide seminars for supervisors to alert them to the typical dual-career conflicts that may come up.

• Develop their third-party skills in counseling, coaching, and listening.

• Provide simulations in handling employee problems caused by spouse and family needs.

Setting up of interorganizational cooperative arrangements. The most helpful resources a company can have in managing two-career relocations are contacts in other companies and organizations. These provide a base for helping the spouse relocate. These contacts are often used informally by personnel managers, but there is a growing need in many companies for a more systematic network of cooperation.

Providing flexible work environments. More within the grasp of the company, however, are policies regarding working hours and days off. Flexible working hours is probably the single most effective technique companies have instituted to meet working parents' needs. The establishment of family emergency days or "personal days" is another. Some companies, such as research and consulting firms, allow employees to work at home when necessary to do "think work," write reports, and accomplish other tasks for which the office may be too distracting.

Evaluating the effectiveness of the program. The final component is measuring the effects of your efforts against bottom-line-related results and costs. To do this, we suggest that you first establish goals and criteria based on current turnover, problem incidents, days lost, and so on, as well as on the basis of your initial or annual dual-career audit results. The evaluation design should *precede* the program design so that baseline data will be recorded and interventions measured.

CONCLUSION

In this paper we have attempted to highlight the issues associated with an emerging corporate phenomenon: the dual-career couple. In an earlier paper (*Organizational Dynamics,* Summer 1976), we referred to the dual-career employee as a "corporate time bomb," because the impact will be greatest about five years from now, when the dual-career employee (now mainly at entry level) will be in a more responsible, critical position, will be starting a family, and will be facing various relocation opportunities and pressures. As professional and management employees move from early career positions into mid-career, they will become less willing to sacrifice family and personal needs to corporate requirements. To cope successfully with these stresses, couples will need to develop coping mechanisms, flexibility, and a mutual commitment to each other's careers and to invest large amounts of time and energy. With more married women and couples entering the workforce, companies will experience greater difficulties in recruiting, scheduling, and transferring professional personnel. Problems regarding travel, benefits, conflicts of interest, and career pathing are also sure to grow.

Companies are just becoming aware that there are problems. They admit the problems exist, but feel that the problems belong to the employee, not to them. When they do react, it is on a case-by-case basis. Few actual programs for dual career employees have been developed. Orientation programs for the spouse are the most frequent action taken to date.

Other recommended company actions include auditing dual-careers; revising development, transfer, and nepotism policies; providing assistance to couples in dual-career management; training supervisors in counseling and coaching skills; providing intercompany cooperation; and providing more flexible work environments. Most of these necessary steps are not unique to dual-career issues; they are important in any program to develop and utilize human talents more effectively. The dual career is just one more manifestation of a new corporate phenomenon: more employees are coming to see their work lives as protean careers. As Douglas Hall said in *Careers in Organizations:*

> The protean career is a process which the person, not the organization, is managing. It consists of all of the person's varied experiences in education, training, work in several organizations, changes in occupational field, etc. The protean career is *not* what happens to the person in any one organization. The protean person's own personal career choices and search for self-fulfillment are the unifying or integrative elements in his or her life. The criterion of success is internal (psychological success), not external. In short, the protean career is shaped more by the individual than by the organization and may be redirected from time to time to meet the needs of the person. (p. 201)

Like it or not, this increasing desire for self-direction in one's career is a fact to which organizations will have to adapt. Some companies may try to resist this trend by selecting more passive or easily socialized people. In our opinion, this is a short-term solution with very high long-term costs (increasing corporate rigidity). The other corporate response, which makes a lot more sense to us, is to develop more flexible management policies and practices so that the potential for growth and creativity of the protean employee is not only tolerated but utilized for increased corporate, as well as personal, success.

Plotting a Route to the Top

Business Week

It has been more than 20 years since Shepherd Mead's *How to Succeed in Business Without Really Trying* laid out a comic path to the peaks of corporate power. But some of its tips—attract attention to yourself, be a politician, get yourself a mentor—had just enough of the ring of truth to establish them in the grand tradition of executive-suite gamesmanship. *How to Succeed* also gave career plotting a bad reputation it has yet to live down.

Today, though, the young executive who engages in "career pathing" is anything but a caricature of the ruthless opportunist climbing gingerly over fallen bodies. In the best sense, career pathing is merely career planning, and if you want to make something of yourself—or make something more of yourself if you are already well on your way—it is no less essential than planning is to the company you work for.

"Blind fate," says Max M. Ulrich, president of the recruiting firm of Ward Howell Associates, "accounts for at least 60% of what happens in careers." Most managers agree. Still, a goal-setting plan, if kept flexible enough, can spur you to action when your progress has halted and help you evaluate with clearer insight the alternative opportunities.

Charted course. The real point is to have a sound basis for a decision when one must be made. If you are offered a new job, a promotion, or a transfer, it's nice to say yes or no on the basis of something more reasoned than a weekend's confused weighing of the apparent pros and cons.

Nevertheless, career plotting still is more art than science. In its purest form, it involves setting down in the form of a chart, or plotting on a graph, your major goals and interim objectives. It also means establishing the benchmarks that will let you know whether you are on track and on schedule. If you are an MBA in your 20s, for example, a milestone on your graph, plotted in at the appropriate age, might be "corporate vice-president by 35."

It can cover one year or five. It can prescribe a course of study or map out a program of community involvement. It can even estimate your salary as far as you wish to project.

Four or five alternate graphs are better than one. They will encourage you to think in terms of the optional paths probably available to you.

Private project. "To a far greater degree than most people imagine, a career can be managed," asserts Marion S. Kellogg, a management development specialist at General Electric Co. John Rogers, vice-president of personnel for Cleveland Trust Co., puts it another way: "People can never abdicate the fundamental responsibility of their own career planning to a corporation or to anyone else."

Everybody's path will be different, depending on goals and circumstances, but you can fill in the blanks to suit your own situation and shoot for:

• Supervision of a given number of employees by a certain age. Obviously, it makes a difference what job you hold. Supervising 100 professionals may enhance your career more than overseeing 1,000 hourly workers.
• A target salary within a specified number of years. Circumstances should temper your planning. Salaries vary by industry. If your peers are closemouthed about what they make, get a feel from recruiters for what a manager your age in your business can expect, and strive to beat it.
• A title by some outside date. Here you can compare yourself with executives in your own company as well as outside it. Take an inventory. If most of the vice-presidents are 35, while you are 37 and still an assistant, it probably is time for a reappraisal.

Fundamentally, your plan is nothing more than an instrument of self-awareness, intended to bring forth your best effort. It should begin with a look at yourself and what you want out of life. In *Career Management*, for example, Kellogg's "career-launching checklist" includes fundamental questions such as: "Do I know the things I like best?" and "How hard am I willing to work physically and mentally?"

The essence of a career plan is thinking smart and looking ahead. It means taking into account the advice and counsel of those who have already scaled the peaks, following a few simple rules, and realistically appraising yourself, warts and all. Then you will be ready to decide—less on the basis of emotion than of logic—which company to work for and when to move out of it, what expertise to acquire and which mentor to follow, when to make yourself heard and when to keep quiet. And, it must be said, when to ignore your plan and follow your instincts.

PAY AND PRESTIGE

A Cram Course for Your Early 20s

The earlier career planning begins the better, although it's possible to carry even that to

extremes. It happens. Richard W. Walker, general manager of M. David Lowe Personnel Services, Inc., of Houston, and his son Mike have already committed to paper a blueprint for Mike's business career, carrying him to the presidency of a medium-sized company, even though Mike, at 18, has so far progressed little beyond summer lifeguard.

Your early 20s are the years to get a jump on many of your peers. Here are some guidelines:

Pick your industry carefully. Your likes and dislikes should be controlling, of course. But consider an industry's salary levels since pay scales vary widely; when selecting a company, think about the quality of management.

The industry you choose is important because, over a lifetime, assuming you stay put, it can mean a tremendous difference in how many of life's pleasures you can afford. Unless you really are fascinated by retailing, utilities, or meat processing, avoid them. A study by McKinsey & Co. shows that at least the top jobs in companies in these industries pay well under the average, and chances are good their salaries are below par at all career levels.

Find out where the industry fits into the compensation picture. You may elect to go into a low-paying business but at least you will do it with your eyes open. In choosing an industry, look at its growth curve. "Electronics," says one pather, "is a place where you don't have to spend 20 years waiting in line for an opportunity." In steel, you might.

On the other hand, don't worry so much about money as about management and reputation when you are choosing your first company. Stay away from a troubled company, if you're not the chief executive credited with turning it around. A big corporation is probably a better entry vehicle than a small one. Even in a large bureaucracy you can get broad exposure if you resist attempts to cram you into a narrow niche of specialization. And you are more likely to be on the cutting edge of up-to-date management practice. Moreover, just the fact that you have put in time with a big company will dress up your résumé.

Get out of your specialty fast, unless you decide that's all you ever want to do. This means rapid rejection of the notion that you are a professional engineer, lawyer, scientist, or anything but a manager. W. Donald Bell, 37-year-old president of Electronic Arrays, Inc., of Mountain View, Calif., recalls staying with his first employer—a division of Rockwell International Corp.—only 18 months before he concluded the engineer's road was too slow and too limited. "I felt like I was part of a stockpile of bodies," he says.

The earlier in your career you move through several functions—engineering, sales, production—the easier it will be. "And get your financial training up front," counsels recruiter Spencer Stuart. "It's the language of top management." Some managers, in fact, say a bank or accounting firm can be a dandy first employer. But the sooner you become a generalist the better.

Take time out for an MBA. If you didn't stay in school to pick up your advanced degree, don't worry. It is probably better that you waited until you had a few years' experience anyway. Some of the more prestigious schools are becoming more selective, though. Harvard B-School had 3,729 applicants this year, 10% more than last year. It accepted only 752 freshmen, 7% fewer than last year.

Surprisingly, a lot of companies prefer graduates from anywhere but Harvard, since not everyone likes the cockiness typical of the B-School grad. Wharton, Stanford, and the University of Chicago are among the favorites.

Stay mobile. That may mean switching companies, so get used to the idea. In your early 20s and early 30s you are expected to move around. Experience at two or three companies during this time broadens your perspective. A recent study of more than 6,000 graduates of 16 B-Schools by two Harvard professors shows that 40% to 45% change jobs at least once in the first five years after graduation.

"Too many companies don't accommodate young men in the first six to eight years of their careers as well as they can accommodate themselves," says Donald Williams, senior vice-president of the search firm of Heidrick & Struggles, Inc.

The higher you go, the more loyalty you will feel for your corporation. But remember that even chief executives do a lot of job hopping these days. One-third of the 225 presidents recently surveyed by Walden Public Relations for its search firm clients had been recruited from outside the company. And the outsiders tended to reach the top spot fastest.

FROM ROY GILBERT TO LEE IACOCCA

Some Well-Plotted Success Stories

The plan for your career path doesn't have to be in writing. But sometimes it helps to put everything down in black and white. The discipline can help focus your planning on fundamental goals, a crucial element in career pathing. As Yogi Berra once put it: "You've got to be very careful if you don't know where you are going, because you might not get there."

At the same time, don't be afraid to fill in the details, down to such imponderables as a planned stop in government service or a fling as an entrepreneur. You may not make many of the stops in order or on time, and some of them you might end up not making at all, but at least the plan gives you something to shoot for.

Close to targets. Roy Gilbert, 37-year-old executive vice-president of Southern Bancorporation, the holding company of Birmingham Trust National Bank, has made detailed plans of his career since his sophomore year in Davidson College. Armed only with a psychology degree and courses in accounting and commercial law he had completed in the Army, he embarked on a banking career equipped with both one-year and five-year plans.

"I wanted to be the youngest officer in the bank," he says, and he breezed through a 24-month training program in six months. The five-year target was a vice-presidency. His plan called for college-level courses relating to every major department of the bank and extensive outside involvement in civic affairs. In 1968, after picking up an MBA in night school and being named Outstanding Young Man of Birmingham, he became a vice-president—a little behind his plan but not far off target.

By then he had switched to three-year plans. The one he set up in 1970, when he was 33, included "the specific goal to move into top management by age 36." This time he was ahead of schedule. In 1972, at 35, he was elected executive vice-president of the holding company. Lately, Gilbert has been redefining his plan. "It's getting shorter and shorter, but broader and broader," he says.

James R. Wilson, vice-president of administration at Talon, a Textron subsidiary, is 33. Wilson believes in planning, but not in tight time frames or specific job titles. "If you say, 'By 45 I want to do this . . . ,' well, in 10 years that function may not even exist," he says. Nevertheless, Wilson has set some mileposts. "I wanted to be a corporate vice-president at Textron by the time I was 35," he says. "I got there when I was 32."

Charting your career. If you are lucky enough to be in a company like General Electric, IBM, or Exxon, which help managers plan their careers, half your work is done for you. But if not, you can easily map your own way to the top. An annual personal review—by you, not your company—may be all you need. But a career plan that is plotted as a chart or graph can incorporate your goals, your achievements, and your aspirations. After you have decided where you want to go and after you have evaluated yourself, you can set up a timetable. But don't court frustration by shoehorning yourself into a calendar.

Even with a loose schedule you can define some targets: that you expect, say, to gain an entry-level management job by 25; to earn an MBA degree by 26, a "visible" job by 32, a show of your own by 35; and that you expect to be making $20,000, $30,000, or $40,000 at specific stops along the way.

If you want, you can plot age against salary, age against promotion, age against years (or months) in a particular job. If you are really aiming at the top, you should start "making your age"—or the inflationary equivalent—in salary when you are around 30. By mid-career, of course, your age is no longer much of a benchmark. Increments of $1,000 or

even $2,000 per year add up to a sorry record for a man shooting for top management.

Your career plot can look like a project description, which in a real sense it is. Richard J. Censits, a modishly dressed pather who at 36 is controller of IU International, a $1.5-billion conglomerate, has a goal on the top line of his current chart, followed by a line with four objectives. Then there is a place to tick off achievements leading to the objectives.

To Censits, an objective can simply be learning your boss's job before you have to. "Get a job description of the guy you're working for and learn what he has to do so you're prepared to take his job," advises Censits. His own copy of a Conference Board publication entitled *Duties and Responsibilities of the Chief Financial Officer,* the next slot in his own career path, is copiously covered with bright yellow underlinings.

But focusing on career stops can sometimes blind you to major objectives. "In my experience the guy who says he has to do all these things to round out his career is the guy you meet at the age of 50 and he's still trying to get experience," says Wilfred J. Corrigan, who became chief executive of Fairchild Camera & Instrument Corp. last July at 36.

In laying out your strategy, keep these basic points in mind:

Know when to leave. Most plotters agree that you should plan to stick with your first job only two to five years unless the company has been shuttling you around to different functional areas and heaping responsibility on you.

Says Joseph C. Kaminski, at 30 the treasurer of Bowmar International in New York: "Three or four years in any one area is probably all you should allow yourself. In the first two or three months it's a total learning experience. In the next 9 to 12 months you begin pulling your own weight, and in the next year you're self-sufficient, the master of the job. After that, you should look for something bigger or resign yourself to being in that spot forever."

Another bonus of moving, beyond broadening your experience, is inflating your paycheck. You can expect a raise of at least 20% to 25% for a transfer outside the company, and in a high-risk situation you should demand considerably more. In the long run, several judicious moves can put you miles ahead of the competition. Companies don't like to admit it, but some have made studies that confirm that their long-term employees make less than newcomers doing the same work.

If you have a challenging job but feel you are grossly underpaid, that is a clear sign something is wrong. Henry B. Turner, 37, who recently resigned as No. 3 man in the Commerce Dept., has had six jobs and four employers since he left Harvard B-School 12 years ago, and at times he has earned an income well into six figures. But he recalls leaving the job of treasurer and director of corporate planning at StarKist Foods, a subsidiary of H. J. Heinz, after two years because he was squirming under the modest salary of $16,000.

Finally, if you are blocked by a superior who is not moving, it is time that you did.

Warning: Don't run every time something goes wrong. Staying where you are is better than leaving if you are relatively happy with your progress. The Walden study of presidents showed that more than half come to the top through a single company.

Moreover, while a few moves embellish your résumé, more than three or four in 15 years are a blemish. "Job-hopper" and "corporate gypsy" are still dirty words in many personnel offices.

Land in a good place. Aim for a spot where you can see the business in toto early on, suggests Peter Huang, 39, executive vice-president of City Investing Co. "I always said I learned businesses from the top down," says Huang, whose specialty once was acquiring companies but now is running them. "Don't look at the pyramid from the bottom up."

Some good jobs for an overview: assistant to the president, a corporate staff position, investment banking. And if you are stuck in a niche and are looking for breadth, you might consider a stint with a consulting firm, which is not a bad way to make contacts, either.

Fit in. "It is important," says a marketing manager for a major insurance company, "to be politically 'in' from the beginning of your career. If you don't feel politically connected within two years, something is wrong."

How do you tell? "If someone you don't respect stays even with you or passes you," he suggests, "it's time for a change because you are not 'in.' Ditto if you're spending more time in a particular job than your boss did when he was in that position."

Be visible. Despite the stereotype of the executive as conformist, the manager who rises to the top is most often an innovator, and he does anything but hide that fact.

As the management pyramid narrows, making yourself known becomes absolutely essential. "Next to talent, the second most important factor in career success is taking the time and effort to develop visibility," says recruiter Richard M. Ferry of Korn/Ferry International. With the right exposure, he adds, a man can cut five years off his trip to the summit.

There are some obvious ways to bring attention to yourself. Get your name in print, give speeches, take industry association jobs, take time off for a stint in government. One sure-fire technique: broadening the scope of your job. Southern Bancorp's Roy Gilbert early in his career sold an officer on the idea of letting him develop an in-bank teller training program. He added zing by taking along a cake he baked himself when he met branch tellers for the 7:30 a.m. sessions.

Avoid the administration of trivia, but seek out additional duties that count for something. William J. Edwards, a career plotter at Cleveland Trust Co., Ohio's largest bank, once asked his boss for a specific district with a large volume of lending so he could prove himself when he was an assistant vice-president. "From then on it was my ball game," he recalls. The move helped him become the youngest vice-president in the bank's history.

Mellon Bank's 36-year-old comptroller Jerry A. Lemmons admits he worked at looking better than his peers, taking the advice of a boss who told him: "It doesn't matter how you get your name mentioned, just get it mentioned. And don't sit quietly. Make sure you're always doing something. Ask people a lot of questions."

You could do worse than to emulate Ford Motor President Lee A. Iacocca, a perfect example of an executive who set himself apart from the managerial crowd. In 1964, when Iacocca shepherded to market the original Mustang, he accompanied the introduction with a massive campaign of careful leaks and interviews, making sure he was billed as "Father of the Mustang." It put him on the cover of *Time* and *Newsweek* the same week.

Play on the team. "Executives move up in twos and threes, bringing with them their key subordinates, who are considered crucial to their superior's effectiveness and mobility," says Dr. Eugene Jennings, professor of management at Michigan State University's graduate business school and author of *The Mobile Manager.* "In other words, a man may be chosen president because of his team as much as for himself. And that means that if you make your superior look good you are likely to move up when he does."

Iacocca had several mentors at Ford, including Robert S. McNamara and finally Henry Ford II himself, and in turn many Ford executives rose to top jobs clinging to Iacocca's coattails. They have become known as the Chester gang because so many of them worked in the Chester (Pa.) office, an early stop for Iacocca.

Find good advice. Unfortunately, there is no single place where you can get unbiased, useful career advice, and executives lament that good counsel is particularly hard to come by when a change of jobs is contemplated.

Many executives and most recruiters advise against using executive placement counselors, conveyors of a whole catalog of services ranging from résumé preparation and mailing to psychological testing. They can set you back several thousand dollars and their help in actually finding you a job may be nil. On the other hand, if you suspect your career and your interests are beginning to take off in different

directions, try testing by an industrial psychology firm ($300 to $500). A recruiting acquaintance can probably direct you to a good one. There you will learn from aptitude, intelligence, and interest testing how far where you are is from where you should be.

One of your biggest problems may be evaluating an actual job offer. If the company is in a different town or industry, you may have more questions than answers even after a series of meetings with your prospective boss. If you are serious about the overture, ask to talk to more of the company's executives. If the job is vice-president of finance, request interviews with the vice-presidents in marketing and manufacturing. "I don't think the average man asks to see enough people," says Fred H. Sides, a recruiter with Ward Howell Associates. "The company probably would be impressed if they did." At a senior level, you should also insist on meeting the directors.

Search firms (not the ones that sought you out for the job) are good sources of information. You should try to make a friend or two in that field before you need them. It is not their job, but a recruiter spends much of his time counseling managers about job changes his firm is not even involved in. An experienced search man can tell you much about a company's reputation, its executive turnover, how its pay stacks up. They are also good leads to executives who have left the company—sometimes a better source of information than the ones still there.

At a job-hopping juncture you really need all the information you can get, whether it comes from your father-in-law, a banker, or a friend of a friend. No single source is likely to help you much, but together they may.

THE MOBILE MANAGER

The Drawbacks to Company Loyalty

"Twenty years ago, the typical executive gave his whole loyalty to the company, and that was it," says William F. Breitmayer, president of General Executive Services, a clearing house for executives who are looking for a better job but don't want it known. "It was often quite a shock later when the company closed down a project he was working on, and he found he was out of a job through no fault of his own. People can become redundant. As they have found this out, they have said to themselves 'Why don't I look after my own career?'"

Still, managers probably do not think enough about their own progress. "I have repeatedly been impressed with how well many businessmen can run a company," says recruiter Charles Pope of New Canaan, "but don't reasonably run their own careers."

If your company never heard of a "fast track" for achievers—or has one but did not put you on it—you should start thinking about yourself. Graef Crystal, vice-president of Towers, Perrin, Forster & Crosby, Inc., a consulting firm, has gone so far as to call company loyalty "an inappropriate ingredient" in a business relationship today. Companies, he said recently, should strive for a "symbiotic relationship—I need you, you need me."

In fact, three circumstances lately have tended to make the company's need greater than yours: the declining pool of employees in the 33 to 44 age range (the Depression babies)

from which lower top management is drawn; the proliferation of search firms; and the conviction that a good manager can manage almost anything.

Expert for hire. You don't have to advertise the fact, but don't feel guilty about contemplating a move out of your company, especially if you have groomed a talented replacement, as you should have. "The mobile manager considers himself to be a professional who hires himself out to a corporation for an indefinite period of time," declares MSU's Jennings. "Professionalism has replaced employeeism."

It is when you finally decide to move that you may find that loyalty has cost you where least expected. "Loyalty to a company, and long tenure with a company, have in the past been viewed as helpful," says David O. Bailey, senior vice-president of the recruiting firm of Paul R. Ray & Associates. "What we're finding now is completely counter to this. Our clients are reluctant to take someone with a one-company background. They generalize that he's inflexible, perhaps overly security-conscious." And what is more, says Bailey, they are right most of the time.

Section 9

Organizational Strategies for Career Management

The basic responsibility for managing a career is shared by the individual and the organization. The organization's responsibilities, however, are most often fulfilled by the immediate supervisor and the human resources department. This section identifies several activities which can be developed by the organization to improve the management of employees' careers.

The first selection by Morgan, Hall, and Martier identifies the career development programs which are being implemented in organizations today. Seven major areas of activity are identified: (1) career counseling; (2) career pathing; (3) manpower planning; (4) career information systems: (5) management development activities; (6) job skills training; and (7) programs for special groups.

In the second selection, several key problems in the area of career management are identified. These problems are addressed from the perspective of both the individual and the organization. In addition, several innovative coping strategies are suggested.

Career Paths have been an important aspect of career activities for many years. Employees want to know more about the career opportunities in an organization in order to help set their own career objectives. However, career paths need to be specific and practical, rather than general and idealized. Wellbank, Hall, Morgan, and Hamner describe a career planning system which relies on the use of job skills to identify relevant career paths for a particular target job.

The last reading in this section raises the question of whether career planning systems are of benefit to the organization. Walker argues effectively that such systems are not only of great benefit to the individual employee but to the organization itself.

Career Development Strategies in Industry: Where Are We and Where Should We Be?*

Marilyn A. Morgan
Douglas T. Hall
Alison Martier

Career management and development programs have been widely used over the past few years due to increasing concern about the quality of work life, EEO legislation and affirmative action pressures, rising educational level and occupational aspirations, accompanied by slow economic growth and reduced advancement opportunities. In an attempt to learn more about current programs, we conducted a telephone survey of 56 companies in the Chicago metropolitan area aimed at exploring several very basic issues. What types of career programs are being conducted in organizations—counseling, pathing? How did the program start? What is the degree of commitment or support from top management? Is the program integrated into the regular management function?

Participants in the career-program survey included a majority of manufacturers and dis-tributors and a mix of banks, retail companies, insurance companies, a newspaper, an airline, and a public utility, ranging in size from 130 to 125,000 employees.

WHAT ARE CAREER PROGRAMS?

Career programs in these organizations can be grouped into seven main categories: career counseling, individual career planning, organizational human resources planning, career information systems, management or supervisory development, training, and programs for special groups. Many of these programs are not new—viewed in terms of human resources development, they come down to good management practice at the individual and corporate levels. Other approaches represent innovative career programs that go beyond the tradi-

*The research reported here was supported by the research fund from the Earl Dean Howard Chair, Graduate School of Management, Northwestern University. The authors are extremely grateful to the personnel executives who participated in this study with such a high level of interest and cooperation.

tional—such as the growing use of outplacement programs. Figure 1 lists a wide sample of these specific career development activities.

WHY BE CONCERNED WITH CAREER PROGRAMS?

By and large, survey respondents viewed career development programs as a positive means of increasing individual and organizational efficiency. By developing more competent employees, the organization is better able to identify future managers. "Growing" managers for tomorrow, through concerted efforts to train and provide lower-level employees with the necessary job experiences, develops a pool of human resources from which companies select their next group of managers.

Benefits of such efforts for the individual are seen in terms of better jobs, more money, increased responsibility, mobility, and the acquisition of skills that can lead to increased productivity. Little attention is paid to more personalized benefits, such as increased satisfaction, development of a career rather than job orientation, increased involvement, exposure and visibility, better understanding of what is expected or available, and identification of additional areas of career interest.

For the organization, career programs serve to assure maximum contributions from individual employees, as well as reduced underemployment. These activities also enable organizations to practice promotion policies from within by assuming that they have developed competent employees for replacements. Overall, organizations encourage these career programs, hoping to improve performance and profitability.

Performance, adaptability, improved attitudes, and employee identity are some measures for career-effectiveness. Top managers are also beginning to recognize the need for greater adaptability and technical updating. Many of these needs can be satisfied as part of the career development process. Employee attitudes are strongly affected by career processes, and formalized programs in organizations can

do much to increase levels of employee commitment, involvement, and satisfaction. Finally, career development is a process that serves to increase the fit between occupational requirements and the employee's personal identity.

Thus, objectives and benefits of career programs and activities may be more extensive than those seen by the personnel directors in our survey. While performance may be the most recognized benefit of these career activities, several unanticipated payoffs should be considered.

SPECIFIC CAREER ACTIVITIES

Figure 1 lists career activities that were generated by survey participants. Many of these are self-explanatory. However, some companies have implemented particularly noteworthy activities, and we will describe a few of these programs in detail.

Advanced Management Program

Each year 10 to 12 promising middle managers in one company are identified as candidates for upper management. These managers are relieved of their major responsibilities in order to attend an intensive eight-week program dealing with all aspects of the company. Candidates have increased opportunities for exposure outside their own departments as well as broader and deeper understanding of the total corporation. After this in-house training, candidates attend a management institute for two weeks. During this session they are exposed to the current techniques of management—leadership styles, problem-solving skills, and motivation. After successfully completing this development program, managers are "marked" as high potential candidates for key management positions.

Unfortunately, this program creates unrealistic expectations. Most often managers are ready to assume their new responsibilities after completing the advanced training. However, the company is not always ready to move them up. Sometimes a manager may wait as long as

Figure 1 Specific career activities

Career Counseling

Career counseling during the employment interview.
Career counseling during the performance appraisal session.
Psychological assessment and career alternative planning.
Career counseling as part of the day-to-day supervisor/subordinate relationship.
Special career counseling for high-potential employees.
Counseling for downward transfers.

Career Pathing

Planned job progression for new employees.
Career pathing to help managers acquire the necessary experience for future jobs.
Committee performs an annual review of management personnel's strengths and weaknesses and then develops a five-year career plan for each.
Plan job moves for high-potential employees to place them in a particular target job.
Rotate first-level supervisors through various departments to prepare them for upper-management positions.

Human Resources

Computerized inventory of backgrounds and skills to help identify replacements.
Succession planning or replacement charts at all levels of management.

Career Information Systems

Job posting for all nonofficer positions; individual can bid to be considered.
Job posting for hourly employees and career counseling for salaried employees.

Management or Supervisory Development

Special program for those moving from hourly employment to management.
Responsibility of the department head to develop managers.
Management development committee to look after the career development of management groups.
In-house advanced management program.

Training

In-house supervisory training.
Technical skills training for lower levels.
Outside management seminars.
Formalized job rotation programs.
Intern programs.
Responsibility for manager for on-the-job training.
Tuition reimbursement program.

Special Groups

Outplacement programs.
Minority indoctrination training program.
Career management seminar for women.
Preretirement counseling.
Career counseling and job rotation for women and minorities.
Refresher courses for midcareer managers.
Presupervisory training program for women and minorities.

two years before advancing into upper management. During this time the manager becomes restless. Thus, in implementing such a program, care must be taken to make sure candidates are aware that the major purpose is to prepare them for future job responsibilities, but that the opportunity for promotion may be delayed.

Management Development Committee

Some companies have established committees to oversee the career development of management-level employees. In one midsize company (15,000 employees) this committee is composed of all department heads, vice-presidents, and the president. Their main purpose is to oversee movement among management-level employees, but in so doing they annually review the strengths and weaknesses of each manager. A five-year career plan is then developed in consultation with the individual manager, and the committee oversees the individual's development in terms of this plan. This information is also used in the selection of new replacements.

A program such as this provides useful information that can be helpful in making replacement decisions. It can also provide useful information to the individual manager. Since the development of the five-year program is a joint venture between individual manager and committee, there is greater opportunity for assuring congruence between individual and organizational goals. The program often contains ideas about planned experiences, job assignments, and formalized training so the individual has definite steps to follow in an effort to reach career goals.

Career Pathing

In some organizations, such as a retailing firm, there are clear career tracks. In order to advance to a particular level in the organization, there are only one or two routes. However, in most organizations the route to the top is not quite as clear.

One company practices planned job rotation or progression for early career employees.

This means that for the first few years in the organization a new employee moves into a new department every 9 to 12 months. After this variety of experiences, the young manager is ready to assume the responsibilities of second-level management. Once a member of second-level management, however, all attempts at formalized job rotation or planned job progression stop.

Other companies have implemented programs of planned job rotation for women and minority employees. Hiring women and minority-group members is the first objective of affirmative action programs. The second objective is to develop these employees. Planned job rotation seems to be an effective way of doing this.

Job rotation or progression need not be limited to special groups. In fact, job experiences apparently contribute more to managerial success than does individual ability. With this in mind it seems reasonable to argue for the identification of reasonable career paths in organizations that will contribute to successful performance of a particular target job.

Midcareer Update

Obsolescence is a major concern for midcareer managers. In response to this problem, a large manufacturing firm has established a program to systematically update the skills of their midcareer managers. Special seminars are offered in such areas as finance, marketing, computer applications, and human behavior. Enrollment in these seminars is limited to midcareer managers so that they are not threatened by some young "hot shot" MBA. The sessions are inexpensive to run since they are in-house and provide an older manager with the opportunity to learn new skills in a nonthreatening environment.

Preretirement Counseling

Transition from active worklife to retirement is an increasingly important concern for organizations. A large midwestern utility has developed a rather complete series of retirement seminars. A year before planned retirement, employees attend seminars to help them prepare for the transition. Topics such as pension and benefits are covered, as you would expect. However, experts in other areas meet with this group and discuss such issues as insurance, social security, leisure time, psychological adjustments, relocation, and second careers. In other words, this particular organization recognizes that their retired employees will experience severe changes and attempts to prepare them for that transition.

Downward Transfers?

We typically view careers in terms of upward movement. While this advancement is common, alternative patterns are emerging. One medium-size manufacturing firm with 8,000 employees has recently begun to counsel employees to accept downward transfers.

When individuals are promoted into jobs with responsibilities beyond their level of competence, unacceptable performance levels result. An employer has the option of dismissing a poor performer or finding a job that the employee can successfully handle. This particular organization gives unacceptable performers the option of leaving the organization or of stepping down to a more manageable position—often the same job the employee held earlier in the same company.

An example may serve to clarify this idea. An outstanding salesman in one manufacturing organization had performed at exceptional levels for many years. Two years after promotion to district manager, he was referred to the personnel department for career counseling by his supervisor because of his poor performance. After a series of counseling sessions, the manager decided he would like to take the "demotion" and return to the job of salesman. He liked sales work and he was good at it, but he recognized that he was not a manager. He is now back among the ranks of the top sales force. This cooperative effort on the part of an individual and an organization has brought about increased levels of satisfaction for both parties.

This is not a unique example—there are many others in this same organization. Fifty percent of the employees referred to personnel on the basis of unacceptable performance choose to go back to a job they know they can handle.

While this example serves to highlight the issue of downward transfers for poor performers, there are other occasions that support the use of such a transfer pattern. Some mid-career managers reach the point where they no longer want to work a 12-hour day. Perhaps they want to spend more time on leisure activities or with their families. Perhaps there are health problems.

Another case might involve a manager who realizes he or she's in a dead-end career track. It may be possible to transfer into another area at a lower level and then advance along this new path. Each of these situations could be handled through a downward transfer, satisfying both individual and organizational needs. Downward transfers can be acceptable ways of managing organizational careers. This is certainly one way of handling career issues in a realistic yet innovative way.

HOW DO CAREER PROGRAMS DEVELOP?

Our survey suggests that many formalized career activities develop as the result of a directive from top management. In most cases top management recognizes the need to train managers and encourages the personnel department to identify ways of doing so. The general purpose of career programs, identified by numerous participants, is to enable organizations to practice promotion policies from within by assuring that they develop competent employees for replacement. In fact, many career programs are established for this very reason.

"... One company developed a special presupervisory training program in the hopes of better preparing women and minorities for advancement. This became a regular program for all employees who advanced to supervisory levels. . . .Other companies have extended this service to all employees."

In a few cases, requests for particular career programs came from the employees themselves. Employees of one manufacturing firm felt that the information about job openings was inadequate. They asked the personnel department to set up procedures for a more systematic means of job posting. In another organization the employees requested that a position for career counseling be created within the personnel department. It is encouraging to see employees identify the importance of particular career activities for it suggests that they recognize that both the individual and the organization share the responsibility for career development. However, cases of employee initiative are exceptions. We find that top management or a member of the personnel department often initiates a particular activity. There are no reports of supervisors who identify the need for a particular activity without the encouragement of top management. This is a very interesting finding, since many organizations feel that the immediate supervisor has the ultimate responsibility for facilitating the career development of subordinates.

A final point worth making is that programs for "special groups" such as women and minorities are so successful that they are often expanded to include all employees. For example, one company developed a special pre-supervisory training program in the hopes of better preparing women and minorities for advancement. This became a regular program for all employees who advanced to supervisory levels. Other companies started career counseling for women and minorities and, after discovering their usefulness, have extended this service to all employees. Thus, what began as a temporary program for special groups, has become a career activity available to all. In this way, then, affirmative action benefits *all* employees, not only women and minorities.

Management Support

It is no surprise that top management supports career development. However, it is more diffi-

cult to determine exactly how management demonstrates this backing. A commonly cited example is the budget. Respondents feel that the greatest proof of support is management's willingness to pay for these programs. More than 50 percent of the respondents indicate significant increases in the budget for career activities during recent years. It is interesting to note for whom career activities are a budget item. One-third of the respondents indicate that such programs are a personnel budget item, one-third state that they are part of individual departments' operating budgets, and one-third emphasize that the cost of these activities is shared by personnel and the individual department.

But there are a few examples of management support other than paying operating costs. Several respondents mentioned that management demonstrated their support by asking questions about the career programs. In a couple of cases, the president reported to the board of directors on career-development progress. There were also several examples of top management involvement in these programs that directly reflected their support and commitment.

While there appears to be widespread agreement about the level of support from top management, there is some evidence to suggest that this is not always true. In two cases there had been several formal career programs that seemed to be operating rather well, but as soon as the organization began to experience an economic decline they were cancelled. It is not uncommon to see programs in the area of human resources terminated when the business is experiencing difficulties. However, this fact does raise certain questions about the degree of support from top management.

Whose Responsibility?

Let's move on to the issue of responsibility. One could view career development as the responsibility of the organization (through the personnel department), the manager or supervisor, the individual employee, or some combination therein. Most often the responsibility for administering career programs is that of the personnel department. However, when asked about the responsibility for career development in general, the results suggest shared responsibility between the personnel department and the manager. In most of these cases, the importance of the individual manager assuming responsibility for the development of subordinates was stressed while the role of the personnel department was to facilitate this managerial practice. It is interesting to note that in only a few cases was the individual employee's responsibility mentioned.

This lack of recognition of the individual's role in his career development raises an interesting question about selection. In more than 80 percent of the cases we found that participants in the career programs were nominated by the manager, the personnel department, or by someone in top management. Self-nomination was encouraged in only a few cases.

Lack of Career Program Evaluation

Program evaluation or effectiveness is another important issue. We found few respondents concerned with evaluation. There were even some responses that indicated no concern at all—"we don't try to evaluate our programs" or "we just have faith in them." There were, however, several attempts to look at indicators of effectiveness throughout the organization and attribute program effectiveness to these results. Profit-and-loss statements, turnover, sales performance, and the ability to fill positions from the internal labor market were most often cited. Others indicated that they relied upon the feedback from participants at the end of a program. A few admitted that they did not know how to evaluate programs such as these.

Future Career Issues

We asked about the organization's future plans in the area of career development. No one mentioned increased efforts to evaluate program effectiveness, but there were a couple of other ideas. The most common response was to continue with the same programs that were in existence but to intensify and expand them.

Several organizations plan to increase the emphasis placed on manpower planning. More automated and computerized systems were suggested. Due to the increased concern for affirmative action goals, it was no surprise to learn that several organizations were planning to increase developmental opportunities for women and minorities. But generally, there were very few specific plans for the future. People were more concerned about working with what they already had.

While it was difficult for our respondents to describe future plans, they had no problem discussing the crucial issues that they have identified as they have become involved with career activities. The most interesting and frequently cited issues or problems are summarized in Figure 2.

Most of the issues identified in Figure 2 deal with the unintended consequences of success in career development programs: What does a company do *after* the person is ready for career movement? After people set career plans and

Figure 2 Issues and problems in relation to career programs and activities

Matching opportunities with expectations.
Awareness of managers that one of their major roles is to develop people.
Servicing the great demand for this type of program.
Encouraging people to assume responsibility for their own careers.
Overdevelopment of people.
Crown prince effect—danger of certain people getting on the inside track.
People becoming impatient and feeling they aren't moving fast enough.
Raising the expectations of individuals.
Promotion opportunities seen as only possible outcome of such activities.
Lack of information about evaluation of these programs.
Unwillingness of people to relocate.
Conflict over long-run versus short-run objectives: Can we afford to take people away from their jobs and develop them when they could be working?
Lack of time for managers to work on career development issues and activities.
The more you give people, the more they want.
Emphasis on minority groups, which causes reverse discrimination from the standpoint of the white male.

goals, there may not be sufficient opportunities in the organization to implement those plans. This problem is reflected in issues such as matching opportunities with expectations— people becoming overdeveloped, impatient, as well as feeling that "the more you give, the more people want."

This problem does not arise, however, in programs that incorporate realistic information about future career opportunities as an input to planning. This can be done with data on career paths, number of projected future job openings in management, and so on. With better company data, expectations can be more realistic.

WHAT CAN WE CONCLUDE ABOUT CAREER PROGRAMS?

The original objective of this survey was to learn more about career practices in organizations. At this point we are ready to draw several conclusions about the state of the art.

• *Career programs are not new.* Although practitioners talk about a new emphasis on careers, this is not quite as new or innovative as we might suspect. When asked about career programs our respondents most often defined them in terms of traditional personnel or human resources activities. Thus, for the most part, today's career programs have evolved from older programs.

• *Many of the career programs are informal.* There are many career activities for which there are no formal programs. In other words, while personnel managers suggest that their organization does some career counseling or career pathing, there may not be a formal program in this area. It is common to discover that training is a specific program but often the other aspects of career activities have not yet been formalized within the organization.

• *The responsibility for career development is shared.* A tripartite approach to career development is probably the most realistic. In other words, the organization, the supervisor, and the individual share responsibility for career devel-

opment. Although the level of individual involvement is not always recognized formally in organizational practices, few managers could argue against this cooperative approach.

• *The supervisor should be a career specialist.* Career development is often thought of in terms of programs or activities. However, our respondents constantly emphasized the importance of day-to-day activities on the job. Thus, career development should be integrated into the regular management function.

• *Career-program objectives are viewed in terms of an organization not an individual.* The purpose and benefits of career development programs are stated in terms of the organization. Even though we talk about the individual's career, the primary concern is for organizational performance and effectiveness.

• *There is a paucity of efforts to evaluate the effectiveness of career programs.* The common forms of evaluation are inadequate. Participants are often asked about their reactions to the program content. These data may indicate weak areas but say nothing about the overall effectiveness of career activities. Some organizations use global organizational measures, such as profit and turnover, to identify the effectiveness of these programs. However, such measures are so far removed from the career program or activity that the relationship must be questioned. Nonetheless, there is a need to focus more attention on assessing the results of these efforts. Too many costly resources are being invested to ignore this issue.

• *Unrealistic expectations on the part of participants are a major problem.* Career development programs have the effect of raising expectations of participants. Employees often see promotion opportunities as the major outcome from such programs, and if there is no position for them, then they become disappointed and frustrated. It is a disservice to establish norms of upward mobility when in reality there are not always jobs available. Emphasizing additional career effectiveness indicators, such as identity, adaptability, and job attitudes, will help to alleviate this problem.

• *Both large and small organizations can implement effective career programs.* One might suspect that only the larger organizations are able to support career programs. The results of this survey indicate few differences between the career activities of large and small organizations. The major difference appears to be that large organizations have more formal programs while the smaller organization has more informal programs. However, many of the small organizations support such activities as job posting, career pathing, and supervisory development. Also, when the supervisor is viewed as the career development specialist, similar managerial practices can be adopted in large or small organizations.

NEW DIRECTIONS

Based on where we are now in the evaluation of career development activities, where should we be headed? What are the next steps firms should be taking?

Less is More

First, let us point out what should *not* be done. We should not plan large, formal career development programs. One attractive feature of present career activities is that they have been an appropriate size: large enough to meet specific career needs that have emerged, yet small enough to do the job efficiently and flexibly. We know from recent experiences with T-groups, MBO, job enrichment, and behavior modification that useful techniques are often prematurely escalated into major companywide OD programs that often become ends in themselves and generate more resistance than results. (A good recent example of this process is the "failure of success" in General Foods' job-redesign activities in Topeka.) Therefore, let your career activities grow as they need to, but avoid developing a major career program just for the sake of having a major career program.

Focus on the Immediate Supervisor as a Career Development Agent

The best way to keep your career activities from outgrowing the needs they serve is to focus on

the immediate supervisor. The supervisor probably has more impact on the person's career than any other person, but is often reluctant to get too involved in career discussions with subordinates because (1) they lack necessary skills in developing people, and (2) there are few rewards for developing people. Great strides can be made in employee career development simply by giving supervisors training in certain basic skills: employee counseling and coaching, performance appraisal and feedback, mutual goal setting (both job performance goals and career goals), and job redesign (to provide subordinates with more skill-building activities within the present job). The beauty of starting with these skills is that they are basic supervisory skills that will lead to better management as well as to better development of employees. There's nothing fancy about them and they don't have to be billed as part of a special career program; they are simply good management skills.

Before you start skill building for supervisors, you may want to perform a supervisory audit. This is simply a diagnostic survey of the skills that your supervisors already have and those that they need to develop. For example, a supervisory audit may show that your supervisors are already performing certain activities (for instance, coaching and counseling) fairly well; then you might be able to concentrate your training in the other skill areas. A supervisory audit need not be a massive questionnaire survey; it can often be done in two or three days of small group interviews.

Another key piece of information you could seek in your supervisory audit would be the extent to which supervisors feel that employee development is rewarded. In most organizations, supervisors feel that this is an unrewarded activity, and it usually costs significant amounts of time and money, so that it is seen as negatively rewarded. This survey could help identify barriers and inconsistency in your corporate reward system that might be changed to provide more inducements for supervisors to help employees grow. For example, one large company has a policy that supervisors cannot be considered for promotion until they have demonstrated that at least one subordinate is ready for promotion. Linking the supervisor's career development to the subordinate's is a striking way of making development worthwhile for the supervisor.

Use Personnel Specialists as Third-Party Agents

If the major unit for career development is the employee and the immediate supervisor, this suggests that the personnel specialist should not be directly involved in this process, for at least two reasons: (1) if the personnel specialist becomes too involved, this may take the supervisor "off the hook," and (2) no company, regardless of size, has enough personnel resources to provide individual career counseling in the personnel department.

> "The supervisor probably has more impact on the person's career than any other person, but is often reluctant to get too involved in discussions with subordinates."

What would be the responsibilities of the personnel third-party role? First, the personnel specialist (PS) would be responsible for making available the supervisory training described in the previous section. Second, the PS could ensure that the supervisor and employee meet periodically (say, at least once a year) to discuss the employee's career plans and progress. Third, the PS could provide information about career opportunities elsewhere in the organization (often supervisors and managers are just as ignorant about other parts of the organization as are employees). And fourth, the PS could be a "career agent of last resort," providing guidance to the employee about other sources of career help beyond the supervisor's expertise (for example, specialized occupational testing, outplacement, or professional counseling). Another way the PS can function as an agent of last resort is in cases where the supervisor simply does not provide the assistance expected.

Provide Realistic Career Opportunity Information

As we have seen, one negative side effect of many career programs is that people engage in

self-assessment, goal setting, and planning, and lose touch with reality. In the process of freeing people to dream of and aspire to more satisfying lives, career planning agents often overlook the realities and constraints in most work organizations. While it is true that most people are employing only a small fraction of their potential skills, most organizations do not have the ability to absorb more skills because jobs are designed to be simple and because slow economic growth means fewer promotional opportunities are opening up. Therefore, as part of the information-gathering process in career planning activities, you should be sure to provide realistic company opportunities to employees: What are the prospects for promotion or transfer from the present job? What percentage of employees reach a certain target level in this organization? What are the pay ranges at various job levels? Where is the fastest growth (and, therefore, best promotion opportunity) in the company? If I have reached a dead end, what are paths for moving down so I can move up faster somewhere else? How do I go about requesting a transfer without alienating my boss?

In our experience, corporate career planning activities focus too much on self-assessment, such as identifying personal values, and too little on corporate opportunity assessment. Some companies prefer to withhold career-opportunity information, treating it as a confidential matter, such as pay. One cost of this policy, however, is inflated employee expectations that eventually are frustrated, bringing problems in morale, performance, and turnover.

Don't Focus Only on Advancement

Another way that unrealistic expectations develop is through an assumption implicit in many career development activities. For example, career development means advancement. We are finding problems with this assumption in two ways. First, as employees become more concerned with personal fulfillment and quality of life, they may place these outcomes ahead of upward mobility, especially if advancement involves sacrifices in lifestyle and fulfillment. Second, companies simply do not have enough high-level positions open to make upward mobility a realistic option for large numbers of employees.

Therefore, career planning should focus on helping the employee make a better fit between his own desires and the realistic opportunities available in the company. Planning should focus on activities that would provide satisfaction and *psychological success* for the employee, and these may or may not entail future promotions. If the employee has been in a dead end for 15 years, with few promotion prospects, perhaps the objective would be a lateral move that would provide variety and new challenge. If the employee is in midcareer, perhaps identifying new activities consistent with his new identity (as a middle-aged person, or as a middle manager) is necessary.

Another outcome of career development that has been underutilized to date is the objective of keeping employees flexible and adaptive as they grow older. You must look at the objectives that are important to your company and to your employees. Don't assume yourself into the upward-mobility trap—it's a promise you can't deliver, and even if you could, it would not provide full satisfaction.

Provide for Different Needs in Different Career Stages

People have different needs for development at different stages in their careers. In the *trial* stage, the person is testing different jobs and companies and is seeking a good fit, a good place to "settle down." In the establishment or advancement stage, the person has found a niche and is concerned with good performance and upward mobility. In midcareer, the person has achieved many earlier career goals (or learns how many will not be attained) and is making the adjustment to a new identity. This may also entail a shift in the relative importance of work and home roles to one's overall sense of identity. In late career, there is also a shift in identity, to "senior statesman" status, and later to a gradual detachment from the organization.

With changes in mandatory retirement leave, along with fast advancement for younger, high-potential employees in some organizations, the midcareer stage may be getting longer. As yet, most development activities are geared to new, young employees. As the average age of the work force increases, we will be forced to develop specific learning opportunities for employees in particular career stages. Figure 3 lists stage-specific development.

One Way to Start—A Sample Career Planning Workshop

A question we are often asked by managers or company personnel people is, "How do we get started with career development?" As we have said before, our advice is to start small and build organically, as needs indicate. For instance, start with a supervisory career-skill audit. This is a strategy for developing career competencies across several departments.

Another strategy is to focus on one department where a need or opportunity exists. A line manager may be interested in providing a career development program for his group, or it may be a group that has requested some career assistance. We have found that a one-day career planning workshop is a good way to introduce employees and managers to the career-planning process. The workshop is based upon five career competencies identified by John Crites: self-assessment, career opportunity information, goal setting, planning, and problem solving. The outline for the workshop is shown in Figure 4.

In our experience, the critical career need for most employed people is for more information on career opportunities. Therefore, the entire morning of the workshop is devoted to a discussion of career need and company opportunities. An expert in careers (either a personnel specialist or an outside consultant) provides a general framework about what a career is and what opportunities and activities are necessary for career growth. Most important, however, is specific company information about what career paths are available, how to move from point A to point B, how moves should be timed,

Figure 3 Training needs within career stages

Stage	Task Needs	Emotional Needs
Trial	Varied job activities Self-exploration	Make preliminary job choices Settling down
Establishment and/or Advancement	Job challenge Develop competence in a specialty area Develop creativity and innovation Rotate into new area after 3 to 4 years	Deal with rivalry and competition; face failures Deal with work—family conflicts Support Autonomy

Midcareer	Technical updating
	Develop skills in training and
	    coaching others (younger
	    employees)
	Rotation into new job requiring
	    new skills
	Develop broader view of work and own
	    role in organization
		Express feelings about midlife
		Reorganize thinking about self in relation
		    to work, family, and community
		Reduce self-indulgence and
		    competitiveness

Late career	Plan for retirement
	
	Shift from power role to one of
	    consultation and guidance
	Identify and develop successors
	Begin activities outside the organization
		Support and counseling to see one's work
		    as a platform for others
		Develop sense of identity in extra-
		    organizational activities

From D. T. Hall and M. Morgan, "Career development and planning," in W. C. Hamner and F. Schmidt (eds.), *Contemporary Problems in Personnel* (Rev. Ed.), Chicago: St. Clair Press, 1977.

Figure 4 One-day career planning workshop

Morning (9:00–12:00)   Basic Career Information

1½ hours   Introduction to career planning (given by specialist on career processes). Topics: What is a career? Career decision competencies. Career stages. Methods of self-managing a career.

1½ hours   Information about career opportunities in Corporation X (given by at least one key line manager and one personnel specialist). Topics: What career paths are available in this organization? (Show sample paths, if possible.) Costs and strategies for career planning. At what times do various important decisions have to be made?

Lunch (12:00–1:00)   Lunch-Group Assignment

        Example: What are the critical career choices a person must make in this organization?

Afternoon (1:00–5:00)   Career Planning

1 hour   Needs and current job assessment exercise.
1½ hours   Individual exercises on career assessment, goal setting, and planning. (Includes refreshment break.)

1 hour   Discussion of career plan and problem solving with career counselor or resource person (for example, a personnel specialist or interpersonally skilled manager).

½ hour   Wrapup and discussion of next step.

and so on. One key resource here is the line manager who supervises the group of people in the workshop. A second key resource is a personnel specialist (or two or more) from corporate headquarters who can provide information about opportunities about the company as a whole. Ideally, this would be a person who plays an active role in transfer and promotion decisions and will then be a credible source of information and advice. At this point, much nitty-gritty information about the costs and benefits of various career strategies in the company is exchanged, and this is perhaps the most valuable part of the day.

The afternoon shifts to individual exploration. First, there is a self-assessment exercise, aimed at clarifying career-related needs or values; there are plenty of these available in the market. Second, the person identifies tentative career goals and plans. We advocate doing this more quickly than many other people who work in this area for two reasons: first, many people have already given their goals and plans some thought, and second, we want people to get feedback before they go too far with their goals and plans. Therefore, the next step is to meet individually with one of the resource people (either the external specialist, one of the personnel people, or the line manager) for feedback (including reality testing), discussion, and problem solving. The objective of this session should be a more realistic set of goals and plans that would be discussed in detail with the immediate superior at a later date. The final activity would be a discussion of these individual meetings with the boss.

It is critical to point out all along the way that this one-day meeting is just one part of the career planning process. It helps greatly if people have thought about their career aspirations in advance of the meeting, and much follow-up work will be necessary to carry out their plans. If enough interest is generated, other career activities could be added later, such as training managers in career-aiding skills and setting up information systems on career opportunities. On the other hand, if little interest is generated, at the very least the one-day session has produced some useful career information without raising unrealistic expectations. Such a workshop is a low-cost, low-risk activity that can possibly lead to a wider range of career development activities, without necessarily committing you to them.

INSIGHTS

From this survey, it appears that most organizations are involved in some form of career development activity. Most programs have grown up organically around specific company human resources development needs, rather than starting as full-blown formal career programs. We recommend that this process be continued and offer several methods of "working small" in providing development opportunities, with primary focus on the immediate supervisor.

Our final recommendation is both obvious and usually ignored: evaluate your career development activities. Evaluation of career activities, as is the case with other personnel activities, is rarely done, but it provides the feedback that is essential for the improvement of your programs. Furthermore, if the evaluation is planned jointly by personnel experts and line managers (so that you are sure to measure outcomes that are important to managers), the outcome of your evaluation will have the credibility necessary to gain wider support for your activities.

During our talks with personnel administrators, we were impressed by the degree of untapped career potential in industry today. Employees have great capabilities for developing new skills and higher levels of performance to aid corporate objectives, and companies have numerous unexplored options for improving employee-company fit in many ways that do not necessarily involve more pay or promotions. There seems to be a growing realization that career development offers a useful way to realize more of this potential and increase the congruence between the needs of the employee and the goals of the company.

REFERENCES

Campbell, J.P., M.D. Dunnette, E.E. Lawler, K.E. Weick, *Managerial Behavior, Performance, and Effectiveness.* New York: McGraw-Hill, 1970.

Hall, D.T., *Careers in Organizations.* Pacific Palisades, California: Goodyear Publishing Co., 1976.

Hall, D.T. and E.E. Lawler, "Unused Potential in Research and Development Organizations." *Research Management,* 12, 1969, pp. 339-54.

Hall, D.T. and M.A. Morgan, "Career Development and Planning," in W.C. Hamner and F. Schmidt (Eds.), *Contemporary Problems in Personnel* (Rev. Ed.), Chicago: St. Clair Press, 1977.

Morgan, M.A., The Impact of Job History on Managerial Career Success. Unpublished Ph.D. Dissertation, Northwestern University, 1977.

What's New in Career Management

Douglas T. Hall
Francine S. Hall

In many organizations, the largest item in the corporate budget consists of wages and salaries. For this reason, financial problems that dictate cost reductions and increased efficiency usually boil down to problems of personnel and human resource management. Therefore, more creative, flexible, and efficient utilization of human resources through better corporate career planning can be a powerful means of dealing with some of the current headaches of managing a stable or shrinking organization in a stagnant economy. In this article, we will review some current (and probably all-too-familiar) human-resource management problems and report on how some organizations are coping with them through creative techniques for career management. We will also point out what is being neglected in the area of career development. And we will conclude with some general principles about how to make corporate career planning more effective.

PROBLEM 1: HOW CAN WE REDUCE
TURNOVER AMONG RECENTLY HIRED
EMPLOYEES?

Students often graduate from college or business school with unrealistically high expectations about the amount of challenge and responsibility they will find in their first job. Then they are put through a job-rotation training program or into a fairly undemanding entry-level job, and they get turned off. They experience "reality shock." The result is low morale, low productivity, and high turnover. Some companies lose as many as one-third or one-half of their new recruits in the first year or two of employment. One company was hiring 130 people at one time in order to have 30 at the end of the first year!

The cost of turnover is tremendous, especially among professionals and management candidates. Michael Alexander, of Touche, Ross & Co., calculated in 1973 that the total cost (including recruiting expenses, training, reduced performance during orientation, and so on) of replacing a manager was $25,000 to $30,000. After three years of inflation, that figure might be closer to $40,000. Therefore, if your company hires 100 new MBAs this year and loses 25 of them in the first year, that first year of "reality shock" may be adding $1,000,000 annually to your operating expenses.

Obviously, then, you can save a lot of money by managing the entry and first year of new employees in a more satisfying way. As companies like AT&T and General Electric have found, making initial jobs more challenging and "stretching" not only decreases turnover, but also improves long-term career performance. In one study of two AT&T operating companies, David E. Berlew and Douglas T. Hall (1966) found that management trainees who received the most challenging first-year jobs were the most successful performers five to seven years later.

Select a challenging first job. Granted, then, that one answer to Problem One is to make the first job more challenging. Just how do you go about it? First, instead of simply putting the new employee into any open job, give the matter more careful thought. If more than one job assignment is available, purposely slot the new employee into the most demanding one. "But," you ask, "how can I be sure he or she can handle it?" Good question; obviously, you can't be sure. However, our research shows that managers are quite conservative on this issue and usually err in the direction of making the first assignment too easy. This may eliminate the possibility of failure, but it also prevents the employee from achieving *psychological success*, the exhilarating sense of accomplishment that results only from achieving a task that entailed a reasonable probability of failure. More likely than not, the new recruit will perform well in a tough assignment—especially if you are available to provide help and support when needed.

Provide job enrichment. A second way of enhancing the first job is to provide a measure of job enrichment. How? Add more responsibility to the job, give the new employee increased authority, and let the new person deal directly with clients and customers (not through you); if new employees are doing special projects and making recommendations to you, let them follow through and implement these ideas. AT&T is currently training supervisors of certain new employees in the skills of job enrichment as a way of making initial jobs more of a "stretching" experience.

Assign the new recruit to demanding bosses. A third way of improving the first job is to give more care and thought to selecting the supervisor to whom you assign the new recruit. As J. Sterling Livingston has shown, there is a "Pygmalion effect" in the relationship between a new employee and his or her boss. The more the boss expects and the more confident and supportive the boss is of the new employee, the better the recruit will perform. So don't assign a new employee to a "dead wood," undemanding, or unsupportive supervisor. Choose high-performing supervisors who will set high standards for the new employee during the critical, formative first year.

Give realistic job previews. If it's not possible to upgrade the first job experience, the opposite strategy is to provide the employee with realistic expectations during the recruiting process. Several organizations (Prudential Insurance Company, Texas Instruments, the Southern New England Telephone Company, and the U.S. Military Academy) have employed *realistic job previews* (RJPs) in the form of booklets, films, visits, or talks that convey not only the positive side of organizational life, but some of the problems and frustrations as well (example: the close supervision, lack of variety, limited socializing opportunities, and criticism experienced by telephone operators).

"But we'll never be able to hire anyone if we tell them the bad news about the job," you may be thinking. Research by John Wanous and others has shown, however, that these fears are unjustified. The recruitment rate is the same for people receiving RJPs as for those who get the more traditional one-sided information.

The big return comes later, after the person starts work: Among the recipients of RJPs, turnover and dissatisfaction are significantly lower than for people on the receiving end of traditional job previews. So to retain more of your new recruits, as the (now somewhat dated) saying goes, "Tell it like it really is!"

A somewhat different form of the RJP has been experimentally introduced into management classrooms at the University of Wisconsin—Parkside in cooperation with the Goodyear Tire and Rubber Company's North Chicago Hose Plant. When a new recruit reacted to his first job with, "We never learned this in a classroom!" training manager Ernie LaBrecque gradually began to bring supervisors into Parkside's classes on a regular basis. The purpose is quite simple: to provide tomorrow's hires with first-hand knowledge of what to expect.

While the Parkside-Goodyear efforts have been limited, the model has significant potential for companies that recruit on a regular basis at particular universities. Not only are business leaders generally welcome in classes, but the opportunity to establish an ongoing relationship has obvious mutual benefits.

PROBLEM 2: HOW CAN WE QUICKLY DEVELOP HIGH-POTENTIAL CANDIDATES (ESPECIALLY WOMEN AND MINORITIES) FOR MANAGEMENT POSITIONS?

The problem of identifying and selecting high-potential management candidates has been well researched over the years and is pretty well understood. Job sampling and other ways of simulating management jobs, such as assessment centers, have been shown to be effective though expensive ways of identifying managerial talent. The real problem is how we can best *train and develop* these promising candidates once they are identified.

Assessment centers for development. Assessment centers were originally developed for selection purposes, to identify high-potential candidates for hiring or promotion. When used for selection purposes, the results of the assessment process are used by managers responsible for these personnel decisions and are often not fed back to the employee. More recently, however, assessment centers have also been used successfully for employee development. When they are used in this way, the emphasis is on feedback of results to the employee following the assessment experience. In a feedback ses-

sion, a trained staff member points out the candidate's strong and weak points, illustrating them with examples of the candidate's behavior in the assessment activities. After the employee understands and accepts the feedback, the discussion turns to counseling and planning for future training experiences and developmental assignments that would lead to a particular target job in management.

Many companies, viewing the results of the assessment center experience as classified information, are reluctant to feed back this information to the employee. This secrecy represents a waste of extremely valuable developmental input, particularly in view of the high cost of putting the employee through the two- or three-day experience. Such secrecy also probably leads the candidate to develop unrealistically high expectations (as in the first job). If, on the other hand, assessment results are used for feedback and career counseling, several benefits are reaped: (1) The candidate's expectations are more realistic; (2) the candidate is helped in overcoming weaknesses; (3) the candidate has a specific career plan; and (4) the company is viewed as a partner rather than an adversary in career planning, something better calculated to result in career satisfaction.

Job pathing. The AT&T research cited earlier showed the impact the first job can have on the employee's development. A logical extension of this idea is that a *sequence of jobs* can have even greater effects on the person's career growth. In fact, we would argue that *carefully sequenced job assignments have greater impact on a person's development than any other kind of training experience.* Job requirements demand that a person learn certain job-related skills. Training programs, by contrast, by and large do not demand learning. Job activities and job-related learning are by definition integrated into the ongoing work environment, whereas off-the-job training programs are often hard to reconcile with the "back home" job environment.

The critical factors in using jobs for developmental purposes are to identify (1) the skills and experience a person needs to reach a certain target job and (2) which jobs, in what sequence, will provide these skills and experiences in small enough increments so the person will not be overwhelmed, but in large enough jumps so that the person is always being stretched—thus minimizing career time to reach the target job.

One large retailing organization, for example, is undertaking just such a job-pathing program in an attempt to reduce the amount of time it takes to "grow" a store manager. Conventional wisdom in the organization is that it takes around fifteen years, but initial experiences with careful job plotting indicate that it can probably be done in five. Another widely held belief in this organization is that there are one or two main paths to the store manager's position. Yet examination of several alternative paths, which are quite feasible but for some reason never used, indicates that the company has more flexibility in plotting career paths than it is currently using. Plotting paths through several different functions makes it possible to grow "broader" managers.

Talent development among hourly employees. Several existing methods of developing managerial talent among hourly workers may need to be reexamined in light of the need to comply with legislation on equal employment opportunity. Companies are beginning to address the question: "How can we attract a substantial number of women and minorities into these presupervisory programs?" To answer this question, some have begun to assess employee *perceptions* of upward mobility opportunities, organizational barriers to or support mechanisms for upward mobility, and the self-perceptions and role perceptions held by women and minorities. When, for example, a plant manager in a brewing company queried a woman on the reasons she *resisted* the opportunity to move into management, she replied, "I thought a production supervisor had to be a 'Two-Ton Tony.'" Obviously, this woman's resistance stemmed at least in part from the discrepancy between her perception of the role requirements and her self-image.

Another approach has been the use of in-

service training institutes conducted by professional or trade organizations. While these are common in manufacturing (the Midwest Manufacturing Association, for example, has sponsored numerous "certificate" programs), organizations such as the National Association of Banking Women are also seeking ways of developing their numbers. Frequently, women and minorities view the opportunity for training through these associations as being less competitive and more supportive than company-sponsored programs.

PROBLEM 3: HOW CAN WE INCREASE PROMOTION OPPORTUNITIES IN A STABLE OR CONTRACTING ORGANIZATION?

For many organizations, the current push for career development, especially for women and minority candidates, comes in an economic period when career growth is hardest to provide: a period of corporate slow-down or retrenchment. When many new management positions are opening up in an organization, career opportunities abound; when they dry up, career advancement requires more careful planning. How can we make the most of these declining opportunities?

Cross-functional moves. One developmental method is the cross-functional or lateral transfer. Such rotational transfers may occur often at the beginning of a person's career. After a certain point, however, organizations tend to keep people in a particular functional area in which they can become highly trained and specialized and spend enough time to pay off the company's investment. In the long run, this policy leads to obsolescence; the person who is not forced to learn about new areas from time to time ends up stale, bored, and increasingly less creative and productive. Cross-functional transfers throughout the career keep a person fresh and open to new learning and give him or her a broader perspective on the company as a whole.

An example of this sort of transfer occurred at Union Carbide, where three executive vice-presidents traded jobs. The reason for the move was to give each one a better "big picture" view of the total organization and prepare them better for the presidency. One of the men, Warren M. Anderson, explained the value of the move in an article in *Business Week* (July 14, 1975, pp. 82, 84):

> We were a holding company until the mid-1950s, and you could count on your fingers the number of people who moved from division to division. You grow up in a division, and you get about four miles tall but not very broad. . . . Everybody had sneered at lateral transfers. Now, they can point to us. I feel this gives me a chance to see the whole business.

Job pathing enables us to identify jobs *at the same organizational level* that demand more skills in certain areas than do other jobs. Thus the great potential of lateral moves for development is more effectively tapped. After two people trade jobs, as one retailing organization found, it is possible for each to end up in a more demanding position!

A critical issue in any kind of lateral move is how the transfer decision is made. When personnel staff specialists make the decisions, the moves may make good, sound technical sense—but may be unacceptable to the bosses of the people to be moved. Also, this kind of decision-making process implies that career planning is purely a staff function, and not the manager's job.

Management-personnel committees. One way of getting managers more involved in career planning is through the mechanism of management-personnel committees. In this structure, which is employed by the Southern New England Telephone Company (SNET), each personnel committee is made up of managers from all the functions at the same level of management. Each committee meets once every week or two to decide what transfers will be made between their departments among people who report to them. They also make recommendations on promotions. Employees are assessed in terms of their management potential, ranging from Category 1 (high-level potential) to Category 6 (not promotable even if the company is on the verge of going out of business).

According to Robert Neal, director of human resources development for SNET, this process results in a high quality of personnel decisions and in personnel actions that generally are well accepted by those affected—both the bosses and the transferred employees. The process does deal with tough issues of bargaining ("I'll take one from your Category 5, but let's agree in writing that you'll take him back in two years"). Actual contracts are written and signed, in much the way that "player swaps" are handled in professional sports. Another benefit of this system, according to Neal, is that a "Cat. 5" in one department—say, marketing—may blossom into a "Cat. 2" in traffic. Employees are periodically reassessed in light of *recent* performance, since these transfers enable an employee to demonstrate potential that might otherwise have been hidden forever if he or she had stayed in one function or department.

One disadvantage of this process, of course, is that like most committee structures, it takes a fair amount of time. However, the benefits seem to justify the time invested. Another management "plus" of this system is that the managers who serve on personnel committees develop a greater identification with the company as a whole. The decision process involved forces them to rise above their own department loyalties and look at decisions from a broader perspective. The rate of interfunctional movement has increased from 5 percent of all transfers in 1968 to 50 percent now.

Whenever we discuss developmental lateral moves with executives, the response is usually surprisingly strong, either pro or con. Some people see it as a radical, impractical idea because the need for retraining would be great, as would the organizational risk of having managers who are inexperienced in their new function or department. Lateral moves also buck a common norm in many organizations—namely, that the only good move is a promotion. Other managers report that they are beginning to experiment with cross-functional moves, and their experiences are generally favorable. Still others report they have never really thought about cross-functional moves, but they get very excited about this "creative new idea." There is nothing new or creative about lateral moves, however; the fact is that in many companies promotion policies are simply taken for granted, like "organization wallpaper," when they might quite easily and profitably be changed.

Fallback positions. One risk of a cross-functional transfer or promotion, especially when it occurs at a senior level, is that the person may fail in the new job simply because it's too demanding. Because many organizations are reluctant to move people down a level, there is some risk that the cross-functional transferee may become stuck in a position beyond his or her level of competence—the Peter Principle in action.

A novel way of reducing this risk in a high-level job move is to identify a fallback position into which the person can move if he or she is not successful after promotion or transfer. The fallback position assures the person of a position equal in status and pay to his or her original job if things don't work out in the new one. Establishing a fallback position in advance lets everyone involved know that (1) there is some risk in the promotion or transfer, (2) the company is willing to accept some of the responsibility for it, and (3) moving into the fallback position does not constitute failure. As a result, the ratchet effect of upward-only movement is partially eliminated, and the organization's degree of freedom in manpower planning is substantially increased.

Consider this illustration of the fallback-position concept: In the Heublein organization, one management-information systems expert was moved to finance, and a human-resources specialist was transferred to a job in production management. Without the fallback position, neither person might have been willing to take the risk. With it, people who have become highly specialized (perhaps overspecialized) can be helped to work their way back into general management. Among the other com-

panies that have employed fallback positions are Procter and Gamble, Continental Can, and Lehman Brothers (*Business Week,* September 28, 1974).

Downward transfers. More dramatic than the establishment of fallback positions is the policy of legitimizing downward transfers (demotions). Being able to move people down as well as up introduces considerably more flexibility in manpower planning. As organizational growth decreases, and as more people elect to "stay put" in their present job (or are compelled to), the result could be corporate stagnation—with few people entering or leaving the organization. To maintain flexibility, therefore, new ways of creating internal mobility become critical. For every person moved downward, a shot at a promotion is created for numerous people below this level. Where there is a policy against moving people down, the only way a vacancy could open up would be through retirement or death (assuming no organization growth or turnover).

The problem with downward transfers, obviously, is the strong norm in our society against moving down. Moving up is good, moving laterally is suspect, and moving down spells *failure.*

The upward-mobility norm is a tough one to buck, but it is being challenged on several fronts:

1. As concern over the quality of life increases, more people are turning down promotions or accepting lower-level jobs in order to move to or to stay in such desirable geographical areas as San Diego, Minneapolis, Atlanta, and Seattle. When, for example, the department of psychology at San Diego State University advertised an opening for an assistant professor (a position generally filled by someone fresh out of graduate school), the department received many applications from full professors and department chairmen who were willing to move down in order to live in San Diego.

2. Realizing that growth opportunities are becoming more limited, people are willing to move down into a new area or company as a possible base from which to move up later on.

3. Given the option of being terminated or being demoted, people are often willing to accept a move down. As with many decisions in life, the attractiveness of a demotion often depends upon the nature of the alternatives. In recent cuts of technical personnel, companies such as General Electric and Chrysler first tried to place as many employees as possible in lower-level jobs rather than terminate them. Those who were moved down rather than out were viewed as being quite fortunate.

4. As the economy settles into a period of slower growth, expectations of rapid advancement may diminish and the upward-mobility norm may weaken. There is already evidence that the American success ethic is moving away from advancement and money as success symbols, toward self-fulfillment. As Daniel Yankelovich put it:

> Since World War II most Americans have shaped their ideas of success around money, occupational status, possessions, and the social mobility of their children. Now, ideas about success are beginning to revolve around various forms of self fulfillment. If the key motif of the past was "keeping up with the Joneses," today it is, "I have my own life to live, let Jones shift for himself."

As part of this quest for personal self-fulfillment (which does not necessarily have to occur on the job), people may be more likely to take a lower-level job that gives them more autonomy or challenge or simply more freedom to pursue fulfillment off the job.

Other organizations are using downward transfers to open up management training and mobility options that otherwise would not exist. One large Canadian oil company has been experimenting with downward transfers at senior executive levels. This company has learned certain principles that increase the success of downward transfers. First, the people who are chosen to be moved down should be people who are known (by themselves and other employees) to be outstanding performers. This helps dissociate downward movement from failure (and, it is to be hoped, may even associate it with

success). Over time, if enough obviously competent people are moved down, the norm of promotion-as-a-sign-of-success may be replaced with movement-as-a-sign-of-success. People to be moved down should be informed well in advance and told that they may be moved back to their present levels later.

Why are outstanding performers moved down? First, because even if a person is performing successfully at his or her job, there are still many equally promising people at the next level down, waiting for a higher-level challenge. Moving one person down temporarily gives many more people a good opportunity for development. The obviously successful person would be more secure and more effective in a downward move than would a less outstanding performer. Second, there may be "hot spots" at a lower level in the organization that call for the temporary trouble-shooting services of a successful higher-level person. Perhaps a tough marketing problem needs to be solved or maybe a department needs reorganizing. A key executive could come in on a one-year assignment, clean things up, and then move back to his previous level or to a new "hot spot."

A second principle is that important ground rules must be established: (1) No one will suffer a cut in pay as a result of a downward move, and (2) no one moved down will be terminated (to make it clear that the next move after moving down isn't out the door). People moved down thus received a sort of "tenure" that gave them more security than most other employees.

What are some of the preliminary results of the downward-transfer system in this firm? The most obvious is that intraorganizational mobility and flexibility have increased. More young people can move up into high-responsibility positions faster than before. They can also move back down and into other functional areas more easily.

What about the effects on the people moved down? According to the personnel director, the first few people (as one might anticipate) had mixed emotions about it. After several months, however, they began to appreciate the freedom from higher-level responsibilities and pressures. They appreciated having a bit more time to spend with their families, getting to know their grandchildren, and so on. They also enjoyed the stimulation of working with younger managers—learning new ideas and techniques from them and transmitting wisdom and experience to them.

An unintended consequence of these downward transfers has been an improvement in two-way communication, especially in the upward direction.

Corporate Tenure

Some of the career-management policies we have just discussed, such as cross-functional transfers and downward moves, are often difficult to implement because of the threats they may pose to the person's security in the organization. One way to increase employees' sense of security, and at the same time to establish tougher performance standards and feedback, is through a system of corporate tenure.

Such a novel system has been used in a medium-sized Pennsylvania manufacturing firm. The president of this firm, Robert Seidel, took a look at how various types of organizations develop personnel. He decided that universities, for all their problems, did have one promising feature: the tenure system. The tenure system forces the university to take a good hard look at a person's performance and to give him or her straight feedback: "up or out."

Seidel modified the tenure system in this way. When a new employee is hired, he or she is put on a short-term probation period, a customary procedure in many organizations. At the end of the period, the employee's immediate superior and a personnel expert carefully appraise the person's performance. If it has been satisfactory, the employee is encouraged to stay on.

At this point, however, a novel twist occurs. The two evaluators make a second judgment: If there were to be a economic downturn and we had to make a 20 percent staff cut, would this person be in the 20 percent we would terminate? The answer to this question, which is fed back to the employee, gives him a realistic idea of where he stands with the company. People who are not in this 20 percent marginal group are thus granted a form of organizational tenure. Knowing that their jobs are secure, they feel freer to assume the risks of interdepartmental transfer, promotion, or demotion. Interestingly, this tenure does not result in "slacking off," perhaps because of clear standards of high performance in the organization.

What about the effect on the people in the 20 percent group? Often they elect to remain in the organization. In some cases, the feedback results in improved performance. One major advantage of this tenure system is that it forces the organization to appraise new employees all the time, not just on a "crash" basis when a personnel cut is necessary.

The Need for Internal Mobility

The common theme in all these methods of providing for better career development in a slower growth economy is increased intraorganizational mobility. If job changes are not going to be facilitated so much by the entrance or departure of people or by the opening up of new positions, we will have to find new ways to move people around within the organization.

We know from the work of Paul Lawrence and Jay Lorsch and others that organizations have to become more flexible if they are to adapt to changes and uncertainty in the external environment. The methods we have been discussing (downward transfers, cross-functional moves, and so on) are all specific ways in which the organization can increase its own flexibility and that of its human resources.

Executives are rethinking their norms about what kind of movement is appropriate. Both employees and the organization have to plan career moves more carefully and work harder at career development, because the economy is no longer doing the job for us. In an ironic twist, a slow growth economy is giving (or forcing upon) individuals and organizations more control over the way careers unfold.

WHAT IS NOT BEING DONE ABOUT CAREER DEVELOPMENT?

So much for the good news; now let's see where less progress is being made.

Integrating Career Development and Manpower Planning

Work on organizational careers has a schizophrenic aspect. On the one hand, there are attempts to facilitate the careers of individual employees through career counseling, goal setting, and so forth (the micro approach). At the other extreme, manpower planners chart the moves of large numbers of people through various positions in the organization—identifying future staffing gaps, "fast tracks," and the like (the macro approach). But these two types of career planning are rarely integrated.

Most organizations, in fact, use only one of these approaches—an unfortunate practice no matter which one they choose. The company that focuses on individuals, for example, may well do a good job of developing people—but if overall corporate manpower needs are ignored, these individuals may be "all developed with no place to go" or find themselves being routed into dead-end jobs.

On the other hand, the organization that develops corporate manpower plans without adequately developing and training people to move through various positions (or to move through a different sequence of positions) is not really managing and planning careers, but merely monitoring them. Even in the organization that is doing both micro and macro career planning, most of the potential of each approach is lost if (as is often the case) the micro and macro people don't talk to each other.

It seems almost trite to suggest that the micro and macro facets of career management be integrated because it seems so straightforward and reasonable. One wonders why this integration does not occur more often. One reason is that organizations large enough to need systematic career management generally have career counseling and manpower planning in different departments. Practitioners in each area often come out of different professional disciplines—counselors from psychology, and manpower planners from economic or systems analysis. And it is difficult to integrate the two—to undertake sound manpower forecasts and then to translate them into specific training and development activities.

Dealing with Second-Generation EEO Problems

Many organizations are now into what we might call Phase II of affirmative action. The main need in Phase I, which concerned recruitment and selection, was to get more women and minority employees to enter managerial and professional positions. Now that more women and minorities *are* entering these positions, other problems arise—such as the need for training and development, meeting new needs of new kinds of employees, and coping with the reactions of white male employees.

The problem of providing organizational support. A subtle pattern seems to be evolving, in which some executives subvert EEO goals while apparently implementing them. The equation for this process is "Equal opportunity + low support = discrimination." If a woman or minority employee is hired for a position traditionally occupied by white males, the new person will probably need some technical training as well as informal advice, coaching, and support. In fact, most of us need—and receive—all kinds of informal help and support in any new job. However, when female or minority employees are placed in a nontraditional position (that is, given equal employment opportunity), they are often socially isolated from peers and senior colleagues who could give them words of wisdom, feedback prodding, encouragement, "Dutch uncle" talks, and the like; these new employees are simply left alone to do their job—and frequently to fail. One young woman, for example, was hired by a high-prestige (and high-pressure) university despite the concern some people felt about her lack of experience and confidence in dealing with the demanding students she would encounter. A senior faculty member assured the others that he would take her "under his wing" and help her cope with her environment. So she was hired—the first woman in her department—and all eyes were on her. And the senior professor left for a sabbatical as soon as she arrived! No one else was willing to act as a substitute sponsor in his absence. Without support or counsel, she floundered in the classroom. She spent so much time working on her teaching that she didn't spend much time on research—and no one "bugged" her to do any publishing. Now the reaction of her colleagues is, "Well, we tried giving a woman a chance; I guess we'd better not make *that* mistake again." Thus with equal opportunity and low support, low initial expectations for the person's success can create a vicious self-fulfilling prophecy.

The problem of meeting the needs of the white male. Because of the slow economy, promotions are harder to come by these days—and those that *are* available are often used to advance women and minority employees. Consequently, the white male often feels frustrated and demotivated. It is no consolation to him to say that this reverse discrimination is a temporary corrective measure to make up for past generations of discrimination in favor of white males. After all, he wasn't responsible for what happened earlier, so why should he suffer now?

The group being hurt most is white males of average competence. Outstanding performers will always have corresponding career opportunities. And poor performers are likely always to have problems—but right now, EEO activity is giving them a handy scapegoat. It is the average white male who is most likely to lose out in competition with women and minorities who show equal performance and qualifications.

Most companies seem aware of this problem, but see little they can do about it. They often handle the issue by cloaking promotion data in great secrecy—perhaps in the hope that if white males aren't told they're not getting anywhere, maybe they won't notice it! The irony here is that in many companies white males tend to overestimate their relative disadvantage. More open information would probably show that white males are moving faster than their perceptions would suggest.

One way to deal with this issue is to be sure that white males receive at least as much career counseling and assistance in career planning as do women and minorities, because the former group may need to plan their career moves more carefully. The white male may have a greater need for occupational information inside and outside the company than do other, higher-

priority groups. In fact, many companies started career-planning programs for women and minorities only and then opened them up to all employees. In these organizations, white males have more career-planning services now available than they ever would have had without EEO pressures.

Another strategy—a high-risk, but high-potential one—would be to hold career workshops in which male and female employees, black and white, meet to discuss their feelings about career opportunities and explore methods of aiding their career development. Such group sessions could meet employees' need for: (1) ventilating feelings, (2) being counseled, (3) getting career information, (4) doing some self-assessment, and (5) solving career problems.

Managing Dual Careers

As more women embark upon full-time work careers, more dual-career families come into existence. When both husband and wife have full-time careers, their personal career flexibility decreases (if they want to live together), so career planning becomes more difficult and necessary. It is, of course, more difficult to transfer a dual-career employee to a different city or, if the spouse is transferred by his or her firm, to attempt to make a similar move for the partner who works for you. You may find yourself losing good people because of a spouse's career. Alternatively, you might find it difficult to attract someone whose spouse could not find good career opportunities in your organization's geographical area.

The best way for organizations to deal with dual careers is not clear. Many executives do not yet see the problem as an important one. The first step, therefore, is to demonstrate to managers the ways in which dual careers can affect their organization. Our preliminary research indicates that the main problem caused by dual careers comes in making personnel transfers. Recruitment and hiring do not seem to be so strongly affected, although again managers may just be less aware of the dual-career people they lose in the hiring process than of the ones they hire and can't transfer.

Companies seem to be dealing with the transfer problem by adopting a more flexible attitude toward people who turn down transfers. An employee is now informally granted more transfer refusals without prejudice to future promotions than in the past. There also seems to be more effort to find developmental moves within the same geographic location. This is another reason why cross functional moves may become more common.

Another corporate response to dual careers is an increasing awareness that the organization has some stake in the spouse's career, even if the spouse works elsewhere. Thus various supportive services, mainly informal, are being extended to unemployed spouses (for example, help in setting up job interviews with other organizations.) Nepotism rules are also being relaxed, making it easier for husband and wife to work for the same organization or even in the same department. (The emerging norm in many organizations is that spouses can work in the same department as long as one is not supervising the other.) Flexible workhours are helpful, too.

Some organizations are finding that attracting dual-career people requires dual recruiting, or helping to find a job for the spouse as well as the primary candidate. This may require cooperative, interorganizational recruiting. Dealing with another organization's personnel executives, over whom you have no control, can be a real test of managerial and persuasive skills. The fact is, however, that the spouse's career opportunities have become a bargaining point in recruiting and retaining talented dual-career employees. This issue is just beginning to show up with younger, more junior people. In time, these will become key people and then the problem will be critical. The executive who responds that this is the couple's problem, not the organization's, will lose many good employees. The issue, we feel, is a real organizational "time bomb."

GENERAL PRINCIPLES OF EFFECTIVE CAREER PLANNING

So far, we've examined what novel ideas are being tried and what isn't being done. Let's conclude with a few general guidelines about what *should* be done in developing employee careers.

Utilize the Career-Growth Cycle

First, let's consider just how career growth occurs. This process, shown in Figure 1, is triggered by a job that provides challenging,

Figure 1

The career-growth cycle

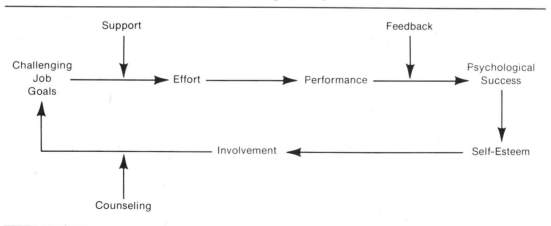

stretching goals. The clearer and more challenging the goals, the more effort the person will exert—and the more effort exerted, the more likely it is that good performance will result. If the person does a good job and receives positive feedback, he or she will feel successful (psychologically successful). Feelings of success increase a person's feelings of confidence, self-worth, or self-esteem. This internal gratification leads the person to become more involved in work, which in turn leads to the setting of future stretching goals. Let us consider more specifically how a company might use this growth cycle.

Plan and Utilize the Job Itself

Since the career-growth cycle is triggered by challenging work goals, the person's job should be made as challenging as possible (as we explained earlier). Too many companies see career development only as something done by "those people in personnel." Each job should represent a challenge, and the sequence of jobs should be planned to provide a systematic and continuing growth of career skills.

Goal setting. In general, people tend not to set work goals for themselves. But when they do, the results can be dramatic. This doesn't mean that you need a formal MBO system—just mutual agreement between you, your boss, and your subordinate on a few specific objectives over the next few months that will help the employee focus his or her efforts.

Frequent performance review and feedback. Although most organizations have formal policies regarding performance appraisals, few performance appraisals are actually handled properly for the benefit of employees. People need feedback to help assess how well they have performed and where changes should be made. Such feedback can be given informally, on a continuing basis, instead of in a stressful, formal, once-a-year ordeal. It is also easier to provide feedback if specific goals have been set; then you can talk not only about how well activities were carried out, but also about whether certain ones were carried out at all.

Counseling and support from the boss. When building the conditions for career success into the job, don't forget the boss. As a source of support (in translating goals into action) and counseling and planning (for translating involvement into future goals), supervisors can be far more influential than any personnel or career specialist. The supervisor is also the best person to provide goal-setting stimulation and performance feedback.

Train and Reward Supervisors for Career-Planning Skills

If the supervisor is to be expected to provide support, feedback, and counseling, don't think this will happen easily. One reason supervisors don't do more along these lines now is that they don't feel comfortable doing it. And they feel uncomfortable for a number of reasons. One is that they often lack the necessary skills. A second reason is that they often experience role conflict between being a "boss" and being a "helper." A two- or three-day training program would be an enormous aid for supervisors, enabling them to learn both how to conduct good performance appraisals and how to be good informal agents of career planning. This approach to career planning is already being taken in one of the major auto manufacturers, with good results.

Tying employee development specifically into the supervisor's own performance appraisal is another good way to reward these activities. This is a simple idea, but it is rarely practiced. General Electric has been successful in including managers' affirmative action progress in their performance appraisals. The result has been a great increase in EEO attainments. A large Canadian computer company requires each manager to pick and develop a successor before the manager will be considered for promotion. This is a very clear and powerful way of linking the career development of subordinates to the career progress of the manager.

Personnel specialists as monitors. Tying career development into the everyday work environment of supervisors frees personnel specialists to act in an indirect, support role (which is what a staff function is intended to be, anyway). Personnel people can work in two ways: (1) They can train the supervisors in the career-developing skills just discussed, and (2) they can monitor the process to make sure that periodic goal setting, feedback, and career planning are discussed. The following application of these ideas gives more details.

An illustrative example: AT&T. Several of these principles are illustrated in career programs being used at AT&T. Joel Moses, a personnel specialist, cites one early identification program—the Initial Management Development Program—for noncollege employees being considered for management positions. The employees first go through a one-day assessment program. Then they are given feedback by a trained person (either in personnel or in the person's own department), who then continues to function as the employee's *career counselor.* Explicit career plans are made. Then the person and the boss jointly set work targets to help achieve the career plan. Although most of the planning is done within the employee's department, the personnel specialist functions as monitor of the process. The third-party career counselor is useful because of the high turnover in superior-subordinate relationships.

Another program is a successor to the Initial Management Development Program, but is more "user oriented" than IMDP. The stress is on *boss training* in the areas of job design, joint target setting, and appraisal skills. At the end of the first year of employment, the person goes through a two-day assessment program. Following this is a meeting with the person's boss, a member of the assessment center, and a personnel coordinator. One of three decisions is made: Terminate, don't promote, or prepare for middle management. A feedback meeting is held with the employee to discuss the results of the assessment process. Then in the second year a career plan is drawn up—entailing a target job, the training needed, interim assignments, and a time frame. The three parties review this plan and the progress made every six months.

The following principles are reflected in these AT&T programs:

1. Emphasize the development of high-potential people. Don't try to change people who lack management potential.

2. Set specific development objectives. Identify specific job experiences and skills the person needs (for example, "ability to supervise a central office PBX group.")

3. Train the supervisor to provide the day-to-day job experiences (for example, challenging goals and feedback) that facilitate career development.

4. Give personnel experts the responsibility for structuring and monitoring the development *process*, but reserve for the employee and the supervisor the responsibility for its actual content.

CONCLUSION

The more we use the job itself and the superior-subordinate relationship for career development and call upon the personnel department for outside resources and process monitors, the better use we are making of the respective resources of each.

We hope that the new process of career development will not be accepted or implemented without careful thought and planning, since it could become just another management fad. Rather, career development, the enhancement of human talent, should be viewed as a management function that has always been performed in effective organizations—yet one that can benefit from being conceptualized and practiced in new ways.

SELECTED BIBLIOGRAPHY

A comprehensive source on career theory, factors in career success, organizational career-management practices, and self-management of careers is Douglas T. Hall's *Careers in Organizations* (Goodyear Publishing Company, 1976). For the more technical readers, a test of the model of career development in this paper and a description of the careers of priests are found in Douglas T. Hall and Benjamin Schneider's *Organizational Climate and Careers: The Work Lives of Priests* (Seminar [Academic] Press, 1973). A good discussion of the impact of the first job and the first boss is found in J. Sterling Livingston's "Pygmalion in Management," (*Harvard Business Review*, July-August, 1969, pp. 81-89). A thorough and highly readable report of how individual differences and early job experiences affect employee career development is found in Douglas W. Bray, Richard J. Campbell, and Donald L. Grant's *Formative Years in Business: A Long-Term*

Study of Managerial Lives (John Wiley & Sons, Inc., 1974). For a comprehensive review of the research on obsolescence and midcareer development, see H. G. Kaufman's *Obsolescence and Professional Career Development* (AMACOM, a division of American Management Associations, 1974). Several perspectives on women's careers are found in Francine E. Gordon and Myra Strober's *Bringing Women into Management* (McGraw-Hill, Inc., 1975). And finally, an excellent, entertaining, and professional source book for self-directed career planning is Richard N. Bolles's *What Color Is Your Parachute? A Practical Manual for Job Hunters and Career Changers* (Ten Speed Press, 1974).

Planning Job Progression for Effective Career Development and Human Resources Management

Harry L. Wellbank
Douglas T. Hall
Marilyn A. Morgan
W. Clay Hammer

There are three important problems with the way many career development and human resources management systems are currently designed and operated. First, there is rarely any connection between career planning and development, aimed at individual employees, and corporate human resources planning and management, aimed at organizational staffing needs. Second, much career development activity takes place in isolation or in classroom settings and is unrelated to actual job needs and experiences. Much career development has little connection with either the employee's organizational career or actual development. Third, many career development systems are unnecessarily complex, consisting of exotic planning exercises, computerized self-assessment instruments, or mathematical models.

To overcome these problems, Sears, Roebuck and Co. is developing a new method of job-based career development and human resources management, which it thinks will resolve these critical career management problems. To do this, it is using a highly potent, but very common, everyday training and development instrument: the job.

Sears has a long history of using job assignments for management development, though perhaps the "new" methods aren't really so new. For example, for years college recruits at Sears started on the back dock and rotated through six or eight other job assignments during the first 12 to 18 months. At the end of this period, the individual was assigned to his or her first supervisory position, as a department manager. During ensuing years, if the individual was still considered promotable, he or she was assigned to a variety of store staff positions—perhaps as many as five, six, or seven—ending with assistant store manager and store management.

All of these moves were made by the corporation on the basis of a feeling for what would be appropriate in terms of the company's past experience, that is, on the basis of "what worked." But with the human resources needs of today, unanalyzed past experience is not an adequate basis on which to proceed, and so Sears is adopting new methods.

JOB ASSIGNMENT SEQUENCES FOR CAREER DEVELOPMENT

To provide the foundation for the new approach, Sears is proposing several critical principles of career development:

• *The most important influences on career development occur on the job.* As the work at AT&T indicates, everyday job challenges and demands are powerful socializing and skill-building devices. The job itself undoubtedly has more influence on development than formally planned development experiences, such as classroom training and workshops.

• *Different jobs demand the development of different skills.* A supervisory job, for example, stimulates the development of greater human relations skills, while a staff specialist's job may stretch the person's technical skills.

• *Development occurs only when the person has not yet developed the skills demanded by a particular job.* If a person is put into a job that demands skills the person has already mastered, little or no new learning will take place. For a job to provide development experiences, it must stretch the person to learn new skills or improve existing ones. This principle seems painfully obvious, but it often is violated in many corporate personnel moves.

• *By identifying a rational sequence of job assignments for a person, the time required to develop the necessary skills for a chosen target job can be reduced.* If one job produces a certain amount of skill development, then a series of job assignments can be selected to produce even more development over the course of the person's career.

This last point is the key principle in the new Sears system—the use of a well-planned sequence of job assignments to maximize career development. Without a systematic way of analyzing job demands, job assignments often overlap greatly. Even promotions, if they are within the same functional area, often do not encourage the learning of new skills. But with a systematic method of evaluating job content, job progressions can be planned to minimize the overlap in job demands and maximize skill stretching.

USING A JOB EVALUATION SYSTEM FOR MORE RATIONAL JOB PROGRESSION

Although job evaluation systems are generally used for compensation purposes, they also have great potential in career development since they provide systematic procedures for assessing the skills required in a particular job. The Hay system is used at Sears. However, the career management process to be discussed here can be used with various job evaluation systems, not just the Hay method.

The Hay system measures three basic competencies for each job: know-how, problem solving, and accountability. Know-how can be further broken down into three kinds of job knowledge: technical, managerial, and human relations. Problem solving and accountability also have several dimensions. Scores for each of these three competencies are assigned to each job, and a total value for each job is then computed. Thus, for any planned job transfer, the amount of increase (or decrease) the next job represents in each of the component skill areas, as well as in the total point value, can be computed. At Sears, any further job that is one scale unit or more above the previous job on any skill dimension requires significant learning on that dimension. Similarly, any transfer to a job representing a 10 percent or greater increase in total points is a growth-demanding assignment. Further, it is also desirable at Sears for a person to have a combination of experiences in different functional areas. Using these criteria, developmental career paths can be constructed to provide the following experiences:

—An increase in at least one skill area on each new assignment.

—An increase of at least 10 percent in total points on each new assignment.
—Assignments in several different functional areas.

ACHIEVING MULTIPLE OBJECTIVES IN A JOB PROGRESSION DEVELOPMENT PROGRAM

Once an organization has a way to evaluate the skill requirements of different job assignments, job progression plans can be designed to achieve a number of objectives for both the organization and the employee. Several different objectives of a job progression development program and how each one might be achieved follow.

1. *Identifying rational paths to target jobs.* One of the most important purposes of a systematic job progression plan is to identify all of the logically feasible paths to any target job, such as store manager, a key job in a retailing organization. In most organizations, certain paths become established as the "best" routes to a particular job without a clear reason. Putting together rational career paths on the basis of an objective assessment of the skills that the paths will impart is a way of moving from folklore to facts about what jobs will best add career growth.

Having done this, an organization may find that the range of rationally possible career paths to a given target job is wider than those paths in present use. A comparison of rationally feasible paths with actual paths (based upon job histories of present employees) may suggest alternative routes for developing employees who may have been overlooked in the past. This can increase both the organization's flexibility in meeting staffing needs and employees' development needs at the same time.

The set of rational paths should be screened carefully, of course, since it is possible that some make no sense because of practical constraints and needs. For example, it may be possible, in terms of the three previously mentioned criteria, to move a person from a merchandise manager to store manager in two moves, but the company would probably want to give the person more interim assignments just to learn more about the organization. To be most useful, the rational paths should be screened by many personnel specialists and managers in different functional areas to eliminate those that are unworkable. (However, paths should be screened out only for rational reasons; they should not be eliminated just because they have never been tried before. Those are exactly the paths an organization may *want* to try!)

2. *Identifying rational "fast tracks" to a target job.* Once a set of feasible rational paths to a target job has been identified, the paths that entail the fewest moves—that is, those that prepare the person for the target job in the shortest period of time—can be identified. For example, many Sears personnel believe that it takes from 14 to 16 years to "grow" a store manager. However, preliminary analyses using job evaluations indicate that it is technically feasible to develop store managers in far less time.

This kind of analysis has great value for affirmative action purposes or for high-potential employees whom the organization may desire to move up as fast as their abilities will permit. Rapid promotions call for especially careful analysis on each job move, and the job evaluation system can reduce the risk of hurting the person's career through a series of inappropriate assignments that do not adequately prepare him or her for the responsibilities of the target job.

3. *Identifying rational lateral moves (that is, slower career growth).* Many organizations in today's economy are not as much concerned about rapid promotions as they are about slower promotions. If an organization is in a fairly stable state—not growing, growing very slowly, or perhaps shrinking—it can be difficult to provide satisfying career experiences to bright, ambitious young employees when there are few promotion opportunities opening up. Are there alternatives to promotion that can provide career growth and fulfillment?

One viable alternative to promotions is increased use of lateral transfers, moves to jobs at the same level that demand quite different skills and therefore require career growth. Unfortunately, lateral moves as practiced in many firms now are simply reassignment to the same kind of job in a new location; this provides all the disadvantages of a geographical transfer (uprooting the family and so on) with no compensating benefits in the job itself. Therefore, lateral moves are not eagerly anticipated by many employees. In the eyes of many employees—and many executives, too—the only good move is an upward move.

But lateral moves can be used more creatively. With a job evaluation system, an organization can identify many jobs at about the same rank and pay level that represent a wide range of skills and responsibilities. At Sears, there are ample numbers of jobs at the same level that require acquisition of significant new skills in human relations, technical know-how, managerial competence, or problem solving. For example, movement from the job of merchandise manager in a medium-size store to operating superintendent would result in an increase in both managerial responsibilities and the kind of technical skills used. If organizational realities demand that promotions in a firm be slower, it will become especially important to plan for other methods of providing career fulfillment and maintaining employee commitment. Job progression planning is a useful tool for well-managed lateral transfers that maintain a high level of stimulation from the intrinsic features of the job itself.

4. Identifying rational downward moves. Why not make more conscious, if sparing, use of downward moves as a way of developing people and meeting organizational needs better? If an organization had the option of moving people down just one level, imagine how much more flexibility it would have in its human resources planning.

One reason a downward move may be needed for employee development is that the organization wants to move a person into a new functional area, such as from finance to marketing. The person may be at too high a level for a

lateral move into a marketing job at the same level; he or she simply may not have the technical skills to be able to handle that job. So, with the job evaluation data, the organization can look for a lower-level marketing job in which technical skill demands are more within the person's reach. Rather than make a guess at which job is at the appropriate level, the organization uses job evaluation scores to help it make a better informed decision. It can then put the person in this lower-level job for, say, six or eight months until he or she masters the new area, and then it can start advancing the employee in the marketing department.

Another situation that may occur is that a lower-level job may make significantly greater skill demands on one or two job dimensions than the job the person currently holds and the development of that skill may be critical to the person's career development. For example, consider a person who has advanced to a fairly high-level job in a technical staff function (for example, marketing research or engineering) but who has had no supervisory or management experience. In many cases like this, the next career move up for talented people is to be a manager of a technical group. But the promotion may be based on demonstrated technical proficiency, not managerial skill. Rather than risk a major promotion into management, the organization can identify a lower-level supervisory job in line management that may have lower total job points than the person's previous technical job but which demands considerable human relations skills. Using this job, the organization would try the person out for a year or so. Then if it wants to promote him or her to a management job, it can do it on the basis of demonstrated supervisory performance. But first it must use its job evaluation system to identify a good supervisory "trial" job.

5. Identifying career path clusters. One problem with analyzing individual career paths, especially in large organizations, is information overload—there may be simply too many feasible paths available. Once an organization knows the characteristics of individual jobs, it can identify clusters of similar jobs. Then it can identify paths connecting various clusters of jobs on the way to the target job.

Similarly, the organization can identify paths within particular functions, departments, or specialties. For example, at Sears some people specialize in marketing and merchandising, which may involve a series of staff positions in territorial or corporate headquarters. Others take a store management route with positions mainly in the stores rather than in headquarters. These career specialties are actually more general concepts, and they provide a way to comprehend a larger set of job progression paths.

This kind of general information on job clusters and career specialties is usually clear and simple enough to be presented in recruiting or orientation literature. In fact, showing the recruit what the various career ladders are in the company seems to be a recent trend in the recruiting practices of many companies. ARCO's recruiting booklet does an especially good job of illustrating career ladders and of giving a recruit a short, self-directed career planning exercise as well.

6. Identifying good development moves from a given job.   Once an organization has identified the complete paths from present job to target job, it can move in for a close-up. This means identifying all the possible next jobs that are available and that provide either a 10 percent increase in total points or a significant increase in at least one job skill. The information display may include the total profile on all job dimensions for each of the possible next jobs. An example of this information is shown in Figure 1.

Figure 1 identifies nine jobs to be considered as reasonable next moves that would be considered promotions for someone who is the merchandising manager of a smaller store (sales volume $4 to $8 million). If the individual needs more merchandising experience, he or she may be assigned to the position of merchandising manager in a larger store to gain greater technical responsibilities. Assignment to the

job of operating superintendent, personnel manager, or group advertising manager would provide the opportunity to develop a different set of technical skills. Selection of the most reasonable next assignment would be worked out with both the individual and his or her supervisor. Such factors as previous experience, identified target job, and job availabilities would have to be considered.

7. Identifying training needs for future jobs. Another important use for the job evaluation data when next moves are being planned is to focus on the job dimensions where very large increases in skill will be needed. If the person is being stretched to an unusual degree on any one dimension, this may be a "red flag" that training is needed to support and supplement the on-the-job learning that will be taking place. In this way an organization can do a better job of integrating training activities with the actual training needs indicated by the job evaluation data in the new assignment. This analysis of the increments between the new and the old job profiles can also help an organization avoid wasting training in areas where it is not needed.

8. Identifying "people pools" for open jobs: staffing. Career management also has a more "macro" or corporate objective: providing a pool of people who are developed and ready to assume increased job responsibilities. A job evaluation system can also be used to identify the pool of candidates for any given job. In other words, a job evaluation system can be used to select people for jobs as well as to select jobs for people.

When a position becomes open, for example, it would be possible to search the organization's personnel files and identify the people for whom the job would represent career growth, that is, people for whom the job would represent a gain of at least 10 percent in total job points or a significant stretching of skill on at least one job dimension. The organization would obviously supplement this information with other data, such as the employee's career preferences

Figure 1   Sears, Roebuck and Co. Career counseling information: possible job moves

Current Job: Merchandise manager; store volume, $4 to $7.9 million.
Job Ratings*: Technical, D; Managerial, II; Human relations, 3; and Challenge, 3.

Possible Job Moves	Change in Job Dimensions
Percent change = 7.13	
Group advertising manager	
Store volume = Over $400 million	+T†, −M
Technical, E; Managerial, I; Human Relations, 3	
Percent change = 14.73	
Merchandise manager	
Store volume = $8 to $14.9 million	+T
Technical, E; Managerial, II; Human Relations, 3	
Percent change = 14.73	
Auto center manager	
Store volume = $1 to $2.9 million	+T
Technical, E; Managerial, II; Human Relations, 3	
Percent change = 7.13	
Group display manager	
Store volume = Under $76 million	+T
Technical, E; Managerial, II; Human Relations, 3	
Percent change = 14.73	
Operating superintendent, 1	
Store volume = Under $4 million	+T
Technical, E; Managerial, II; Human Relations, 3	
Percent change = 7.13	
Group installation manager	
Store volume = Under $5 million	+T
Technical, E; Managerial, II; Human Relations, 3	
Percent change = 14.73	
Operating superintendent, 2	
Store volume = $4 to $7.9 million	+T
Technical, E; Managerial, II; Human Relations, 3	
Percent change = 4.04	
Personnel manager, 1	
Store volume = $8 to $14.9 million	+T
Technical, E; Managerial, II; Human Relations, 3	
Percent change = 4.04	
Personnel manager, 2	
Store volume = $15 to $29.9 million	+T
Technical, E; Managerial, II; Human Relations, 3	

*These are the job evaluation ratings on these four factors using the Hay system.
†Increases or decreases in the technical, managerial, and human relations demands of the job in comparison with the present job are shown in this column.

and performance appraisals. But the basic process of matching people to career-growing jobs is the same, whether the organization is looking at the employee's career planning objectives or its human resources planning and selection needs.

IMPLEMENTATION

How should this kind of job evaluation/job progression system be put to use in a corporate setting? Carefully, very carefully. Career management involves working with important information about people's work histories that will affect their future careers. An acceptable system, therefore, must have the following features:

—Checks on the accuracy of the information used.
—Opportunity for the employee to examine data on his or her work history and to remove incorrect information.
—Provisions for inputs from the employee when decisions about his or her career are made.
—Safeguards for the confidentiality of the data.

There are three likely users or consumers of the information provided through such a system. First, individual employees may use it in thinking about their own careers. Second, line managers and employee development and training specialists may use it for developing managers. Job progression can be related to performance appraisal and advancement potential to provide the most stretching experiences possible for the organization's most talented employees. And, last, corporate and human resource planning experts may use the information for present and future staffing activities.

More specifically, information about job progressions may be used in the following ways:

• *For job posting.* Along with possibly posting vacant jobs, an organization may also post the skill profile for each job and the various paths

from each posted job to some generally valued target job.

• *For widespread dissemination of basic career paths.* An organization may want to identify general clusters of paths, or career specialties. These can be printed and disseminated on posters, in pamphlets, in the company newspaper, or in other media for distribution to all employees to give them some clear, simple information about advancement possibilities in different parts of the organization. Such information is in extremely short supply in most organizations—but in high demand. The result is that the need for information is filled with rumors, myths, and other inaccuracies. Like pay, careers are the subject of much secrecy and much dysfunctional rumor in most organizations. Accurate, useful information on basic career paths can be quite easy to provide.

• *For on-line computer access.* An organization may also want to store information on job evaluations and employees' career histories in an interactive computer system. The employee, a personnel specialist, or a manager can enter the number of a particular job and then request to have different kinds of information displayed: various career paths from that job to a target job, possible next jobs, their job evaluation profiles, training required, and perhaps salary ranges. A list of people for whom the job in question represents a significant growth experience can also be generated.

• *For input to employees, line managers, and personnel specialists.* The three parties most interested in this information are the individual employee, the line manager, and the personnel specialist. The employee can use the data for his or her own career planning, and the manager and the personnel specialist can use the information to aid and counsel the employee in that process. The manager and personnel specialist can also use the information to assist in making different personnel decisions: hiring, transfers, promotions, demotions, and so on.

• *For input to and from corporate planning.* Organizations need to have as much coordination as possible between corporate planning, human resources planning, and individual career planning. Usually, these three kinds of planning operate in isolation, although they are all quite dependent on one another. For example, an employee may map out a career path in automotive sales, but the company may plan to get out of the automotive business. Similarly, an organization may plan a large expansion of its engineering operations, but it may lack qualified engineers and they may be in very short supply in the external labor market. A high-level planning committee that includes corporate planning, human resources planning, and career planning is one method of achieving this degree of integration.

CONCLUSION

The notion of using job evaluation schemes for purposes other than compensation is still in the early stages of application. Although the system is used at Sears, other point systems for evaluating jobs can be used for career planning. The important thing is to have an objective method of measuring the skills demanded by various jobs and of putting them together in a way that will stimulate growth in desired directions. This kind of system can lift career planning out of the informal corporate "old boy" network and reduce the employee's dependence upon a well-informed boss. Although there are many pitfalls in any centralized information system, if used carefully a job evaluation-based job progression system can be a useful way of increasing the employee's self-direction and career fulfillment and of providing for a more efficient utilization of the organization's human resources.

Does Career Planning Rock the Boat?

James W. Walker

Is individual career planning consistent with the objectives and practices of a well-managed business? Or does it "rock the boat?" Many executives support career planning as a worthwhile concept but fear that implementation of a formal career planning program will raise expectations, increase turnover, burden supervisors and imply a management commitment to career development that is not realistic. This article examines the risks in career planning and outlines a program that minimizes these risks while achieving the desired benefits.

WHAT IS CAREER PLANNING?

Career planning is the personal process of planning one's life work. It entails evaluating abilities and interests, considering alternative career opportunities, establishing career goals and planning practical development activities. The process results in decisions to enter a certain occupation, join a particular company, accept or decline job opportunities (relocations, promotions or transfers, etc.) and ultimately leave a company for another job or for retirement.

Some companies have responded to employee desires for assistance in career planning by introducing formal programs. These programs typically include:

—career counseling by personnel staff or by supervisors
—group workshops to help employees evaluate their skills, abilities and interests and to formulate development plans
—self-directed workbooks aimed at guiding career planning and analysis by the individual
—communication of job opportunities through job posting, videotapes, reading materials, publications, etc.

To date, most career planning programs have been experimental and of limited scope. Many employers have been reluctant to intervene in matters such as personal assessments, life planning and career goal setting. Accordingly, most corporate career planning programs have been limited to work-related matters that:

—help employees conduct their own career planning by raising questions that need to be answered and providing information on available opportunities and resources
—guide employees in taking advantage of systems available for career development, such as job posting, performance reviews,

Reprinted from *Human Resource Management*, Vol. 17, No. 1, Spring 1978, pp. 2-7, Graduate School of Business Administration, University of Michigan, Ann Arbor, MI 48109.

training and educational assistance programs

—increase employee confidence in the company's career management and demonstrate to outside parties that the company is concerned with career development particularly for minorities and females.

In some companies programs have been designed for non-exempt employees; in others, for managerial, professional and technical employees. Because of difficulties in extending the programs to smaller units or outlying locations, some companies have limited their career planning programs to major locations, such as headquarters offices. A few companies offer their programs company-wide for all salaried employees. The differences in approaches and participants exist because career planning is new, relative to other personnel programs. At this stage of practice, therefore, a "proper" career planning program is what best fits an organization's needs.

WHAT ARE THE RISKS?

Career planning has both positive and negative effects (see Figure 1). However, some executives see only the risks inherent in career planning and none of the potential rewards. These executives feel that career planning raises individual expectations and puts additional strains on personnel systems such as training, educational assistance, internal placement and job posting, and increases employee anxiety about future work in relation to personal interests, abilities and goals.

In some companies, supervisors are concerned that career planning will increase their work loads by requiring them to provide counseling and on-the-job development. Many already feel burdened by other personnel programs (appraisals, employee interviewing and selection procedures, job descriptions, etc.) and other administrative demands (budgeting, salary administration, etc.).

Career planning may also lead to greater employee demand for career development re-

sources. Participants in career planning programs rely on the company for training, educational assistance (tuition reimbursement) and staff counseling. In addition, employees may request more information on job vacancies, pay practices and career opportunities.

It is also feared that raised expectations may increase employee anxiety. Fundamental questions regarding individual strengths, weaknesses and goals sometimes are raised for the first time. Group workshops, workbooks and counseling rarely equip an individual to deal adequately with these issues. Accompanying the expectation that life somehow will be different is general anxiety about the uncertainty of career decisions and future events.

Anxiety caused by raised expectations can be beneficial if it leads to increased employee motivation. But some executives believe that unfulfilled expectations can lead only to employee disappointment and reduced commitment to the organization. As a result, some employees may slack off and others may seek work elsewhere.

WHY GET INVOLVED?

In spite of these concerns, companies are developing and implementing career planning programs. Pressures for company-sponsored programs have emerged from several sources:

—High-talent candidates (particularly minorities and females) often give preference to employers who can demonstrate that career advancement opportunities do exist.

—Women, employees in mid-career and college recruits in particular are asking for career planning assistance. Popular publications have raised employee awareness of the need for career planning.

—Affirmative Action programs and court-approved settlements of discrimination suits frequently require companies to set up career development programs for protected classes.

—Company growth and changing staffing

requirements necessitate individual career development to help assure that needed talent will be available.

Some companies have adopted career planning programs to reduce turnover, improve the "quality of working life," help minimize the chance of white-collar unionization and improve on-the-job performance.

Others have initiated career planning programs specifically to help those employees whose career expectations are too *low*. These companies have found that it is in their own interest as well as the employee's interest to stimulate career aspirations toward more ambitious career goals—to actually *raise* employee expectations. In fact, several companies have focused on "achievement motivation training" as a central component of career planning workshops.

Career planning can be useful, yet at the same time risky, as shown in Figure 1. Companies that have pioneered in introducing career planning, including such major corporations as Gulf Oil, IBM, General Electric, Xerox, TRW and General Motors, have sought to minimize the risks of "rocking the boat" while obtaining the desired benefits.

BUILDING MORE REALISTIC EXPECTATIONS

The key to effective career planning appears to lie in developing *more realistic—not raised—* career expectations. Companies that have been successful in their career planning efforts have guided employees toward opportunities and resources that are actually available.

Moreover, they have tried to dispel the "up or out" notion of a career. After all, an employee need not feel it necessary to be promoted to "get ahead." Lateral careers and careers within specialized job areas or locations can be attractive to many employees, and this can be a significant element of realistic career planning. Promotional opportunities are, by definition, limited in a hierarchical organization. If career information focuses on personal development, work content and job importance rather than

on promotability, potential and career ladders, career planning can help create more realistic career expectations and help minimize career dissatisfaction.

As shown in Figure 1, realistic expectations lead to clarification of supervisors' roles and career development responsibilities, more effective employee use of a company's career development system and strengthened individual abilities to carry out career planning in a practical, meaningful way.

Rather than burdening supervisors unduly, career planning can clarify and support supervisory responsibilities. After all, realistic career planning focuses on current job responsibilities and mastery of job requirements. Current job performance and skills development are usually considered appropriate concerns of every supervisor. It is unlikely that all supervisors can or should even try to become career counselors. Rather, their primary role should be to discuss openly with each employee the *current job* goals, requirements and performance results. This job-related support is the most important "enabling system" a company can offer employees for career development.

Many companies have been training supervisors to conduct effective performance planning and review discussions with employees. Now new support is emerging from the employees. Through career planning, employees are better prepared to participate in the appraisal process. In fact, it has been found that individuals tend to be more critical of their own performance than are their appraisers.

Several large corporations require managers to meet with employees at least annually—more often if the employees desire—to review career progress and future career plans. As difficult as the task may seem, these companies have found that most managers do, in fact, have the abilities and that performance reviews are not unduly burdensome. Supervisory training on career development matters is essential, they report, along with adequate third-party staff support.

Career planning can also equip employees to make better use of available career development systems. Rather than raising expecta-

Figure 1

The effects of career planning

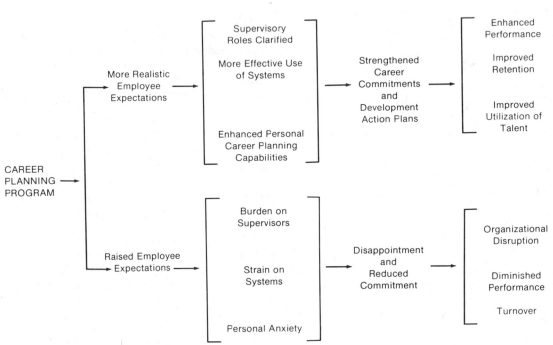

tions with promises that cannot be fulfilled, many companies candidly describe what their systems can and cannot do and the job opportunities they anticipate. Career planning provides an opportunity to demonstrate how performance appraisal, training and development, performance incentives, compensation and other systems relate to personal needs and plans. These systems are the primary means by which personal career goals are achieved and company staffing needs met.

Effective career planning requires facts to stimulate and guide individual training. Individuals ask, "How can I know what I want to do if I don't know the alternatives?" Career planning should help answer questions such as this by providing information about job requirements and alternative career paths, compensation opportunities and available development resources. Company information may be communicated through workbooks, videotapes, booklets or other ways. Cases and readings on career-related issues also can be provided. As part of the information, it is important that employees learn about the company's business—what it is doing and why, its plans and objectives, and future career opportunities. Telling employees a straight story about career options builds employee commitment to the company and helps avoid "rocking the boat."

Rather than leading to heightened individual anxiety, career planning can enhance self-confidence and self-determination. Experience suggests that the key to a successful program is *depth*—of information provided to employees, of employee thinking and of career planning skills developed. Career planning cannot be a superficial exercise, nor merely another self-development program. To avoid "rocking the boat," career planning needs to be an intensive, voluntary, recurring and self-directed process of self-examination. Moreover, it must lead to the development of realistic personal goals and action plans.

END RESULTS

The primary aim of a career planning program is not to help employees lay out a career plan, *per se*. Rather, the objective is to help employees acquire the skills essential for planning their own careers. For example, when a major oil company designed a pilot study to evaluate its new career planning program, a detailed questionnaire was developed to measure changes in participant career attitudes, information adequacy and specific career planning skills. The intent of the program, stated the company, was to equip employees with the skills needed to develop their own career plans.

Of course, to maintain employee interest in an in-depth program, workbooks and related materials must be attractive, interesting and relevant. Experience indicates that a high degree of structure (checklists and short-answer questions as opposed to open-ended exercises), bite-sized sections (so that they are not overwhelming) and attractive graphics are necessary to gain and hold the employee's interest. Readings and exercises should be simple and interesting, yet challenging. When supplemented with counseling, group workshops and other resources, self-directed materials are tools that will build individual career planning capabilities.

More realistic career planning, as described above, generally results in strengthened employee commitment to their careers and personal development action plans. Some employees who contemplate leaving the company may decide to stay after discovering that desired opportunities do, in fact, exist. Proponents of career planning observe that today's work force is increasingly mobile as the "student activists" of the sixties become "activist" employees seeking careers. Of course, career planning may accelerate decisions to change occupations or companies. But this should actually result in better matching of individuals and jobs and improved utilization of capabilities.

At best, corporate career planning presents the company's needs and resources in an open, candid and helpful manner. Rather than disrupting an organization, it can only strengthen the commitment among employees who represent the core of its talent. Of course, the risks are greater for a stable or contracting organization than for a growing one, because opportunities are limited. But even in these cases, career planning can help stimulate employees and guide them toward the personal development and alternative work opportunities best suited to them.

The function of current job activities and skill development as a step in career planning may result in a better employee focus on the work to be done. By reinforcing performance planning and appraisal activities, career planning may contribute to improved performance productivity.

A SUGGESTED STRATEGY

A career planning process that will have positive effects must be carefully developed and implemented. Figure 2 outlines the steps necessary.

Figure Two Implementing a career planning program

I.   **Define Needs and Develop Strategy**

II.   **Develop Necessary Resources**

Support Systems
Career Opportunities Data
Workbooks

III.   **Pilot Introduction**

Evaluation
Refinement

IV.   **Full Introduction**

Inform Managers
Communicate to Employees
Establish Resource Center

First, an organization should conduct an audit to identify the needs it wants to satisfy and to develop a strategy for implementing the program. A large consumer products company, for example, conducted a series of interviews with employee relations staff members to find out whether employees wanted a career planning program and what techniques they thought would be most applicable. The company obtained factual inputs from 20 individuals, including top corporate personnel executives, employee relations managers in the operating divisions, all members of the training and development staff and representatives from compensation, data systems, manpower planning and other employee relations functions. The result was a plan of action that became part of the following year's budget activity.

In other companies, inputs have been obtained from other staff and operating managers. This helps establish a supportive climate for introducing the program once it is developed. Participation by managers in the early development of a career planning program helps allay concerns that it will burden them or otherwise "rock the boat" and also builds commitment to the program.

The second step is to develop the tools necessary to implement the program. Personnel systems supporting career development should be checked and any shortcomings corrected. For example, an insurance company had several performance appraisal systems in use, but felt that greater consistency was needed. A new appraisal process was developed that served both performance and development aspects, and this process was introduced through management workshops. In other companies, needs have been identified in other areas: counseling staff, training and development programs, personnel data systems or inventories, job posting, job description, salary administration, manpower planning (staffing requirements), recruitment and selection, personnel policies, etc.

In another company, a sophisticated personnel data system was in place, but was not widely understood or used for purposes of identifying candidates for job vacancies. The company developed a "career profile" printout for each employee and strengthened the procedures for making use of the data base.

But, perhaps the most common void in the resources needed to support career planning is realistic information on career opportunities. The best strategy is to build career information gradually, starting with simple charts that show job titles in each unit or function by organizational level. Salary level or grade need not be used, because the purpose is to identify only the possible job opportunities. To back up such a chart, a food products company published brief descriptions of the content and qualifications of each job. In another case, a bank published a manual containing all of these basic facts, sorted by department.

With the basic data in place, refinements may be made. For example, job titles can be grouped into "families" of similar jobs and possible job progression lines (career paths) among jobs and job families drawn. A computer company provides detailed information on level and job vacancies. And an oil company has published career paths within its financial and engineering functions.

Career planning workbooks are useful as basic, self-directed tools. Although many varieties of published workbooks are available, experience suggests that the tailored approach provides the realistic in-depth information and exercises needed. IBM, Xerox, General Motors and other companies have developed their own workbooks, tailored to their particular needs. These workbooks generally provide exercises on self-analysis, career planning and career goal setting.

Information may also be included on the company's personnel systems, EEO/AA policies and practices, career opportunities, salary administration and other policies. Articles may be included to stimulate and guide individual thinking; illustrations help maintain interest. A major oil company developed a series of five workbooks that included these features. Employees receive each in sequence over a period of weeks: Know Yourself, Know Your Interests, Know Your Opportunities, Know Your Job, Develop Your Plan. A food products company developed a similar series of three workbooks: Know Yourself, Know Your Opportunities, Know Your Plan.

It is also advisable to pre-test workbook materials. In this way management can assess the effectiveness of the tools in achieving their intended purposes and make whatever modifications are necessary. Such a study may be limited to one location or represent a cross-section of all employees. In one company employees from all divisions were included; in another, the pilot group was comprised of the financial staff.

Finally, before the program is introduced, all supervisors and managers should be informed about the program so that they can answer employee questions. A Career Resource Center may be established (usually as part of the employee development function) to conduct the program and handle referrals from supervisors. The Center may provide:

—individual counseling on career matters and referral to other counselors for additional kinds of information
—group workshops, arranged in response to requests
—self-instructional development materials and courses
—information on career paths and job requirements.
—company and external training and development programs such as seminars and courses, and

—additional reading materials on career planning.

The procedure for participating in the program should be widely communicated, so that all interested employees know that it is available, what is involved and how to sign up. Under Affirmative Action requirements, communication is often a significant task. One company was required to inform certain employees in writing about the program. In addition, it had to receive a signed statement from each individual affirming that she or he had the opportunity to participate in the program.

CONCLUSION

Effective career planning should help employees come to grips with what they want out of their working lives and translate their wants into realistic action plans that get results with the support of company resources. At the same time, career planning should not disrupt the functioning of the organization. It is one thing to force employees to analyze personal needs and set personal goals. It is another to make personal career plans fit into the company's organization plans, needs and ways of doing business. To avoid rocking the boat and at the same time fully achieve its objective—increasing employee confidence in the company—career planning needs to be a broadly based program.